THE
DAY OF THE LORD
and the COMING KINGDOM

A New and Biblical Framework for the End Times

BRANDON L. EMCH

THE DAY OF THE LORD and the COMING KINGDOM:
A New and Biblical Framework for the End Times

Copyright © 2017 Brandon L. Emch
endtimessimplified.com

NOTABLE DAY PUBLISHING
notabledaypublishing.com

ISBN: 978-0-9989288-0-7 (softcover)
ISBN: 978-0-9989288-1-4 (ebook)
LCCN: 2017905901

All rights reserved. No part of this book may be reproduced in any form (whether electronic, mechanical, photocopy, or otherwise), except for brief quotations in printed reviews, without permission in writing from the publisher.

All Scripture is quoted from the King James Version, public domain. Emphasis in Scripture quotations is the author's.

The Mississippi Delta diagram in the introduction is from https://commons.wikimedia.org/wiki/File:Mississippiriver-new-01.png. Created by Shannon1 and licensed under CC BY 3.0.

Cover design: Brandon Emch and Katherine Lloyd
Back cover illustration: Timon Emch
Interior design and typeset: Katherine Lloyd, thedeskonline.com

*This book is dedicated to all those who
live and prepare for the great and notable day of the Lord,
looking for the blessed hope and His glorious appearing.*

TABLE OF CONTENTS

Acknowledgments vii

Introduction **Seeing the Big Picture of Prophecy** 1

Chapter 1 **The Great and Notable Day of the Lord** 25
    I.   THE PRECEDING COSMIC EVENTS   31
    II.   RESURRECTION AND RAPTURE   34
    III.   JUDGMENT AND REWARDS   41
    IV.   SALVATION OF REMNANT ISRAEL   44
    V.   THE WRATH OF GOD   64

Chapter 2 **An Eschatological Framework** 81
    I.   DANIEL'S PROPHECY OF SEVENTY WEEKS   82
    II.   THE APPOINTED TIMES   106
    III.   THE ESCHATOLOGICAL TIME PERIODS OF SCRIPTURE   114
    IV.   LINKING THE MOEDIM WITH THE ESCHATOLOGICAL TIME PERIODS   119
    V.   DID JESUS SAY THAT NO ONE WILL EVER KNOW THE DAY OF HIS RETURN?   131

Chapter 3 **The Revelation of Jesus Christ** 141
    I.   BRIEF HIGHLIGHTS OF REVELATION CHAPTERS 1–5   142
    II.   CHRONOLOGY OF THE BOOK OF REVELATION   148
    III.   A BIG-PICTURE OVERVIEW OF THE TRIBULATION AND ITS TIMING   150
    IV.   SEALS, TRUMPETS, AND VIALS— A DETAILED COMPARISON AND STUDY   153
    V.   REVELATION 10—THE MYSTERY OF THE SEVEN THUNDERS   177

VI.	REVELATION 13—THE BEASTS AND THE MARK, NAME, AND NUMBER OF ANTICHRIST	185
VII.	REVELATION 7 AND 14—THE 144000 AND THE HARVEST OF THE EARTH	194
VIII.	REVELATION 19—A GLARING DICHOTOMY	205

Chapter 4 The Book of Daniel 211

I.	THE FUTURITY OF DANIEL'S VISIONS	212
II.	THE KINGDOMS OF DANIEL 2 AND REVELATION 17	216
III.	LINKING THE DANIEL AND REVELATION BEAST KINGDOMS	222
IV.	STUDY AND COMPARISON OF DANIEL 7–8	224
V.	THE RISE OF THE LITTLE HORN/ANTICHRIST	233
VI.	DANIEL 10–12, THE FIFTH VISION	234

Chapter 5 The Olivet Road Map of the End Times: What Did Jesus Say? 241

COMPARISON AND REVIEW OF MATTHEW 24, MARK 13, AND LUKE 21   242

Chapter 6 The Egyptian Corollary of the End Times 265

Concluding Remarks 277

Appendix 1 **The Kingdom of God at Jesus's Second Coming** 283

Appendix 2 **Are There Mansions in Heaven?** 293

Appendix 3 **End-Times Chart**. 300

Bibliography. 302

Scripture Index 303

About the Author 311

ACKNOWLEDGMENTS

Above all, I would like to thank my God for His faithfulness to me, not only for the prompting but for coming alongside and aiding me on this journey. And Lord, please forgive me where I still don't see clearly enough, or if I have misrepresented truth in any way.

I also want to thank Wayne Anliker, Mark Schmidgall, Carol Klopfenstein, and my wife Maria for their willingness to read through my rough draft and offer helpful comments. Wayne, your steady hand of encouragement and support to "press on for His name's sake" helped me greatly.

Well deserved credit also goes to Rachel Starr Thomson for her expertise in editing and for assisting me with comments and suggestions. Your help was an immeasurable benefit. I can't thank you enough.

Maria—thank you for your commitment and selfless dedication to our family. Thank you for your love. Thank you for your pure, unbridled passion to cultivate the hearts of our children to the ways of God. Thank you for your encouragement to me throughout my journey in responding to God's provocation.

Anna, Timon, Jesse, Alice, Milan, Jonas, and Lydia: You are all precious gifts from above. I love and treasure you dearly. I pray that your hearts will remain soft before the Lord. Never forget how much God loves you. I pray that our family vision will be fulfilled on the day of the Lord.

Introduction

SEEING THE BIG PICTURE OF PROPHECY

A thorough study of prophecy was not on my agenda, but the Lord pressed hard on my heart and I couldn't shake it.

I have been a student of Scripture for many years. The past few years were different. Unprecedented for me. My life was poured into a study of the Word of God. When I look back, it is an understatement to say that I am thankful to God beyond measure for His provocation. My feelings align with a lesson that I was taught long ago: nothing good or worthwhile comes easily or without effort. The journey has been a supreme blessing, and it isn't over.

I never dreamed that there would be a message on my heart worthy enough to share with an audience. But such a message, one that I believe is timely and helpful, spills now out of my heart—a direct result of these years of study.

What I see today is a fuller, deeper, more detailed and picturesque landscape. The "story" of the Bible makes more sense to me. The entirety of Scripture is more alive. The continuity of the Old Testament into the New Testament is more discernable. I was always a student of the Scriptures, but had I inadvertently glossed over words and details simply because my personal understanding, the context in which I saw Scripture, was not as foundationally strong as it should have been? I believe so.

God is abundantly faithful. What was once, only a few short years ago, an insurmountable topic for me has come alive in my heart with vibrancy and clarity. I can't explain it as anything other than a work of God by His Spirit. But I am not special. What I have experienced is what I believe any of God's children can experience with prayer and substantial personal time, combined with devotion and confidence in the Word of God. When you take the time to build a solid Old Testament foundation, the Scriptures are transformed.

Be assured, I fully recognize that I don't have all of the answers and that I am prone to error. But thanks to God, the Bible *does* have all of the answers, and it is not prone to error! The passage of time will prove true all that is contained within Holy Scripture. The more I learn from the Scriptures, the greater my confidence, faith, and awe of the completeness and fullness that is contained within His Word grows.

I am not an alarmist, but as I compare Scripture with world events, I can only conclude that the time of the end is drawing near. Rightly or wrongly, I have a growing sense that I could live to see the return of Christ Jesus. The Lord specifically told Daniel that the understanding of his visions were closed up and sealed until the time of the end (Daniel 12:9). I believe the prophecies of the Holy Scriptures are being unsealed in our time and that we very well could be that last generation. And if the New Testament writers often exhorted their hearers to be prepared for the appearing of our Lord, what do we, nearly two thousand years later, have to lose by committing ourselves more fully to the copious writings of the inspired prophets, and indeed of the entirety of God's Word? Can the church benefit from greater understanding, greater sobriety, and greater preparation? I believe so. We are to "exhort one another: and so much the more, as ye see the day approaching" (Hebrews 10:25).

In our time we see an abundance of evil called good and good called evil. In this climate, the long-held charge to the follower of God is "to seek good, and not evil, that ye may live" (Amos 5:14). One of the most effective means of seeking good is to draw nigh to God's heart and build our faith through His precious, life-giving Word. With reverence and humility, let's seek the Lord earnestly. Let's look to God our Maker for help, for wisdom, for discernment, and for a double portion of devotion in these days so that we may follow His guiding hand. Without a doubt, we need strong faith and abundant grace to overcome the darkness, confusion, and turmoil that are present in this evil world.

I will be pleased if this book sparks a deep and honest Berean-like study of the Holy Scriptures. The topic of Bible prophecy is big and complex. Although the final book of Scripture, the Revelation of Jesus Christ, has become clear to my heart, I'm hopeful that my writing goes much deeper than interpretations and analysis of prophecy. I hope that the embers in your heart become warm, that you are inspired to pay attention to all that God has written to you for edification, exhortation, and comfort (1 Corinthians 14:3).

In light of the future appearing of the Lord Jesus, Christians have a high calling and worthwhile endeavor before us today (1 Timothy 6:14, 1 Peter 1:7, 2 Peter 3:14). The great and notable day of the Lord will be so monumental—nearly beyond description—that it is important to peer into these things. Simply put, we are exhorted to love, look forward to, and eagerly anticipate the promise of righteousness associated with His return in power and glory (2 Timothy 4:8, Titus 2:13, 2 Peter 3:10–14). Can we more effectively heed this counsel if we pray for God's help and open our hearts and minds to the prophetic Scriptures? I think so.

While we enjoy supreme blessings in Christ today (Ephesians 1:3), this is only a down payment of our future inheritance (Ephesians 1:14). As the apostle Paul prayed for the Ephesian believers, may the Lord give us the spirit of wisdom and revelation in the knowledge of Him so that our understanding is enlightened! Why? So that we can grasp the blessedness of the hope, the richness of the glorious inheritance, and the mighty power of the future resurrection and rapture (Ephesians 1:17–20)!

When it comes to understanding prophecy, there are certain themes and principles that can aid our quest for understanding. The following is an attempt to lay some of that groundwork. Let's get started.

PRINCIPLE #1: UNDERSTAND THE PRIMARY PURPOSE OF PROPHECY IS TO REVEAL JESUS CHRIST

While there are many prophecies in Scripture with a near-term or contemporary fulfillment, the ultimate trajectory of the Bible's prophetic accounts takes us all the way to the day of the Lord: that great and notable day when Jesus is given everlasting dominion and authority as King of kings and Lord of lords (Daniel 2:44, 7:13–14; Revelation 11:15, 19:16). The general "spirit" of prophecy is the testimony of Jesus.

> And I fell at his feet to worship him. And he said unto me, See thou do it not: I am thy fellowservant, and of thy brethren that have the testimony of Jesus: worship God: for the testimony of Jesus is the spirit of prophecy. (Revelation 19:10)

To understand this pictorially, let's use an analogy with the Mississippi River. According to Wikipedia, the Mississippi River flows for over 2,300 miles through the center of the continental United States and discharges into the Gulf of Mexico. The headwaters originate in northern Minnesota at Lake Itasca. As an interesting point of trivia to help bolster our analogy, the name "Itasca" was coined from a combination of two Latin words: *veritas* ("truth") and *caput* ("head"). While the waters of the Mississippi sometimes flow east, west, or north, their general direction is from north to south. Numerous tributaries then feed into the Mississippi, some later and some earlier, flowing in many directions as they make their way to eventually support the river's broad current. Yet all the flowing water that begins at Lake Itasca and is bolstered and supported by the water-carrying tributaries ends up at the same place.

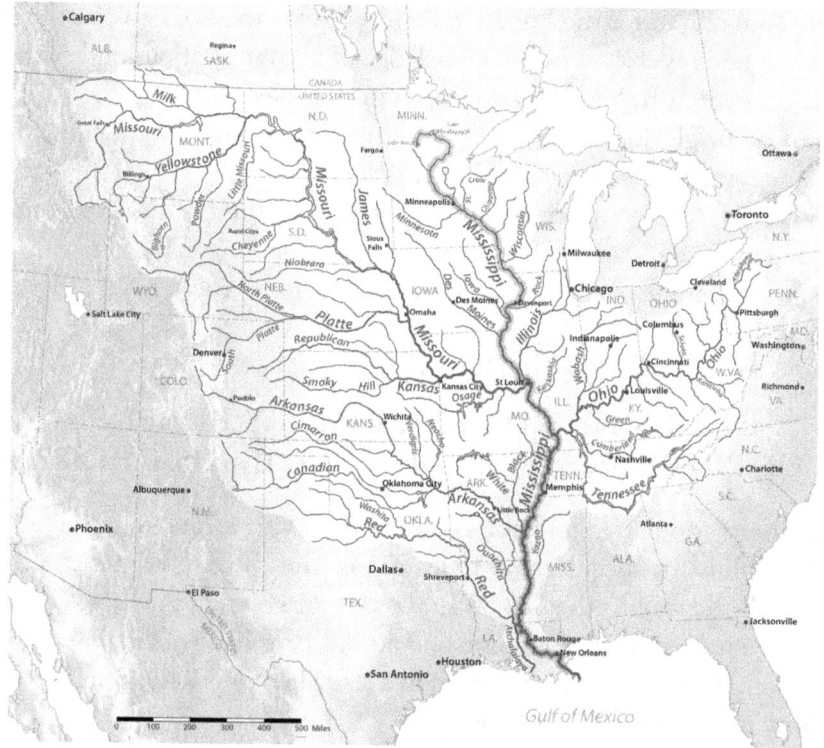

The same is true of prophetic Scripture. Consider the inspiration of the Spirit as the headwaters, the tributaries that support and feed into the Mississippi as the prophets, and the consolidated words of prophecy as the Mississippi River itself. The ultimate trajectory of these inspired "waters" is toward a common destination: the first and second comings of Jesus Christ. I have heard some say that the Holy Bible contains nearly 30 percent prophecy.

If we equated the United States of America to the Holy Bible itself and the placement of the Mississippi and its tributaries to prophecy, what would we find lies at the heart of Scripture? Prophecy. And what is the heart of the message of prophecy? Jesus Christ.

PRINCIPLE #2: UNDERSTAND THE NECESSITY OF TWO "COMINGS"

In hindsight, it is simple for us to see two "comings" of Jesus Christ laid out in the prophetic Scriptures. But this wasn't the case prior to the crucifixion of Jesus. No one expected the King of the Jews to suffer and die, not even the evil powers, "for had they known it, they would not have crucified the Lord of glory" (1 Corinthians 2:8).

Clear fulfillment of the prophecies regarding the first coming has occurred with the prophesied virgin birth of a king from the seed of David, born in Bethlehem (Genesis 3:15, Isaiah 7:14, Matthew 1:20–23, Isaiah 9:6–7, Matthew 2:2, Micah 5:2, Matthew 2:5–6). However, with Satan still prominently positioned as "prince of the power of the air" (Ephesians 2:2) and "god of this world" (2 Corinthians 4:4), we must acknowledge that we live in a presently evil world (Galatians 1:4). We therefore conclude that the evil kingdoms and powers of this world have yet to be crushed. The day is yet future when Jesus will be given everlasting dominion and when we find the prophesied Messiah King sitting on the everlasting throne of his father David, reigning righteously over the house of Jacob in an everlasting kingdom (2 Samuel 7:12–13, 1 Chronicles 17:11–14, Jeremiah 33:15–16, Luke 1:32–33, Revelation 11:15). Has the glory of the LORD vibrantly filled the holy mountain Jerusalem (Isaiah 66:18–20), or do we see King Jesus worshipped consistently (Isaiah 66:23)? The prophecies related to the second coming clearly remain unfulfilled.

If we look keenly at this span of time between the first coming and the still future second coming, we start to see the glow from the light of the hidden mystery of the Scriptures (1 Corinthians 2:7; Ephesians 2:12–14, 19–20, 3:3–4, 9, 5:32, 6:19; Colossians 1:26–27). What is this mystery? The mystery is this present church age and our suffering Savior, who was "slain from the foundation of the world" (Revelation 13:8). According to the will of God and His foreordained plans, the path of salvation through Christ was made available for all humankind, but it occurred somewhat unexpectedly! While it is possible to detect the mystery of Christ from a position of hindsight (Acts 17:2–3), it truly was kept secret from the beginning of the world (Romans 16:25).

With the first coming having been accomplished, and with the suffering Savior having been crucified and resurrected, we now await His second coming. Thus, the primary thrust of prophecy in Scripture points us toward this second coming and Jesus's future return on the day of the Lord.

PRINCIPLE #3: UNDERSTAND THAT MANY PROPHETIC TRUTHS ARE LIKE AN OVERLAY

Comparing Scripture with Scripture is a biblically sound method of interpretation and helps us to gain a full and complete understanding of the teachings of God. In the same manner that we can do this for nonprophetic Scriptures, it is mandatory that we utilize this technique with prophecy. God is particularly repetitive through the writings of the prophets.

This principle was demonstrated to me in 2005 when I was preparing a Bible study on the parable of the sower. The parable of the sower is recorded in Matthew 13, Mark 4, and Luke 8. What stood out to me was what Jesus taught about the good ground. It was recorded in the following way by the gospel writers:

- But he that received seed into the good ground is he that heareth the word, and *understandeth it;* which also beareth fruit, and bringeth forth, some an hundredfold, some sixty, some thirty. (Matthew 13:23)
- And these are they which are sown on good ground; such as hear the word, and *receive it*, and bring forth fruit, some thirtyfold, some sixty, and some an hundred. (Mark 4:20)
- But that on the good ground are they, which in an honest and good heart, having heard the word, *keep it*, and bring forth fruit with patience. (Luke 8:15)

Each of the disciples heard the same story and then heard the parable explained by Jesus. Yet, the Holy Spirit inspired the gospel writers to use unique and different words to convey the teaching. When we layer each verse upon another, it adds depth and fullness to the simple teaching. So what must we do with the truth of the gospel, according to the Scriptures? Upon hearing the Word with an honest and good heart, we must:

- Understand it (Strong's G4862—"to comprehend; by implication to act piously: — consider, understand, be wise")
- Receive it (Strong's G3858—"to accept near, that is, admit or (by implication) delight in: — receive")
- Keep it (Strong's G2722—"have, hold (fast), keep (in memory), let, possess, retain, seize on, stay, take, withhold")

In my personal study I have used this technique with the Olivet Discourse in Matthew 24, Mark 13, and Luke 21 and with different themes in the books of Revelation and Daniel. I have also attempted to gather together many of the common passages from the Old Testament prophets regarding the day of the Lord.

A few points about studying in this way:

- This method of study is biblically sound and can help detect commonalities and consistencies, adding fullness to our understanding of events.
- This method of study can bring what could be a disjointed or partial understanding into a greater completeness.
- In addition, and importantly, it can increase one's faith substantially in the authority, power, majesty, and might of Almighty God! When we read promises in the prophets beginning with the two words "I will," coming from the lips of God Himself, we can think of nothing less than our Creator, who is Faithful and True. Do we have the faith to believe that He will do what He says He will do? See Isaiah 13:9–19, Micah 5:10–15, and Zephaniah 1:1–18 for a sampling of these commitments of God.

PRINCIPLE #4: UNDERSTAND THAT THE TIME OF THE END HAS BEEN PREDETERMINED BY GOD

God will orchestrate events and circumstances to accomplish His purposes at the set time.

Psalm 102 refers to a time when God will have mercy upon Zion in the last days and when the LORD will appear in His glory at the second coming. Verse 13 states, "Thou shalt arise, and have mercy upon Zion: for the time to favour her, yea, the set time, is come."

Set time (*moed*), Strong's H4150—"properly an appointment, that is, a fixed time or season; specifically a festival; (set, solemn) feast, (appointed, due) season, (set) time (appointed)"

This psalm ties in wonderfully with the book of Daniel. In Daniel, we likewise read that God has an appointment with His creation. The time of the end is an appointed time; it will occur at the set time as ordained by Almighty God and exactly as recorded in the prophetic accounts of Daniel and Revelation.

- As Gabriel spoke to Daniel he said, in Daniel 8:19, "Behold, I will make thee know what shall be in the last end of the indignation: for *at the time appointed* [moed] the end shall be."
- Referring to the time when the Antichrist will be in power (this of course is during the "end times"), Daniel 11:27 says, "for yet the end shall be *at the time appointed* [moed]."
- Also in Daniel 11:35 we read, "And some of them of understanding shall fall, to try them, and to purge, and to make them white, even to the time of the end: because it is yet for *a time appointed* [moed]."

We also see this principle in the book of Acts, chapter 17. Acts 17:31 states, "Because *he hath appointed a day*, in the which he will judge the world in righteousness by that man whom he hath ordained; whereof he hath given assurance unto all men, in that he hath raised him from the dead." Additionally, Acts 15:18 states, "Known unto God are all his works from the beginning of the world."

The *moedim*, or appointed times, are typically referred to in the Scriptures as God's feast days. They are spoken of in several places but are presented together in Leviticus 23. More is discussed about the relevance of these feast days in the "Eschatological Framework" chapter of this book, but suffice it to say, our Lord Jesus Christ perfectly fulfilled the spring feasts with His death (on Passover), His lying in the tomb (during Unleavened Bread), His resurrection (on Firstfruits), and the sending of the Holy Spirit fifty days later (on Pentecost). This was God's design.

There is a prophetic significance to each of the spring and fall feasts. It is remarkable that our Lord truly accomplished and fulfilled, to the very day, all of the spring feasts in a literal way with His first advent on this earth as the Son of Man. Could this pattern of perfect fulfillment also hold true for the fall feasts at the second coming? It is against my native understanding, but the

Lord has led me to the point whereby I fully believe and wholeheartedly trust that the Scriptures confirm this to be so.

PRINCIPLE #5:
UNDERSTAND OUR PRESUPPOSITIONS

We all come to the Scriptures with presumptions, opinions, and conjectures. Nevertheless, in answering God's call to study biblical prophecy, I did not come with many preformulated ideas. Perhaps this was a good thing. Frankly, I'm not a big book reader—so as a result, I was an open slate in a stage of asking, seeking, and knocking.

This book will likely challenge some of your own presuppositions. In particular, it strongly questions the soundness of a future seven-year tribulation period. Though common, this interpretation of Daniel 9 may not be as rock solid and foundationally secure as many think. This common teaching and my challenge to it are laid out in the "Eschatological Framework" chapter.

If we are biblically correct in our premises, there shouldn't be any Scriptures that lack agreement with us. The framework should self-support, align, and fitly come together in a united and acceptable manner. The ruling authority is the pure, unadulterated Word of God. The less human intervention and assumptions required in our interpretation the better, and when we come to Scripture in this way, it can blossom our faith and awe of the God of the Bible. Especially with a topic such as the end times, which is filled with disparity, disunity, and opposition of views, I simply ask that you prayerfully read and consider ideas that may be new to your consideration—interpretations generated using Scripture to interpret Scripture and that require fewer human opinions and assumptions.

While opinions and assumptions are a part of life, we know that assumptions increase the probability for errors. There is a principle called Occam's razor that is good to consider. It states, "Other things being equal, simpler explanations are generally better than more complex ones."

PRINCIPLE #6:
UNDERSTAND THAT ISRAEL AND THE MIDDLE EAST ARE THE FOCUS OF THE LAST DAYS

In my study of the end times, I was provoked to spend considerable time in the Old Testament. As I did, the numerous passages referring to Israel's future and permanent restoration to the Holy Land were difficult to dismiss. While I knew that God's chosen people were "the apple of his eye," I was personally focused on the New Testament church. But we cannot discount the heritage of faith that began with Abraham (Genesis 15:4, Romans 4:16). I had neglected to see with clarity the bigger picture. Now my focus has been expanded, and my affection for the Jews has increased. I long to see the believing remnant's permanent restoration to the promised land. It is the will of God.

Please don't misunderstand. I am eternally grateful and thankful for this church age and the blessed way of redemption through Jesus Christ. He is the way, the truth, and the life, and no man can come to our Father God except by Jesus. However, God has not forever cast away Israel and replaced them with the church. It is not one or the other. Nothing has been taken away; it is simply that more has been revealed and given to us in this new era, which has gone on now about two thousand years. The great mystery of Christ, foreordained before the foundation of the world, became manifest (1 Peter 1:20) in the first coming. What was hidden in God from the beginning of the world became known (see Ephesians 3:2–11, especially verses 5 and 9).

Let me explain. My former understanding relegated Israel and the Old Testament to a lower standing in comparison to what Jesus brought to us with the New Testament. Indeed, there is a major distinction between the Old Testament and the New Testament church dispensation. But for some of the following reasons, it is less of a distinction to me now than it was formerly.

First, our resurrection/rapture will be the same resurrection as the Old Testament saints! Scripturally, I find it very hard to differentiate a resurrection and rapture for the "church" that is separate from the Old Testament saints. The following verses, among many others that will be reviewed later, point to a singular resurrection event at the day of the Lord Jesus: John 6:39–40, 44, 54; John 11:24; 1 Corinthians 5:5; 2 Corinthians 1:14.

Second, it is the New Testament church members who are grafted into Israel's olive tree (Romans 11:17, 24), and not into an entirely separate and distinct tree. We are not a replacement of that tree; rather we have become a part of that tree. We, the New Testament church, are the circumcision (Philippians 3:3), which means that New Testament followers of Jesus are part of true Israel and the family or offspring of God (Galatians 6:16). Through Jesus Christ, we have the privilege and opportunity to become the sons and daughters of the one true God (YWHW or Jehovah).

Third, the Old Testament saints are fellow citizens with New Testament followers of Jesus Christ (Ephesians 2:12–22). Ephesians 3:6 says that we Gentiles are fellow heirs and of the same body with the Old Testament saints! How many bodies are there? God says that there is only one body (Ephesians 4:4–6).

And last, though it is a mystery to me, verses like 1 Peter 1:11 indicate that the prophets had the Spirit of Christ. The fathers of old drank of that spiritual Rock that was Christ (1 Corinthians 10:4)! Other verses, like Matthew 22:31–32; Galatians 3:16, 26, 29; and Galatians 4:29 hint at a root of faith in Christ Jesus, the "I am" (John 8:58), going all the way back to Abraham and his seed.

This brings me to make a final point. God is not going to be satisfied, and the Holy Scriptures will not be fulfilled, until all of remnant Israel is redeemed through Jesus Christ. How will this occur? When will this occur?

I can't imagine another Holocaust-type event, but the Scriptures seem to indicate that many of God's chosen will be sifted and purged and experience death in the latter days (Amos 9:8–9 and Zechariah 13:8–9). The tribulation and travail that God's special people will endure in the latter days is difficult to swallow and accept (Deuteronomy 4:29–31). Yet, the fruit of this suffering will lead to the corporate salvation of remnant Israel at the day of the Lord, when they look upon the One whom they pierced, repent, mourn, experience a cleansing and a new heart, and receive the pouring out of God's Spirit (Revelation 1:7; Romans 11:25–26; Zechariah 9:16, 12:10; Joel 3:16–20; Isaiah 66:19–23; Jeremiah 23:3–6; Jeremiah 31:31–34; Ezekiel 36:24–29; Isaiah 59:18–21; Deuteronomy 30:4–6).

As followers of the Lord Jesus, the question for us to contend with is what, if any, role God would have us play to aid and assist the Jewish people in that time, and moreover how we can best shine unto them the light of truth about the Lord Jesus in advance of that day. May the Lord help us, and may His will be done.

In addition to the end-time focus on the people of Israel, I also needed to come to grips with the primary geographical focus of the end times. Simply put, the *main* focal point of the end times is not America, Japan, Sweden, or Italy. Jerusalem and the Middle East are the main areas of focus. It is in a (future) temple at Jerusalem that Antichrist will commit the blasphemous abomination of desolation. The Middle East is where the revived beast kingdom will primarily have its location and headquarters, as most actions and activities of Antichrist depicted in Daniel 11:21–45 are in a clear Middle Eastern context. It is Jerusalem that, in Luke 21:20, becomes surrounded by armies. And it is to a place called Armageddon that Revelation 16:14 says the spirits of devils, working miracles, will direct and influence the evil opposition to come together to the battle of that great day of God Almighty, when the winepress of the wrath of God is trampled (Revelation 14:19 and Revelation 19:15).

Because of this, I don't know the depth to which North Americans, Central Americans, Europeans, and so forth will be affected by the Antichrist. I expect *all the world* to be severely impacted, because Revelation 13:7 says that it is given to the Antichrist to make war with the saints and to overcome them: "and power was given him over all kindreds, and tongues, and nations." This power and influence could be economic or religious (and these two may become interconnected). Spiritually, his reach and influence will no doubt be far and wide and serious, because the flames of spiritual deception can spread fast, especially when the fear of Almighty God is a rare commodity in the world. However, the Antichrist's dominion is not likely to be a worldwide government, because we read where nations will oppose his beast kingdom (Daniel 11:30, 40–44). And since I believe Antichrist comes into view at the opening of the fourth seal, the context of his physical rule is a one-fourth part of the earth (Revelation 6:8). Therefore, I believe a tyrannical, worldwide dominancy is questionable.

PRINCIPLE #7: UNDERSTAND WHERE WE ARE ON THE TIMELINE OF HISTORY AND WHAT LIES AHEAD

This section could almost be titled, "The Second Peter 3 Timeline." The Scripture places three "worlds" on its timeline. The "first world" lasted until the flood (2 Peter 3:6). The "current world" is ordained to last until the day of the Lord, or the day of judgment (2 Peter 3:7), and is described as "this present evil world" (Galatians 1:4). And the "world to come" is future and will come to fruition after the day of the Lord (2 Peter 3:10–13), a monumental and great day of transition.

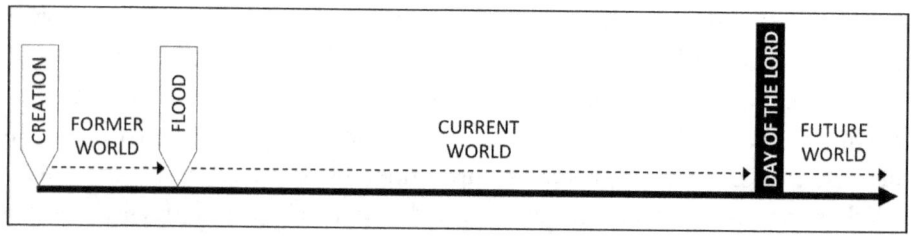

I contend that this transition does not remove the present world, but rather transforms it. According to Ecclesiastes 1:4, "one generation passeth away, and another generation cometh: but the earth abideth forever." But isn't the earth going to "melt" and "pass away"? I'm not so certain about that assumption. Personally, this subject has been transformative in my own mind and heart to where my fond hope and expectation have been altered from a heavenly view to a future that is more earthly. I could be wrong, but this is the view I believe the Scriptures teach. So much influence (Greek philosophy in this case) has unknowingly impregnated our minds and influenced our interpretation of the Bible!

Peter does speak of this world melting and passing away, yes. Yet the former world perished by water (2 Peter 3:6) at the time of Noah. In that time, the earth's topography was altered substantially, but the primary substance that perished was that of evil mankind. "The wickedness of man was great in the earth, and every imagination of the thoughts of his heart was continually evil" (Genesis 6:5). What then was the objective of the flood when it repented the LORD that he had made man on earth and was grieved in his heart (Genesis 6:6)? We read the answer in the following verse: "And the LORD said, I will destroy man whom I have created from the face of the earth; both man, and beast, and the creeping thing, and the fowls of the air; for it repenteth me that I have made them" (Genesis 6:7). It was an evil people and culture that experienced destruction and death. It was a world of wickedness that perished, not the world itself.

We now find ourselves in the current world, in the era of the gospel of Jesus Christ. While righteousness is a component of the current world, evil is ragingly predominant. Our charge in the current world is to live and promote the gospel of Jesus Christ. It is the will of God that all come to belief and repentance (2 Peter 3:9). Sadly, we recognize that few will be found on the path that leads to God's everlasting kingdom, and many will be found traveling on the broad path that leads to destruction (Matthew 7:13–14). Nevertheless, we press on! During our lifetimes, Jesus teaches that we are not to love and seek after the things of this world, but to trust and follow Him with an eternal focus. We are mere mortals on earth today, and our hope and prize, Jesus Christ, is in heaven (1 Corinthians 9:24, Philippians 3:14, Colossians 1:5). The Scripture teaches of a reward in heaven that will be distributed to the redeemed (Matthew 5:12, 6:1, 16:27; 2 Corinthians 5:10; Revelation 11:18), and that what God has for us in heaven is not subject to being stolen, nor is it subject to rust or corruption (Luke 12:33, I Peter 1:4). Note that this doesn't mean our reward *is* heaven; rather, the idea is that Jesus maintains our reward in heaven, ready for distribution to the saints on the appointed day when the resurrected and raptured faithful stand before the judgment seat of Christ. And although we will stand before the Lord on that day with glorified and immortal bodies, it doesn't mean that heaven is our permanent destination.

This brings us to the great transition event, the day of the Lord, when the current world will be destroyed. The seventh trumpet will sound (Revelation 11:15). Jesus will be given dominion over all the kingdoms of the world and will then reign for ever and ever (Revelation 11:15; Daniel 2:44, 7:13–14). The dead will be resurrected and receive rewards in heaven before the judgment seat of Christ (Revelation 11:18). The wrath of God will be dispensed upon earth, and evil will be destroyed (Revelation 11:18). Much like the ark in Noah's day or Lot's family fleeing Sodom, the redeemed will be raised into heaven to escape the wrath and destruction on the earth.

The day of the Lord will bring about a similar earth-altering consequence as the flood, only this time the current world will pass through fire (2 Peter 3:10). Satan's rule as "prince of the power of the air" (Ephesians 2:2) and "god of this world" (2 Corinthians 4:4) will be destroyed, and he will be bound and thrust into the bottomless pit, an ultimate fulfillment of the "mother prophecy" in Genesis 3:15. Evil powers and kingdoms will be crushed. The wrath of God on the day of the Lord will bring about the destruction of the ungodly. The lust of the flesh, the lust of the eyes, and the pride of life will pass away, "but he that doeth the will of God abideth forever" (1 John 2:15–17).

The future world is described as the "new heavens and a new earth, wherein dwelleth righteousness" (2 Peter 3:13). We cannot dismiss this key point: due to the subduing and frankly the annihilation of evil, the theme of the new earth will be righteousness.

So will the earth utterly perish, or will this "passing" be akin to its former death, when evil was eradicated and destroyed in Noah's day? I believe it wise to consider the larger biblical context; when we do, it will start nudging us toward the most accurate answer. If the future world is to be comprised of new heavens *and a new earth*, why is the focus of most believers on heaven only? Or is there biblical support that can help us tilt our focus toward a new and fresh earth that has been ridden of evil? Please realize that my desire is to plant seeds of consideration at this point, and not to exhaustively cover the subject.

But I hope this book will bring you to take a new look at the Bible's view of the timeline of earth.

PRINCIPLE #8: UNDERSTAND THE FUTURE RESTORATION OF EARTH

Many New Testament Scriptures confirm the principle of an earthly restoration, renovation, and renewal; see for example Acts 1:6–8, Acts 3:21, and Matthew 19:27–28. The "restitution" in Acts 3:21 is *apokatastasis* (Strong's G5605), defined by Thayer's Greek Lexicon as "the restoration of a true theocracy and of the perfect state before the fall." This promise of restoration meshes with numerous Old Testament Scriptures that denote a time of peace, righteousness, and prosperity on earth, the likes of which we cannot comprehend. King Jesus will say "Come, ye blessed of my Father, inherit the kingdom prepared for you from the foundation of the world" (Matthew 25:34). What existed at creation? It was paradise, or the garden of Eden.

Ezekiel 36:35 and Isaiah 51:3–16 seem to convey this transformation as well. In the context of this transition event from old to new when Jesus establishes a permanent righteousness upon earth and when the heavens shall vanish away like smoke, Isaiah 51:3 states, "For the LORD shall comfort Zion: he will comfort all her waste places; and he will make her wilderness like Eden, and her desert like the garden of the LORD; joy and gladness shall be found therein, thanksgiving, and the voice of melody." It will be so beautifully glorious that "the former shall not be remembered, nor come into mind" (Isaiah 65:17). The glory of the LORD will vibrantly fill the holy mountain Jerusalem (Isaiah 66:18–19), and King Jesus will be worshipped consistently by all mankind (Isaiah 66:23). But most importantly, beyond the beauty and splendor of any earthly transformation, the heavens and the earth will be transformed from the rule of Satan and his evil spirits to the dominion of King Jesus and His pure and righteous reign. Upon the destruction of the Wicked by the spirit of His mouth and the brightness of His coming, the Lord Jesus will rule in righteousness (Isaiah 11:4–5, 2 Thessalonians 2:8, Revelation 19:15–16).

Thanks to God, the power of Satan today can be subdued and overcome with God's help and grace. But again, at the transitional day of the second coming of the Lord Jesus, the seed of the woman will deal an overwhelming blow to the head of Satan (Genesis 3:15). Here we will see the ultimate fulfillment of prophecy.

PRINCIPLE #9: UNDERSTAND THE FUTURE KINGDOM OF GOD

Spiritually, the kingdom of God is already present in the heart of every child of God (Luke 17:20–21, Colossians 1:13). However, we need to recognize that viewing the kingdom of God in a purely spiritual context gives only a faint realization of what the kingdom of God truly is and is but a foretaste of what is to come. It is a "now but not yet" concept because one day, the current "king" of this earth will be destroyed, and Jesus will rule on earth from Jerusalem as King of kings and Lord of lords (Zechariah 14:9, Revelation 19:16). At that time, all of the kingdoms of the world will be destroyed (broken in pieces and consumed), and God's kingdom will be formally established. God's kingdom shall then never be destroyed (Daniel 2:44–45). (See Appendix 1 to review a list of verses which I believe depict the future kingdom of God in the New Testament and the book of Daniel.)

Jesus will have reign and dominion over all the earth during a millennial (that is, a thousand-year) kingdom (Daniel 7:13–14, 26–27; Revelation 11:15; Zechariah 14:9; Isaiah 11:9; Isaiah 60:19–21; Isaiah 66:22–23; Psalm 72:8; Revelation 20:4). Jesus will be king, and out of the Lord's house and out of Zion shall go forth the law, and the word of the Lord from Jerusalem (Isaiah 2:2–3). During the millennium, the resurrected and raptured will have immortal, glorified bodies like the angels (Luke 20:35–36). The resurrected and raptured will live and reign with Christ for a thousand years as priests of God and of Christ (Revelation 3:21; 20:4, 6). Did you hear that? Those who are resurrected and raptured at the appearing or second coming of Jesus will *reign* with Christ as *priests*. In His kingdom we will in some manner function as intercessors and ambassadors on behalf of His royal and righteous rule, not completely unlike our role today as stewards of the gospel.

A debatable question to me is "From where will we live and reign with Christ during the millennium?" I tend to think that we will live and reign with Christ from an earthly position and location for the following reasons:

- Jesus and His glory will be located in Jerusalem during the millennium, and we are to be "ever with the Lord" (Isaiah 66:18–20, Zechariah 14:8–9, 1 Thessalonians 4:17).
- Some of us may have responsibilities over a few cities and others over five or ten (Luke 19:15–19).
- With the disciples, Jesus will drink of the fruit of the vine in the kingdom of God (Matthew 26:29).

- Many will come from the east and west to sit down with Abraham, Isaac, and Jacob in the kingdom of God (Matthew 8:11).
- We will enter the kingdom of the Lord Jesus Christ after our pilgrim journey of faith is over (2 Peter 1:11).
- I don't see an indication that once the "wife" of Christ descends to earth with Him for the final battle of Armageddon a reascension to heaven will occur (Revelation 19:7, 14). The focus remains on earth. Likewise, at the end of the millennium, the new Jerusalem comes "down from God out of heaven" (Revelation 3:12; 21:2, 10), when Almighty God dwells "with man" forever.

That said, based on Revelation 3:12 and also the "bride" language in Revelation 21:2 and 9, I can't totally eliminate the possibility that the resurrected and raptured faithful may have their "millennial headquarters" in heaven with God. I don't think this position is as scripturally strong as an earth-based location, but nonetheless, either circumstance is wonderfully rich to contemplate. The utter privilege and blessing to be resurrected or raptured at the first resurrection, to be in a body and a state where "death has no power," and to "live and reign with Christ a thousand years" (Revelation 20:6) is beyond comprehension. Then, after the millennium, it will be ours to think of and look forward to a seemingly greater and richer inheritance with streets of gold, gates of pearls, a crystal-clear river of life, and the incomprehensible brightness of the glory of Almighty God and the Lamb completely filling a city of 1,400 square miles!

But why a millennium before eternity with God? It seems the millennial reign of Christ will be an opportunity for God Almighty, through redeemed Israel, to vindicate His holy covenants, His will, and His Word. Significant Israel-centric promises remain unfulfilled. Along with the everlasting and irrevocable promises of God to Israel of a specific region of land (Genesis 15:5–21) and of a king from the seed of David who sits on an everlasting throne (Luke 1:32–33, Matthew 2:2, 2 Samuel 7:10–16, 1 Chronicles 17:11–15), we also see a multitude of prophecies for the corporate salvation of remnant Israel (Romans 11:25–27; Jeremiah 31:31–34, 32:37–42; Ezekiel 36:22–38; Zechariah 12:8–11). When we combine these promises with the understanding that the kingdom of God will become a physical reality upon the second coming of Jesus Christ, more details emerge to form the remarkable picture that is developing. The millennium will be the fulfillment of the prayer, "thy kingdom come, thy will be done, on earth as it is in heaven" (Matthew 6:10). At long last, it will be the time of Israel's faithful and forever abiding in the Spirit and new covenant righteousness!

So what is one calling, of many, for the Gentile church today? Through our new-birth experience with the Spirit of the living God dwelling in our hearts, we are to exemplify and reflect the power, the truth, the grace, and the love of God by faithfully abiding in Christ. Through a personal conversion experience, God affords His children the capacity to relate to what is prophesied corporately for Israel. And it is through the Gentile believer that His elect will be provoked to jealousy (Romans 11:11). As such, Gentile believers are not to be proud of our current position and opportunity through Christ, but we are called to humbly and faithfully continue in God's ways (Romans 11:21–22). Reflecting the light of God is our calling and opportunity today!

The word "reign" raises a question: who are the subjects of this millennial kingdom? I can identify two groups. One is Israel and the other is the "nations." It appears that the main subjects under the rule and reign of Christ and the redeemed will be the corporate remnant of Israel, who were recently converted at the day of the Lord (Isaiah 10:20–21, 11:11–12, Jeremiah 30:7–11, 31:10–11, 32:37–38, Hosea 3:5. Zechariah 12:9–11). Redeemed Israel will actually reside and prosper in the promised land (Isaiah 60:21, Ezekiel 39:27–28, Amos 9:11–15), and Jerusalem will be a praise in the earth (Isaiah 62:7, 11–12). There will be joy and gladness, and sorrow and sighing shall flee away (Isaiah 35:10, Jeremiah 30:17–22, 31:12). Israel will live in new covenant faithfulness forever (Isaiah 59:20–21; Jeremiah 31:31–33, 32:38–40; Ezekiel 36:25–28, 37:25–28).

In the millennium, there will at last be just and righteous governance on earth (Jeremiah 33:15–16). Can you comprehend the righteous leadership of King Jesus over the earth as recorded in Isaiah 11:1–5? After the second coming when Jesus reigns as King of kings and Lord of lords, the rebuilt millennial city of Jerusalem will be called, "The LORD is there" (Ezekiel 48:35). Can you comprehend an earth no longer under curse and bondage, where a wolf and lamb are peacefully at rest with each other and a child leads a young lion or plays by a nest of vipers and doesn't get hurt (Romans 8:19, 21–22, Isaiah 11:6, 8)? A time when the earth is full of the knowledge of the LORD as the waters cover the sea (Isaiah 11:9)? I cannot contain the joy in my heart at such a thought, and frankly, I am unable to process all that the Lord has prepared for His return in power and glory. Jerusalem will be the throne of the LORD (Jeremiah 3:17). The LORD will be praised in the city of our God, in the mountain of His holiness (Psalm 48:1). Indeed, as the "city of the great King," Mount Zion will be the joy of the whole earth (Psalm 48:2)!

After the day of the Lord, there will be "nations" that remain. The prophets tell us that "all the families of the earth" will be required to come to Jerusalem to worship the king, the LORD of hosts. If families of the earth do not go, they and their land will be plagued with no rain (Zechariah 14:16–19). The glorified, immortal saints, along with King Jesus, will rule and reign over the nations with a rod of iron (Revelation 2:26–29). The "nations" who survive the day of the Lord will enter the millennium in mortal bodies (Matthew 25:31–32) and sin and death amongst these mortals will exist during the millennium (Psalm 72:9, Isaiah 65:20). While the millennium is a wonderfully pure and rich state, the perfect state will not come until the conclusion of the millennium when the final revolt is finished and death and hell are cast into the lake of fire (Revelation 20:7–15).

There is no question that the salvation of Israel will only happen through faith in Christ Jesus, repentance, and a new heart filled with the Spirit of God. The recipe for entrance into the family of God won't change, it is the same for everyone. However, one difference for Israel during the millennium as compared to the experience of believers today is the existence of a temple, filled with the glory of the LORD, and an altar (Ezekiel 43: 2–5, 13–17). Priests of Israel, it appears, will make sacrifices and offerings during the thousand-year reign of Jesus. And while still "a priest forever" made after the power of "an endless life" (Hebrews 7:16-17), Jesus will occupy a new role, and physically rule as the long-prophesied king from the seed of David.

What will be the purpose of these sacrifices? It is clear that no longer will these sacrifices look forward to the coming lamb of God, as they did in Old Testament times. Perhaps, much like when believers today partake of Holy Communion, they will look back in time to what the Lord did on the Jews' behalf. That is my guess for the sacrifices, although it is unnatural to me and beyond my understanding. I'm thankful that our calling today (between the first advent and the second) is to walk by faith, to offer the Lord a sacrifice of praise, to yield to Him a broken spirit and heart, and to present our bodies as a living sacrifice. We are not to conform our lives to this present evil world, but rather, to the ways of Almighty God and the perfect pattern that the Lord Jesus left for us.

There is much that I don't understand about Ezekiel 40–48. I do find it amazing that the millennium will offer glimpses of the amazing new Jerusalem, which will descend out of heaven to the earth after the millennium. The glory of the Lord will be present (Ezekiel 43). A river of life will issue out from under the threshold of the temple, and trees will grow on either side of the river, yielding fruit each month and possessing leaves for medicine (Ezekiel 47). And surrounding the city will be twelve gates, with three gates per side according to the tribes of Israel (Ezekiel 48). The millennial kingdom will be a rich and fruitful experience for all, especially with King Jesus on the throne and righteousness covering the earth. Unimaginable—but worth the effort to imagine.

PRINCIPLE #10: THE NEW JERUSALEM TRANSITION

A great transition will also occur at the end of the millennium. We are told that the devil has the "power of death" (Hebrews 2:14). Jesus will reign until all enemies are put under His feet, and the last enemy that shall be destroyed is death (1 Corinthians 15:25–26). When will the devil, who has the power of death, be destroyed? According to Revelation 20:7–10, after the thousand-year reign of Jesus, the devil will be loosed for a time. He will go throughout the four quarters of the earth and will deceive from the nations a contingent as numerous as the sand of the sea. This large number of deceived people will go up to battle at Jerusalem, only to be met with fire from God out of heaven that will devour them. The devil will then be cast into the lake of fire and brimstone, where he will be tormented day and night forever.

After all things have been subdued before Jesus and the last enemy, death, has been destroyed, in the millennial transition Jesus will deliver up the kingdom to God and then subject Himself "unto him that put all things under him, that God may be all in all" (1 Corinthians 15:28). I believe the following verses from 1 Corinthians 15:24–28 portray this transition. It is a time when God Himself will descend from heaven with the new Jerusalem, the City of God, and proceed to dwell with the redeemed on earth for ever and ever (Revelation 21:2–3, 10)!

> Then cometh the end, when he shall have delivered up the kingdom to God, even the Father; when he shall have put down all rule and all authority and power. For he must reign, till he hath put all enemies under his feet. The last enemy that shall be destroyed is death. For he hath put all things under his feet. But when he saith all things are put under him, it is manifest that he is excepted, which did put all things under him. And when all things shall be subdued unto him, then shall the Son also himself be subject unto him that put all things under him, that God may be all in all. (1 Corinthians 15:24–28)

In the spirit, and from the vantage point of a high mountain (Revelation 21:10), the apostle John first takes note that the heaven and earth have been made new. The restoration is clearly evident, and likely has been for nearly one thousand years. Next, he states "and there was no more sea." As new Jerusalem descends out of heaven, where will it eventually land? A reasonable guess is that it's right on top of old Jerusalem! Or, among several options, God could preserve the promised land and set the eastern edge of new Jerusalem along the present-day shore of the Mediterranean Sea. With an enormous length and width of nearly 1400 miles, whatever the ultimate destination, a removal of hundreds of miles of the Mediterranean Sea (far beyond where John's eye could see) seems likely.

As the vision continues, the apostle John describes the magnificent city, complete with the glory of God, and without the need for the light of the sun or moon within its beautiful walls and gates, descending to earth! There will be no more temple, for God Almighty and the Lamb will be the temple of new Jerusalem. And the gates, which are of course made for going "in and out," will never be shut.

PRINCIPLE #11: UNDERSTAND TWO KEY PRINCIPLES FOR STUDYING THE SCRIPTURE

After God laid a charge to my heart to study His future plans, I felt there was only one correct response. Admittedly, though, I had some reluctance due to negative connotations associated with the topic and being aware of the multitudes of discrepancies and inconsistencies within the realm of Bible prophecy advocacy. I needed discernment.

So I went forward with two fundamental and long-held principles in mind. One, my conviction that the most effective and Bible-based method of interpreting the Scriptures is that which is as literal, plain, and simple as possible. And two, a firm belief that the answers for understanding Bible prophecy were contained within the pages of Scripture itself (Revelation 22:18). I really believed (and believe) this! I have been encouraged from my youth up of the wisdom in *sola scriptura*, "by Scripture alone"—the belief that the Bible is the supreme authority in all matters of life and doctrine.

While I was confident that Scripture itself would ultimately reveal and yield the fruit of understanding for this difficult topic, I prayerfully sought guidance. I was confident the Lord knew my needs . . . but was He expecting me to gain insight all on my own, or were there works from the labors of other Bible students worth considering? Could such works help me as I used the two core principles to study the prophecies in a Berean-like manner?

I believe that God led me to two helpful sources. The first was a Bible prophecy study manual that took me several months to work through. I carried three primary and prized gems of truth and encouragement from that experience. The first was a reinforcement of the core principle of interpreting the Scriptures as literally as reasonably possible. The second was the need to marry the visions of Daniel together with Revelation when possible.

The third, but not least important, was the need to appreciate and value aspects of the Old Testament that I had never considered and to understand that Almighty God has "appointed times and seasons" through the Jewish holidays and feasts of Leviticus 23. These appointed times ultimately bring relevancy and understanding to the time periods referenced throughout the books of Revelation and Daniel (i.e. 1260 days, 1290 days, 1335 days, 2300 evenings and mornings, 42 months, and 3.5 years). Without that study manual experience, the eschatological framework in this book (which I believe is best supported by Scripture) would not exist. Although I differ with many of the conclusions in the overall work, I am ever grateful for the dedication and work of the author, Kevin Swift.

Another major source of encouragement and help came from Joel Richardson. While doing some research on Daniel 8, I came across some work of his, and one thing led to another. I was impressed with the honesty and candidness with which Joel presented his understanding of that chapter in Daniel. This led me to purchasing and reading two books that Joel had authored, *Mideast Beast* and *When a Jew Rules the World*. I have been blessed by his humble approach, his research, and his insight and understanding of Scripture.

At this point, I felt the Lord give me the encouragement to settle in and spend time with the Scriptures in a period of personal devotion and study like never before. Many of my usual priorities were set aside as this became my primary vocation. This study occurred over a lengthy period of time and continues to this day.

The writing of this book generally took place during the first five months of 2016. Unless otherwise noted, the following resources were used to assist in my writing:

The e-Sword Bible software (www.e-sword.net) on my laptop was my primary tool. I have used this software on my computer for over ten years, and it is fantastic. I also use it on my phone every day in some way as a reference tool, to look up a verse, and so on. Incorporated into my e-Sword application is the Greek Old Testament (Septuagint) with Strong's Numbers, Hebrew Old Testament (Tanach) with Strong's Numbers, *Strong's Bible Dictionary*, published in 1890, *Thayer's Greek Definitions*, published in 1886, as well as *Webster's Dictionary*, published in 1828.

Along with stacks of personal study notes, my personal Bible and the handwritten scribbles therein were my most important tool. I have always used the King James Version, so that is the version of my personal Bible and also what I have loaded onto e-Sword.

I wrote out each section of this book separately with no thought that one day it would be compiled and published. This was a personal journey that the Lord had set me on. This work was not the product or fulfillment of a long-held dream or ambition. At the end of the day, however, it became clear to me that each section could be tied together by an overarching theme. That theme is the day of the Lord, the heartbeat of prophetic Scripture.

Please be warned, this isn't a novel and it isn't easy reading. It is ultimately a Bible study, and I am not ashamed to include copious full-length Scripture citations. The Scripture is the main focus of this book, and ultimately our main authority.

With that, I invite you to journey with me into the heart of Scripture and the purpose of all history.

Chapter 1

THE GREAT AND NOTABLE DAY OF THE LORD

The day of the Lord will be the most monumental, transitional day in all of life's history. It is a day of events referred to more than any other in the Word of God.

All the way back in Genesis, God promised Satan that from the "seed of the woman" One would come to crush his head (Genesis 3:15). While this is clearly a prophecy of Jesus Christ, I believe the ultimate fulfillment of this promise will occur on the day of the Lord. While God's help supplies us with the means to overcome the Evil One today, Satan is still wildly active and successful on the earth. Would Satan continue to achieve the level of success that he currently enjoys if his abilities and power had been fully broken at the time of the cross or resurrection of Jesus? Of course not. This is one more reason to yearn for that great and notable day! Surely that great victory will occur sooner than later (Romans 16:20, Revelation 1:1).

Spiritually it is true and feasible for us to consider Jesus as our king today. However, the day of the Lord will bring about events that make His kingship a physical reality as well.

I do not profess to understand how everything will specifically unfold on the day of the Lord. For instructive purposes, I have broken out the events of this day into five main categories that will lead to the inauguration of Jesus Christ as king of the earth for one thousand years.

I did my best to find and assemble the relevant Scriptures that pertain to each phase. There is a great deal of overlap, because the Bible, especially throughout the prophets, contains a flood of Scriptures that point to the events of this great day—in fact, you will probably think of additional relevant material that I overlooked! As such, a vivid story is told of this most comprehensive, powerful, sober, and joyful day that will ever be. It is that great, historic, and transitional day when the Lord Jesus, by the authority of Almighty God, is given reign over all the earth.

Below are the five main components that I see occurring on that day:

- I. Cosmic events that *precede* the great and notable day of the Lord
- II. Resurrection and rapture at the last trumpet; shout and roar of the Lord
- III. Judgment and rewards
- IV. Salvation of remnant Israel
- V. The wrath of God poured out

Based on my study of the book of Revelation, and also due to the high-level yet detailed eschatological framework I have come to understand, I believe the day of the Lord will come at the time of the seventh seal, the seventh thunder, the seventh trumpet, and the seventh vial.

It is my understanding that each of these events, all recorded in the book of Revelation, will occur at the same time. Each denotes a climactic point in time, and they share many similarities. The "voices, thunderings, lightnings," and "an earthquake" are shared by the seventh seal, seventh trumpet, and seventh vial. The angel voice declares finality with the word "finished" and "done," as recorded in the seventh thunder and seventh vial, respectively. And a plague of great hail is mentioned with both the seventh trumpet and the seventh vial. In addition, the resurrection of the dead referred to with the seventh trumpet lends day of the Lord context as well as coinciding with the popular "last trump" message of 1 Corinthians 15:52. The day of the Lord context is also applicable with the seventh vial, as this final vial judgment comes right after the thief-like day of the Lord warning just two verses prior.

The Seventh Seal: And when he had opened the seventh seal, *there was silence in heaven about the space of half an hour.* And the angel took the censer, and filled it with fire of the altar, and cast it into the earth: and there were *voices, and thunderings, and lightnings, and an earthquake.* (Revelation 8:1, 5)

The Seventh Thunder: But in the days of the voice of the seventh angel, when he shall begin to sound, *the mystery of God should be finished,* as he hath declared to his servants the prophets. (Revelation 10:7)

The Seventh Trumpet: And the seventh angel sounded; and there were great voices in heaven, saying, *The kingdoms of this world are become the kingdoms of our Lord, and of his Christ; and he shall reign for ever and ever.* And the four and twenty elders, which sat before God on their seats, fell upon their faces, and worshipped God, saying, We give thee thanks, O Lord God Almighty, which art, and wast, and art to come; because thou hast taken to thee thy great power, and hast reigned. And the nations were angry, and thy wrath is come, and *the time of the dead, that they should be judged, and that thou shouldest give reward unto thy servants the prophets, and to the saints, and them that fear thy name, small and great; and shouldest destroy them which destroy the earth.* And the temple of God was opened in heaven, and there was seen in his temple the ark of his testament: and there were *lightnings, and voices, and thunderings, and an earthquake, and great hail.* (Revelation 11:15–19)

The Seventh Vial: And the seventh angel poured out his vial into the air; and there came a great voice out of the temple of heaven, from the throne, saying, *It is done.* And there were *voices, and thunders, and lightnings; and there was a great earthquake,* such as was not since men were upon the earth, so mighty an earthquake, and so great. And the great city was divided into three parts, and the cities of the nations fell: and great Babylon came in remembrance before God, to give unto her the cup of the wine of the fierceness of his wrath. And every island fled away, and the mountains were not found. And there fell upon men *a great hail out of heaven,* every stone about the weight of a talent: and men blasphemed God because of the plague of the hail; for the plague thereof was exceeding great. (Revelation 16:17–21)

Will there be fourteen plagues (seven trumpet plagues and seven vial/bowl plagues) inflicted on the earth? Or twenty-one plagues (to include the seven thunder plagues)? Or could there be as many as twenty-eight plagues (to include the seven seal judgments)?

I think the events recorded in the visions given to John can be more simply understood. All of the plague judgments of God are targeted against the unrepentant followers of Antichrist. Before dishing out these horrific and difficult plagues, I believe God will provide ample warning and notice so the recipients assuredly know they are in defiance of a living and Almighty God. It is my opinion that the *voice* of thunder and *sound* of a trumpet are warnings for each forthcoming vial plague. I don't believe that the thunders will be plagues in and of themselves, nor do I believe the trumpet blasts will be plagues. They simply are what they are: thunderous words of warning and loud, long warning blasts. Consistent with Ezekiel 33, the precedent for the trumpet blast is to serve as a herald or warning for impending judgment. Such warnings in advance of the plague judgments seem consistent with the heart of God. There will not be room for ignorance in the hearts of the followers of Antichrist.

A biblical precedent for this is when the hearts of Pharaoh and the Egyptians became (and remained) defiant to God's power via the plagues. Will it be different this time? To be brutally honest, the Scripture doesn't foretell a great awakening and turning for those who are aligned with Antichrist. But that won't stop our merciful God from making a clear declaration of warning to the inhabitants of earth as time moves swiftly toward the last trumpet and the second coming of Jesus on the day of the Lord. Also, these same warnings from God, and their related immunity from the plagues, will no doubt be an immense encouragement for the saints of God to persist in faith (Revelation 12:11). Therefore, the warnings and related plagues will serve as both a blessing and a curse, just as they did in Egypt. This subject of the seals, thunders, trumpets, and vials is discussed in much more detail in the chapter on Revelation.

How long will the day of the Lord last? Some may believe that the day of the Lord will not be a twenty-four-hour day. I am a literalist when interpreting the Scripture; at least I try to be, unless it is unreasonable or irresponsible based on the text. Therefore, I see a high likelihood that these events will occur in one day, starting with the resurrection/rapture and continuing all the way to Armageddon. The continual refrain of the day of the Lord passages is "in that day" and "on that day" and "at that day." As is discussed later in this book, my confidence that these events will occur in one literal day is simply the result of my confidence in an eschatological framework that ties the Jewish feast days perfectly to all of the Scripture-provided time frames pertaining to the end times. After all, the day of the Lord is in fact called the "day" of the Lord!

We also read that the resurrection will occur on the "last day" and it will happen in a moment and in the twinkling of an eye (John 6:39–40, 44, 54, 11:24; 1 Corinthians 15:52). The transformation and corporate salvation of remnant Israel will occur in "one day" (Isaiah 66:8; Ezekiel 39:22, 25–29; Zechariah 9:16, 12:9–11; Zephaniah 3:15–16; Matthew 23:39; Romans 11:26). And the wrath of God (the "day" of judgment) is likewise depicted as a single day (Isaiah 13:9, 13; Isaiah 24:21, 34:8; Ezekiel 38:19, 39:8; Micah 5:10; Zephaniah 1:15; Malachi 4:1; 2 Peter 3:7, 12; Revelation 16:14).

This will be discussed in detail later on, but I believe the day of the Lord will occur on the Day of Atonement, or Yom Kippur. The Day of Atonement is of course a single day on the calendar. This is a tremendous amount of anticipated activity for one day. But I say this: with God all things are possible!

As noted above, I have categorized the events of the day of the Lord into five parts and assembled relevant, contextual Scriptures for each phase. I believe the text itself explains remarkably well what the Bible calls the "great and notable day," a day the prophets of old have long pointed to. Reading through each of the Scriptures alone is all that is necessary to develop a deep appreciation for the exhaustive, intense, and dramatic events of that day. But I will first give a high-level summary of these events in my own words.

I believe the cosmic events will occur basically at the "midnight hour," just prior to the beginning of the day of the Lord. The Scriptures indicate that the cosmic events *precede* the second coming and the day of God's wrath.

It then seems most likely that the resurrection and rapture will chronologically occur first on the day of the Lord. The Scripture teaches us that the saints of the Lord today are referred to as the "bride" of Christ. It is my understanding that the "wife" of Christ (per Revelation 19:7) will return with Jesus to the earth for the trampling of the winepress, when the fierceness and wrath of Almighty God are unleashed at Armageddon. The bride of Christ then, by necessity, needs to have already met up with Jesus in the clouds and to have been escorted to heaven prior to the time of God's wrath (1 Thessalonians 5:9) and prior to the marriage of the Lamb to His bride (Revelation 19:7–8).

Those believers in Jesus who are resurrected and raptured on the day of the Lord when the last trumpet sounds are in much the same situation as Noah's family boarding the ark. Essentially, those dead in Christ and the living followers of the Lord Jesus will be *lifted off the earth* and taken to heaven to stand before the throne of God. In heaven there will be silence for a half-hour (Revelation 8:1). I tremble with somber joy and delight when I think of this half-hour space of time! At this point we will have glorified bodies, and we will be face-to-face with our Creator, knowing the things of God even as we are known (1 Corinthians 13:12). Judgment, rewards, and responsibilities will be given to the saints of God (Revelation 11:18 and 2 Corinthians 5:9–10).

Meanwhile, on earth there will be utter chaos, confusion, darkness, blindness, and destruction. I can't imagine a starker contrast of events between the scene in heaven and what is taking place on the earth. Among other things, some of the earthly events of that day will be:

1. A raining down of great hail (Revelation 16:17–21, Isaiah 30:30, Ezekiel 38:22)
2. Darkness and gloom during the daytime (Zechariah 14:6–7; Zephaniah 1:15; Amos 5:18, 20; Joel 2:2)
3. The Lord will cause men to kill each other as in the day of Midian (Isaiah 10:26, Zechariah 14:13, Ezekiel 38:21–22)
4. A flesh-consuming plague will smite all people who have fought against Jerusalem (Zechariah 14:12)
5. Distress, fear, pestilence, confusion, and blindness among sinners (Zephaniah 1:15–17, Isaiah 24:17–18, Habakkuk 3:5)
6. A fiery judgment on the earth (2 Peter 3:7; Isaiah 9:19, 24:6, 34:4, 9; Ezekiel 39:6; Zephaniah 1:15–18; Malachi 4:1)

Then, toward the end of this great and notable day, the saints of God will follow Christ to earth to put the finishing touches upon the evil sinners at Armageddon. At this same time it appears that the Lord will be gathering one by one the children of Israel, who are mourning because of the great salvation they have experienced (Isaiah 27:12, Zechariah 12:10–11). I can't conceive how this will be done. It is reminiscent of the sword of the Lord (which will be coming out of the mouth of Jesus—Revelation 19:15) that is two-edged. On one side it will smite the ungodly and slay the remaining wicked as He marches through the land in indignation, and on the other side it will cut forth unto the salvation of His chosen people, who will have been transformed with new hearts by the Spirit (Habakkuk 3:12; Revelation 19:21; Habakkuk 3:13; Jeremiah 31:33, 32:39; Ezekiel 36:26–27; Zechariah 12:10). At the conclusion of the battle of Armageddon, the fowls of the air will gather for a great supper (Revelation 19:17, 21; Matthew 24:28; Ezekiel 39:17–20).

The return of Jesus to earth along with the resurrected saints will likely happen toward the evening of the day. As was mentioned, it will be cloudy, dark, and gloomy during the daytime hours. Then, in Zechariah 14:7 we read that at evening time it shall be light. Perhaps this will be a reflection of Jesus Christ coming to earth with the saints, His glorious church. The culmination of the great and notable day is described in Zechariah 14:8–9:

And his feet shall stand in that day upon the mount of Olives, which is before Jerusalem on the east, and the mount of Olives shall cleave in the midst thereof toward the east and toward the west, and there shall be a very great valley; and half of the mountain shall remove toward the north, and half of it toward the south. And ye shall flee to the valley of the mountains; for the valley of the mountains shall reach unto Azal: yea, ye shall flee, like as ye fled from before the earthquake in the days of Uzziah king of Judah: and *the* LORD *my God shall come, and all the saints with thee.* And it shall come to pass in that day, that the light shall not be clear, nor dark: but it shall be one day which shall be known to the LORD, not day, nor night: but it shall come to pass, that *at evening time it shall be light.* And it shall be *in that day, that living waters shall go out from Jerusalem*; half of them toward the former sea, and half of them toward the hinder sea: in summer and in winter shall it be. And the LORD shall be king over all the earth: *in that day shall there be one* LORD, *and his name one*.

Let me warn you that the rest of this chapter doesn't contain much commentary, but I'm not going to apologize for making you read so much Scripture. Truly, it is the Scripture itself that has spoken to my heart so vividly and enhanced my faith. I have never been so confident in the words of the Holy Bible than I am as I write this today. Comparing common Scripture passages to one another is a wondrous, profitable blessing. What builds our faith? The Word of God (Romans 10:17).

Be prayerful as you proceed through these passages. And as you go through them, may the journey forever alter your perspective of this great day of God.

I. THE PRECEDING COSMIC EVENTS

As you read through the passages pertaining to the cosmic events that precede the great and notable day of the Lord, please steer away from the tendency to spiritualize such things because they are too difficult to visualize. Bear in mind that God's power and ability have not diminished since the time of Christ. According to Genesis 1:14, the lights in the sky are for times and seasons. This Hebrew word for seasons, *moed* (Strong's H4150), is the same as mentioned previously and refers to an appointment or a fixed time. Recall that God used a peculiar light in the sky to guide the wise men to Jerusalem when the King was born (Matthew 2:2, Numbers 24:17). When the Lord Jesus hung on the cross, God easily brought darkness over all the land (Matthew 27:45) and made the earth to quake (Matthew 27:54, 28:2). The second advent of Christ is no less important than the first and will be preceded by an unprecedented cosmic display.

Ever since Satan lured humankind into sin and gained leverage over the creation, earth's curse has been sustained. This transformative day will become the fulcrum of a great reversal. Through a restoration, creation will transition back to a paradise-like state where the wolf will dwell with a lamb (Acts 1:6, 3:21; Matthew 19:27–28; Isaiah 11:6–8). Such a new and glorious future under the reign of Christ will not come quietly. Simply put, the theme of this great day is the power and glory of God. We should humbly recognize these things and appreciate the repetition of truth embedded in the Holy Word of God. Taken at face value, the Scriptures make it clear this will be a major earth-shaking event.

> Immediately after the tribulation of those days shall *the sun be darkened, and the moon shall not give her light, and the stars shall fall from heaven, and the powers of the heavens shall be shaken:* and then shall appear the sign of the Son of man in heaven: and then shall all the tribes of the earth mourn, and they shall see the Son of man coming in the clouds of heaven with power and great glory. And he shall send his angels with a great sound of a trumpet, and they shall gather together his elect from the four winds, from one end of heaven to the other. (Matthew 24:29–31)

> But in those days, after that tribulation, *the sun shall be darkened, and the moon shall not give her light, and the stars of heaven shall fall, and the powers that are in heaven shall be shaken.* And then shall they see the Son of man coming in the clouds with great power and glory. And then shall he send his angels, and shall gather together his elect from the four winds, from the uttermost part of the earth to the uttermost part of heaven. (Mark 13:24–27)

> *And there shall be signs in the sun, and in the moon, and in the stars;* and upon the earth distress of nations, with perplexity; the sea and the waves roaring; men's hearts failing them for fear, and for looking after those things which are coming on the earth: for *the powers of heaven shall be shaken.* And then shall they see the Son of man coming in a cloud with power and great glory. And when these things begin to come to pass, then look up, and lift up your heads; for your redemption draweth nigh. (Luke 21:25–28)

> And I will shew wonders in heaven above, and signs in the earth beneath; blood, and fire, and vapour of smoke: the sun shall be turned into darkness, and the moon into blood, *before* that great and notable day of the Lord come: and it shall come to pass, that whosoever shall call on the name of the Lord shall be saved. (Act 2:19–21)

The sun shall be turned into darkness, and the moon into blood, *before the great and the terrible day of the* LORD *come.* And it shall come to pass, that whosoever shall call on the name of the LORD shall be delivered: for in mount Zion and in Jerusalem shall be deliverance, as the LORD hath said, and in the remnant whom the LORD shall call. (Joel 2:31–32)

Put ye in the sickle, for the harvest is ripe: come, get you down; for the press is full, the fats overflow; for their wickedness is great. Multitudes, multitudes in the valley of decision: for the day of the LORD is near in the valley of decision. *The sun and the moon shall be darkened, and the stars shall withdraw their shining.* The LORD also shall roar out of Zion, and utter his voice from Jerusalem; and *the heavens and the earth shall shake*: but the LORD will be the hope of his people, and the strength of the children of Israel. (Joel 3:13–16)

Enter into the rock, and hide thee in the dust, for fear of the LORD, and for the glory of his majesty. The lofty looks of man shall be humbled, and the haughtiness of men shall be bowed down, and the LORD alone shall be exalted in that day. For the day of the LORD of hosts shall be upon every one that is proud and lofty, and upon every one that is lifted up; and he shall be brought low: and upon all the cedars of Lebanon, that are high and lifted up, and upon all the oaks of Bashan, and upon all the high mountains, and upon all the hills that are lifted up, and upon every high tower, and upon every fenced wall, and upon all the ships of Tarshish, and upon all pleasant pictures. And the loftiness of man shall be bowed down, and the haughtiness of men shall be made low: and the LORD alone shall be exalted in that day. And the idols he shall utterly abolish. And they shall go into the holes of the rocks, and into the caves of the earth, for fear of the LORD, and for the glory of his majesty, when he ariseth to *shake terribly the earth*. In that day a man shall cast his idols of silver, and his idols of gold, which they made each one for himself to worship, to the moles and to the bats; to go into the clefts of the rocks, and into the tops of the ragged rocks, for fear of the LORD, and for the glory of his majesty, when he ariseth *to shake terribly the earth*. Cease ye from man, whose breath is in his nostrils: for wherein is he to be accounted of? (Isaiah 2:10–22)

Behold, the day of the LORD cometh, cruel both with wrath and fierce anger, to lay the land desolate: and he shall destroy the sinners thereof out of it. *For the stars of heaven and the constellations thereof shall not give their light: the sun shall be darkened in his going forth, and the moon shall not cause her light to shine.* And I will punish the world for their evil, and the wicked for their iniquity; and I will cause the arrogancy of the proud to cease, and will lay low the haughtiness of the terrible. I will make a man more precious than fine gold; even a man than the golden wedge of Ophir. Therefore *I will shake the heavens, and the earth shall remove out of her place,* in the wrath of the LORD of hosts, and in the day of his fierce anger. (Isaiah 13:9–13)

And I beheld when he had opened the sixth seal, and, lo, there was *a great earthquake;* and *the sun became black as sackcloth of hair, and the moon became as blood; and the stars of heaven fell unto the earth,* even as a fig tree casteth her untimely figs, when she is shaken of a mighty wind. And the heaven departed as a scroll when it is rolled together; and every mountain and island were moved out of their places. And the kings of the earth, and the great men, and the rich men, and the chief captains, and the mighty men, and every bondman, and every free man, hid themselves in the dens and in the rocks of the mountains; and said to the mountains and rocks, Fall on us, and hide us from the face of him that sitteth on the throne, and from the wrath of the Lamb: for the great day of his wrath is come; and who shall be able to stand? (Revelation 6:12–17)

II. RESURRECTION AND RAPTURE

Next to occur, I believe, is the resurrection and rapture of the saints. The timing of the resurrection and rapture is discussed in greater detail in the chapter on the Olivet Discourse. It is also discussed in the chapter on Revelation in the review of the seals, trumpets, vials, and thunders, as well as the harvest of the earth. Briefly, I believe in a post-tribulation resurrection and rapture on the *last day.* Jesus referred to the resurrection occurring "at the last day" (John 6:40, 44, 54), as did also Martha (John 11:23–24). After cosmic events, I believe the seventh trumpet will sound. In context, Scriptures teach that the day of the Lord and the "gathering together" are accompanied by the great sound of a trumpet, also referred to as the *last trump* (Matthew 24:31, 1 Thessalonians 4:16, 1 Corinthians 15:52, et al).

The resurrection/rapture is not imminent. Our "gathering together" to Him at "the coming of our Lord Jesus Christ" (2 Thessalonians 2:1) will not occur until after the time of Antichrist and the abomination (2 Thessalonians 2:3–4). The "coming" in verse 1 is the *parousia* (Strong's G3952), defined by

Thayer's Greek Lexicon as "the advent, i.e. the future, visible, return from heaven of Jesus, the Messiah, to raise the dead, hold the last judgment, and set up formally and gloriously the kingdom of God." The occurrence of Antichrist's abomination before the second coming is simply and plainly taught by the apostle Paul. He tells the church not to be "shaken in mind" or "troubled" that the day of the Lord is present or will be coming in an instant (2 Thessalonians 2:2). The Greek word Paul uses is *enistemi* (Strong's G1764), which teaches that the day of the Lord is not imminent, nor is it even presently on hand! Paul further writes, don't let anyone deceive you, for that day shall not come (i.e. the *parousia*) except there first comes a defection from the truth and the man of sin is revealed (2 Thessalonians 2:3). Essentially Paul is calming their anxious hearts by stating that a specific event must occur before the second coming. That event is the revealing of the Antichrist and later his abomination where he "exalts himself" so that "he as God sits in the temple of God showing himself that he is God" (2 Thessalonians 2:3)!

Is the resurrection and rapture of the church distinct and separate from the future resurrection of the Old Testament saints? What did the apostle Paul know when he wrote to the Corinthian church? What we know is that his inspired letter was penned decades before John's Revelation. And we know that Paul was well acquainted with the Old Testament. In that light, he ties together our future resurrection/rapture with that noted by the prophets Isaiah (Isaiah 25:8) and Hosea (Hosea 13:14) by quoting Isaiah in 1 Corinthians 15:54; "then shall be brought to pass the saying that is written, Death is swallowed up in victory," and Hosea in 1 Corinthians 15:55; "O death, where is they sting? O grave, where is thy victory?" I believe the Scriptures most plainly teach a resurrection of all the righteous dead, both the church and the Old Testament saints, at the last day and at the last trump. "Blessed and holy is he that hath part in the *first resurrection*" (Revelation 20:6).

It is a wondrous thought that the resurrection and rapture will include the righteous saints of old along with the church, who we recognize are all part of a singular body (Ephesians 2:12–22, 3:6, 4:4–6), though with clear distinctions since Pentecost. The fact that Isaiah remarked on his personal resurrection in the context of the day of the Lord and indicated that "in that day" a great trumpet would be blown is marvelous (Isaiah 26:19, 27:13). And it stirs my heart to consider the faith of Job and the longing in his heart to picture the day when he himself would be resurrected and behold God with eyes made new (Job 19:25–27). Job understood death and the resurrection of the body in the context of Job 14:12, a verse that states clearly "So man lieth down, and riseth not: till the heavens be no more." This is unmistakably the day of the Lord when the "heavens shall pass away with a great noise" (2 Peter 3:10).

Will the resurrection/rapture be a sneaky event with no advance warning? Absolutely not. The believer who is watching, waiting, and "of the day" (1 Thessalonians 5:4–6) will be armed with awareness due to the warnings and signs from Scripture leading up to that powerful and glorious day.

From the following Scriptures, we can be confident that the resurrection and rapture will be:

- Preceded by the aforementioned cosmic events
- Audible (there will be a trumpet sound, the voice of the archangel, and the Lord will roar and shout)
- Visible (Jesus will be seen coming in the clouds)

Without further ado, here are the Scriptures to consider.

Immediately after the tribulation of those days shall the sun be darkened, and the moon shall not give her light, and the stars shall fall from heaven, and the powers of the heavens shall be shaken: and then shall appear the sign of the Son of man in heaven: and then shall all the tribes of the earth mourn, and they *shall see the Son of man coming in the clouds* of heaven with power and great glory. And he shall send his angels *with a great sound of a trumpet*, and *they shall gather together his elect* from the four winds, from one end of heaven to the other. (Matthew 24:29–31)

But in those days, after that tribulation, the sun shall be darkened, and the moon shall not give her light, and the stars of heaven shall fall, and the powers that are in heaven shall be shaken. And then *shall they see the Son of man coming in the clouds* with great power and glory. And then shall he send his angels, and shall *gather together his elect from the four winds, from the uttermost part of the earth to the uttermost part of heaven*. (Mark 13:24–27)

And there shall be signs in the sun, and in the moon, and in the stars; and upon the earth distress of nations, with perplexity; the sea and the waves roaring; men's hearts failing them for fear, and for looking after those things which are coming on the earth: for the powers of heaven shall be shaken. And then *shall they see the Son of man coming in a cloud* with power and great glory. And when these things begin to come to pass, *then look up, and lift up your heads; for your redemption draweth nigh*. (Luke 21:25–28)

Behold, I shew you a mystery; We shall not all sleep, but we shall all be changed, in a moment, in the twinkling of an eye, *at the last trump: for the trumpet shall sound, and the dead shall be raised incorruptible, and we shall be changed*. For this corruptible must put on incorruption, and this mortal must put on immortality. So when this corruptible shall have put on incorruption, and this mortal shall have put on immortality, then shall be brought to pass the saying that is written, *Death is swallowed up in victory. O death, where is thy sting? O grave, where is thy victory?* (1 Corinthians 15:51–55)

For this we say unto you by the word of the Lord, that we which are alive and remain unto the coming of the Lord shall not prevent them which are asleep. For *the Lord himself shall descend* from heaven *with a shout, with the voice of the archangel, and with the trump of God: and the dead in Christ shall rise first: then we which are alive and remain shall be caught up together with them in the clouds*, to meet the Lord in the air: and so shall we ever be with the Lord. Wherefore comfort one another with these words. (1 Thessalonians 4:15–18)

But in the days of *the voice of the seventh angel, when he shall begin to sound*, the mystery of God should be finished, as he hath declared to his servants the prophets. (Revelation 10:7)

And *the seventh angel sounded*; and there were great voices in heaven, saying, The kingdoms of this world are become the kingdoms of our Lord, and of his Christ; and he shall reign for ever and ever. And the nations were angry, and thy wrath is come, and *the time of the dead, that they should be judged*, and that thou shouldest give reward unto thy servants the prophets, and to the saints, and them that fear thy name, small and great; and shouldest destroy them which destroy the earth. (Revelation 11:15, 18)

Please note for the Revelation 14 reference below that it is my understanding that the first sickle (Revelation 14:14–16) represents the resurrection and rapture (i.e. the harvest of the wheat/fruit), while the second sickle (Revelation 14:17–20) represents the wrath of God upon the followers of Antichrist and the enemies of God at Armageddon (i.e. the harvest of the tares).

And I looked, and behold *a white cloud, and upon the cloud one sat like unto the Son of man*, having on his head a golden crown, and *in his hand a sharp sickle*. And another angel came out of the temple, crying with a loud voice to him that sat on the cloud, Thrust in thy sickle, and reap: *for the time is come for thee to reap; for the harvest of the earth is ripe.* And he that sat on the cloud thrust in his sickle on the earth; and *the earth was reaped*. (Revelation 14:14–16)

Let's now review several Old Testament passages that depict the resurrection itself, and/or its audible and visible nature (i.e. the sound of a trumpet, a loud voice and shout, and the presence of clouds). Please note, in some of these selected passages you will see an intermixing of details related to war, wrath, destruction, fire, or even deliverance for Israel. However, this should be expected because the timing of these events on the day of the Lord are compact and pressed together. Really, this is no different than what we read in 2 Thessalonians 1:7–10. In this passage, a strong cohesion in timing between the judgment (verses 8–9) and the glorification of the saints (verse 10) is clearly portrayed.

> And to you who are troubled rest with us, when the Lord Jesus shall be revealed from heaven with his mighty angels, In flaming fire taking vengeance on them that know not God, and that obey not the gospel of our Lord Jesus Christ: Who shall be punished with everlasting destruction from the presence of the Lord, and from the glory of his power; When he shall come to be glorified in his saints, and to be admired in all them that believe (because our testimony among you was believed) in that day. (2 Thessalonians 2:7–10)

Please note that the following passage is the one I referenced previously as being quoted by the apostle Paul in 1 Corinthians 15:54:

> And in this mountain shall the Lord of hosts make unto all people a feast of fat things, a feast of wines on the lees, of fat things full of marrow, of wines on the lees well refined. And he will destroy in this mountain the face of the covering cast over all people, and the vail that is spread over all nations. *He will swallow up death in victory; and the Lord God will wipe away tears from off all faces;* and the rebuke of his people shall he take away from off all the earth: for the Lord hath spoken it. And it shall be said in that day, Lo, this is our God; we have waited for him, and he will save us: this is the Lord; we have waited for him, we will be glad and rejoice in his salvation. (Isaiah 25:6–9)

The following verse is the one I referenced previously, where Isaiah references his own personal resurrection in the context of the day of the Lord!

Like as a woman with child, that draweth near the time of her delivery, is in pain, and crieth out in her pangs; so have we been in thy sight, O Lord. We have been with child, we have been in pain, we have as it were brought forth wind; we have not wrought any deliverance in the earth; neither have the inhabitants of the world fallen. *Thy dead men shall live, together with my dead body shall they arise. Awake and sing, ye that dwell in dust*: for thy dew is as the dew of herbs, and *the earth shall cast out the dead*. Come, my people, enter thou into thy chambers, and shut thy doors about thee: hide thyself as it were for a little moment, until the indignation be overpast. For, behold, the Lord cometh out of his place to punish the inhabitants of the earth for their iniquity: the earth also shall disclose her blood, and shall no more cover her slain. (Isaiah 26:17–21)

And it shall come to pass *in that day*, that the Lord shall beat off from the channel of the river unto the stream of Egypt, and ye shall be gathered one by one, O ye children of Israel. And it shall come to pass *in that day*, that *the great trumpet shall be blown*, and they shall come which were ready to perish in the land of Assyria, and the outcasts in the land of Egypt, and shall worship the Lord in the holy mount at Jerusalem. (Isaiah 27:12–13)

For, lo, I begin to bring evil on the city which is called by my name, and should ye be utterly unpunished? Ye shall not be unpunished: for I will call for a sword upon all the inhabitants of the earth, saith the Lord of hosts. Therefore prophesy thou against them all these words, and say unto them, *The Lord shall roar* from on high, *and utter his voice from his holy habitation; he shall mightily roar* upon his habitation; *he shall give a shout, as they that tread the grapes, against all the inhabitants of the earth. A noise shall come even to the ends of the earth*; for the Lord hath a controversy with the nations, he will plead with all flesh; he will give them that are wicked to the sword, saith the Lord. Thus saith the Lord of hosts, Behold, evil shall go forth from nation to nation, and a great whirlwind shall be raised up from the coasts of the earth. And the slain of the Lord shall be at that day from one end of the earth even unto the other end of the earth: they shall not be lamented, neither gathered, nor buried; they shall be dung upon the ground. Howl, ye shepherds, and cry; and wallow yourselves in the ashes, ye principal of the flock: for the days of your slaughter and of your dispersions are accomplished; and ye shall fall like a pleasant vessel. And the shepherds shall have no way to flee, nor the principal of the flock to escape. A voice of the cry of the shepherds, and an howling of the principal of the flock, shall be heard: for the LORD hath spoiled their pasture. And the peaceable habitations are cut down because of the fierce anger of the LORD. *He hath forsaken his covert, as the lion:* for their land is desolate because of the fierceness of the oppressor, and because of his fierce anger. (Jeremiah 25:29–38)

The great day of the LORD is near, it is near, and hasteth greatly, even *the voice of the day of the* LORD: the mighty man shall cry there bitterly. That day is a day of wrath, a day of trouble and distress, a day of wasteness and desolation, *a day of darkness and gloominess, a day of clouds and thick darkness, a day of the trumpet and alarm* against the fenced cities, and against the high towers. And I will bring distress upon men, that they shall walk like blind men, because they have sinned against the LORD: and their blood shall be poured out as dust, and their flesh as the dung. Neither their silver nor their gold shall be able to deliver them in the day of the LORD's wrath; but the whole land shall be devoured by the fire of his jealousy: for he shall make even a speedy riddance of all them that dwell in the land. (Zephaniah 1:14–18)

And the LORD shall be seen over them, and his arrow shall go forth as the lightning: and *the Lord* GOD *shall blow the trumpet,* and shall go with whirlwinds of the south. The LORD of hosts shall defend them; and they shall devour, and subdue with sling stones; and they shall drink, and make a noise as through wine; and they shall be filled like bowls, and as the corners of the altar. And the LORD their God shall save them in that day as the flock of his people: for they shall be as the stones of a crown, lifted up as an ensign upon his land. (Zechariah 9:14–16)

And at that time shall Michael stand up, the great prince which standeth for the children of thy people: and there shall be a time of trouble, such as never was since there was a nation even to that same time: and at that time thy people shall be delivered, every one that shall be found written in the book. And *many of them that sleep in the dust of the earth shall awake, some to everlasting life, and some to shame and everlasting contempt.* And they that be wise shall shine as the brightness of the firmament; and they that turn many to righteousness as the stars for ever and ever. (Daniel 12:1–3)

The following verse is the one I referenced previously, where Job speaks of his own personal resurrection in the context of a time when the redeemer shall stand upon the earth in the latter day!

> Oh that my words were now written! oh that they were printed in a book! That they were graven with an iron pen and lead in the rock for ever! For I know that my redeemer liveth, and that he shall stand at the latter day upon the earth: and *though after my skin worms destroy this body, yet in my flesh shall I see God: whom I shall see for myself, and mine eyes shall behold, and not another*; though my reins be consumed within me. (Job 19:23–27)

III. JUDGMENT AND REWARDS

It appears that immediately after the resurrection and rapture, the bride of Christ is escorted to the throne of God in heaven by Jesus and the angels. What a euphoric time—the time when the bride meets up with the Bridegroom! A complete review of Revelation 7 is included in the chapter on Revelation. It is my opinion that these verses capture the picture in heaven at this very time. It is a most glorious portrayal:

> After this I beheld, and, lo, a great multitude, which no man could number, of all nations, and kindreds, and people, and tongues, stood before the throne, and before the Lamb, clothed with white robes, and palms in their hands; and cried with a loud voice, saying, Salvation to our God which sitteth upon the throne, and unto the Lamb. And all the angels stood round about the throne, and about the elders and the four beasts, and fell before the throne on their faces, and worshipped God, saying, Amen: Blessing, and glory, and wisdom, and thanksgiving, and honour, and power, and might, be unto our God for ever and ever. Amen. (Revelation 7:9–12)

Once the saints are gathered around the throne, it is a time for judgment and rewards.

Recompense comes at the resurrection of the just (Luke 14:14). This is sharply distinct from the judgment of the wicked: the time when the prophets, the saints, and the small and great who fear the Lord stand before God's throne isn't a time for judging whether someone lives forever or is cast into hell. The mere fact that this uncountable multitude is surrounding the throne of God *in heaven* reflects that a divine judgment of "life" has already been given. To be a part of the first resurrection is to literally pass from death and to taste and experience the blessedness of eternal life (Revelation 20:6).

All who are resurrected or raptured in this scene have been found "in Christ" (Philippians 3:9–11). They are confident and without shame (1 John

2:28). They receive a crown of glory that never fades; they love the appearing of Jesus in the clouds and receive a crown of righteousness (1 Peter 5:4, 2 Timothy 4:8). They receive too a crown of life for enduring faithfully (James 1:12, Revelation 2:20), for they have lived soberly, righteously, and godly in this present world, looking for that blessed hope and the glorious appearing of Jesus Christ (Titus 2:12–13).

In this scene, it is Jesus who will sit on the judgment seat. No witnesses will be needed. Jesus knows us fully inside and out, and it is unnecessary for anyone to testify on our behalf (John 2:24–25).

Jesus spoke a parable in Luke 19:11–27 about ten servants and ten pounds, with one pound given to each servant. The purpose of the parable was to shed light on what will occur once the kingdom of God comes to earth. In view of the judgment seat of Christ and the reality of judgment and the distribution of rewards (2 Corinthians 5:10, Romans 14:10, Revelation 11:18), I believe it is instructive to consider the parable. How shall it be with us? What are we doing, so to speak, with our pound? As He said in the last verse of the parable, if we are unwilling to surrender and let Jesus reign in our lives now, we will forfeit the opportunity to reign with Christ when His kingdom is established on earth.

The parable of the talents in Matthew 25:14–30 proclaims the same message in the same context (that of the coming kingdom). With clarity, the very words of Jesus teach us that roles and responsibilities for those resurrected/raptured in the kingdom of God will be dependent on how we live by faith under the guidance of the Holy Spirit and the Word of God.

The theme of varying rewards is hinted at again in the "resurrection chapter," 1 Corinthians 15. It states that a variation in illumination exists between the sun, the moon and the stars. And likewise, from star to star the degree of glory emitted differs. The text goes on to say, "so also is the resurrection of the dead" (1 Corinthians 15:42). As such, in our immortal state we will see variation in the rewards, roles, and responsibilities given. Revelation 22:12 says, "Behold, I come quickly; and my reward is with me, to give every man according as his work shall be." Oh, may the Lord help us that our lights can shine for Him today in a dark and sinful world!

> And the seventh angel sounded; and there were great voices in heaven, saying, The kingdoms of this world are become the kingdoms of our Lord, and of his Christ; and he shall reign for ever and ever. And the four and twenty elders, which sat before God on their seats, fell upon their

THE GREAT AND NOTABLE DAY OF THE LORD • 43

faces, and worshipped God, saying, We give thee thanks, O Lord God Almighty, which art, and wast, and art to come; because thou hast taken to thee thy great power, and hast reigned. And the nations were angry, and thy wrath is come, *and the time of the dead, that they should be judged, and that thou shouldest give reward unto thy servants the prophets, and to the saints, and them that fear thy name, small and great*; and shouldest destroy them which destroy the earth. And the temple of God was opened in heaven, and there was seen in his temple the ark of his testament: and there were lightnings, and voices, and thunderings, and an earthquake, and great hail. (Revelation 11:15–19)

Wherefore we labour, that, whether present or absent, we may be accepted of him. For we must all appear before the judgment seat of Christ; that every one may receive the things done in his body, according to that he hath done, whether it be good or bad. (2 Corinthians 5:9–10)

For none of us liveth to himself, and no man dieth to himself. For whether we live, we live unto the Lord; and whether we die, we die unto the Lord: whether we live therefore, or die, we are the Lord's. For to this end Christ both died, and rose, and revived, that he might be Lord both of the dead and living. But why dost thou judge thy brother? or why dost thou set at nought thy brother? *for we shall all stand before the judgment seat of Christ.* For it is written, As I live, saith the Lord, every knee shall bow to me, and every tongue shall confess to God. So then every one of us shall give account of himself to God. (Romans 14:7–12)

. . . *and hath given him authority to execute judgment also, because he is the Son of man.* Marvel not at this: for the hour is coming, in the which all that are in the graves shall hear his voice, and shall come forth; they that have done good, unto *the resurrection of life*; and they that have done evil, unto *the resurrection of damnation*. I can of mine own self do nothing: *as I hear, I judge: and my judgment is just*; because I seek not mine own will, but the will of the Father which hath sent me. (John 5:27–30)

And I saw an angel come down from heaven, having the key of the bottomless pit and a great chain in his hand. And he laid hold on the dragon, that old serpent, which is the Devil, and Satan, and bound him a thousand years, and cast him into the bottomless pit, and shut him up, and set a seal upon him, that he should deceive the nations no more, till the thousand years should be fulfilled: and after that he must be loosed a little season. *And I saw thrones, and they sat upon them, and judgment was given unto them:* and I saw the souls of them that were beheaded for the witness of Jesus, and for the word of God, and which had not worshipped the beast, neither his image, neither had received his mark upon their foreheads, or in their hands; and they lived and reigned with Christ a thousand years. But the rest of the dead lived not again until the thousand years were finished. This is the first resurrection. Blessed and holy is he that hath part in the first resurrection: on such the second death hath no power, but they shall be priests of God and of Christ, and shall reign with him a thousand years. (Revelation 20:1–6)

IV. SALVATION OF REMNANT ISRAEL

Along with Scriptures specifically pertaining to Israel in the day of the Lord, I have included here a few Scriptures to help lay the groundwork as to why and how Israel is still relevant and important to God to this very day. This includes the covenant background and the everlasting nature of God's promises to His chosen people.

The Abrahamic Covenant. The following passage in Genesis 15 contains the covenant made to Abraham that a specific region of land was promised for an inheritance to his seed. Does God lie or fail in His promises? This is an irrevocable promise of God that essentially says Israel is the rightful owner of this land parcel. But while it was (and is) an unconditional promise of ownership, the ability to keep and stay in the land was based upon obedience (Deuteronomy 4:29–31; 7:9, 12).

> And he brought him forth abroad, and said, Look now toward heaven, and tell the stars, if thou be able to number them: and he said unto him, So shall thy seed be. And he believed in the LORD; and he counted it to him for righteousness. And he said unto him, I am the LORD that brought thee out of Ur of the Chaldees, *to give thee this land to inherit it.* And he said, Lord GOD, whereby shall I know that I shall inherit it? And he said unto him, Take me an heifer of three years old, and a she goat of three years old, and a ram of three years old, and a turtledove, and a young pigeon. And he took unto him all these, and divided them in the midst, and laid each piece one against another: but the birds divided he not. And when the fowls came down upon the carcases, Abram drove them away. And when the sun was going down, a deep sleep fell upon Abram; and, lo, an horror of great darkness fell upon him. And he said unto Abram, Know of a surety

> that thy seed shall be a stranger in a land that is not theirs, and shall serve them; and they shall afflict them four hundred years; and also that nation, whom they shall serve, will I judge: and afterward shall they come out with great substance. And thou shalt go to thy fathers in peace; thou shalt be buried in a good old age. But in the fourth generation they shall come hither again: for the iniquity of the Amorites is not yet full. And it came to pass, that, when the sun went down, and it was dark, behold a smoking furnace, and a burning lamp that passed between those pieces. *In the same day the* LORD *made a covenant with Abram, saying, Unto thy seed have I given this land,* from the river of Egypt unto the great river, the river Euphrates: the Kenites, and the Kenizzites, and the Kadmonites, and the Hittites, and the Perizzites, and the Rephaims, and the Amorites, and the Canaanites, and the Girgashites, and the Jebusites. (Genesis 15:5–21)

According to the Lord, the Israelites are a special and elect people chosen by God above all peoples who are upon the face of the earth.

> *For thou art an holy people unto the* LORD *thy God: the* LORD *thy God hath chosen thee to be a special people unto himself, above all people that are upon the face of the earth.* The LORD did not set his love upon you, nor choose you, because ye were more in number than any people; for ye were the fewest of all people: but because the LORD loved you, and because he would keep the oath which he had sworn unto your fathers, hath the LORD brought you out with a mighty hand, and redeemed you out of the house of bondmen, from the hand of Pharaoh king of Egypt. *Know therefore that the* LORD *thy God, he is God, the faithful God, which keepeth covenant and mercy with them that love him and keep his commandments to a thousand generations;* and repayeth them that hate him to their face, to destroy them: he will not be slack to him that hateth him, he will repay him to his face. Thou shalt therefore keep the commandments, and the statutes, and the judgments, which I command thee this day, to do them. Wherefore it shall come to pass, *if ye* hearken to these judgments, and keep, and do them, that the LORD thy God shall keep unto thee the covenant and the mercy which he sware unto thy fathers. (Deuteronomy 7:6–12)

The Mosaic or Sinaitic Covenant. God Almighty established law and order in the form of the commandments given to Moses in Exodus 20 (see also Deuteronomy 5). These commandments were established for the Israelites primarily because God is holy and deserving of being served wholeheartedly.

This covenant was conditional from the standpoint that if Israel was obedient, then God would bless them, but if they disobeyed God would punish them (Deuteronomy 28).

> And God spake all these words, saying, I am the LORD thy God, which have brought thee out of the land of Egypt, out of the house of bondage. Thou shalt have no other gods before me. Thou shalt not make unto thee any graven image, or any likeness of any thing that is in heaven above, or that is in the earth beneath, or that is in the water under the earth: thou shalt not bow down thyself to them, nor serve them: for I the LORD thy God am a jealous God, visiting the iniquity of the fathers upon the children unto the third and fourth generation of them that hate me; and shewing mercy unto thousands of them that love me, and keep my commandments. Thou shalt not take the name of the LORD thy God in vain; for the LORD will not hold him guiltless that taketh his name in vain. Remember the sabbath day, to keep it holy. Six days shalt thou labour, and do all thy work: but the seventh day is the sabbath of the LORD thy God: in it thou shalt not do any work, thou, nor thy son, nor thy daughter, thy manservant, nor thy maidservant, nor thy cattle, nor thy stranger that is within thy gates: for in six days the LORD made heaven and earth, the sea, and all that in them is, and rested the seventh day: wherefore the LORD blessed the sabbath day, and hallowed it. Honour thy father and thy mother: that thy days may be long upon the land which the LORD thy God giveth thee. Thou shalt not kill. Thou shalt not commit adultery. Thou shalt not steal. Thou shalt not bear false witness against thy neighbour. Thou shalt not covet thy neighbour's house, thou shalt not covet thy neighbour's wife, nor his manservant, nor his maidservant, nor his ox, nor his ass, nor any thing that is thy neighbour's. And all the people saw the thunderings, and the lightnings, and the noise of the trumpet, and the mountain smoking: and when the people saw it, they removed, and stood afar off. (Exodus 20:1–18)

> **The Davidic Covenant.** God Almighty promised law and order in the form of a king and kingdom ruling over the land of Israel. By its very nature a kingdom isn't complete with land only; it must have laws and a king or it is no kingdom at all. The Lord said that He would establish an everlasting kingdom and throne through the seed of David. Ultimately this points to Jesus Christ sitting on the throne and ruling the everlasting kingdom (Luke 1:32–33; Matthew 2:2; Jeremiah 30:9, 33:14–17; Hosea 3:5).

Moreover I will appoint a place for my people Israel, *and will plant them, that they may dwell in a place of their own, and move no more;* neither shall the children of wickedness afflict them any more, as beforetime, and as since the time that I commanded judges to be over my people Israel, and have caused thee to rest from all thine enemies. Also the LORD telleth thee that he will make thee an house. And when thy days be fulfilled, and thou shalt sleep with thy fathers, I will set up thy seed after thee, which shall proceed out of thy bowels, and I will establish his kingdom. He shall build an house for my name, and *I will stablish the throne of his kingdom for ever.* I will be his father, and he shall be my son. If he commit iniquity, I will chasten him with the rod of men, and with the stripes of the children of men: but my mercy shall not depart away from him, as I took it from Saul, whom I put away before thee. *And thine house and thy kingdom shall be established for ever before thee: thy throne shall be established for ever.* (2 Samuel 7:10–16)

And it shall come to pass, when thy days be expired that thou must go to be with thy fathers, that *I will raise up thy seed after thee, which shall be of thy sons; and I will establish his kingdom.* He shall build me an house, and *I will stablish his throne for ever.* I will be his father, and he shall be my son: and I will not take my mercy away from him, as I took it from him that was before thee: *but I will settle him in mine house and in my kingdom for ever: and his throne shall be established for evermore.* According to all these words, and according to all this vision, so did Nathan speak unto David. (1 Chronicles 17:11–15)

With such a glorious destiny promised them, why did Israel fall away from God? The problem throughout the history of the children of Israel was a hard heart, pride, and iniquity:

O that there were such an heart in them, that they would fear me, and keep all my commandments always, that it might be well with them, and with their children for ever! (Deuteronomy 5:29)

Yet the LORD hath not given you an heart to perceive, and eyes to see, and ears to hear, unto this day. (Deuteronomy 29:4)

Nevertheless, God Almighty will not forget or fail His covenants made with Abraham and his seed. God's covenant promises are as sure as the sun rising in the morning and going down in the evening (Jeremiah 33:24–26).

The ultimate solution will come through travail and tribulation in the latter days (Deuteronomy 4:30–31). Although an enormous death toll will occur, it appears that roughly one-third of the people of Israel will be refined by fire, and call on the name of the Lord, and experience everlasting salvation (Zechariah 13:8–9). This believing remnant will then faithfully serve "David" their king, whom the Lord will raise up unto them (Jeremiah 30:9, 33:14–17).

> If they shall confess their iniquity, and the iniquity of their fathers, with their trespass which they trespassed against me, and that also they have walked contrary unto me; and that I also have walked contrary unto them, and have brought them into the land of their enemies; if then their uncircumcised hearts be humbled, and they then accept of the punishment of their iniquity: *then will I remember my covenant with Jacob, and also my covenant with Isaac, and also my covenant with Abraham will I remember; and I will remember the land.* The land also shall be left of them, and shall enjoy her sabbaths, while she lieth desolate without them: and they shall accept of the punishment of their iniquity: because, even because they despised my judgments, and because their soul abhorred my statutes. And yet for all that, when they be in the land of their enemies, I will not cast them away, neither will I abhor them, to destroy them utterly, and to break my covenant with them: for I am the Lord their God. *But I will for their sakes remember the covenant of their ancestors*, whom I brought forth out of the land of Egypt in the sight of the heathen, that I might be their God: I am the Lord. (Leviticus 26:40–45)

> *In that day will I raise up the tabernacle of David that is fallen*, and close up the breaches thereof; and I will raise up his ruins, and I will build it as in the days of old: that they may possess the remnant of Edom, and of all the heathen, which are called by my name, saith the Lord that doeth this. Behold, the days come, saith the Lord, that the plowman shall overtake the reaper, and the treader of grapes him that soweth seed; and the mountains shall drop sweet wine, and all the hills shall melt. And I will bring again the captivity of my people of Israel, and they shall build the waste cities, and inhabit them; and they shall plant vineyards, and drink the wine thereof; they shall also make gardens, and eat the fruit of them. *And I will plant them upon their land, and they shall no more be pulled up out of their land which I have given them*, saith the Lord thy God. (Amos 9:11–15)

But if from thence thou shalt seek the LORD *thy God, thou shalt find him, if thou seek him with all thy heart and with all thy soul. When thou art in tribulation, and all these things are come upon thee, even in the latter days, if thou turn to the* LORD *thy God, and shalt be obedient unto his voice; (for the* LORD *thy God is a merciful God;) he will not forsake thee, neither destroy thee, nor forget the covenant of thy fathers which he sware unto them.* (Deuteronomy 4:29–31)

The word that came to Jeremiah from the LORD, *saying, Thus speaketh the* LORD *God of Israel, saying, Write thee all the words that I have spoken unto thee in a book. For, lo, the days come, saith the* LORD, *that I will bring again the captivity of my people Israel and Judah, saith the* LORD: *and I will cause them to return to the land that I gave to their fathers, and they shall possess it. And these are the words that the* LORD *spake concerning Israel and concerning Judah. For thus saith the* LORD; *We have heard a voice of trembling, of fear, and not of peace. Ask ye now, and see whether a man doth travail with child? wherefore do I see every man with his hands on his loins, as a woman in travail, and all faces are turned into paleness? Alas! for that day is great, so that none is like it: it is even the time of Jacob's trouble; but he shall be saved out of it. For it shall come to pass in that day, saith the* LORD *of hosts, that I will break his yoke from off thy neck, and will burst thy bonds, and strangers shall no more serve themselves of him: but they shall serve the* LORD *their God, and David their king, whom I will raise up unto them. Therefore fear thou not, O my servant Jacob, saith the* LORD; *neither be dismayed, O Israel: for, lo, I will save thee from afar, and thy seed from the land of their captivity; and Jacob shall return, and shall be in rest, and be quiet, and none shall make him afraid.* (Jeremiah 30:1–10)

And it shall come to pass, that in all the land, saith the LORD, *two parts therein shall be cut off and die; but the third shall be left therein. And I will bring the third part through the fire, and will refine them as silver is refined, and will try them as gold is tried: they shall call on my name, and I will hear them: I will say, It is my people: and they shall say, The* LORD *is my God.* (Zechariah 13:8–9)

God Almighty has promised through the prophets of old that the days will come when He will make a new covenant with the house of Israel, plant them assuredly in the promised land, and give them a new heart and a new spirit. While individuals, whether Jew or Gentile, are afforded the new covenant opportunity today, the time referred to below infers a corporate salvation experience that will occur after a great travail as the people look upon Jesus, the One whom they pierced, at the second coming. Corporately, the blindness of Israel won't be lifted until they come to a point of brokenness and thus repent in sorrow, recognizing that salvation is only through the redeemer Christ Jesus. And corporately, the house of Israel will be desolate of new covenant salvation until they say, "Blessed is he that cometh in the name of the Lord" (Matthew 23:39, Romans 11:25–27).

> And it shall come to pass, when all these things are come upon thee, the blessing and the curse, which I have set before thee, and thou shalt call them to mind among all the nations, whither the Lord thy God hath driven thee, and shalt return unto the Lord thy God, and shalt obey his voice according to all that I command thee this day, thou and thy children, with all thine heart, and with all thy soul; that then the Lord thy God will turn thy captivity, and have compassion upon thee, and will return and gather thee from all the nations, whither the Lord thy God hath scattered thee. If any of thine be driven out unto the outmost parts of heaven, from thence will the Lord thy God gather thee, and from thence will he fetch thee: *and the Lord thy God will bring thee into the land which thy fathers possessed, and thou shalt possess it;* and he will do thee good, and multiply thee above thy fathers. *And the Lord thy God will circumcise thine heart, and the heart of thy seed, to love the Lord thy God with all thine heart, and with all thy soul, that thou mayest live.* (Deuteronomy 30:1–6)

> Behold, the days come, saith the Lord, that *I will make a new covenant with the house of Israel, and with the house of Judah:* not according to the covenant that I made with their fathers in the day that I took them by the hand to bring them out of the land of Egypt; which my covenant they brake, although I was an husband unto them, saith the Lord: but this shall be the covenant that I will make with the house of Israel; After those days, saith the Lord, *I will put my law in their inward parts, and write it in their hearts; and will be their God, and they shall be my people.* And they shall teach no more every man his neighbour, and every man his brother, saying, Know the Lord: for they shall all know me, from the least of them unto the greatest of them, saith the Lord: for I will forgive their iniquity, and I will remember their sin no more. (Jeremiah 31:31–34)

> Behold, *I will* gather them out of all countries, whither I have driven them in mine anger, and in my fury, and in great wrath; and *I will* bring them

again unto this place, and *I will* cause them to dwell safely: and they shall be my people, and *I will* be their God: and *I will give them one heart, and one way, that they may fear me for ever,* for the good of them, and of their children after them: and *I will* make an everlasting covenant with them, that *I will* not turn away from them, to do them good; but *I will* put my fear in their hearts, that they shall not depart from me. Yea, *I will* rejoice over them to do them good, and *I will plant them in this land assuredly with my whole heart and with my whole soul.* For thus saith the Lord; Like as I have brought all this great evil upon this people, so will I bring upon them all the good that I have promised them. (Jeremiah 32:37–42)

Therefore say unto the house of Israel, Thus saith the Lord God; *I do not this for your sakes, O house of Israel, but for mine holy name's sake,* which ye have profaned among the heathen, whither ye went. And I will sanctify my great name, which was profaned among the heathen, which ye have profaned in the midst of them; and the heathen shall know that I am the Lord, saith the Lord God, *when I shall be sanctified in you before their eyes.* For I will take you from among the heathen, and gather you out of all countries, and will bring you into your own land. *Then will I sprinkle clean water upon you, and ye shall be clean: from all your filthiness, and from all your idols, will I cleanse you. A new heart also will I give you, and a new spirit will I put within you: and I will take away the stony heart out of your flesh, and I will give you an heart of flesh. And I will put my spirit within you, and cause you to walk in my statutes, and ye shall keep my judgments, and do them. And ye shall dwell in the land that I gave to your fathers; and ye shall be my people, and I will be your God.* I will also save you from all your uncleannesses: and I will call for the corn, and will increase it, and lay no famine upon you. And I will multiply the fruit of the tree, and the increase of the field, that ye shall receive no more reproach of famine among the heathen. Then shall ye remember your own evil ways, and your doings that were not good, and shall lothe yourselves in your own sight for your iniquities and for your abominations. Not for your sakes do I this, saith the Lord God, be it known unto you: be ashamed and confounded for your own ways, O house of Israel. Thus saith the Lord God; *In the day* that I shall have cleansed you from all your iniquities I will also cause you to dwell in the cities, and the wastes shall be builded. And the desolate land shall be tilled, whereas it lay desolate in the sight of all that passed by. And they shall say, This land that was desolate is become like the garden of Eden;

and the waste and desolate and ruined cities are become fenced, and are inhabited. Then the heathen that are left round about you shall know that I the LORD build the ruined places, and plant that that was desolate: *I the LORD have spoken it, and I will do it.* Thus saith the Lord GOD; I will yet for this be enquired of by the house of Israel, to do it for them; I will increase them with men like a flock. As the holy flock, as the flock of Jerusalem in her solemn feasts; so shall the waste cities be filled with flocks of men: and they shall know that I am the LORD. (Ezekiel 36:22–38)

In that day shall the LORD defend the inhabitants of Jerusalem; and he that is feeble among them at that day shall be as David; and the house of David shall be as God, as the angel of the LORD before them. And it shall come to pass in that day, that I will seek to destroy all the nations that come against Jerusalem. *And I will pour upon the house of David, and upon the inhabitants of Jerusalem, the spirit of grace and of supplications: and they shall look upon me whom they have pierced, and they shall mourn for him, as one mourneth for his only son, and shall be in bitterness for him, as one that is in bitterness for his firstborn.* In that day shall there be a great mourning in Jerusalem, as the mourning of Hadadrimmon in the valley of Megiddon. (Zechariah 12:8–11)

The above passages reveal God's covenant faithfulness and a massive salvation experience for Israel after tribulation in the latter days. When taken at face value, numerous other Scriptures reveal that God Almighty has not, and will not, forsake Israel.

And it shall come to pass *in that day*, that the remnant of Israel, and such as are escaped of the house of Jacob, shall no more again stay upon him that smote them; *but shall stay upon the* LORD, *the Holy One of Israel, in truth. The remnant shall return*, even the remnant of Jacob, *unto the mighty God.* For though thy people Israel be as the sand of the sea, yet a remnant of them shall return: the consumption decreed shall overflow with righteousness. For the Lord GOD of hosts shall make a consumption, even determined, in the midst of all the land. (Isaiah 10:20–23)

They shall not hurt nor destroy in all my holy mountain: for the earth shall be full of the knowledge of the LORD, as the waters cover the sea. And in that day there shall be a root of Jesse, which shall stand for an ensign of the people; to it shall the Gentiles seek: and his rest shall be glorious. *And it shall come to pass in that day*, that the Lord shall set his hand again the second time to recover the remnant of his people, which shall

THE GREAT AND NOTABLE DAY OF THE LORD • 53

be left, from Assyria, and from Egypt, and from Pathros, and from Cush, and from Elam, and from Shinar, and from Hamath, and from the islands of the sea. *And he shall set up an ensign for the nations, and shall assemble the outcasts of Israel, and gather together the dispersed of Judah from the four corners of the earth.* (Isaiah 11:9–12)

And he will destroy in this mountain the face of the covering cast over all people, and the vail that is spread over all nations. He will swallow up death in victory; and the Lord God will wipe away tears from off all faces; and the rebuke of his people shall he take away from off all the earth: for the Lord hath spoken it. And it shall be said *in that day*, Lo, this is our God; we have waited for him, and he will save us: *this is the Lord; we have waited for him, we will be glad and rejoice in his salvation.* (Isaiah 25:7–9)

And it shall come to pass *in that day*, that the Lord shall beat off from the channel of the river unto the stream of Egypt, and *ye shall be gathered one by one, O ye children of Israel.* And it shall come to pass in that day, that the great trumpet shall be blown, and they shall come which were ready to perish in the land of Assyria, and the outcasts in the land of Egypt, *and shall worship the Lord in the holy mount at Jerusalem.* (Isaiah 27:12–13)

And *in that day* shall the deaf hear the words of the book, and the eyes of the blind shall see out of obscurity, and out of darkness. The meek also shall increase their joy in the Lord, and the poor among men shall rejoice in the Holy One of Israel. *For the terrible one is brought to nought*, and the scorner is consumed, and all that watch for iniquity are cut off: that make a man an offender for a word, and lay a snare for him that reproveth in the gate, and turn aside the just for a thing of nought. Therefore thus saith the Lord, who redeemed Abraham, concerning the house of Jacob, *Jacob shall not now be ashamed, neither shall his face now wax pale.* But when he seeth his children, the work of mine hands, in the midst of him, *they shall sanctify my name, and sanctify the Holy One of Jacob, and shall fear the God of Israel. They also that erred in spirit shall come to understanding, and they that murmured shall learn doctrine.* (Isaiah 29:18–24)

But Israel shall be saved in the Lord with an everlasting salvation: ye shall not be ashamed nor confounded world without end. For thus saith the Lord that created the heavens; God himself that formed the earth and made it; he hath established it, he created it not in vain, he formed it to be inhabited: I am the Lord; and there is none else. I have not spoken in secret, in a dark place of the earth: I said not unto the seed of Jacob, Seek ye me in vain: I the Lord speak righteousness, I declare things that are right. Assemble yourselves and come; draw near together, ye that are escaped of the nations: they have no knowledge that set up the wood of their graven image, and pray unto a god that cannot save. Tell ye, and bring them near; yea, let them take counsel together: who hath declared this from ancient time? who hath told it from that time? have not I the Lord? and there is no God else beside me; a just God and a Saviour; there is none beside me. *Look unto me, and be ye saved, all the ends of the earth: for I am God, and there is none else.* I have sworn by myself, the word is gone out of my mouth in righteousness, and shall not return, That unto me every knee shall bow, every tongue shall swear. Surely, shall one say, in the Lord have I righteousness and strength: even to him shall men come; and all that are incensed against him shall be ashamed. *In the Lord shall all the seed of Israel be justified, and shall glory.* (Isaiah 45:17–25)

For a small moment have I forsaken thee; *but with great mercies will I gather thee.* And all thy children shall be taught of the Lord; and great shall be the peace of thy children. *In righteousness shalt thou be established: thou shalt be far from oppression; for thou shalt not fear: and from terror; for it shall not come near thee.* Behold, they shall surely gather together, but not by me: whosoever shall gather together against thee shall fall for thy sake. Behold, I have created the smith that bloweth the coals in the fire, and that bringeth forth an instrument for his work; and I have created the waster to destroy. No weapon that is formed against thee shall prosper; and every tongue that shall rise against thee in judgment thou shalt condemn. *This is the heritage of the servants of the* Lord, *and their righteousness is of me, saith the* Lord. (Isaiah 54:7, 13–17)

According to their deeds, accordingly he will repay, fury to his adversaries, recompence to his enemies; to the islands he will repay recompence. So shall they fear the name of the Lord from the west, and his glory from the rising of the sun. When the enemy shall come in like a flood, the Spirit of the Lord shall lift up a standard against him. And *the Redeemer shall come to Zion,* and unto them that turn from transgression in Jacob, saith the Lord. As for me, *this is my covenant with them, saith the* Lord; My spirit that is upon thee, and my words which I have put in thy mouth, shall not depart out of thy mouth, nor out of the mouth of thy seed, nor out of the mouth of thy seed's seed, saith the Lord, *from henceforth and for ever.* (Isaiah 59:18–21)

Violence shall no more be heard in thy land, wasting nor destruction within thy borders; but thou shalt call thy walls Salvation, and thy gates Praise. The sun shall be no more thy light by day; neither for brightness shall the moon give light unto thee: but *the* Lord *shall be unto thee an everlasting light, and thy God thy glory.* Thy sun shall no more go down; neither shall thy moon withdraw itself: for the Lord shall be thine everlasting light, and the days of thy mourning shall be ended. *Thy people also shall be all righteous: they shall inherit the land for ever,* the branch of my planting, the work of my hands, *that I may be glorified.* A little one shall become a thousand, and a small one a strong nation: I the Lord will hasten it in his time. (Isaiah 60:18–22)

For Zion's sake will I not hold my peace, and for Jerusalem's sake I will not rest, until the righteousness thereof go forth as brightness, and the salvation thereof as a lamp that burneth. And the Gentiles shall see thy righteousness, and all kings thy glory: and thou shalt be called by a new name, which the mouth of the Lord shall name. Thou shalt also be a crown of glory in the hand of the Lord, and a royal diadem in the hand of thy God. *Thou shalt no more be termed Forsaken; neither shall thy land any more be termed Desolate*: but thou shalt be called Hephzibah, and thy land Beulah: for the Lord delighteth in thee, and thy land shall be married. For as a young man marrieth a virgin, so shall thy sons marry thee: and as the bridegroom rejoiceth over the bride, so shall thy God rejoice over thee. I have set watchmen upon thy walls, O Jerusalem, which shall never hold their peace day nor night: ye that make mention of the Lord, keep not silence, *and give him no rest, till he establish, and till he make Jerusalem a praise in the earth.* The Lord hath sworn by his right hand, and by the arm of his strength, Surely I will no more give thy corn to be meat for thine enemies; and the sons of the stranger shall not drink thy wine, for the which thou hast laboured: but they that have gathered it shall eat it, and praise the Lord; and they that have brought it together shall drink it in the courts of my holiness. Go through, go through the gates; prepare ye the way of the people; cast up, cast up the highway; gather out the stones; lift up a standard for the people. *Behold, the* Lord *hath proclaimed unto the end of the world, Say ye to the daughter of Zion, Behold, thy salvation cometh; behold, his reward is with him, and his work before him. And they shall call them, The holy people, The redeemed of the* Lord: *and thou shalt be called, Sought out, A city not forsaken.* (Isaiah 62:1–12)

> For I know their works and their thoughts: it shall come, that I will gather all nations and tongues; and they shall come, and see my glory. And I will set a sign among them, and I will send those that escape of them unto the nations, to Tarshish, Pul, and Lud, that draw the bow, to Tubal, and Javan, to the isles afar off, that have not heard my fame, neither have seen my glory; and *they shall declare my glory among the Gentiles*. And they shall bring all your brethren for an offering unto the LORD out of all nations upon horses, and in chariots, and in litters, and upon mules, and upon swift beasts, to my holy mountain Jerusalem, saith the LORD, as the children of Israel bring an offering in a clean vessel into the house of the LORD. And I will also take of them for priests and for Levites, saith the LORD. For as the new heavens and the new earth, which I will make, shall remain before me, saith the LORD, *so shall your seed and your name remain*. And it shall come to pass, that from one new moon to another, and from one sabbath to another, shall all flesh come to worship before me, saith the LORD. And they shall go forth, and look upon the carcases of the men that have transgressed against me: for their worm shall not die, neither shall their fire be quenched; and they shall be an abhorring unto all flesh. (Isaiah 66:18–24)

The Olivet Discourse alludes to the "end times" as a time that will bring birth pangs or contractions. What do contractions lead to?

In the context of the day of the Lord's return and the sound of the trumpet, we see desolation in the land and blackness in the heavens, and we read of the "great tribulation" that brings travail like no other time in history (Jeremiah 4:19, 27–28, 31). This Scripture in Jeremiah makes the point that the day of the Lord is the climax of the birth pains. This is true not only because it makes sense that this great transitional day of the Lord would be the climax and monumental turning point of earth's history, but also because it is this gathering to Jerusalem that causes the climax point of pain and suffering through spoil, death, anguish, and travail. However, what does it bring forth? A new birth!

Jeremiah 4 equates this point in time with "her that bringeth forth" her first child. The day of the Lord brings salvation and corporate rest to remnant Israel! But it cannot come without pain, sorrow, and travail that ultimately lead to a soft, repentant heart that the Lord God Almighty can fill with His Spirit and new covenant grace.

> My bowels, my bowels! I am pained at my very heart; my heart maketh a noise in me; I cannot hold my peace, because thou hast heard, O my soul, *the sound of the trumpet, the alarm of war. Destruction upon destruction is*

cried; for the whole land is spoiled: suddenly are my tents spoiled, and my curtains in a moment. *How long shall I see the standard, and hear the sound of the trumpet?* For my people is foolish, they have not known me; they are sottish children, and they have none understanding: they are wise to do evil, but to do good they have no knowledge. I beheld the earth, and, lo, it was without form, and void; and the heavens, and they had no light. I beheld the mountains, and, lo, they trembled, and all the hills moved lightly. I beheld, and, lo, there was no man, and all the birds of the heavens were fled. *I beheld, and, lo, the fruitful place was a wilderness, and all the cities thereof were broken down at the presence of the* Lord, *and by his fierce anger.* For thus hath the Lord said, *The whole land shall be desolate;* yet will I not make a full end. For this shall the earth mourn, and *the heavens above be black:* because I have spoken it, I have purposed it, and will not repent, neither will I turn back from it. *The whole city shall flee* for the noise of the horsemen and bowmen; they shall go into thickets, and climb up upon the rocks: every city shall be forsaken, and not a man dwell therein. *And when thou art spoiled, what wilt thou do?* Though thou clothest thyself with crimson, though thou deckest thee with ornaments of gold, though thou rentest thy face with painting, in vain shalt thou make thyself fair; thy lovers will despise thee, they will seek thy life. *For I have heard a voice as of a woman in travail, and the anguish as of her that bringeth forth her first child,* the voice of the daughter of Zion, that bewaileth herself, that spreadeth her hands, saying, Woe is me now! for my soul is wearied because of murderers. (Jeremiah 4:19–31)

And I will gather the remnant of my flock out of all countries whither I have driven them, and will bring them again to their folds; and they shall be fruitful and increase. And I will set up shepherds over them which shall feed them: and they shall fear no more, nor be dismayed, neither shall they be lacking, saith the Lord. Behold, the days come, saith the Lord, that *I will raise unto David a righteous Branch, and a King shall reign and prosper, and shall execute judgment and justice in the earth. In his days Judah shall be saved, and Israel shall dwell safely: and this is his name whereby he shall be called,* The Lord Our Righteousness. (Jeremiah 23:3–6)

For it shall come to pass *in that day,* saith the Lord of hosts, that I will break his yoke from off thy neck, and will burst thy bonds, and strangers shall no more serve themselves of him: *But they shall serve the* Lord *their God, and David their king, whom I will raise up unto them.* Therefore fear thou not, O my servant Jacob, saith the LORD; neither be dismayed, O Israel: for, lo, *I will save thee from afar, and thy seed from the land of their captivity; and Jacob shall return, and shall be in rest, and be quiet, and none shall make him afraid.* For I am with thee, saith the LORD, to save thee: though I make a full end of all nations whither I have scattered thee, yet will I not make a full end of thee: but I will correct thee in measure, and will not leave thee altogether unpunished. For thus saith the LORD, Thy bruise is incurable, and thy wound is grievous. There is none to plead thy cause, that thou mayest be bound up: thou hast no healing medicines. All thy lovers have forgotten thee; they seek thee not; for I have wounded thee with the wound of an enemy, with the chastisement of a cruel one, for the multitude of thine iniquity; because thy sins were increased. Why criest thou for thine affliction? thy sorrow is incurable for the multitude of thine iniquity: because thy sins were increased, I have done these things unto thee. Therefore all they that devour thee shall be devoured; and all thine adversaries, every one of them, shall go into captivity; and they that spoil thee shall be a spoil, and all that prey upon thee will I give for a prey. *For I will restore health unto thee, and I will heal thee of thy wounds, saith the* LORD; *because they called thee an Outcast, saying, This is Zion, whom no man seeketh after.* Thus saith the LORD; Behold, I will bring again the captivity of Jacob's tents, and have mercy on his dwellingplaces; and the city shall be built upon her own heap, and the palace shall remain after the manner thereof. *And out of them shall proceed thanksgiving and the voice of them that make merry: and I will multiply them, and they shall not be few; I will also glorify them, and they shall not be small.* Their children also shall be as aforetime, and their congregation shall be established before me, and I will punish all that oppress them. And their nobles shall be of themselves, and their governor shall proceed from the midst of them; and I will cause him to draw near, and he shall approach unto me: for who is this that engaged his heart to approach unto me? saith the LORD. *And ye shall be my people, and I will be your God.* (Jeremiah 30:8–22)

As I live, saith the Lord GOD, surely with a mighty hand, and with a stretched out arm, and with fury poured out, will I rule over you: and I will bring you out from the people, and will gather you out of the countries wherein ye are scattered, with a mighty hand, and with a stretched out arm, and with fury poured out. And I will bring you into the wilderness of the people, and there will I plead with you face to face. Like as I pleaded with your fathers in the wilderness of the land of Egypt, so will I plead with you, saith the Lord God. And I will cause you to pass under the rod, and *I will bring you into the bond of the covenant*: and I will purge out from among you the rebels, and them that transgress against me: I will bring them forth out of the country where they sojourn, and they shall not enter into the land of Israel: and ye shall know that I am the Lord. As for you, O house of Israel, thus saith the Lord God; Go ye, serve ye every one his idols, and hereafter also, if ye will not hearken unto me: but pollute ye my holy name no more with your gifts, and with your idols. *For in mine holy mountain, in the mountain of the height of Israel, saith the Lord God, there shall all the house of Israel, all of them in the land, serve me: there will I accept them*, and there will I require your offerings, and the firstfruits of your oblations, with all your holy things. I will accept you with your sweet savour, when I bring you out from the people, and gather you out of the countries wherein ye have been scattered; and *I will be sanctified in you* before the heathen. And ye shall know that I am the Lord, when I shall bring you into the land of Israel, into the country for the which I lifted up mine hand to give it to your fathers. And there shall ye remember your ways, and all your doings, wherein ye have been defiled; and ye shall lothe yourselves in your own sight for all your evils that ye have committed. *And ye shall know that I am the Lord, when I have wrought with you for my name's sake*, not according to your wicked ways, nor according to your corrupt doings, O ye house of Israel, saith the Lord God. (Ezekiel 20:33–44)

And say unto them, Thus saith the Lord God; Behold, I will take the children of Israel from among the heathen, whither they be gone, and will gather them on every side, and bring them into their own land: and I will make them one nation in the land upon the mountains of Israel; and one king shall be king to them all: and they shall be no more two nations, neither shall they be divided into two kingdoms any more at all: neither shall they defile themselves any more with their idols, nor with their detestable things, nor with any of their transgressions: but I will save them out of all their dwellingplaces, wherein they have sinned, and will cleanse them: so shall they be my people, and I will be their God. And David my servant shall be king over them; and they all shall have one shepherd: they shall also walk in my judgments, and observe my statutes, and do them. And they shall dwell in the land that I have given unto Jacob my servant, wherein your fathers have dwelt; and *they shall dwell therein, even they, and their children, and their children's children for ever*:

and my servant David shall be their prince for ever. Moreover I will make a covenant of peace with them; *it shall be an everlasting covenant with them: and I will place them, and multiply them, and will set my sanctuary in the midst of them for evermore.* My tabernacle also shall be with them: yea, *I will be their God, and they shall be my people.* And the heathen shall know that I the LORD do sanctify Israel, when my sanctuary shall be in the midst of them for evermore. (Ezekiel 37:21–28)

So will I make my holy name known in the midst of my people Israel; and I will not let them pollute my holy name any more: and the heathen shall know that I am the LORD, the Holy One in Israel. *So the house of Israel shall know that I am the LORD their God from that day and forward.* And the heathen shall know that the house of Israel went into captivity for their iniquity: because they trespassed against me, therefore hid I my face from them, and gave them into the hand of their enemies: so fell they all by the sword. According to their uncleanness and according to their transgressions have I done unto them, and hid my face from them. Therefore thus saith the Lord GOD; *Now will I bring again the captivity of Jacob, and have mercy upon the whole house of Israel,* and will be jealous for my holy name; after that they have borne their shame, and all their trespasses whereby they have trespassed against me, when they dwelt safely in their land, and none made them afraid. When I have brought them again from the people, and *gathered them out of their enemies' lands, and am sanctified in them* in the sight of many nations; then shall they know that I am the LORD their God, which caused them to be led into captivity among the heathen: but *I have gathered them unto their own land, and have left none of them any more there.* Neither will I hide my face any more from them: for *I have poured out my spirit upon the house of Israel, saith the Lord* GOD. (Ezekiel 39:7, 22–29)

Therefore, behold, I will allure her, and bring her into the wilderness, and speak comfortably unto her. And I will give her her vineyards from thence, and the valley of Achor for a door of hope: and she shall sing there, as in the days of her youth, and as in the day when she came up out of the land of Egypt. And it shall be at that day, saith the LORD, that thou shalt call me Ishi; and shalt call me no more Baali. For I will take away the names of Baalim out of her mouth, and they shall no more be remembered by their name. *And in that day* will I make a covenant for them with the beasts of the field, and with the fowls of heaven, and with the creeping things of the ground: and I will break the bow and the sword and the battle out of the earth, and will make them to lie down safely. *And I will betroth thee unto me for ever; yea, I will betroth thee unto me in righteousness, and in judgment, and in lovingkindness, and in mercies. I will even betroth thee unto me in faithfulness: and thou shalt know the* Lord. And it shall come to pass in that day, I will hear, saith the Lord, I will hear the heavens, and they shall hear the earth; and the earth shall hear the corn, and the wine, and the oil; and they shall hear Jezreel. And I will sow her unto me in the earth; and *I will have mercy upon her that had not obtained mercy; and I will say to them which were not my people, Thou art my people; and they shall say, Thou art my God.* (Hosea 2:14–23)

Then said the Lord unto me, Go yet, love a woman beloved of her friend, yet an adulteress, according to the love of the Lord toward the children of Israel, who look to other gods, and love flagons of wine. So I bought her to me for fifteen pieces of silver, and for an homer of barley, and an half homer of barley: and I said unto her, Thou shalt abide for me many days; thou shalt not play the harlot, and thou shalt not be for another man: so will I also be for thee. For the children of Israel shall abide many days without a king, and without a prince, and without a sacrifice, and without an image, and without an ephod, and without teraphim: *afterward shall the children of Israel return, and seek the* Lord *their God, and David their king; and shall fear the* Lord *and his goodness in the latter days.* (Hosea 3:1–5)

I will go and return to my place, till they acknowledge their offence, and seek my face: in their affliction they will seek me early. Come, and let us return unto the Lord: for he hath torn, and he will heal us; he hath smitten, and he will bind us up. After two days will he revive us: *in the third day he will raise us up, and we shall live in his sight.* Then shall we know, if we follow on to know the Lord: his going forth is prepared as the morning; and he shall come unto us as the rain, as the latter and former rain unto the earth. (Hosea 5:15–6:3)

The sun and the moon shall be darkened, and the stars shall withdraw their shining. The Lord also shall roar out of Zion, and utter his voice from Jerusalem; and the heavens and the earth shall shake: *but the* Lord *will be the hope of his people, and the strength of the children of Israel.* So shall ye know that I am the Lord your God dwelling in Zion, my holy mountain: then shall Jerusalem be holy, and there shall no strangers pass through her any more. And it shall come to pass in that day, that the mountains shall drop down new wine, and the hills shall flow with milk, and all the rivers of Judah shall flow with waters, and a fountain shall come forth of the house of the LORD, and shall water the valley of Shittim. Egypt shall be a desolation, and Edom shall be a desolate wilderness, for the violence against the children of Judah, because they have shed innocent blood in their land. *But Judah shall dwell for ever, and Jerusalem from generation to generation. For I will cleanse their blood that I have not cleansed: for the* LORD *dwelleth in Zion.* (Joel 3:15–21)

And I will bring again the captivity of my people of Israel, and they shall build the waste cities, and inhabit them; and they shall plant vineyards, and drink the wine thereof; they shall also make gardens, and eat the fruit of them. And *I will plant them upon their land, and they shall no more be pulled up out of their land which I have given them, saith the* LORD *thy God.* (Amos 9:14–15)

And I will make her that halted a remnant, and her that was cast far off a strong nation: and *the* LORD *shall reign over them in mount Zion from henceforth, even for ever.* (Micah 4:7)

In that day shalt thou not be ashamed for all thy doings, wherein thou hast transgressed against me: for then I will take away out of the midst of thee them that rejoice in thy pride, and thou shalt no more be haughty because of my holy mountain. I will also leave in the midst of thee an afflicted and poor people, and they shall trust in the name of the LORD. *The remnant of Israel shall not do iniquity, nor speak lies; neither shall a deceitful tongue be found in their mouth: for they shall feed and lie down, and none shall make them afraid.* Sing, O daughter of Zion; shout, O Israel; be glad and rejoice with all the heart, O daughter of Jerusalem. The LORD hath taken away thy judgments, he hath cast out thine enemy: *the king of Israel, even the* LORD, *is in the midst of thee: thou shalt not see evil any more.* In that day it shall be said to Jerusalem, Fear thou not: and to Zion, Let not thine hands be slack. The LORD thy God in the midst of thee is mighty; he will save, he will rejoice over thee with joy; he will rest in his love, he will joy over thee with singing. I will gather them that are sorrowful for the solemn assembly, who are of thee, to whom the reproach of it was a burden. Behold, at that time I will undo all that afflict thee: and I will save her that halteth, and gather her that was driven out; and I will get them praise and fame in every land where they have been put to shame. *At that time will I bring you again, even in the time that I gather you: for I will make you a name and a praise among all people of the earth, when I turn back your captivity before your eyes, saith the* LORD. (Zephaniah 3:11–20)

And the LORD *their God shall save them in that day* as the flock of his people: for they shall be as the stones of a crown, lifted up as an ensign upon his land. (Zechariah 9:16)

O Jerusalem, Jerusalem, thou that killest the prophets, and stonest them which are sent unto thee, how often would I have gathered thy children together, even as a hen gathereth her chickens under her wings, and ye would not! Behold, your house is left unto you desolate. For I say unto you, Ye shall not see me henceforth, *till ye shall say,* Blessed is he that cometh in the name of the Lord. (Matthew 23:37–39)

O Jerusalem, Jerusalem, which killest the prophets, and stonest them that are sent unto thee; how often would I have gathered thy children together, as a hen doth gather her brood under her wings, and ye would not! Behold, your house is left unto you desolate: and verily I say unto you, Ye shall not see me, *until the time come when ye shall say,* Blessed is he that cometh in the name of the Lord. (Luke 13:34–35)

Therefore *let all the house of Israel know assuredly,* that God hath made that same Jesus, whom ye have crucified, both Lord and Christ. Now when they heard this, they were pricked in their heart, and said unto Peter and to the rest of the apostles, Men and brethren, what shall we do? Then Peter said unto them, Repent, and be baptized every one of you in the name of Jesus Christ for the remission of sins, and ye shall receive the gift of the Holy Ghost. *For the promise is unto you, and to your children, and to all that are afar off, even as many as the Lord our God shall call.* (Acts 2:36–39)

I say the truth in Christ, I lie not, my conscience also bearing me witness in the Holy Ghost, that I have great heaviness and continual sorrow in my heart. For *I could wish that myself were accursed from Christ for my brethren, my kinsmen according to the flesh: who are Israelites; to whom pertaineth the adoption, and the glory, and the covenants, and the giving of the law, and the service of God, and the promises;* whose are the fathers, and of whom as concerning the flesh Christ came, who is over all, God blessed for ever. Amen. Esaias also crieth concerning Israel, Though the number of the children of Israel be as the sand of the sea, *a remnant shall be saved*: for he will finish the work, and cut it short in righteousness: because a short work will the Lord make upon the earth. (Romans 9:1–5, 27–28)

> For I would not, brethren, that ye should be ignorant of this mystery, lest ye should be wise in your own conceits; that blindness in part is happened to Israel, until the fulness of the Gentiles be come in. *And so all Israel shall be saved: as it is written, There shall come out of Sion the Deliverer, and shall turn away ungodliness from Jacob: for this is my covenant unto them, when I shall take away their sins.* As concerning the gospel, they are enemies for your sakes: but as touching the election, they are beloved for the fathers' sakes. For the gifts and calling of God are without repentance. For as ye in times past have not believed God, yet have now obtained mercy through their unbelief: even so have these also now not believed, that through your mercy they also may obtain mercy. For God hath concluded them all in unbelief, that he might have mercy upon all. O the depth of the riches both of the wisdom and knowledge of God! how unsearchable are his judgments, and his ways past finding out! For who hath known the mind of the Lord? or who hath been his counsellor? Or who hath first given to him, and it shall be recompensed unto him again? For of him, and through him, and to him, are all things: to whom be glory for ever. Amen. (Romans 11:25–36)

V. THE WRATH OF GOD

The final event of the day of the Lord is the wrath of God poured out at Armageddon. As reviewed earlier, the Lord's wrath will not come upon those who are in Christ, as this "day of judgment" is reserved for the ungodly. The escape of those who are in Christ will occur as the seventh trumpet sounds and the first sickle gathers the harvest of righteous souls (Luke 21:36). Then the ungodly will be met with a day of judgment like none other.

> But of the times and the seasons, brethren, ye have no need that I write unto you. For yourselves know perfectly that the day of the Lord so cometh as a thief in the night. For when they shall say, Peace and safety; then sudden destruction cometh upon them, as travail upon a woman with child; and they shall not escape. But ye, brethren, are not in darkness, that that day should overtake you as a thief. Ye are all the children of light, and the children of the day: we are not of the night, nor of darkness. Therefore let us not sleep, as do others; but let us watch and be sober. For they that sleep sleep in the night; and they that be drunken are drunken in the night. But let us, who are of the day, be sober, putting on the breastplate of faith and love; and for an helmet, the hope of salvation. *For*

God hath not appointed us to wrath, but to obtain salvation by our Lord Jesus Christ, who died for us, that, whether we wake or sleep, we should live together with him. Wherefore comfort yourselves together, and edify one another, even as also ye do. (1 Thessalonians 5:1–11)

But the heavens and the earth, which are now, by the same word are kept in store, *reserved unto fire against the day of judgment and perdition of ungodly men.* But, beloved, be not ignorant of this one thing, that one day is with the Lord as a thousand years, and a thousand years as one day. The Lord is not slack concerning his promise, as some men count slackness; but is longsuffering to us-ward, not willing that any should perish, but that all should come to repentance. But the day of the Lord will come as a thief in the night; in the which the heavens shall pass away with a great noise, and the elements shall melt with fervent heat, the earth also and the works that are therein shall be burned up. Seeing then that all these things shall be dissolved, what manner of persons ought ye to be in all holy conversation and godliness, looking for and hasting unto the coming of *the day of God,* wherein the heavens being on fire shall be dissolved, and the elements shall melt with fervent heat? Nevertheless we, according to his promise, look for new heavens and a new earth, wherein dwelleth righteousness. (2 Peter 3:7–13)

For they are the spirits of devils, working miracles, which go forth unto the kings of the earth and of the whole world, *to gather them to the battle of that great day of God Almighty.* Behold, I come as a thief. Blessed is he that watcheth, and keepeth his garments, lest he walk naked, and they see his shame. And he gathered them together into a place called in the Hebrew tongue Armageddon. And the seventh angel poured out his vial into the air; and there came a great voice out of the temple of heaven, from the throne, saying, It is done. And there were voices, and thunders, and lightnings; and there was a great earthquake, such as was not since men were upon the earth, so mighty an earthquake, and so great. And the great city was divided into three parts, and the cities of the nations fell: and great Babylon came in remembrance before God, *to give unto her the cup of the wine of the fierceness of his wrath.* And every island fled away, and the mountains were not found. And there fell upon men a great hail out of heaven, every stone about the weight of a talent: and men blasphemed God because of the plague of the hail; for the plague thereof was exceeding great. (Revelation 16:14–21)

As mentioned earlier, the first sickle (Revelation 14:14–16) represents the resurrection/rapture (i.e. the harvest of the wheat/fruit), and the second sickle (Revelation 14:17–20) represents the wrath of God upon the followers of Antichrist and the enemies of God at Armageddon (i.e. the harvest of the tares).

> And another angel came out of the temple which is in heaven, he also having a sharp sickle. And another angel came out from the altar, which had power over fire; and cried with a loud cry to him that had the sharp sickle, saying, Thrust in thy sharp sickle, and gather the clusters of the vine of the earth; for her grapes are fully ripe. *And the angel thrust in his sickle into the earth, and gathered the vine of the earth, and cast it into the great winepress of the wrath of God.* And the winepress was trodden without the city, and blood came out of the winepress, even unto the horse bridles, by the space of a thousand and six hundred furlongs. (Revelation 14:17–20)

> And I saw heaven opened, and behold a white horse; and he that sat upon him was called Faithful and True, and in righteousness he doth judge and make war. His eyes were as a flame of fire, and on his head were many crowns; and he had a name written, that no man knew, but he himself. And he was clothed with a vesture dipped in blood: and his name is called The Word of God. And the armies which were in heaven followed him upon white horses, clothed in fine linen, white and clean. And out of his mouth goeth a sharp sword, that with it he should smite the nations: and he shall rule them with a rod of iron: *and he treadeth the winepress of the fierceness and wrath of Almighty God.* And he hath on his vesture and on his thigh a name written, KING OF KINGS AND LORD OF LORDS. And I saw an angel standing in the sun; and he cried with a loud voice, saying to all the fowls that fly in the midst of heaven, Come and gather yourselves together unto the supper of the great God; that ye may eat the flesh of kings, and the flesh of captains, and the flesh of mighty men, and the flesh of horses, and of them that sit on them, and the flesh of all men, both free and bond, both small and great. And I saw the beast, and the kings of the earth, and their armies, gathered together to make war against him that sat on the horse, and against his army. And the beast was taken, and with him the false prophet that wrought miracles before him, with which he deceived them that had received the mark of the beast, and them that worshipped his image. These both were cast alive into a lake of fire burning with brimstone. And the remnant were slain with the sword of him

that sat upon the horse, which sword proceeded out of his mouth: and all the fowls were filled with their flesh. (Revelation 19:11–21)

Let's now walk through the field of the Old Testament prophets where we find this same unmistakably clear forecast of judgment and wrath on the day of the Lord. Though heart-wrenching, the harvest of the tares is an integral component of that day. This day is referred to as the "wrath of the Lord" (Isaiah 9:19, 13:9, 13; Jeremiah 10:10, Ezekiel 7:19, 22:31; Zephaniah 1:18).

> For thou hast broken the yoke of his burden, and the staff of his shoulder, the rod of his oppressor, as in the day of Midian. For every battle of the warrior is with confused noise, and garments rolled in blood; but this shall be with burning and fuel of fire. *Therefore the* LORD *will cut off from Israel head and tail, branch and rush, in one day.* The ancient and honourable, he is the head; and the prophet that teacheth lies, he is the tail. For the leaders of this people cause them to err; and they that are led of them are destroyed. Therefore the LORD shall have no joy in their young men, neither shall have mercy on their fatherless and widows: for every one is an hypocrite and an evildoer, and every mouth speaketh folly. For all this his anger is not turned away, but his hand is stretched out still. For wickedness burneth as the fire: it shall devour the briers and thorns, and shall kindle in the thickets of the forest, and they shall mount up like the lifting up of smoke. *Through the wrath of the* LORD *of hosts is the land darkened, and the people shall be as the fuel of the fire:* no man shall spare his brother. (Isaiah 9:4–5, 14–19)

I pointed out previously that many of the prophecies in the Old Testament seem to have had application at or near the time of the prophets. The Assyrian and Babylonian empires dealt severe and oppressive blows to God's people, and many of these prophecies seem directly linked to them. But does that mean these prophecies have no relevance to us—no future fulfilment?

To answer this question, I often go back to the principle spirit of prophecy, which is the testimony of the Lord Jesus (Revelation 19:10). These prophecies were without a doubt inspired by the Spirit of God. While Assyria and Babylon were chief nemeses to Israel in their time, the judgments that came on those nations—and on Israel through them—were only partial fulfillments. The prophecies repeatedly stretch their view to the "end times" and an ultimate fulfillment that results in the destruction of the wicked one (i.e. Antichrist), the rule of a Messiah King, and a forever, faithful, and saved remnant Israel. For example, the term "the Assyrian" is used by Isaiah eight times, by Ezekiel once, by Hosea twice, and by Micah twice. Due to the ultimate end-time context of these passages, the Assyrians of their day can be considered a type of fulfillment, while for our consideration today "the Antichrist" is in view when we read "the Assyrian." Similarly, many places that reference Babylon and the king of Babylon can be placed in an ultimate end-time context as well. In fact, we see this very language in use in the book of Revelation.

> O *Assyrian*, the rod of mine anger, and the staff in their hand is mine indignation. I will send him against an hypocritical nation, and against the people of my wrath will I give him a charge, to take the spoil, and to take the prey, and to tread them down like the mire of the streets. Wherefore it shall come to pass, that *when the Lord hath performed his whole work upon mount Zion and on Jerusalem, I will punish the fruit of the stout heart of the king of Assyria, and the glory of his high looks.* For he saith, By the strength of my hand I have done it, and by my wisdom; for I am prudent: and I have removed the bounds of the people, and have robbed their treasures, and I have put down the inhabitants like a valiant man: and my hand hath found as a nest the riches of the people: and as one gathereth eggs that are left, have I gathered all the earth; and there was none that moved the wing, or opened the mouth, or peeped. Shall the axe boast itself against him that heweth therewith? or shall the saw magnify itself against him that shaketh it? as if the rod should shake itself against them that lift it up, or as if the staff should lift up itself, as if it were no wood. Therefore shall the Lord, the Lord of hosts, send among his fat ones leanness; and *under his glory he shall kindle a burning like the burning of a fire. And the light of Israel shall be for a fire, and his Holy One for a flame: and it shall burn and devour his thorns and his briers in one day;* and shall consume the glory of his forest, and of his fruitful field, both soul and body: and they shall be as when a standardbearer fainteth. And the rest of the trees of his forest shall be few, that a child may write them. *And it shall come to pass in that day, that the remnant of Israel, and such as are escaped of the house of Jacob, shall no more again stay upon him that smote them; but shall stay upon the* LORD, *the Holy One of Israel, in truth.* The remnant shall return, even the remnant of Jacob, unto the mighty God. (Isaiah 10:5–6, 12–21)

The following Scripture, Isaiah 11:4, as well as Isaiah 30:27–28 and 31, can be coupled together with 2 Thessalonians 2:8, which states, "And then shall that Wicked be revealed, whom the Lord shall consume with the spirit [Strong's G4151—"a current of air, that is breath"] of his mouth, and shall destroy with the brightness of his coming." The similarities noted between the writings of Paul and Isaiah regarding the breath of the Lord slaying the Wicked (i.e. the lawless one or Antichrist) are amazing! We know from another New Testament writer that a sword will be coming from the mouth of the Lord (Revelation 19:15). Isn't such consistency what we should expect from the Word of God?

> But with righteousness shall he judge the poor, and reprove with equity for the meek of the earth: and *he shall smite the earth with the rod of his mouth, and with the breath of his lips shall he slay the wicked.* And righteousness shall be the girdle of his loins, and faithfulness the girdle of his reins. (Isaiah 11:4–5)

Note that the "day of the Lord" context of Isaiah 13 is unavoidable. Not only do you have the reference to "the day of the Lord" in verse 9, but you also have the cosmic events in verse 10 as well as the Lord Himself bringing punishment upon evil and causing a great shaking "in the day of his fierce anger."

> Behold, *the day of the* Lord *cometh, cruel both with wrath and fierce anger,* to lay the land desolate: and he shall destroy the sinners thereof out of it. For the stars of heaven and the constellations thereof shall not give their light: the sun shall be darkened in his going forth, and the moon shall not cause her light to shine. And *I will punish the world for their evil, and the wicked for their iniquity; and I will cause the arrogancy of the proud to cease, and will lay low the haughtiness of the terrible.* I will make a man more precious than fine gold; even a man than the golden wedge of Ophir. Therefore *I will shake the heavens, and the earth shall remove out of her place, in the wrath of the* Lord *of hosts, and in the day of his fierce anger.* And it shall be as the chased roe, and as a sheep that no man taketh up: they shall every man turn to his own people, and flee every one into his own land. Every one that is found shall be thrust through; and every one that is joined unto them shall fall by the sword. Their children also shall be dashed to pieces before their eyes; their houses shall be spoiled, and their wives ravished. Behold, I will stir up the Medes against them, which shall not regard silver; and as for gold, they shall not delight in it. Their bows also shall dash the young men to pieces; and they shall have no pity on the fruit of the womb; their eye shall not spare children. *And Babylon, the*

glory of kingdoms, the beauty of the Chaldees' excellency, shall be as when God overthrew Sodom and Gomorrah. It shall never be inhabited, neither shall it be dwelt in from generation to generation: neither shall the Arabian pitch tent there; neither shall the shepherds make their fold there. But wild beasts of the desert shall lie there; and their houses shall be full of doleful creatures; and owls shall dwell there, and satyrs shall dance there. And the wild beasts of the islands shall cry in their desolate houses, and dragons in their pleasant palaces: and her time is near to come, and her days shall not be prolonged. (Isaiah 13:9–22)

And it shall come to pass *in the day* that the Lord shall give thee rest from thy sorrow, and from thy fear, and from the hard bondage wherein thou wast made to serve, that thou shalt take up this proverb against the king of Babylon, and say, How hath the oppressor ceased! the golden city ceased! The Lord hath broken the staff of the wicked, and the sceptre of the rulers. He who smote the people in wrath with a continual stroke, he that ruled the nations in anger, is persecuted, and none hindereth. The whole earth is at rest, and is quiet: they break forth into singing. (Isaiah 14:3–7)

The land shall be utterly emptied, and utterly spoiled: for the Lord hath spoken this word. The earth mourneth and fadeth away, the world languisheth and fadeth away, the haughty people of the earth do languish. The earth also is defiled under the inhabitants thereof; because they have transgressed the laws, changed the ordinance, broken the everlasting covenant. Therefore hath the curse devoured the earth, and they that dwell therein are desolate: *therefore the inhabitants of the earth are burned, and few men left.* Fear, and the pit, and the snare, are upon thee, O inhabitant of the earth. And it shall come to pass, that he who fleeth from the noise of the fear shall fall into the pit; and he that cometh up out of the midst of the pit shall be taken in the snare: for the windows from on high are open, and *the foundations of the earth do shake.* The earth is utterly broken down, *the earth is clean dissolved,* the earth is moved exceedingly. The earth shall reel to and fro like a drunkard, and shall be removed like a cottage; and the transgression thereof shall be heavy upon it; and it shall fall, and not rise again. *And it shall come to pass in that day, that the Lord shall punish the host of the high ones that are on high, and the kings of the earth upon the earth.* (Isaiah 24:3–6, 17–21)

Behold, the name of the Lord cometh from far, burning with his anger, and the burden thereof is heavy: his lips are full of indignation, and his tongue as a devouring fire: and his breath, as an overflowing stream, shall reach to the midst of the neck, to sift the nations with the sieve of vanity: and there shall be a bridle in the jaws of the people, causing them to err. Ye shall have a song, as in the night when a holy solemnity is kept; and gladness of heart, as when one goeth with a pipe to come into the mountain of the LORD, to the mighty One of Israel. And the LORD shall cause his glorious voice to be heard, and shall shew the lighting down of his arm, with the indignation of his anger, and with the flame of a devouring fire, with scattering, and tempest, and hailstones. *For through the voice of the* LORD *shall the Assyrian be beaten down, which smote with a rod.* And in every place where the grounded staff shall pass, which the LORD shall lay upon him, it shall be with tabrets and harps: and in battles of shaking will he fight with it. For Tophet is ordained of old; yea, for the king it is prepared; *he hath made it deep and large: the pile thereof is fire and much wood; the breath of the* LORD, *like a stream of brimstone, doth kindle it.* (Isaiah 30:27–33)

Note the theme of "the Lord" as the one who fights against the ungodly. Not a day of man's victory or glory, it is rather the day of "the Lord."

For thus hath the LORD spoken unto me, Like as the lion and the young lion roaring on his prey, when a multitude of shepherds is called forth against him, he will not be afraid of their voice, nor abase himself for the noise of them: *so shall the* LORD *of hosts come down to fight for mount Zion, and for the hill thereof.* As birds flying, so will the LORD of hosts defend Jerusalem; defending also he will deliver it; and passing over he will preserve it. Turn ye unto him from whom the children of Israel have deeply revolted. For in that day every man shall cast away his idols of silver, and his idols of gold, which your own hands have made unto you for a sin. *Then shall the Assyrian fall* with the sword, not of a mighty man; and the sword, not of a mean man, shall devour him: but he shall flee from the sword, and his young men shall be discomfited. *And he shall pass over to his strong hold for fear, and his princes shall be afraid of the ensign, saith the* LORD, *whose fire is in Zion, and his furnace in Jerusalem.* (Isaiah 31:4–9)

Come near, ye nations, to hear; and hearken, ye people: let the earth hear, and all that is therein; the world, and all things that come forth of it. *For the indignation of the* LORD *is upon all nations, and his fury upon all their armies: he hath utterly destroyed them, he hath delivered them to the slaughter.* Their slain also shall be cast out, and their stink shall come up out of their carcases, and the mountains shall be melted with their blood. And all *the host of heaven shall be dissolved,* and the heavens shall be rolled together as a scroll: and all their host shall fall down, as the leaf falleth off from the vine, and as a falling fig from the fig tree. For my sword shall be bathed in heaven: behold, it shall come down upon Idumea, and upon the people of my curse, to judgment. *The sword of the* Lord *is filled with blood,* it is made fat with fatness, and with the blood of lambs and goats, with the fat of the kidneys of rams: for the Lord hath a sacrifice in Bozrah, and a great slaughter in the land of Idumea. And the unicorns shall come down with them, and the bullocks with the bulls; and their land shall be soaked with blood, and their dust made fat with fatness. *For it is the day of the* Lord's *vengeance, and the year of recompences for the controversy of Zion.* And the streams thereof shall be turned into pitch, and the dust thereof into brimstone, and *the land thereof shall become burning pitch.* It shall not be quenched night nor day; the smoke thereof shall go up for ever: from generation to generation it shall lie waste; none shall pass through it for ever and ever. But the cormorant and the bittern shall possess it; the owl also and the raven shall dwell in it: and he shall stretch out upon it the line of confusion, and the stones of emptiness. They shall call the nobles thereof to the kingdom, but none shall be there, and all her princes shall be nothing. And thorns shall come up in her palaces, nettles and brambles in the fortresses thereof: and it shall be an habitation of dragons, and a court for owls. The wild beasts of the desert shall also meet with the wild beasts of the island, and the satyr shall cry to his fellow; the screech owl also shall rest there, and find for herself a place of rest. There shall the great owl make her nest, and lay, and hatch, and gather under her shadow: there shall the vultures also be gathered, every one with her mate. Seek ye out of the book of the Lord, and read: no one of these shall fail, none shall want her mate: for my mouth it hath commanded, and his spirit it hath gathered them. And he hath cast the lot for them, and his hand hath divided it unto them by line: they shall possess it for ever, from generation to generation shall they dwell therein. (Isaiah 34:1–17)

It is sobering to personally consider and understand God's role in all of this. First and foremost, it is God who inspired the prophecies and who knows the end from the beginning. It is clear that the Lord is the one who brings His wrath against the enemy to their defeat. But have we seriously pondered the chief cause that provokes this final gathering of Antichrist and the armies of the ungodly against the land of Israel? Can you accept that it too is the Lord's doing? It is truly the Lord Himself who allows and stimulates the Antichrist and His kingdom followers to come against Israel. This fact is noted in several Scriptures, and no doubt in others that I haven't noticed.

In Isaiah 42:24 below, the reason for God's "giving up" Jacob and Israel to the robbers is their disobedience. Consider these references, which support the fact that the great end-gathering against Israel will be provoked by the Lord and give reasons for His doing so:

- Isaiah 10:5—because of hypocritical Jerusalem
- Isaiah 42:24—because of Israel's disobedience
- Ezekiel 38:4—the Antichrist is very willing to go up, but it is the Lord who puts hooks in Antichrist's jaws
- Ezekiel 38:9–10—the gathering toward Jerusalem like a storm and like a cloud to cover the land will occur because of "things that come into thy mind, and thou shalt think an evil thought"
- Revelation 16:14–16—in a day-of-the-Lord context, with the thief-like return of Jesus in the near future, the Lord will allow miracle-working evil spirits to provoke the gathering of the ungodly to the battle of that great day of God Almighty

The LORD shall go forth as a mighty man, he shall stir up jealousy *like a man of war: he shall cry, yea, roar; he shall prevail against his enemies*. I have long time holden my peace; I have been still, and refrained myself: now will I cry like a travailing woman; I will destroy and devour at once. I will make waste mountains and hills, and dry up all their herbs; and I will make the rivers islands, and I will dry up the pools. *And I will bring the blind by a way that they knew not; I will lead them in paths that they have not known: I will make darkness light before them, and crooked things straight*. These things will I do unto them, and not forsake them. They shall be turned back, they shall be greatly ashamed, that trust in graven images, that say to the molten images, Ye are our gods. Hear, ye deaf; and look, ye blind, that ye may see. Who is blind, but my servant? or deaf, as my messenger that I sent? who is blind as he that is perfect, and blind as the LORD's servant? Seeing many things, but thou observest not; opening the ears, but he heareth not. The LORD is well pleased for his righteousness' sake; he will magnify the law, and make it honourable. But this is a people robbed and spoiled; they are all of them snared in holes, and they are hid in prison houses: they are for a prey, and none delivereth; for a spoil, and none saith, Restore. Who among you will give ear to this? who will hearken and hear for the time to come? *Who gave Jacob for a spoil, and Israel to the robbers? did not the* LORD, *he against whom we have sinned? for they would not walk in his ways, neither were they obedient unto his law.* Therefore he hath poured upon him the fury of his anger, and the strength of battle: and it hath set him on fire round about, yet he knew not; and it burned him, yet he laid it not to heart. (Isaiah 42:13–25)

In context of the day of the Lord's return, the sound of the trumpet, and the corporate salvation of remnant Israel, we see the very presence of the LORD Himself, desolation in the land, and blackness in the heavens (Jeremiah 4:19, 21, 26–28).

I beheld the earth, and, lo, it was without form, and void; and the heavens, and they had no light. I beheld the mountains, and, lo, they trembled, and all the hills moved lightly. I beheld, and, lo, there was no man, and all the birds of the heavens were fled. *I beheld, and, lo, the fruitful place was a wilderness, and all the cities thereof were broken down at the presence of the* LORD, *and by his fierce anger.* For thus hath the LORD said, The whole land shall be desolate; yet will I not make a full end. For this shall the earth mourn, and the heavens above be black: because I have spoken it, I have purposed it, and will not repent, neither will I turn back from it. (Jeremiah 4:23–28)

The same presence of the LORD that we saw in Jeremiah 4:26 is noted again in Ezekiel 38:20. This is not trivial. It is Holy Scripture referring to the physical presence of the LORD!

And it shall come to pass at the same time when Gog shall come against the land of Israel, saith the Lord GOD, that *my fury shall come up in my face. For in my jealousy and in the fire of my wrath have I spoken, Surely in that day there shall be a great shaking in the land of Israel;* so that the fishes of the sea, and the fowls of the heaven, and the beasts of the field, and all creeping things that creep upon the earth, and *all the men that are upon the face of the earth, shall shake at my presence,* and the mountains shall be thrown down, and the steep places shall fall, and every wall shall fall to the ground. And I will call for a sword against him throughout all my mountains, saith the Lord GOD: *every man's sword shall be against his brother. And I will plead against him with pestilence and with blood; and I will rain upon him, and upon his bands, and upon the many people that are with him, an overflowing rain, and great hailstones, fire, and brimstone.* Thus will I magnify myself, and sanctify myself; and I will be known in the eyes of many nations, and they shall know that I am the Lord. (Ezekiel 38:18–23)

Therefore, thou son of man, prophesy against Gog, and say, Thus saith the Lord God; Behold, I am against thee, O Gog, the chief prince of Meshech and Tubal: and I will turn thee back, and leave but the sixth part of thee, and will cause thee to come up from the north parts, and will bring thee upon the mountains of Israel: and I will smite thy bow out of thy left hand, and will cause thine arrows to fall out of thy right hand. Thou shalt fall upon the mountains of Israel, thou, and all thy bands, and the people that is with thee: *I will give thee unto the ravenous birds of every sort, and to the beasts of the field to be devoured.* Thou shalt fall upon the open field: for I have spoken it, saith the Lord God. *And I will send a fire on Magog, and among them that dwell carelessly in the isles: and they shall know that I am the* Lord. So will I make my holy name known in the midst of my people Israel; and I will not let them pollute my holy name any more: and the heathen shall know that I am the Lord, the Holy One in Israel. Behold, it is come, and it is done, saith the Lord God; *this is the day whereof I have spoken.* (Ezekiel 39:1–8)

God came from Teman, and the Holy One from mount Paran. Selah. His glory covered the heavens, and the earth was full of his praise. And his brightness was as the light; he had horns coming out of his hand: and there was the hiding of his power. *Before him went the pestilence, and burning coals went forth at his feet. He stood, and measured the earth: he beheld, and drove asunder the nations; and the everlasting mountains were scattered, the perpetual hills did bow: his ways are everlasting.* I saw the tents of Cushan in affliction: and the curtains of the land of Midian did tremble. Was the Lord displeased against the rivers? was *thine anger* against the rivers? was *thy wrath* against the sea, that thou didst ride upon thine horses and thy chariots of salvation? Thy bow was made quite naked, according to the oaths of the tribes, even thy word. Selah. Thou didst cleave the earth with rivers. The mountains saw thee, and they trembled: the overflowing of the water passed by: the deep uttered his voice, and lifted up his hands on high. The sun and moon stood still in their habitation: at the light of thine arrows they went, and at the shining of thy glittering spear. *Thou didst march through the land in indignation, thou didst thresh the heathen in anger. Thou wentest forth for the salvation of thy people, even for salvation with thine anointed; thou woundedst the head out of the house of the wicked, by discovering the foundation unto the neck. Selah. Thou didst strike through with his staves the head of his villages: they came out as a whirlwind to scatter me: their rejoicing was as to devour the poor secretly. Thou didst walk through the sea with thine horses, through the heap of great waters. When I heard, my belly trembled; my lips quivered at the voice: rottenness entered into my bones, and I trembled in myself, that I might rest in the day of trouble: when he cometh up unto the people, he will invade them with his troops. Although the fig tree shall not blossom, neither shall fruit be in the vines; the labour of the olive shall fail, and the fields shall yield no meat; the flock shall be cut off from the fold, and there shall be no herd in the stalls: yet I will rejoice in the* Lord, *I will joy in the God of my salvation. The* Lord *God is my strength, and he will make my feet like hinds' feet, and he will make me to walk upon mine high places. To the chief singer on my stringed instruments.* (Habakkuk 3:3–19)

Thine hand shall be lifted up upon thine adversaries, and all thine enemies shall be cut off. And *it shall come to pass in that day,* saith the Lord, that *I will* cut off thy horses out of the midst of thee, and *I will* destroy thy chariots: and *I will* cut off the cities of thy land, and throw down all thy strong holds: and *I will* cut off witchcrafts out of thine hand; and thou shalt have no more soothsayers: thy graven images also *will I* cut off, and thy standing images out of the midst of thee; and thou shalt no more worship the work of thine hands. And *I will* pluck up thy groves out of the midst of thee: so *will I* destroy thy cities. And *I will* execute vengeance in anger and fury upon the heathen, such as they have not heard. (Micah 5:9–15)

The great day of the Lord is near, it is near, and hasteth greatly, even the voice of the day of the Lord: the mighty man shall cry there bitterly. *That day is a day of wrath, a day of trouble and distress, a day of wasteness and desolation, a day of darkness and gloominess, a day of clouds and thick darkness,* a day of the trumpet and alarm against the fenced cities, and against the high towers. And I will bring distress upon men, that they shall walk like blind men, because they have sinned against the Lord: and their blood shall be poured out as dust, and their flesh as the dung. Neither their silver nor their gold shall be able to deliver them *in the day of the* Lord's *wrath*; but the whole land shall be devoured by the fire of his jealousy: for he shall make even a speedy riddance of all them that dwell in the land. (Zephaniah 1:14–18)

Then shall the LORD go forth, and fight against those nations, as when he fought in the day of battle. And his feet shall stand in that day upon the mount of Olives, which is before Jerusalem on the east, and the mount of Olives shall cleave in the midst thereof toward the east and toward the west, and there shall be a very great valley; and half of the mountain shall remove toward the north, and half of it toward the south. And ye shall flee to the valley of the mountains; for the valley of the mountains shall reach unto Azal: yea, ye shall flee, like as ye fled from before the earthquake in the days of Uzziah king of Judah: and the LORD my God shall come, and all the saints with thee. *And it shall come to pass in that day, that the light shall not be clear, nor dark:* but it shall be one day which shall be known to the LORD, not day, nor night: but it shall come to pass, that at evening time it shall be light. And it shall be in that day, that living waters shall go out from Jerusalem; half of them toward the former sea, and half of them toward the hinder sea: in summer and in winter shall it be. And the LORD shall be king over all the earth: in that day shall there be one LORD, and his name one. All the land shall be turned as a plain from Geba to Rimmon south of Jerusalem: and it shall be lifted up, and inhabited in her place, from Benjamin's gate unto the place of the first gate, unto the corner gate, and from the tower of Hananeel unto the king's winepresses. And men shall dwell in it, and there shall be no more utter destruction; but Jerusalem shall be safely inhabited. And *this shall be the plague wherewith the* LORD *will smite all the people that have fought against Jerusalem; Their flesh shall consume away while they stand upon their feet, and their eyes shall consume away in their holes, and their tongue shall consume away in their mouth.* And it shall come to pass in that day, that *a great tumult from the* LORD *shall be among them; and they shall lay hold every one on the hand of his neighbour, and his hand shall rise up against the hand of his neighbour.* And Judah also shall fight at Jerusalem; and the wealth of all the heathen round about shall be gathered together, gold, and silver, and apparel, in great abundance. And so shall be the plague of the horse, of the mule, of the camel, and of the ass, and of all the beasts that shall be in these tents, as this plague. (Zechariah 14:3–15)

But who may abide the day of his coming? and who shall stand when he appeareth? *for he is like a refiner's fire, and like fullers' soap:* And he shall sit as a refiner and purifier of silver: and he shall purify the sons of Levi, and purge them as gold and silver, that they may offer unto the LORD an offering in righteousness. Then shall the offering of Judah and Jerusalem be

> pleasant unto the Lord, as in the days of old, and as in former years. And I will come near to you to judgment; and I will be a swift witness against the sorcerers, and against the adulterers, and against false swearers, and against those that oppress the hireling in his wages, the widow, and the fatherless, and that turn aside the stranger from his right, and fear not me, saith the Lord of hosts. (Malachi 3:2–5)

> For, behold, *the day cometh, that shall burn as an oven; and all the proud, yea, and all that do wickedly, shall be stubble: and the day that cometh shall burn them up,* saith the Lord of hosts, that *it shall leave them neither root nor branch.* But unto you that fear my name shall the Sun of righteousness arise with healing in his wings; and ye shall go forth, and grow up as calves of the stall. And ye shall tread down the wicked; for they shall be ashes under the soles of your feet in the day that I shall do this, saith the Lord of hosts. Remember ye the law of Moses my servant, which I commanded unto him in Horeb for all Israel, with the statutes and judgments. Behold, I will send you Elijah the prophet before the coming of the great and dreadful day of the Lord: and he shall turn the heart of the fathers to the children, and the heart of the children to their fathers, lest I come and smite the earth with a curse. (Malachi 4:1–6)

To take in the enormity of the great and notable day of the Lord is no small task. If these truths were not in Scripture, we would call them unbelievable. Praise to Almighty God, the evil host of demons and spirits will be crushed on the day of the Lord! The "prince" will be bound and his "power of the air" be burned and dissolved by fire, falling down as a fig from a fig tree (Isaiah 34:4, Ephesians 2:2, 2 Peter 3:10–12). And what comes after such destruction? This is the time of restoration—the new heavens and new earth, wherein dwells righteousness! The time for the "restitution of all things" is when Jesus Christ returns from heaven.

> And all *the host of heaven shall be dissolved,* and the heavens shall be rolled together as a scroll: and all their host shall fall down, as the leaf falleth off from the vine, and as a falling fig from the fig tree. (Isaiah 34:4)

> ... looking for and hasting unto the coming of the day of God, wherein *the heavens being on fire shall be dissolved,* and the elements shall melt with fervent heat? Nevertheless we, according to his promise, look for new heavens and a new earth, wherein dwelleth righteousness. (2 Peter 3:12–13)

... whom the heaven must receive *until* the times of restitution of all things, which God hath spoken by the mouth of all his holy prophets since the world began. (Act 3:21)

The annihilation of evil may not take long, but due to the great shaking of earth and the physical changes that result from the day of the Lord, physical restoration will take time. During the interval between the day of the Lord and the formal inauguration of the kingdom of God, many activities may occur, such as building the tabernacle of David (Amos 9:11), the great gathering to the Lord (Isaiah 60), singing (Zephaniah 3:14, 17, Psalm 47:5–7, Psalm 68:1–4), and rejoicing (Isaiah 35:10, Psalm 24:7–10). Then Jesus will sit on the throne and dwell in Zion (Luke 1:31–33, Isaiah 9:7, Jeremiah 30:9, Ezekiel 37:24, Zechariah 8:3, Joel 3:20–21, Psalm 2:6)!

From this point, we will walk through the Bible and explore several prophecies that take us all the way to this great day, the second coming of Jesus. We will confirm that the trajectory of prophecy convincingly leads to the coming again of Jesus Christ on a notable day of transition, the day of the Lord!

Chapter 2

AN ESCHATOLOGICAL FRAMEWORK

I have never been through the process of building a house from scratch. Before doing so, however, I can imagine a future homeowner sitting down with an architect and builder in a conference room. Before them on the table are several renderings of the finished product based on the agreed-to plans. This framework will ensure that the house takes shape as expected—that the finished product does not turn out to be something entirely different than the homeowner expected!

Up until now, we have caught several glimpses of the finished product of prophecy, the second coming of Jesus. But now it is time to take several steps back and concentrate on the foundation and basic framework that gives these glimpses shape. Upon what type of foundation and framework will our prophetic understanding be constructed?

This won't be easy. We may turn out to be homeowners who have been in possession of skewed plans—of blueprints that don't line up with the vision of the architect and builder. Have we been led astray in our thinking? Are we confident in our assertions and assumptions? Is it reasonable to reconsider the biblical support for an assumed future, seven-year tribulation period? The later sections of this chapter will soundly piece together the framework. But first, we must work through the complicated prophecy of Daniel's seventy weeks.

I. DANIEL'S PROPHECY OF SEVENTY WEEKS

With great effort, let's examine one of the most challenging and important prophecies in Scripture, one that has enormous implications when we begin to frame our prophetic house.

> Seventy weeks are determined upon thy people and upon thy holy city, to finish the transgression, and to make an end of sins, and to make reconciliation for iniquity, and to bring in everlasting righteousness, and to seal up the vision and prophecy, and to anoint the most Holy.
>
> Know therefore and understand, that from the going forth of the commandment to restore and to build Jerusalem unto the Messiah the Prince shall be seven weeks, and threescore and two weeks: the street shall be built again, and the wall, even in troublous times.
>
> And after threescore and two weeks shall Messiah be cut off, but not for himself: and the people of the prince that shall come shall destroy the city and the sanctuary; and the end thereof shall be with a flood, and unto the end of the war desolations are determined.
>
> And he shall confirm the covenant with many for one week: and in the midst of the week he shall cause the sacrifice and the oblation to cease, and for the overspreading of abominations he shall make it desolate, even until the consummation, and that determined shall be poured upon the desolate. (Daniel 9:24–27)

This controversial prophecy is known as the "seventy weeks" of Daniel. There are generally two mainline interpretations of this prophecy. One, that the seventy weeks prophecy has been completely fulfilled. And two, that the first sixty-nine weeks of the prophecy have been completely fulfilled and we are now in a gap period awaiting a future seventieth week.

Could another interpretation be plausible? I believe so, and this will be the thrust of the forthcoming discussion. Not only will we review several shortcomings of the two mainline interpretations, we will also look seriously at what some would call an impossibility—that the seventy weeks prophecy could be entirely future and is best interpreted plainly and literally as 490 days instead of 490 years.

To the suggestion of the futurity of the entire seventy weeks prophecy, most would initially react and state, "Absolutely no way! This is a prophecy that speaks about the death of Jesus Christ; it can't be future." But let's dig into this matter. I contend that in this major prophecy from the book of Daniel, the deepest, ultimate revealing has been hidden for centuries and needs to be unsealed for our current generation (Daniel 12:4).

Without a doubt, the seventy weeks prophecy is messianic in context. The comprehensive accomplishments of Daniel 9:24 highly suggest a day of the Lord context and a great transformative time in history. It is the thrust of all prophetic Scripture!

To briefly summarize, there are six substantial accomplishments that will come to pass at the conclusion of the seventy weeks:

- The transgression will be finished
- Sin will be brought to completion
- Reconciliation for iniquity will be completed
- Everlasting righteousness will be brought in
- The visions and prophecies of Scripture will be wrapped up/finished
- The most holy will be anointed

We will review these accomplishments in more detail later on. In short, however, the conclusion and completion of all of the things decreed to be accomplished by the seventy weeks can be nothing other than the second coming of Jesus at the day of the Lord! It is at the second coming that everlasting righteousness is brought in, that the mystery of God is "finished" and "done," and that the fury of God's wrath is hurled upon Antichrist and the ungodly (Isaiah 10:22, 11:4–5, 62:1–2; Jeremiah 23:6; Hosea 2:19; Malachi 4:2; 2 Peter 3:13, Revelation 10:7, 16:17). But for the moment this is not the issue at hand. We know the destination of this prophecy (i.e. the day of the Lord), but when does the seventy weeks prophecy begin, how long is seventy weeks, and what occurs during the seventy weeks? The difficult questions we face lie in sorting out the details of the prophecy that lead to the day of the Lord.

The language and syntax of the seventy weeks prophecy is complex and difficult to grasp. On top of that, certain translation liberties in past times (the root of which I was unable to put my finger on) turned into a messianic context certain words that the original Hebrew Old Testament and Greek Septuagint did not require to be messianic. So the first controversy I would like to highlight is the apparent messianic context of two phrases used within the prophecy. The first describes a "Messiah the Prince" who will arrive in Jerusalem seven weeks after the decree goes forth (Daniel 9:25). The other describes "Messiah" being cut off (Daniel 9:26).

You know by now that I am an advocate of literal interpretation and plain meaning. So you may wonder why I see a controversy here. How could "Messiah the Prince" (Daniel 9:25) mean anyone other than Jesus Christ? I am not a Bible scholar, so my abilities are limited, but I argue that we need to go deeper than the plain meaning of the *English* transliteration and use the plain meaning of the Hebrew and Greek! Using Strong's Concordance, the Greek Old Testament (the Septuagint), and *The Apostolic Bible Polyglot* (a Greek-English interlinear Bible) with Strong's numbers, I have reviewed each of the Scriptures, and the related context of those Scriptures, where these same Hebrew words (*mashiyach nagid*) and Greek words (*christos* and *chrisma*) are used. *In every other instance* that *mashiyach nagid* is used in the Old Testament, it is translated into a nonmessianic phrase! The English translation is simply "anointed ruler," or "anointed prince," or "the anointed." The same conclusions are true upon review of the words used in the Greek Septuagint, which is the Old Testament that Jesus, the disciples, and the early church used. Why then did the early English Bible translators turn Daniel 9:25–26 into a messianic prophecy?

My simple conclusion is that God provoked the early translators to transliterate the passage into a messianic context as part of the "sealing" of the book of Daniel. Daniel was told that the visions he saw were for the time of the end and would be sealed until then (Daniel 12:9). That is, a sealing will remain until the appropriate time when God sees fit to fully open the eyes of a latter-day generation. If God truly inspired the early translators to place what the Hebrew and Greek text plainly states as "anointed one" and turn the passage into a Messianic context, this would go a long way toward inhibiting the ability of Bible readers to have a complete understanding of the end times. This would be consistent with the implications of Daniel 12:4, which reads, "But thou, O Daniel, shut up the words, and seal the book, even to the time of the end: many shall run to and fro, and knowledge shall be increased."

This sealing means that many shall endeavor to search out the sense and meaning of Daniel's visions, but the visions won't be fully revealed and made known—until the time of the end. Many have labored to interpret and comment on these passages in history. The sealing of the prophecy doesn't mean those people couldn't receive a rich blessing from God for their efforts. Nor does it mean that all of their interpretations were meaningless or unhelpful to their faith. However, efforts to understand the book prior to its unsealing at the time of the end may not provide us a great deal of fruitful, interpretational help in our day. Isaiah 29:10–11 fittingly describes the situation:

For the LORD hath poured out upon you the spirit of deep sleep, and hath closed your eyes: the prophets and your rulers, the seers hath he covered. And the vision of all is become unto you as the words of a book that is sealed, which men deliver to one that is learned, saying, Read this, I pray thee: and he saith, I cannot; for it is sealed. (Isaiah 29:10–11)

I wonder if we are now in the time when this unsealing will occur and understanding of Daniel's visions will increase. After all, we have several tools and capabilities available for our use to allow us to "go to and fro" in the Scriptures with ease. Digital Bible software provides robust search techniques and can include concordance features, maps, and other Bible helps that can be accessed with ease. Still other electronic means allow us to compare related Scriptures on a single page so that we can swiftly go back and forth between verses and chapters. The most important key, however, is this: Is it God's time to unseal? Are we soon to enter the "time of the end"? And equally as important, if we are inspired and directed to learn more about the end times, are we humbly praying to God for His guiding hand to lead the way? Do we tremble at the Word and esteem it highly? If we are in such a time as this, do we recognize both the opportunity and the gravity of what lies ahead?

The entire subject of the end times and the day of the Lord is so much greater than any one person. It will most likely take the collective efforts of many humble and diligent Bereans to unravel the mysteries that God intends to be made known.

To return to our subject, where has the messianic transliteration of Daniel 9 led us in our present-day understanding of the end times? Generally speaking, the messianic wording of this prophecy has put people who try to decipher and understand it into two camps, defined at the beginning of this section. I understand how we ended up in these two camps: although their interpretations are complex, they are understandable destinations. However, I believe both camps continue to hide, muffle, and cloud our ability to see a detailed picture of the events that God will reveal to us and orchestrate at the time of the end. I believe it is time to consider a third camp of understanding.

It may seem complex initially (though not, perhaps, more so than the majority opinions mentioned above), but I believe this third camp provides us with a detailed and precise framework of the end times—a framework that is generally attainable through simple and plain interpretational methods. *I believe that the Scriptures alone contain a sufficiently detailed road map that will lead God's people to the end of time.* The more that we can let the words of

Scripture stand for themselves in a plain, literal hermeneutic (interpretation), and the less that we rely on human assumptions, the more powerful the Scriptures become!

To review briefly, the two major camps of interpretation are:

Camp 1: Bible interpreters who conclude that the prophecy of seventy weeks was completely fulfilled by Jesus Christ when He died on the cross.

Camp 2: Bible interpreters who conclude that part of the seventy weeks prophecy has been fulfilled (i.e. the first sixty-nine weeks or 483 *years*) and that now we are living in a gap period prior to the final week of the prophecy (i.e. the last "week" of seven *years*.). They believe the seventieth week is a future seven-year tribulation period, which is comprised of 3.5 years of tribulation and 3.5 years of great tribulation, marked by a distinct occurrence in the middle of the week called the abomination of desolation.

I propose a very different interpretation.

Camp 3: This interpretation is closely related to camp 2 in that it sees the seventy weeks prophecy as concluding with the second coming of Jesus Christ. However, it departs from camp 2 in these ways:

- In the belief that the seventy weeks are *literally* seventy weeks, and in the future.
- In the belief that a *future decree* will go forth to rebuild a plaza area and wall in Jerusalem in troublous times.
- In the belief that the text calls for the arrival of an "anointed ruler" seven literal weeks after the decree goes forth.
- In the belief that the cutting off of the "anointed" depicts the two witnesses of Revelation 11 being killed by the Antichrist at the start of the seventieth week, after which they will literally lie in the street for 3.5 days. Then, according to Revelation 11:11–13, the Spirit of life from God will enter into them; they will stand upon their feet; a great voice from heaven will say unto them, Come up hither; they will ascend up to heaven in a cloud; their enemies will fearfully behold them; and in the *same hour* there will be a great earthquake killing seven thousand people.
- In the belief that the "anointed ruler" is either one or both of the two witnesses. Zechariah uses the language of two "anointed ones" who stand by the Lord of the whole earth. This exact language is used in Revelation 11:4 in reference to the two witnesses:

- o "These are the two olive trees, and the two candlesticks standing before the God of the earth." (Revelation 11:4)
- o "Then said he, These are the two anointed ones, that stand by the Lord of the whole earth." (Zechariah 4:14)
- In the belief that the abomination of desolation will occur in the middle of the seventieth week (which is the last literal week of seven days of the seventy weeks prophecy). Based on the timing of the two witnesses being cut off at the beginning of the seventieth week and lying in the street for 3.5 days, I estimate that the blasphemous abomination of desolation will occur at or near the time of their resurrection and could potentially occur within the *hour* of their resurrection, just prior to the great earthquake. The Scripture provides such intricate detail of this time!
- In the belief that following the abomination of desolation a swift and sudden destruction will come primarily upon the inhabitants of the city of Jerusalem and in Judea. This great tribulation, unlike anything before in history, *will last for 3.5 literal days* and take us to the end of the seventy weeks prophecy of Daniel and to the second coming of Jesus Christ.

You may consider removing the "messianic" wording quite a stretch. It is true. While I often look at Strong's Concordance to gain a greater depth of knowledge of certain words underlying the text I am reading, I have great respect for the use of every English word in my Bible and do not doubt their correctness. I believe in the infallible and inerrant Word. However, this is one instance where misleading English wording appears to have been purposefully inspired by God. After all, it is a transliteration and not a direct translation from the Hebrew. *And if it wasn't for the beauty and perfection that I have come to see when a simple, literal, and unforced eschatological framework is used for the time of the end, I wouldn't have the confidence to go out on such a limb.* But, after all, is reading and interpreting Scripture as it would have been read by the disciples of Jesus, and even by Christ Himself, a big stretch?

In this light, I conclude that it isn't a big stretch at all. To conclude as camps 1 and 2 have done requires multiple assumptions and broad maneuvering (i.e. turning weeks into years; deciding which decree to use as the starting point; inserting a gap), and yet there is still a lack of precise fulfillment. In comparison, camp 3 requires us only to look at this prophecy as future and use the original Hebrew or Greek text without our English spin. And when this is done and the final seventieth week is overlaid onto other Scripture passages, a perfect, hand-in-glove fit occurs in our eschatological framework. Most helpful is the removal of the need to force fit our eschatological understanding into a seven-year tribulation, where the abomination of desolation occurs 3.5 years prior to the day of the Lord (with little to no consequence) and the great tribulation lasts 3.5 years. All of these points will be discussed in greater detail.

For now, here is a summary of my recommendations for reading and interpreting the seventy weeks prophecy:

- Translate the English messianic transliteration back into the original nonmessianic context
- Interpret the seventy weeks literally, as weeks of days and not "weeks" of years (i.e. 490 days instead of 490 years)
- Interpret the whole of the seventy weeks prophecy as events yet future
- Give respect to the peculiar wording of the seventy weeks chronology, so that it is understood that:
    o the appearance of the "anointed ruler" must occur on day forty-nine, seven weeks after the decree goes forth
    o the street and wall will be rebuilt in troubled times during the first sixty-nine weeks (or 483 days) of the prophecy
    o the "anointed ruler" will die when the sixty-ninth week has ended (and his death will mark the beginning of the final week, the seventieth week)
    o the one (i.e. Antichrist) who kills the anointed ruler will confirm an existing covenant for one week
    o in the middle of the week animal sacrifices will be stopped, and he will cause the abomination of desolation
    o the holy city Jerusalem and the sanctuary will be destroyed and desolated
    o at the end of the seventieth week, just 3.5 days after the abomination of desolation, the decrees spoken to Daniel in verse 24 will be accomplished at the day of the Lord!

When this prophecy is read in literal fashion, and when other truths of Scripture can be overlaid with it, a clear view of God's design for the end times is revealed.

Taking a Leap

If my recommendations above make you uncomfortable because they are unfamiliar, consider the leaps that each of the popular camps must make in order to make the prophecy fit their understanding. In many cases these are big leaps, especially when we set out to study the prophecies in as literal a way as possible. Let's discuss these major leaps and some of their ramifications.

Leap 1—The need to turn seventy weeks (i.e. 490 days) into seventy weeks of years (i.e. 490 years)

For either of the popular camps, one must believe in a year-for-a-day interpretation of the seventy weeks. This requires us to take leave of interpreting the Scripture using a literal, plain reading. "Weeks" (*shabua*—Strong's H7620) literally means "sevened." The word *shabua* is used nineteen times in the Old Testament. In every instance, it means a *literal week of days*. Again, this is *every time* the word *shabua* is used.

One example is in Daniel 10:2–3, where clearly we recognize that Daniel was mourning for twenty-one days, not twenty-one years. Plus, it is easy to understand that Daniel did not eat bread or meat or drink wine or take a bath for twenty-one days, not twenty-one years!

Another example of its use is when Jacob served Laban for Rachel. First he served seven years to receive Rachel as his wife but was tricked and was given Leah instead. He then fulfilled her "week" (a literal seven-day marriage feast week) before marrying Rachel and beginning another term of seven-year service. After this fourteen-year period, Jacob went on to serve Laban another approximate six years for wages. I have heard this passage used as justification for turning the seventy weeks prophecy into seventy weeks of years, but it cannot be done. Read the Scripture below noting specifically the differentiation between the seven years (*shaneh*—Strong's H8141) of service compared to the seven-day (*shabua*—Strong's H7620) marriage feast week.

> And Jacob served seven years [*shaneh*—Strong's H8141] for Rachel; and they seemed unto him but a few days, for the love he had to her. And Jacob said unto Laban, Give me my wife, for my days are fulfilled, that I may go in unto her. And Laban gathered together all the men of the place, and made a feast. And it came to pass in the evening, that he took Leah his daughter, and brought her to him; and he went in unto her. And Laban gave unto his daughter Leah Zilpah his maid for an handmaid.

And it came to pass, that in the morning, behold, it was Leah: and he said to Laban, What is this thou hast done unto me? did not I serve with thee for Rachel? wherefore then hast thou beguiled me? And Laban said, It must not be so done in our country, to give the younger before the firstborn. Fulfil her week [*shabua*—Strong's H7620], and we will give thee this also for the service which thou shalt serve with me yet seven other years [*shaneh*—Strong's H8141]. And Jacob did so, and fulfilled her week [*shabua*—Strong's H7620]: and he gave him Rachel his daughter to wife also. And Laban gave to Rachel his daughter Bilhah his handmaid to be her maid. And he went in also unto Rachel, and he loved also Rachel more than Leah, and served with him yet seven other years [*shaneh*—Strong's H8141]. (Gen 29:20-30)

The other primary example of *shabua*'s use in the Old Testament is in reference to the feast of weeks, an annual celebration: "Even after a certain rate every day, offering according to the commandment of Moses, on the sabbaths, and on the new moons, and on the solemn feasts, three times in the year, even in the feast of unleavened bread, and in the *feast of weeks*, and in the feast of tabernacles" (2 Chronicles 8:13). By necessity, this has to be interpreted as a literal seven-day week, or the feast of weeks could not occur every year.

▸ The leap: To interpret "weeks" in Daniel 9 as year-for-a-day, we must choose to move away from the seven-day week meaning as used in all other Scripture references.

Leap 2—For camp 2, the need to insert a gap between the end of the sixty-ninth week and the beginning of a future seventieth week

One must believe in a "gap theory." In other words, one must *create* the existence of a large span of time between the conclusion of the sixty-ninth week and the beginning of the seventieth week when no such hint of any gap exists from the words of the prophecy.

Granted, there are times in Scripture when long time gaps occur between one verse and the next. One example is Micah 5. Micah 5:2 refers to the place of Christ's birth in Bethlehem. The following verses quickly turn to Israel's travail, their conversion and salvation, and the day of the Lord! However, this Scripture and others like it, which span thousands of years, isn't given in the context of a specific prophetic window of time. Contrast this to the seventy weeks prophecy, in which one would naturally expect that what is prophesied and determined will actually occur within the specific prophesied time frame!

God is the author and inspiration of the prophecy and vision given to Daniel. Is it wise to say that Daniel and his people simply were not aware of a coming "church age" and thus were not privy to understanding a gap in the vision? God was fully aware, and God's prophecies are fully accurate. By inserting and forcing a gap, are we deeming the prophecy inaccurate as it stands in the Holy Scripture? "Seventy weeks" can no longer mean "seventy weeks" if we do this.

▸ The leap: A "gap theory" flies in the face of the language of Daniel 9:24, which plainly says "seventy weeks are determined." A plain reading of this text gives us no reason to look for a potential pause once the decree goes forth that begins the prophecy.

Leap 3—For camp 2, a seven-year end-times framework is required as a result of the gap insertion

The gap theory described above impacts our eschatology significantly. It *forces* us to use a seven-year framework for the time of the end. We do not have the option of understanding things to happen within a day or a few days, or within a single hour. This is much like the foundation of a structure. If the framework is solid and true, the structure and details laid upon the foundation can be effective and long-lasting, able to hold up to pressures and tensions from outside. The gap theory and its related seven-year future tribulation impacts everything that we understand about the time of the end, because if seven years remain for the prophecy to be fulfilled, we must use those seven years to fit and place the numerous details of Scripture related to the end times.

For example, since the gap theory forces a seven-year tribulation framework, the following associated conclusions are required:

- The Antichrist will enter into a league or covenant at the start of the seven-year tribulation (Daniel 11:23). As such, the Antichrist (whose power lasts forty-two months according to Revelation 13:5) must then be a "nonfactor" during the first 3.5 years of the tribulation but a mighty, evil power to be reckoned with during the last 3.5 years.
- The abomination of desolation occurs at the midpoint of the seven years. This marks the time when Antichrist truly comes on the scene and reveals himself as the leader of the unseemly beast kingdom. From that point on, he launches forth with power and

authority for a period of 3.5 years, persecuting Jews and Christians. This is called the 3.5 year "great tribulation."

These points raise some natural questions.

First: Do Daniel 7, 8, and 11 indicate that when the little horn/vile person comes onto the scene he will be more or less a bystander for 3.5 years?

Second: Wouldn't the little horn/vile person/Antichrist already be in a position of power and influence if he is to enter into a league or covenant at the start of a seven-year tribulation period? And relatedly, if he was in such a position of power and influence *seven* years prior to the day of the Lord, how does that reconcile with Daniel 7:25 and Revelation 13:5, verses that clearly limit the duration of Antichrist's power to 3.5 years?

Third: The Scripture gives no hint of an initial 3.5-year ineffective, powerless leader of the beast kingdom. Once he arises into the leadership position, he is described as nothing less than a powerful force. How will we not be able to identify the "little horn" when he rises to power?

Fourth: Does it seem reasonable that Antichrist would exalt himself in the temple of God, blaspheming the Creator (i.e. the abomination of desolation) *before* he has an opportunity to prove himself and grow his devout following? Or is it more reasonable that this exaltation would occur *after* he gains political and religious capital from successful tirades against Jews and Christians and after many great wonders and miracles are performed by the false prophet, which woo many to worship the beast and his image? Doesn't the abomination of desolation seem like a crowning achievement that will bring a swift response, rather than an opening salvo without any immediate ramification?

Fifth: Does a 3.5-year great tribulation really fit the context of Matthew 24, Luke 21, and Mark 13, wherein the Lord Jesus references "flight" and calls the inhabitants of Judea to "flee" because "those days" will be as it was in the time when Lot fled away from the city and utter devastation quickly followed? The prophets Jeremiah, Isaiah, and Zechariah all indicate that this travail of Jacob's trouble is closely connected to a *soon* coming day of the Lord (Jeremiah 30:4–9, Isaiah 13:8–18, Zechariah 14:1–4). This same thought ties closely with 1 Thessalonians 5:2–3 and the Olivet Discourse in Matthew 24:19–22, 28–31 and Luke 21:22–27.

Let's take a closer look at this fifth question. *Do the descriptions of the great tribulation in Scripture more closely fit an eschatological framework that calls for the great tribulation to last for 3.5 years or one that expects it to last 3.5 days? What* we see in the context of the time of Jacob's trouble (i.e. the great tribulation) is that the day of the Lord is *very near*. To me, these Scriptures corroborate the idea that the great tribulation will occur over a very short time period (i.e. three or four days versus 3.5 years). Each is in the clear context of the soon-to-come day of the Lord.

Also supporting this idea are the numerous connections between the distressful time of the great tribulation and that of a woman in labor. My dear wife has given birth to seven children. She has never had an epidural. And though in some instances she has received some pain medication toward the very end, she has delivered some of our children without the aid of any pain medication at all. Here is the summary from my vantage point. Slight contractions can begin weeks prior to delivery. The intensity of these birth pains then increase over time. Though some can be difficult, she would consider the prior contractions to be relatively minor in comparison to what occurs during the final hour or two. It isn't until these final moments that she would categorize her experience as one of severe toil, such as is described in Jeremiah 30:6, Isaiah 13:8, and 1 Thessalonians 5:3.

The experience is summed up very well by the prophets. The prophet Jeremiah sees travail that causes every face to turn pale. I have witnessed this when my wife starts to squeeze my hand and nearly faint for fear of the next major contraction that is just starting. The prophet Isaiah says pangs and sorrows will take hold of everyone, and their faces shall be as flames. In addition to a visible flash or flame of severity, *flame* in this sense (according to Strong's) can be described as a sharply polished blade or the point of a weapon. Both descriptions seem apt—being overcome by a flash of pain as if the point of a weapon were pressed into your skin.

The apostle Paul describes this last-days travail in 1 Thessalonians 5:3 as "sudden destruction" that cannot be "escaped." My point is this: although contractions can occur over days and weeks of time, the "great" contractions normally occur over the final hour(s). As opposed to the common belief that the end times will be comprised of 3.5 years of tribulation followed by another 3.5 years of great tribulation, it is my conviction that the Holy Scripture consistently references an overall time period of 3.5 years for the time of the end, of which the final three or four days leading up to the day of the Lord can be categorized as the "great tribulation"—the last few sharp hours of labor.

I encourage you to study the Scriptures below. For me it is difficult to comprehend that the time of Jacob's trouble will last much longer than a few days.

Just below, in Jeremiah, we see the day of the Lord context in verses 8–9. Verse 7 then puts the time of Jacob's trouble in the context of a short period of time (i.e. "that *day* is great") as opposed to several years. Verse 6 uses the same phraseology of the travailing woman which is also used by Isaiah and the apostle Paul. It seems reasonable to me that these few verses are referencing the climax point that leads to the day of the Lord. This is very similar to the language used in Matthew 24:21–22, which describes a great tribulation that is greater than anything the world has ever seen—and it continues in the next verse by saying that except "those days" be shortened, there should no flesh be saved. I would have to concur. I can't imagine how my wife could live if the severe toil of the "great" contractions lasted any longer than a few hours.

> And these are the words that the LORD spake concerning Israel and concerning Judah. For thus saith the LORD; We have heard a voice of trembling, of fear, and not of peace. Ask ye now, and see whether a man doth travail with child? wherefore do I see every man with his hands on his loins, as a woman in travail, and all faces are turned into paleness? Alas! for that day is great, so that none is like it: it is even the time of Jacob's trouble; but he shall be saved out of it. For it shall come to pass in that day, saith the LORD of hosts, that I will break his yoke from off thy neck, and will burst thy bonds, and strangers shall no more serve themselves of him: but they shall serve the LORD their God, and David their king, whom I will raise up unto them. (Jeremiah 30:4–9)

In Isaiah, below, we also see the day of the Lord context in verse 9. It mentions the same phrase, "as a woman that travaileth," which is associated with Jacob's trouble or the great tribulation. Also, verse 15 mentions a horrific tribulation that reeks of utter despair and heartache, where children are dashed to pieces before their parents' eyes and wives are ravished. It is so horrible that it makes me shudder and tremble to type these words. There is nothing worse to me than seeing one of my children suffer from a smashed finger, a broken bone, or a slammed head in a tough bike crash. Abuse at the hands of another human being would be as bad as it could get. Plus, it is one thing to come quickly to the scene after an incident has occurred. It is altogether more agonizing to see it unfold before our very eyes. This indeed is describing a great tribulation, and it is right in context with the soon-approaching day of the Lord. Do you think these shocking incidents will occur for a few *years*? May God have mercy and shorten "those days" for the elect's sake!

And they shall be afraid: pangs and sorrows shall take hold of them; they shall be in pain as a woman that travaileth: they shall be amazed one at another; their faces shall be as flames. *Behold, the day of the* LORD *cometh, cruel both with wrath and fierce anger, to lay the land desolate: and he shall destroy the sinners thereof out of it.* For the stars of heaven and the constellations thereof shall not give their light: the sun shall be darkened in his going forth, and the moon shall not cause her light to shine. And I will punish the world for their evil, and the wicked for their iniquity; and I will cause the arrogancy of the proud to cease, and will lay low the haughtiness of the terrible. I will make a man more precious than fine gold; even a man than the golden wedge of Ophir. Therefore I will shake the heavens, and the earth shall remove out of her place, in the wrath of the LORD of hosts, and in the day of his fierce anger. And it shall be as the chased roe, and as a sheep that no man taketh up: they shall every man turn to his own people, and flee every one into his own land. *Every one that is found shall be thrust through; and every one that is joined unto them shall fall by the sword. Their children also shall be dashed to pieces before their eyes; their houses shall be spoiled, and their wives ravished.* Behold, I will stir up the Medes against them, which shall not regard silver; and as for gold, they shall not delight in it. Their bows also shall dash the young men to pieces; and they shall have no pity on the fruit of the womb; their eye shall not spare children. (Isaiah 13:8–18)

In Zechariah, we see the day of the Lord context in verse 1. Verse 2 goes on to describe similar events to those we just reviewed in Isaiah 13:16. In addition, we also see the end-times gathering of nations against Jerusalem. This is the same event described in Luke 21:20, which reads "and when ye shall see Jerusalem compassed with armies, then know that the desolation thereof is nigh." It is important to note that the gathering of the armies and the subsequent flight into the mountains (Luke 21:21) is described in context with the abomination of desolation and is described in Luke 21:22 as "the days of vengeance." It is the final, climatic effort of Antichrist and Satan to usurp Almighty God.

I believe this same and final gathering event is referred to in Isaiah 10:5–6, Isaiah 42:24, Ezekiel 38:9–10, Zechariah 12:2–3, and Revelation 16:14–16. Antichrist and his followers are more than willing to go up, but it is *the Lord Himself* who ultimately provokes the gathering near Jerusalem for the final battle of the current world, the great day of God Almighty. Thankfully, the days will be cut short, and the battle will come to a stop with the second coming of Jesus Christ. I believe the day of the Lord will occur just a *few days* after the abomination of desolation. The consistent theme and context of these Scriptures seems to support that conclusion.

> *Behold, the day of the* LORD *cometh*, and thy spoil shall be divided in the midst of thee. For I will gather all nations against Jerusalem to battle; and the city shall be taken, and *the houses rifled, and the women ravished*; and half of the city shall go forth into captivity, and the residue of the people shall not be cut off from the city. Then shall the LORD go forth, and fight against those nations, as when he fought in the day of battle. And his feet shall stand in that day upon the mount of Olives, which is before Jerusalem on the east, and the mount of Olives shall cleave in the midst thereof toward the east and toward the west, and there shall be a very great valley; and half of the mountain shall remove toward the north, and half of it toward the south. (Zechariah 14:1–4)

In Luke's account of the Olivet Discourse, we see the day of the Lord context in verses 25–27. The "days of vengeance" by the Antichrist and his adherents against the people of God bring "great distress . . . and wrath," where many fall by the edge of the sword. This is the same event as described in the preceding accounts, called "Jacob's trouble," the "great tribulation," and a "woman in travail." Again, does this Scripture seem to indicate a time period of several years, or rather a few "days of vengeance"?

> For these be *the days of vengeance*, that all things which are written may be fulfilled. But *woe unto them that are with child, and to them that give suck, in those days! for there shall be great distress in the land, and wrath upon this people.* And they shall fall by the edge of the sword, and shall be led away captive into all nations: and Jerusalem shall be trodden down of the Gentiles, until the times of the Gentiles be fulfilled. And there shall be signs in the sun, and in the moon, and in the stars; and upon the earth distress of nations, with perplexity; the sea and the waves roaring; men's hearts failing them for fear, and for looking after those things which are coming on the earth: for the powers of heaven shall be shaken. And then shall they see the Son of man coming in a cloud with power and great glory. (Luke 21:22–27)

From Matthew's account below, we find that the common threads continue. The day of the Lord context is clearly evident in verses 29–31. And "those days" of "great tribulation" are described in verses 19–21. The brevity of the severe travail is again highlighted in verse 29, where it is taught that the second coming of Jesus Christ will occur "immediately after the tribulation of those days."

> *And woe unto them that are with child, and to them that give suck in those days!* But pray ye that your flight be not in the winter, neither on the sabbath day: *for then shall be great tribulation, such as was not since the beginning of the world to this time, no, nor ever shall be.* And except *those days* should be shortened, there should no flesh be saved: but for the elect's sake those days shall be shortened. For wheresoever the carcase is, there will the eagles be gathered together. *Immediately after the tribulation of those days* shall the sun be darkened, and the moon shall not give her light, and the stars shall fall from heaven, and the powers of the heavens shall be shaken: and then shall appear the sign of the Son of man in heaven: and then shall all the tribes of the earth mourn, and they shall see the Son of man coming in the clouds of heaven with power and great glory. And he shall send his angels with a great sound of a trumpet, and they shall gather together his elect from the four winds, from one end of heaven to the other. (Matthew 24:19–22, 28–31)

From the apostle Paul, below, we see this same time period of great tribulation in the immediate context of the day of the Lord.

> For yourselves know perfectly that the day of the Lord so cometh as a thief in the night. For when they shall say, Peace and safety; then sudden destruction cometh upon them, as travail upon a woman with child; and they shall not escape. (1 Thessalonians 5:2–3)

His writings raise a new question: how is it that we see Israel say "peace and safety" in one breath and in the next experience sudden destruction, all in the context of "those days" as opposed to seven years? I believe this results from Antichrist's confirmation of the existing covenant at the beginning of the last week. As you know by now, it is my understanding that the much-debated prophecy of Daniel's seventy weeks describes a literal period of 490 days. This means the final week will last a total of seven days, not seven years. And it doesn't force us to stretch the "days of vengeance" into 3.5 long, agonizing years.

▶ The leap: Are you comfortable with a seven-year reign of the Antichrist as king of the end-times beast kingdom, when Scripture tells us plainly that he will have power and authority for 3.5 years? Are you comfortable with the timing of the abomination of desolation as a nonclimatic event at the *beginning* of his 3.5 year rule? Are you comfortable with "those days" of the great tribulation being a lengthy 3.5 years, stretching a short and severe time period of days into many years?

Leap 4—Determining which historical decree is the starting point for the seventy weeks prophecy

When was the decree given to rebuild Jerusalem? If the prophecy is applied historically and the weeks turned into years, multiple problems arise. The following paragraph was taken directly from the *Handbook on the Prophets*, page 314–315, by Robert B. Chisholm Jr. Mr. Chisholm is the department chair and senior professor of Old Testament Studies at Dallas Theological Seminary. He authored this book in 2001–2002.

> When was the decree to rebuild Jerusalem given? Most attempt to identify the decree as a royal edict issued by a Persian ruler. The four options are the decrees of Cyrus (in 538 b.c.), Darius (519 or 518), Artaxerxes to Ezra (458 or 457), and Artaxerxes to Nehemiah (444). The decrees of Cyrus (2 Chron. 36:22–23; Ezra 1:1–4, 6:3–5) and Darius (Ezra 6:1–12) pertain to the rebuilding of the temple, not the city per se. Likewise, Artaxerxes' decree to Ezra (Ezra 7:11–26) makes no mention of rebuilding the city. Nehemiah 2:1–9 refers to letters given by Artaxerxes to Nehemiah authorizing the rebuilding of the city. Using this date (444) as a starting point, some calculate that there was a period of sixty-nine weeks (or 483 years) between the decree to rebuild the city and the triumphal entry of the "anointed" one, Jesus the Messiah, who is then "cut off." However, if the syntactical analysis of Daniel 9:25 proposed above is correct, this view cannot be sustained, for the "anointed one" of verse 25 would have to appear around 396 assuming, as this system of reckoning does, that seven weeks is the equivalent of forty-nine years.

It is my understanding that this theory of interpretation (i.e. sixty-nine fulfilled "weeks" with a seventieth "week" of seven years still in the future) was popularized by Sir Robert Anderson (1841–1918) in his book *The Coming Prince*. However, these Bible readers don't simply add 483 years to the year 444 BC, because that would yield 38 AD—which is long after the crucifixion of Christ. More assumptions are piled on, including which decree to use, what date to use for the death of Jesus, whether to use 360 days for a "year" or to use a different number, whether to adjust for leap years or not, and so on. Due to the many assumptions required to make the math work, inconsistencies in the prophetic community abound, and there is not one "biblical" methodology that all gather around to support. It seems to become a more shaky foundation as the usage of human assumptions increases.

But there are additional reasons to doubt the veracity of any of these calculations. Mr. William Struse has researched this extensively. He has authored one of the most detailed chronologies of biblical history in existence, *Daniel's Seventy Weeks: The Keystone of Bible Prophecy*. According to Mr. Struse, biblical evidence shows that Ezra and Nehemiah were contemporaries of Darius "the Great" Artaxerxes, and not of Artaxerxes Longimanus, the Persian king usually credited with giving the decree to rebuild Jerusalem. This would put the starting point used by Sir Robert Anderson nearly sixty years too late in the second temple era, and it presents profound doubts as to the trustworthiness of this interpretation!

The lesson is this. The further we move away from literal biblical hermeneutics, or understanding the Bible in its normal or plain meaning, the greater the variety of conclusions yielded. However, I don't want to unduly criticize these conclusions. I recall as a teenager being shown a chart by my father that depicted a seven-year tribulation. It was good enough for me until a relatively short time ago, when the Lord compelled me to study the prophetic Word and to do so through a principled, literal lens.

Step back and ask yourself these questions.

Is God the author of confusion?

Am I comfortable with adding several impactful, man-derived assumptions to this text in order to come up with an interpretation that appears valid (yet is still subject to reasonable doubt)?

Albeit there are mysteries, but is it God's nature to make His plans and purposes complex and beyond the comprehension abilities of the average student of Scripture?

▶ The leap: There is a wide array of techniques and methods used on which to establish the foundation of a future seven-year tribulation, and a widespread lack of consensus. Are you comfortable with that?

Leap 5—The syntax of the prophecy

The syntax of Daniel's prophecy seems to describe the appearance of the "anointed one" at seven weeks from the initiation of the decree in verse 25.

Both camps 1 and 2 ignore any relevancy in the first seven weeks. But if the seven weeks are irrelevant to the prophecy, then why include them in the text? Only to test our math skills to see if we can properly add seven plus sixty-two to get to the all-important sixty-nine and the beginning of the seventieth week? For its inclusion in the text, something must be noteworthy regarding this time period.

> Know therefore and understand, that *from the going forth of the commandment to restore and to build Jerusalem unto the Messiah the Prince shall be seven weeks*, and threescore and two weeks: the street shall be built again, and the wall, even in troublous times. (Daniel 9:25)

Are you comfortable that the first time phase of the prophecy, the seven weeks portion of the text, is *completely* neglected by the two primary camps of interpretation?

Below is an annotated translation of Daniel 9:24–27 from the book *Handbook on the Prophets*, pages 313–314, authored by Robert B. Chisholm Jr.

> 24 Seventy "weeks" have been determined with respect to your people and your holy city, for the purpose of putting an end to rebellion, bringing to completion sin, atoning for iniquity, bringing about perpetual righteousness, sealing up a prophetic vision, and anointing what is most holy. 25 Now know and understand this: *From the going forth of a decree to rebuild Jerusalem until an anointed one, a ruler [arrives], [there will be a period of] seven "weeks."* And [during a period of] sixty-two "weeks" a plaza and a trench will be rebuilt, but in distressing times. 26 And after [the period of] sixty-two "weeks" an anointed one will be cut off and have nothing. The people of the ruler who is to come will destroy the city and the sanctuary. Its end will be with a flood. Until the end of war, desolation is decreed. 27 He will ratify a covenant with many [for a period of] one "week." In the middle of the "week" he will put an end to sacrifice and offerings. Upon the wing there will be an abomination that makes desolate, until the end that has been decreed engulfs that which makes desolate.

I highlighted three points as I read the Daniel 9 chapter of this handbook. First, the syntax of verse 25 implies that an anointed ruler will arrive on the scene seven weeks after the start of the seventy weeks prophecy. Second, Professor Chisholm does not mandate a messianic interpretation of the text. And finally, the author was unable to find a literal fulfillment of this prophecy in history and thus concluded a likely need to stray from the strict mathematics of the prophecy as it is usually understood.

▸ The leap: Are you comfortable ignoring the syntax of Daniel 9:25?

Leap 6—For camp 1, the ultimate day of the Lord tone reflected in verse 24 must be dismissed.

I acknowledge that a case can be made for seeing Jesus Christ as having accomplished each achievement of the seventy weeks prophecy when He lived perfectly upon this earth and then in great love and humility shed His innocent blood and bore our sins upon Calvary's old rugged cross. Not remaining in the tomb, our Lord and Savior was resurrected as the firstfruits of righteousness and lives in heaven at the right hand of God, interceding on our behalf as our mediator.

However, I don't believe the case is strong enough. The achievements of Daniel 9:24 seem to be more targeted and focused on an ultimate and more literal finality—the end of evil, the final fulfillment of prophecy, the end of earthly kingdoms and the bringing forth of the everlasting kingdom of the Most Holy, and the end of Satan's rule as the prince and power of the air. The prophecy seems most applicable to an end-times era and what the Almighty will accomplish on the great day of God (i.e. the day of the Lord).

Ask yourself:

- Was the transgression finished . . . or is the great and terrible abomination of desolation yet to occur?
- Has sin been brought to completion . . . or is iniquity yet increasing and abounding?
- Has iniquity been "covered up" . . . literally with pitch according to Strong's H3722?
- Has Jesus returned to bring His everlasting kingdom of righteousness, where all dominions serve and obey Him?
- Have Daniel's visions and all prophecies in the Holy Scriptures been accomplished, and are they no longer applicable to us today because the complete fulfillment of prophecy has occurred?
- Has the King of kings and Lord of lords begun His everlasting kingdom reign?

▸ The leap: Proponents of camp 1 claim that Jesus achieved all of Daniel 9 in His first coming, but consistent with the bulk of prophecies in Scripture, they take the reader all the way instead to a greater fulfillment and point us to the day of the Lord. The accomplishments of Daniel 9:24 are no different: the context and plain meaning of every point will experience ultimate fulfillment on that great and notable day.

Finding the Plain Meaning of Daniel 9:24–27

How do we search out and understand the plain meaning of Daniel 9:24–27—this passage that has brought so much confusion to so many? We of course need to start with the text itself, and then stick to it as best we can! I understand that the language and the sentence structure of these verses is extremely difficult. But I don't believe the task is insurmountable.

Below is a verse-by-verse summary of Daniel 9:24–27 in my words, stated to the best of my ability in a straightforward, plain, and literal manner, and followed by bullet points that help expand on the meaning of the prophecy. I am confident in the following interpretation due to the wonderful cohesion and understanding it brings to the overall framework of the end times, as will be discussed and built upon as we move further into the book.

Daniel 9:24

Seventy weeks (i.e. 490 days) have been decreed upon Jerusalem and Daniel's people (the Israelites) that in the end will result in the following accomplishments: the transgression will be finished, sin will be brought to completion, reconciliation for iniquity will be completed, everlasting righteousness will be brought in, visions and prophecies of Scripture will be wrapped up/finished, and the most holy will be anointed.

- The transgression will be finished.
    - i.e. the Antichrist will have stood in the holy temple and proclaimed himself as God.
- Sin will be brought to completion.
    - i.e. evil and wickedness will be destroyed at the day of the Lord. Also, remnant Israel's great day of salvation will come, when their sins will be cleansed and taken away, they will be given a new heart, and God's Spirit will indwell them.
    - This time is described well by the prophet Zephaniah. Zephaniah 3:13–15 says, "*The remnant of Israel shall not do iniquity, nor speak lies; neither shall a deceitful tongue be found in their mouth:* for they shall feed and lie down, and none shall make

them afraid. Sing, O daughter of Zion; shout, O Israel; be glad and rejoice with all the heart, O daughter of Jerusalem. The LORD hath taken away thy judgments, *he hath cast out thine enemy*: the king of Israel, even the LORD is in the midst of thee: *thou shalt not see evil any more.*"

- Reconciliation for iniquity will be completed.
  - o "Reconciliation" means literally "to cover" (specifically with bitumen) according to Strong's H3722. Another word for bitumen is pitch. This basically connotes the day of the Lord's wrath.
  - o This time is described well by the prophet Isaiah. Isaiah 34:8–9 says, "For it is the day of the LORD's vengeance, and the year of recompences for the controversy of Zion. And *the streams thereof shall be turned into pitch*, and the dust thereof into brimstone, and *the land thereof shall become burning pitch.*"
- Everlasting righteousness will be brought in.
  - o i.e. Jesus Christ will come as King of kings.
  - o This time is described well by the prophet Zechariah and also in Revelation.
    - Zechariah 14:9: "And the LORD shall be king over all the earth: in that day shall there be one LORD, and his name one."
    - Revelation 11:15: "And the seventh angel sounded; and there were great voices in heaven, saying, The kingdoms of this world are become the kingdoms of our Lord, and of his Christ; and he shall reign for ever and ever."
- Visions and prophecies of Scripture will be wrapped up/finished.
  - o i.e. The oracles of prophecy will be fulfilled! The seventh trumpet, seventh vial, and seventh thunder reveal this precious fact.
  - o Revelation 11:15: "And the seventh angel sounded; and there were great voices in heaven, saying, *The kingdoms of this world are become the kingdoms of our Lord, and of his Christ; and he shall reign for ever and ever.*"
  - o Revelation 16:17: "And the seventh angel poured out his vial into the air; and there came a great voice out of the temple of heaven, from the throne, saying, *It is done.*"

- o Revelation 10:7: "But in the days of the voice of the seventh angel, when he shall begin to sound, *the mystery of God should be finished, as he hath declared to his servants the prophets.*"
- The most holy will be anointed.
  - o This means to consecrate and dedicate the reign of Jesus Christ as king of the world as cited above in Revelation 11:15.

Daniel 9:25

Know and understand that from the going forth of a commandment or decree to restore and to build Jerusalem to the coming of an anointed ruler/prince shall be a period of seven weeks. Then, after a period of sixty-two weeks, the street and the wall shall be built again, even in troublous times.

- An anointed ruler/prince will arrive in Jerusalem seven weeks after a decree to build Jerusalem goes forth. Based on my study of these Scriptures, I believe it will be one or both of the two witnesses who enter Jerusalem at this time. This isn't a stretch. In fact, the Scriptures tell us that the two witnesses are the two olive trees and the two candlesticks *standing before the God of the earth* (Revelation 11:4). This is exact language from Zechariah 4:11–14. And what does the angel tell Zechariah in verse 14? "These are the two anointed ones, *that stand by the Lord of the whole earth.*"
- By the sixty-ninth week (a seven-week period plus a sixty-two-week period) the street and wall will be built again, but in distressful times.

Daniel 9:26

After the sixty-two week period, the anointed ruler described above will be cut down and have no life in himself. The people of the prince (the followers of the Antichrist) who shall come into the city will destroy the city and the sanctuary with an overflowing flood of destruction through fighting, war, and amazing desolation until the very end.

- At the start of the final, seventieth week, the anointed ruler (one of the two witnesses, along with his companion) will be killed by the Antichrist and proceed to lie in the street for 3.5 days until God pours the Spirit of life into their bodies (Revelation 11:7–14).

- Shortly before the start of the seventieth week, the followers of Antichrist and the enemies of God will be supernaturally incited to gather themselves around Jerusalem and to a place called Armageddon (Luke 21:20, Revelation 16:12–16). This swarm of evil will wreak havoc, especially during the last half of the seventieth week.
- The destruction during this seventieth week is described by Daniel 9:26 as a "flood." This exact language is used in Isaiah 59:19–20 in a clear day-of-the-Lord context and connotes a swift response by the Lord: "When the enemy shall come in like a flood, the Spirit of the Lord shall lift up a standard against him. And the Redeemer shall come to Zion."

Daniel 9:27

After the sixty-two week period, the Antichrist shall confirm an existing covenant with many for one week. In the middle of the week (the final, seventieth week) he shall cause the animal sacrifice and offering to cease, and he shall make the temple desolate for the purpose of his most extreme and idolatrous abomination, even until the consummation or completion of the seventieth week when that which has been decreed by God shall be poured out upon the desolate.

- A covenant will be confirmed either just prior to, at the same time as, or just after the Antichrist kills the two witnesses.
- The Antichrist will desolate the temple and commit the blasphemous abomination of desolation and declare himself to be God at the middle of the week.
- Great tribulation, more than at any time since the beginning of the world, will ensue until the enemies of God are defeated by the Lord Jesus.
- At the end of the seventieth week God will see fit to accomplish all that was determined in verse 24. Judgment will be poured out against evildoers—this is part of the day of the Lord.

The Greater Fulfillment Ahead

The six leaps discussed above are altogether difficult to overcome. And while we don't find the apostle Paul or anyone else in the New Testament hearkening back to Daniel's seventy weeks prophecy as a proof text for Jesus Christ in their spreading of the gospel truth, I don't fault anyone for peering deeply into the Scripture to find a connection and apparent resolution of this prophecy that will meet their satisfaction. In fact, the current misunderstandings could very well be what the Spirit of the Lord desired for a number of generations of believers. There is a benefit to believers when the Lord provides for a "type" of fulfillment in prophecies that otherwise will find their ultimate fulfillment during the time of the end.

Although it wasn't as the Lord ultimately intends, a believer in years past could be encouraged and comforted during the "sealed" time by prophecies that seemed to have occurred and been fulfilled. Fulfilled prophecy builds faith (faith comes by hearing, and hearing by the Word of God), even if it only winds up being a type of fulfillment. With many of Daniel's visions that we read of in chapters 7 through 12, we can find a type of fulfillment throughout the proofs of history. But one day, at the time of the end, we will find a *greater fulfillment* come to pass!

II. THE APPOINTED TIMES

As we have already touched on, God will orchestrate events and circumstances to accomplish His purposes at the set time. Psalm 102 refers to the time when God will have mercy upon Zion in the last days and the LORD will appear in His glory at the second coming. Verse 13 states, "Thou shalt arise, and have mercy upon Zion: for the time to favour her, yea, the set time, is come."

- Set time: *moed*, Strong's H4150—"properly an appointment, that is, a fixed time or season; specifically a festival; a set or solemn feast, an appointed season, a set or appointed time."

This psalm ties in beautifully with the book of Daniel. In Daniel, we likewise read that God has an appointment with His creation. The time of the end is an appointed time, a *moed*; it will occur at the set time as ordained by Almighty God and exactly as recorded in the prophetic accounts of Daniel and Revelation.

- As Gabriel spoke to Daniel, he said in Daniel 8:19, "Behold, I will make thee know what shall be in the last end of the indignation: for *at the time appointed* the end shall be."

- And referring to the time when the Antichrist is in power (this of course is during the end times), it is recorded in Daniel 11:27 that "yet the end shall be *at the time appointed.*"
- Also in Daniel 11:35 we read, "And some of them of understanding shall fall, to try them, and to purge, and to make them white, even to the time of the end: because it is yet for *a time appointed.*"

We also read this truth in the book of Acts, chapter 17. Act 17:31 states, "Because *he hath appointed a day,* in the which he will judge the world in righteousness by that man whom he hath ordained; whereof he hath given assurance unto all men, in that he hath raised him from the dead."

The *moedim*, or appointed times, are typically referred to in the Scriptures as God's feast days. They are spoken of in several places but are presented together in Leviticus 23:

> These are the feasts [i.e. appointed times] of the LORD, even holy convocations, which ye shall proclaim in their seasons. (Leviticus 23:4)

Basically, at the set times, the Lord commanded His people to gather together for a holy purpose during certain seasons of the year.

Jewish Holiday or Feast	Reference	Season	Date
Passover (Pesach)	Lev. 23:5	Spring	Nisan 14
Unleavened Bread (Chag Hamotzi)	Lev. 23:6–8	Spring	Nisan 15–22
Firstfruits (Yom Habikkurim)	Lev. 23:9–14	Spring	Nisan 16 or 17
Pentecost (Shavu'ot)	Lev. 23:15–22	Late Spring/Summer	Sivan 6
Trumpets (Yom Teru'ah)	Lev. 23:23–25	Fall	Tishri 1
Atonement (Yom Kippur)	Lev. 23:26–32	Fall	Tishri 10
Tabernacles (Sukkot)	Lev. 23:33–44	Fall	Tishri 15

It is profitable to understand that our Lord Jesus Christ perfectly fulfilled the spring feasts with His death (on Passover), His lying in the tomb (during Unleavened Bread), His resurrection (on Firstfruits) and the sending of the Holy Spirit fifty days later (on Pentecost). This was God's design. All was fulfilled according to the set or appointed time ordained by God.

Two important points come from this:

- Based on our Lord's fulfillment of the spring feasts, it is apparent that there is a prophetic significance to the feasts, or *moedim*, instituted by God.
- Based on the multiple promises in Daniel that connect events pertaining to the time of the end with the feasts, or *moedim*, should we expect anything different as it relates to the second coming of our Lord Jesus? In other words, could this perfect fulfilling by Jesus of the spring feasts also be a pattern of what is to come and hold true for the fall feasts at His second coming as king?

Many Jews still celebrate and observe these feasts in our day, at their appointed times. From what I can tell, these seven biblical feasts have historical, spiritual, and messianic applications.

Jewish Feast	Historical	Spiritual	Messianic
Passover	The death angel passed over the houses with blood on the doorpost.	The blood of the lamb delivers from sin, slavery, and death.	Jesus died on the cross and shed His blood.
Unleavened Bread	The going out from Egypt with unleavened bread.	The body of our Lord was free from sin. Buried with Christ, sanctified, and separated from evil.	Jesus was buried and in the tomb.
Firstfruits	Crossing through the Red Sea / thanksgiving for spring harvest.	After being buried with Christ, we rise to a newness of life.	Jesus was resurrected from the dead.
Pentecost	Moses was given the law at Mount Sinai / thanksgiving for summer harvest.	The indwelling of the Holy Spirit to comfort us, guide us, teach us, and direct our lives.	The Holy Spirit was given.
Trumpets	Self-examination and repentance / a signal to stop harvesting and to come worship.	A time for self-examination, for repentance, and listening to God.	FUTURE: A signal to repent, to self-examine our lives, to prepare for the second coming.

| Day of Atonement | A day of affliction and atonement for sin / priest enters the Holy of Holies. | Remembering the Lord's supper. | FUTURE: The second coming, The day of the Lord, the accomplishment of the seventy weeks of Daniel. |
| Tabernacles | God provided shelter to the Israelites in the wilderness / thanksgiving for the fall harvest. | Walking in fellowship with the Lord under His protection and guidance. | FUTURE: The Lord will tabernacle with His people after His return as King of kings. |

Crucified on Passover

Passover pointed to our Lord Jesus as the true Passover lamb, who shed His innocent blood for our sins (1 Corinthians 5:7: "For even Christ our Passover is sacrificed for us"). A perfect spotless lamb was sacrificed, and its blood was sprinkled on the top and sides of the doorpost, a shadow of the sacrifice of Jesus Christ. This blood strongly portrays Jesus as that door we must enter for salvation (John 10:9). Our Lord was crucified on the day of preparation for the Passover at exactly the same hour that the lambs were being slaughtered for the Passover meal that evening (John 19:14).

> And it was the preparation of the passover, and about the sixth hour: and he saith unto the Jews, Behold your King! (John 19:14)

Buried and in the Tomb on the Feast of Unleavened Bread

Unleavened Bread pointed to our Lord Jesus's sinless life (as leaven is likened to sin in the Bible), making Him the perfect sacrifice for our sins. During this meal unleavened bread is eaten and signifies how we, as born-again believers, have been released from the bondage of sin by partaking of Jesus Christ (John 6:32–33, 48–51). Jesus's body was in the grave during the first days of this feast, like a kernel of wheat planted and waiting to burst forth as the bread of life. We as believers are also to have this experience, as Christ did (Romans 6:4–5).

> Then Jesus said unto them, Verily, verily, I say unto you, Moses gave you not that bread from heaven; but my Father giveth you the true bread from heaven. For the bread of God is he which cometh down from heaven, and giveth life unto the world. (John 6:32–33)

> I am that bread of life. Your fathers did eat manna in the wilderness, and are dead. This is the bread which cometh down from heaven, that a man may eat thereof, and not die. I am the living bread which came down from heaven: if any man eat of this bread, he shall live for ever: and the bread that I will give is my flesh, which I will give for the life of the world. (John 6:48–51)

> Therefore we are buried with him by baptism into death: that like as Christ was raised up from the dead by the glory of the Father, even so we also should walk in newness of life. For if we have been planted together in the likeness of his death, we shall be also in the likeness of his resurrection. (Romans 6:4–5)

Arose on the Third Day, or the Day of Firstfruits

Firstfruits pointed to Christ's resurrection as the firstfruits of the righteous. Jesus was resurrected on this very day, which is why Paul states in 1 Corinthians 15:20, "But now is Christ risen from the dead, and become the firstfruits of them that slept." And at the time of Jesus's second coming, we have the hope and promise that the dead in Christ will likewise be physically resurrected as Jesus was (1 Corinthians 15:52).

Holy Spirit Given on Pentecost

Pentecost occurred fifty days after the beginning of the Feast of Unleavened Bread and prophetically pointed to the gift of the Holy Spirit. The resurrection led to a counting period of seven weeks (forty-nine days), which ends with Pentecost on the fiftieth day. Based on Acts 1:3, our Lord was on the earth forty days after His resurrection until He ascended to heaven to be at the Father's right hand. Ten days later was the day of Pentecost, and it was on that day the Holy Spirit descended upon the disciples (Acts 2:1–4).

There was a significant response to the gospel message after the pouring out of the Holy Spirit: three thousand Jews responded to Peter's sermon and his first proclamation of the gospel. This could foreshadow another great moving of the Spirit in the end times, which may also be accompanied by the everlasting gospel preached by the angel of God (Joel 2:23–29, Revelation 14:6).

Trumpets—A Time of Preparation

Trumpets is the first of the fall feasts. This is a day of blowing trumpets (shofars), calling all to repent. Traditionally this day is preceded by thirty days of repentance and followed by another ten days of the same. Prophetically this day speaks of the final call and last opportunity to repent before the return of Jesus Christ.

Many believe this day points to the resurrection and rapture of the church, when Jesus will appear from the clouds in the heavens as He comes for His bride, the church. The resurrection/rapture is always associated in Scripture with the blowing of a loud trumpet. Take a look at the verses below:

> And he shall send his angels *with a great sound of a trumpet*, and they shall gather together his elect from the four winds, from one end of heaven to the other. (Matthew 24:31)

> But I would not have you to be ignorant, brethren, concerning them which are asleep, that ye sorrow not, even as others which have no hope. For if we believe that Jesus died and rose again, even so them also which sleep in Jesus will God bring with him. For this we say unto you by the word of the Lord, that we which are alive and remain unto the coming of the Lord shall not prevent them which are asleep. For the Lord himself shall descend from heaven with a shout, with the voice of the archangel, and *with the trump of God*: and the dead in Christ shall rise first: then we which are alive and remain shall be caught up together with them in the clouds, to meet the Lord in the air: and so shall we ever be with the Lord. Wherefore comfort one another with these words. (1 Thessalonians 4:13–18)

> In a moment, in the twinkling of an eye, at the last trump: for *the trumpet shall sound*, and the dead shall be raised incorruptible, and we shall be changed. (1 Corinthians 15:52)

> But in the days of the voice of the seventh angel, *when he shall begin to sound*, the mystery of God should be finished, as he hath declared to his servants the prophets. (Revelation 10:7)

> And *the seventh angel sounded*; and there were great voices in heaven, saying, The kingdoms of this world are become the kingdoms of our Lord, and of his Christ; and he shall reign for ever and ever. (Revelation 11:15)

> And it shall come to pass in that day, that the LORD shall beat off from the channel of the river unto the stream of Egypt, and ye shall be gathered one by one, O ye children of Israel. And it shall come to pass in that day, that *the great trumpet shall be blown*, and they shall come which were ready to perish in the land of Assyria, and the outcasts in the land of Egypt, and shall worship the LORD in the holy mount at Jerusalem. (Isaiah 27:12–13)

> And the LORD shall be seen over them, and his arrow shall go forth as the lightning: and *the Lord GOD shall blow the trumpet,* and shall go with whirlwinds of the south. (Zechariah 9:14)

From above, the fact that a trumpet will blow at the time of resurrection/rapture is undisputable. But will this occur during the Feast of Trumpets?

We should consider that the time span from the Feast of Trumpets to the Day of Atonement is called the ten "Days of Repentance" or "Days of Awe." It represents a time for serious introspection and repentance. From the passage below, I believe the great sound of a trumpet could occur on the next fall feast, the Day of Atonement, the *last trump* on that great and notable day.

> Then shalt thou cause the trumpet of the jubile to sound on the tenth day of the seventh month, in the day of atonement shall ye make the trumpet sound throughout all your land. (Leviticus 25:9)

Day of Atonement—The Second Coming?

This day is a day of complete fasting and affliction. It is the holiest day on the Jewish calendar. It likewise is a day of repentance, the culmination of the preceding days of repentance. With repentance, reconciliation with God takes place. Psalm 51:17 says, "The sacrifices of God are a broken spirit: a broken and a contrite heart, O God, thou wilt not despise."

This was the day that the corporate sins of the Jews were laid upon a scapegoat and cast outside the camp. The Day of Atonement points to a day when Jews mourn, weep, and repent of their rejection of the Lord Jesus Christ, who was our scapegoat (Hebrews 13:12). I believe that this prophetically points to the Day of Atonement for the Jewish remnant, as they "look upon Him whom they have pierced," repent of their sins, and receive Him as their Messiah. I believe this is that great and notable day, the day of the second coming of Jesus!

> Behold, he cometh with clouds; and every eye shall see him, and they also which pierced him: and all kindreds of the earth shall wail because of him. Even so, Amen. (Revelation 1:7)

> In that day shall the LORD defend the inhabitants of Jerusalem; and he that is feeble among them at that day shall be as David; and the house of David shall be as God, as the angel of the LORD before them. And it shall come to pass in that day, that I will seek to destroy all the nations that

come against Jerusalem. And *I will pour upon the house of David, and upon the inhabitants of Jerusalem, the spirit of grace and of supplications: and they shall look upon me whom they have pierced, and they shall mourn for him, as one mourneth for his only son*, and shall be in bitterness for him, as one that is in bitterness for his firstborn. (Zechariah 12:8–10)

I say then, *Hath God cast away his people? God forbid*. For I also am an Israelite, of the seed of Abraham, of the tribe of Benjamin. God hath not cast away his people which he foreknew. Wot ye not what the scripture saith of Elias? how he maketh intercession to God against Israel, saying, Lord, they have killed thy prophets, and digged down thine altars; and I am left alone, and they seek my life. But what saith the answer of God unto him? I have reserved to myself seven thousand men, who have not bowed the knee to the image of Baal. *Even so then at this present time also there is a remnant according to the election of grace*. (Romans 11:1–5)

For I would not, brethren, that ye should be ignorant of this mystery, lest ye should be wise in your own conceits; that blindness in part is happened to Israel, until the fulness of the Gentiles be come in. *And so all Israel shall be saved: as it is written, There shall come out of Sion the Deliverer, and shall turn away ungodliness from Jacob: for this is my covenant unto them, when I shall take away their sins*. As concerning the gospel, they are enemies for your sakes: but as touching the election, they are beloved for the fathers' sakes. For the gifts and calling of God are without repentance. (Romans 11:25–29)

Tabernacles—The Presence of Jesus with Israel

This celebration feast coincided with the final harvest of the year. As they celebrated the harvest, the Jews also moved out of their homes and lived in booths or shelters decorated with branches to commemorate the Israelites' dwelling in tents for forty years during their stay in the wilderness.

Many believe that this feast day points to the Lord's promise that He will once again "tabernacle" with His people when He returns to reign over all the world. This is a celebration that will continue throughout the millennium to celebrate the fact that God dwells with man and is our "shelter" through Jesus, the King of kings and Lord of lords (Zechariah 14)! As indicated on the End-Times Chart in Appendix 3, Tabernacles could literally represent a forty-day period when Jesus physically tabernacles with the Jews leading up to the start of the millennium.

III. THE ESCHATOLOGICAL TIME PERIODS OF SCRIPTURE

While many things about the end times are mysterious, the Bible is also remarkably specific about certain details. One of those details is the specific time periods involved.

The end-times message in Scripture repeatedly speaks of 3.5-year time periods. To briefly summarize, this is the duration of the Antichrist's power, the time of the two witnesses, the time of the Jewish exile from Jerusalem and the Gentiles overtaking Jerusalem, and finally the time period noted in Daniel 12:11, which starts with the removal of the daily sacrifice (or regular, perpetual worship in the temple) and ends with the abomination of desolation. The ultimate question is, when do these events occur? More specifically, are these separate spans of 3.5 years, occurring randomly or consecutively throughout the end times, or do all of these Scriptures speak of one and the same 3.5-year span of time?

In my estimation, it is most logical to see all the prophesied events as occurring during the same 3.5-year time period. What you basically have is a buildup by all parties, good and evil, to a climactic ending that culminates in the day of the Lord. Let's look at the prophecies one by one.

Antichrist's Rule and Power

The time period of the Antichrist's rule and power is approximately 3.5 years.

> And he shall speak great words against the most High, and shall wear out the saints of the most High, and think to change times and laws: and they shall be given into his hand until a *time and times and the dividing of time*. But the judgment shall sit, and they shall take away his dominion, to consume and to destroy it unto the end. (Daniel 7:25–26)

> And there was given unto him a mouth speaking great things and blasphemies; and *power was given unto him to continue forty and two months*. (Revelation 13:5)

Interpreting the "time, times, and the dividing of time" of Daniel 7:25 as 3.5 years is the derivative of Scripture comparison. This same phrase is used in Revelation 12:14, so we can use the context of Revelation 12 to interpret the phrase. This refers to the time when Michael stands up to Satan (Revelation

12:7) and casts him out into the earth. This results in great wrath on the part of the Evil One and those inspired by him. It is a woeful situation for the inhabitants of the earth (Revelation 12:12). One of the targets of his wrath is the "woman" who flees into the wilderness. I believe the woman represents many Jews who will be driven out of Jerusalem as a result of destruction in the glorious land (Daniel 11:16). By comparing the identical details of Revelation 12:6 to Revelation 12:14, one can define a time, and times, and half a time as 1260 days, or 3.5 years. Basically, it is a time (one year), times (two years), and half a time (half a year).

> And *the woman* fled *into the wilderness*, where *she hath a place* prepared of God, that they should *feed her* there *a thousand two hundred and threescore days*. (Revelation 12:6)

> And to *the woman* were given two wings of a great eagle, that she might fly *into the wilderness*, into *her place*, where she is *nourished* for *a time, and times, and half a time*, from the face of the serpent. (Revelation 12:14)

Also note that Antichrist's rule seems to end climatically, with a decisive judgment and removal of his dominion (power and authority—see Daniel 7:26, Isaiah 59:19–20, and 2 Thessalonians 2:8). As we will discuss in great detail later, I contend that this decisive judgment is the result of the blasphemous abomination of desolation that occurs on the 1260th day of Antichrist's reign.

Prophesying of the Two Witnesses

Revelation 11 describes two witnesses of the Lord. The duration for their time of prophesying is approximately 3.5 years.

> And I will give power unto my two witnesses, and *they shall prophesy a thousand two hundred and threescore days*, clothed in sackcloth. These are the two olive trees, and the two candlesticks standing before the God of the earth. (Revelation 11:3–4)

The God of heaven will give these two individuals magnificent power. Examples of this from Revelation 11:5–6 include the following: they possess the ability to devour their enemies with fire; they possess power to shut heaven so it doesn't rain; they possess power to turn waters to blood; and they possess power to smite the earth with all plagues as often as they wish. Their power will end climatically when the Antichrist overcomes and kills them in Jerusalem. Their bodies will lie in the street for 3.5 days, and after 3.5 days, the Spirit of life from God will enter them and they will ascend up to heaven in a cloud. Sadly, their deaths will result in rejoicing across the face of the earth.

In the chapter on Revelation we'll review in more detail the amazing account from Revelation 11 of the works accomplished by the God-given power of the two witnesses. Truly they will be spiritual warriors on the side of the Almighty. And again, their powerful witness on earth will last approximately 3.5 years.

Jerusalem Given to the Gentiles

The holy city Jerusalem will be trodden underfoot by the Gentiles for approximately 3.5 years.

> But the court which is without the temple leave out, and measure it not; for it is given unto the Gentiles: and the *holy city shall they tread under foot forty and two months.* (Revelation 11:2)

This approximate 3.5 year time period also appears to have a climatic ending. Why? Because the treading underfoot by the Gentiles will end after forty-two months when, apparently, the holy city Jerusalem will be restored at the day of the Lord.

Jews Exiled to the Wilderness Where They Are Nourished

Israel, and quite likely Christians also, will flee into the wilderness for approximately 3.5 years.

> And the woman fled into the wilderness, where she hath a place prepared of God, that *they should feed her there a thousand two hundred and threescore days.* And to the woman were given two wings of a great eagle, that she might fly into the wilderness, into her place, where *she is nourished for a time, and times, and half a time,* from the face of the serpent. (Revelation 12:6, 14)

Based on my end-times framework and "future" view of Daniel's fifth vision, I believe that the "glorious land" of Israel will experience a destructive event as prophesied in Daniel 11:16 and then shortly after the Antichrist will *peaceably* rise to power (Daniel 11:21). Many Jews who flee the Jerusalem destruction will eventually find a place in the wilderness miraculously provided by God. Nourishment and a measure of protection will be provided for exactly 1260 days, presumably denoting the time when a final restoration occurs at the day of the Lord.

The Removal of the Daily Sacrifice to the Abomination of Desolation

From the time that the daily sacrifice is taken away until the abomination of desolation is 1290 days (slightly longer than 3.5 years). Scripture also tells us that he is blessed who reaches the 1335th day (or approximately forty-five days after the abomination of desolation).

The abomination of desolation, which occurs just over 3.5 years after the daily worship or sacrifice is removed, is a dreadful, climatic moment in time. After describing it, Daniel states that only forty-five days later there will be blessedness to those who wait and reach the 1335th day. The End-Times Chart shows this as the very day that the millennial reign begins.

> And from the time that the daily sacrifice shall be taken away, and the abomination that maketh desolate set up, there shall be a thousand two hundred and ninety days. Blessed is he that waiteth, and cometh to the thousand three hundred and five and thirty days. (Daniel 12:11–12)

As stated above, I believe Daniel 12:11 teaches a 1290-day time span between the removal of the daily sacrifice and the abomination of desolation. Because of the wording used in Daniel 11:31 and the fact that both a "taking away" and a "setting up" will need to occur for the abomination of desolation, many interpret Daniel 12:11 as meaning that both these events happen at the same time, leaving 1290 days until . . . something. But what? The passage seems incomplete if interpreted in this manner.

One reason to lump together the removal of the daily sacrifice and the abomination of desolation, rather than seeing a 3.5-year span between them as I do, is Daniel 9:27: "And he shall confirm the covenant with many for one week: and in the midst of the week he shall cause the sacrifice and the oblation to cease, and for the overspreading of abominations he shall make it desolate." This clearly links the ceasing of a sacrifice directly with the abomination of desolation—but is it the same sacrifice mentioned in Daniel 12?

In regards to the "daily sacrifice" of Daniel 12:11, the root word that brings forth the translation "daily sacrifice" is *tamiyd*. The meaning is "to stretch; continuance; constant or constantly; always; continual; daily; evermore; perpetual (Strong's H8548)." It is used 104 times in the Old Testament. Multiple times in Scripture it is used in phrases such as, "bind them *continually* upon thine heart"; "seek his face *evermore*"; "and thou shalt set upon the table shewbread before me *always.*" In other places, we find that *tamiyd* is given an object: "continually *eat bread*"; "continual *burnt offering*"; "daily *burnt offering.*" In each of these cases, there is always a Hebrew word in the Scripture to describe the object.

In Daniel 12:11, there is not. The word is simply *tamiyd*, without a Hebrew object added. This is why *sacrifice* in the verse is italicized in the KJV Bible. Italicized words in the KJV are words that were added by the translators to help the reader and to make the text more readable. To make sure everyone knew that these words were not in the underlying manuscripts, they set them in italics. The word *sacrifice* does make sense in this context—however, while it could indicate a burnt offering or an animal sacrifice, it is not a requirement. All the Hebrew tells us, after all, is that this is something continuous, regular, perpetual, or daily.

In contrast, Daniel 9:27 does use a word for *sacrifice*. Daniel 9:27 describes the Antichrist, in the midst of the week, causing the "sacrifice" and the oblation to cease. The word for sacrifice here is *zebach*, which means "a slaughter, that is, the flesh of an animal; by implication a sacrifice (the victim or the act); offering, sacrifice (Strong's H2077)." It implies that by the time of the abomination of desolation, there will be some form of a rebuilt temple structure used for animal sacrifices. More importantly for our purposes here, it leaves the door wide open for a 3.5-year span between the ceasing of a daily offering of some kind and the day when Antichrist causes the animal sacrifice to cease and sets up the abomination of desolation in its place.

Much like we are to present our bodies a living sacrifice, it isn't unreasonable to believe that this "daily sacrifice" might indicate something like the Western Wall in Old City Jerusalem, for example. This is a place where today, daily/continual prayers are offered seeking God's favor and expressing thanks to the Almighty. It is also a place that could be "taken away" through a destructive event in Jerusalem (Daniel 11:16) causing the exile of many Jews from the city at the beginning of the 3.5-year tribulation.

Interpreting this passage boils down to framework. Is the duration of the whole tribulation seven years or 3.5 years? Based on the special fit and alignment discussed in the following section, I strongly favor an overall tribulation period of 3.5 years. There is a reason that 1290 days is an Achilles' heel within a seven-year seventieth week framework!

IV: LINKING THE MOEDIM WITH THE ESCHATOLOGICAL TIME PERIODS

The linking together of the feast days and the eschatological time periods of Scripture is shown in the End-Times Chart. While all of this is in my own words, I must again mention the writings of Kevin Swift, from whose work I became exposed to the incredible connections we are about to discover at the end of this section. What are the detailed facts that we know from Scripture? And what is the overall picture they may be painting?

The Facts: 1290 Days

Daniel 12:11: "And from the time that the daily sacrifice shall be taken away, and the abomination that maketh desolate set up, there shall be a thousand two hundred and ninety days." Like starting with a blank canvas, the chart below is the simple beginning point. From here we'll continue to build and overlay the Scriptures until finally, we apply the finishing touches of the *moedim* to the overall framework!

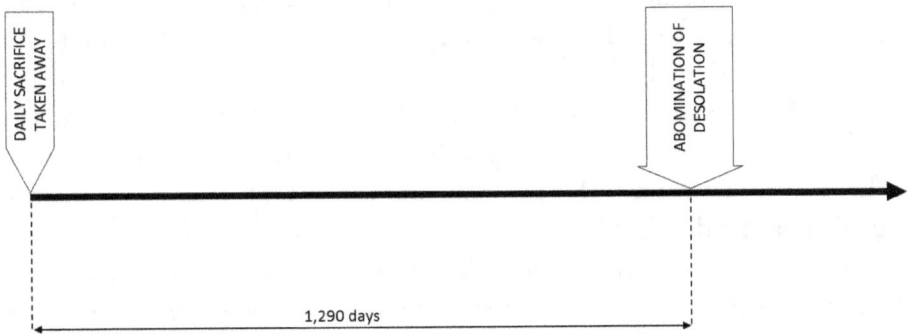

The Facts: A Blessed 1335th Day

Daniel 12:12: "Blessed is he that waiteth, and cometh to the thousand three hundred and five and thirty days." The chart below depicts the time of blessedness forty-five days after the abomination of desolation.

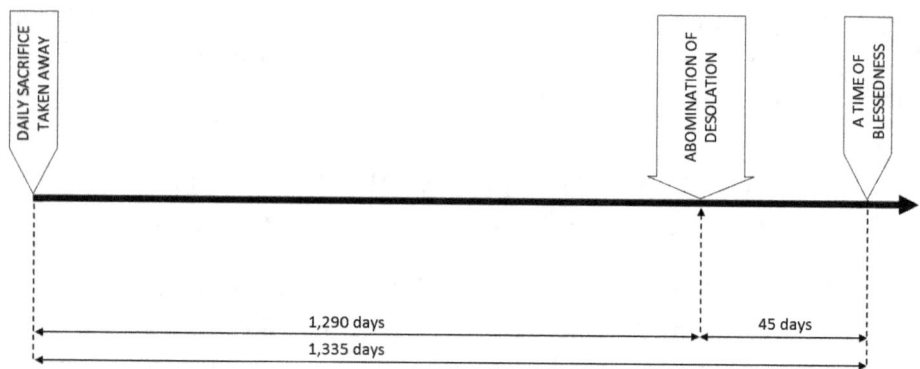

The Facts: Seventy Weeks—And One Great Climactic Week

Daniel 9:24-27: "Seventy weeks are determined upon thy people and upon thy holy city, *to finish the transgression, and to make an end of sins, and to make reconciliation for iniquity, and to bring in everlasting righteousness, and to seal up the vision and prophecy, and to anoint the most Holy* [i.e. to bring us to the day of the Lord and second coming of Jesus Christ]. Know therefore and understand, that from the going forth of the commandment to restore and to build Jerusalem unto the Messiah the Prince shall be seven weeks, and threescore and two weeks: the street shall be built again, and the wall, even in troublous times. *And after threescore and two weeks shall Messiah [mashi-yack—an anointed one] be cut off,* but not for himself: and the people of the prince that shall come shall destroy the city and the sanctuary; and the end thereof shall be with a flood, and unto the end of the war desolations are determined. And he shall confirm the covenant with many for one week: *and in the midst of the week he shall cause the sacrifice and the oblation to cease, and for the overspreading of abominations he shall make it desolate* [i.e. the abomination of desolation], even until the consummation, and that determined shall be poured upon the desolate."

In summary, the chart below depicts the climactic seventieth week, including: the day of the Lord at the conclusion of the seventieth week (Daniel 9:24); the cutting off of the anointed one at the end of the sixty-ninth week (Daniel 9:26); the resurrection of the two witnesses after 3.5 days (Revelation 11:11); and the Antichrist's abomination of desolation at the middle of the week (Daniel 9:27).

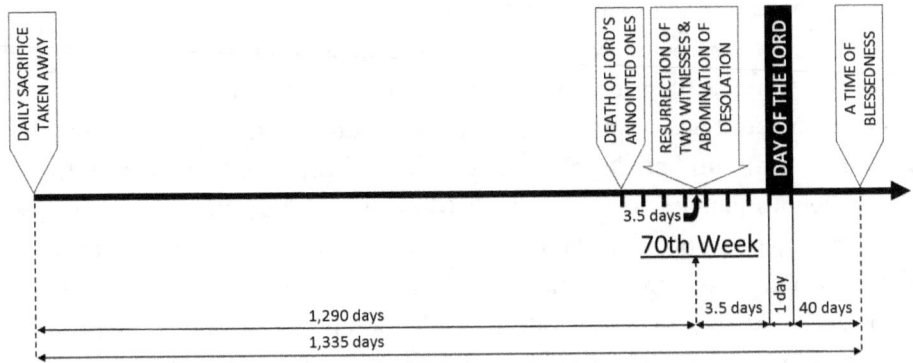

A Question: How Do We Handle the 3.5 Years?

Now, with all this in view, how do we handle the four 3.5-year time periods noted in section 3 above? To recap, they are:

1) Antichrist's rule and power for forty-two months or 3.5 years (Daniel 7:25, Revelation 13:5)
   a. The rule and power of the Antichrist will end climatically, with decisive judgment, with the removal of his dominion as it is consumed and destroyed (Daniel 7:25–26).
2) The prophesying of the two witnesses for 1260 days (Revelation 11:3)
   a. The two witnesses will operate with incredible God-given powers reminiscent of Old Testament times. However, their 3.5-year time on earth will end climatically when the Antichrist overcomes and kills them in Jerusalem. Their dead bodies will lie in the street for 3.5 days and sadly result in much rejoicing all over the earth until they are miraculously resurrected (Revelation 11:3).
3) Jerusalem given to the Gentiles for forty-two months
   a. The Holy City will be trodden underfoot for 3.5 years (Revelation 11:2).
4) Jews exiled to the wilderness where they are nourished for 1260 days
   a. A large contingent of Israelites will leave Jerusalem and go into the wilderness for 1260 days, or 3.5 years (Revelation 12:6, 14).

I reason that each of these 3.5-year time periods *overlap and occur at the same time*. It only makes sense that the Antichrist and the two witnesses will be on the scene at the same time. In my opinion, the purpose of the two witnesses is to counter Antichrist's great persecution of those who are unwilling to bear his mark and pledge allegiance to his unholy, unbiblical realm. In the day of Egypt's plagues, it was through Moses that God inflicted the plagues upon the Egyptian people. I believe it will be a similar experience in the tribulation when God, through the two witnesses, will inflict plagues upon the followers of Antichrist. Likewise, the treading underfoot of Jerusalem surely correlates and is caused by the force and power of the revived beast kingdom led by Antichrist, the little horn.

Each of the 3.5-year periods lead to a climactic point when the Antichrist's power is taken away. This moment is the 1290th day referred to in Daniel 12:11, where "the abomination of desolation" is described. This is the same day when the two witnesses are resurrected, 3.5 days into the seventieth week or in other words, the middle of the week. I believe that Antichrist's fate is sealed once he commits the blasphemous abomination. Not to jump the gun, because we will soon review God's judgment in heaven, but I believe the abomination of desolation is the trigger event for the time when the Son of Man is given the verdict for a kingdom that will never be destroyed, and an everlasting dominion (Daniel 7:13–14, 27).

The 1260 day or 3.5 year or forty-two month periods are depicted below as the tribulation period, ending with the abomination of desolation at the middle of the seventieth-week.

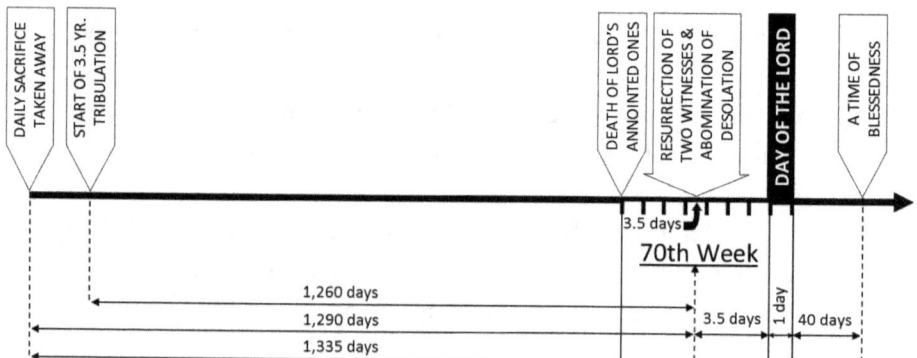

A Supernatural Alignment?

Why and how is there such specificity in the Scriptures, to the exact number of days? The time periods mentioned in Scripture—1260 days, 1290 days, 1335 days, 490 days, 2300 evenings and mornings, two witnesses lying in the street for 3.5 days, and "midst" of the week—are extremely precise. What does it all mean? Could there be a special alignment designed by God, something that makes it easy and simple for God to designate the set time of the end with such precision?

As we have discussed, God has an appointment with His creation. The feast days, or *moedim*, appear to be our connection to discern God's plan.

Let's look hard at the word spoken by Gabriel to Daniel. He said in Daniel 8:19, "Behold, I will make thee know what shall be in the last end of the indignation: *for at the time appointed the end shall be.*" This is very matter-of-fact, quite the opposite of obscure, moveable, or changeable. There surely is a "set time," as noted in Psalm 102:13.

So is it just coincidence that God uses the phrase "set times" for His feasts? Or is there a pattern—a greater picture—here?

I will now demonstrate how particular feast days and key Jewish holidays are integrally connected with God's appointed time of the end, using, as an example, dates from this time of writing in 2016 and overlaying them on this chart. These 2016 and 2019 dates are for demonstration purposes only!

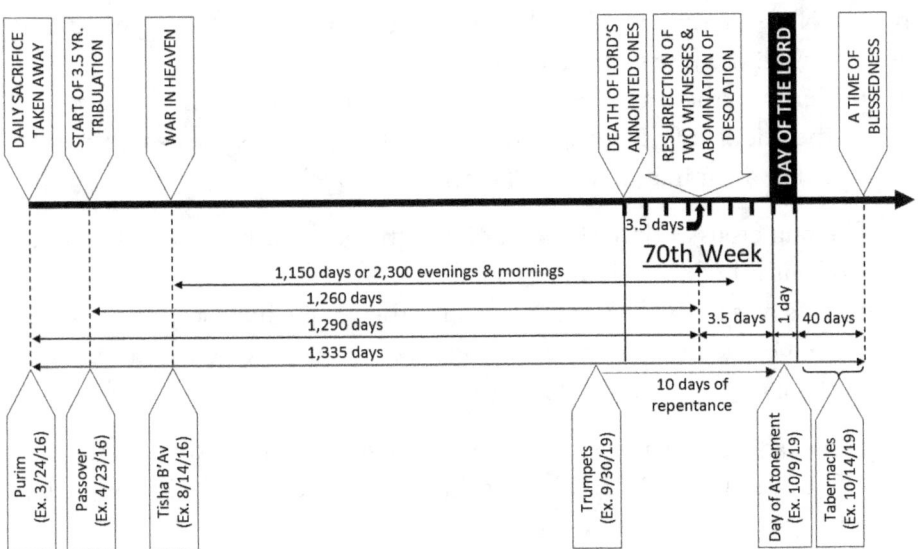

```
        1,290.5 Days (Purim to the abomination of desolation - Daniel 12:11)
+          3.5 Days (Great tribulation during last half of Daniel's seventieth week)
+          1.0 Days (The day of the Lord)
+         40.0 Days (Tabernacle with the Lord from the day of the Lord to the millennium)
        1,335.0 Days - Daniel 12:12

   10/9/2019 Day of Atonement coincides with the day of the Lord
-   4/23/2016 Passover coincides with start of 3.5-year tribulation
    1,264.0 Days
-         3.5 Days (from the day of the Lord back 3.5 days to the abomination of desolation)
    1,260.5 Days - Revelation 11:2-3; 12:6, 14; 13:5; Daniel 7:25-26

   10/9/2019 Day of Atonement coincides with the day of the Lord
-   3/24/2016 Purim coincides with removal of the daily sacrifice or place of continual worship
    1,294.0 Days
-         3.5 Days (from the day of the Lord back 3.5 days to the abomination of desolation)
    1,290.5 Days - Daniel 12:11
```

Notice the correlations, and specifically the timing calculations that work perfectly. And although Purim is not a feast day recorded in Leviticus 23, it is a Jewish holiday that commemorates the saving of the Jewish people from Haman and is recorded in the book of Esther. It is annually observed according to its *appointed time* (Esther 9:26–27) and is always thirty days prior to Passover.

Let's summarize these incredible correlations.

The time from the removal of the daily sacrifice or worship to the abomination of desolation is 1290 days (Daniel 12:11). This time period links perfectly with the Jewish holiday calculation.

- Purim to the Day of Atonement, then adjusting 3.5 days back to the middle of the seventieth week of Daniel, gives the exact time of the abomination of desolation as the 1290th day!

The numerous Scripture references for the 3.5-year time periods also link perfectly with the Jewish holiday calculation.

- Passover to the Day of Atonement, then adjusting back 3.5 days to the middle of the week, is the exact time of the abomination of desolation on the 1260th day!

Daniel states that there will be blessedness to those who wait and reach the 1335th day (Daniel 12:12). This mark of 1335 days has a strong correlation with the Jewish Feast of Tabernacles, or Sukkot.

AN ESCHATOLOGICAL FRAMEWORK • 125

- Purim plus 1335 days equals the start of the millennium, as evidenced by the End-Times Chart, while allowing an appropriate forty-day time period between the day of the Lord and the start of the millennium. Sukkot occurs five days after Yom Kippur (the Day of Atonement) and is representative of the Jews wandering in the wilderness for forty years. This forty-day period may be a literal event magnificently reminiscent of their forty years with Moses. Instead of a cloud by day and fire by night as in the wilderness wander, the people of God may literally shelter under the tender care and presence of their Messiah, Jesus Christ. And Jesus may "tabernacle" with the saved Jews in literal huts due to the utter devastation during the great tribulation and the enormity of earthshaking events at the day of the Lord.

Another Supernatural Alignment?

You will notice one additional eschatological time period in the summary chart above. This relates to Daniel 8:14, with its 1150 days or 2300 evenings and mornings. We'll shortly get into the details of that prophecy, but to highlight, this time period correlates fantastically with the sober fast day, Tisha B'Av.

What is Tisha B'Av? It is an annual day of mourning, or fast day, on the ninth of Av. Numerous Jewish tragedies are said to have occurred on this exact day in history, including the destruction of the first temple by the Babylonians in 586 BC and the destruction of the second temple by the Romans in 70 AD. Amazingly, it is my belief that Tisha B'Av will also correlate with the time when Satan mounts up with pride in heaven, wars against Michael and his angels, and in doing so ransacks *the heavenly temple* before being cast to earth along with his angels.

Counting 1150 days from Tisha B'Av results in a date just after the abomination of desolation and just prior to Yom Kippur, or the day of the Lord. The 1150th day from Tisha B'Av lands right in the last half of the seventieth week of Daniel. What is the significance of this? It marvelously depicts the time when Jesus is given the courtroom verdict from the Ancient of Days and the sanctuary in heaven is cleansed or made right again. Court is adjourned. The evidence, topped off by the climatic, blasphemous, and recently completed abomination of desolation by the Antichrist, is sufficient for judgment to be pronounced and kingship awarded to the Lamb. Jesus is now given dominion and power as king of the earth forever and will await the Father's word to descend for the second coming and fulfill the much prophesied day of the Lord!

When the seventy weeks of Daniel are interpreted plainly and literally as seventy weeks of days (i.e. 490 total days), with a final week of a literal seven days (i.e. the seventieth week), the Scriptures come alive with more detail and precision than ever imagined. And when the seventieth week is interconnected with the Jewish feast days, the *moedim* or "appointed times," the feasts literally match up in identical fashion with the prophesied eschatological time periods of Holy Scripture. Amazingly, the Scripture corroborates that the long prophesied day of the Lord or second coming aligns with the holiest day on the Jewish calendar, the Day of Atonement.

From War in Heaven to the Everlasting Dominion Given to Jesus

As mentioned, we find one additional eschatological time period in Daniel 8:14. The time period is 2300 evenings and mornings and is initiated with a disruption in heaven. Daniel 7 and 8 appear to relate to the war in heaven from Revelation 12. As noted previously, I believe this war in heaven will ensue on Tisha B'Av. But is this prophecy for 2300 days or 1150 days? Let's first understand the rationale for interpreting the prophecy as 1150 days.

The underlying Hebrew words translated as "days" literally means "evenings and mornings." The normal Hebrew word used for days in the Old Testament is *yom* (Strong's H3117), used 2295 times. The word translated "days" in Daniel 8:14 is comprised of two separate Hebrew words, *ereb* and *boqer* (Strong's H6153 and H1242). *Ereb* literally means "evening" and is translated as "even, evening, or eventide" all 134 times it is used in the Old Testament with the exception of Daniel 8:14. And *boqer* literally means dawn or morning and is translated as such all 214 times it is used in the Old Testament, with the exception of Daniel 8:14, Judges 19:26, and 2 Samuel 13:4. Evenings and mornings are the Jewish time for sacrifices; 1150 evening sacrifices plus 1150 morning sacrifices equals a total of 2300 sacrifices. Because of the daily sacrifice/sanctuary context, it is reasonable to conclude that 2300 "evenings and mornings" would occur over the course of 1150 days, with two sacrifices per day. Plus, the Antichrist has power for 1260 days, and this time period must begin after he has come into power according to Daniel 8:9–14, thus the shorter length is appropriate. The 1150 days finds a perfect fit in the End-Times Chart and helps us understand to a greater depth and detail of what is really occurring in heaven during this time.

The chain of events is broken into two sections. Part 1 is the rise of Antichrist, the pride of Satan, and the casting out of Satan from heaven, while part 2 is the heavenly alterations and the courtroom judgment.

Part 1: Rise of Antichrist, pride of Satan, and the casting out of Satan

To help us understand this peculiar event regarding a disruption in heaven, we begin with the rise of the little horn, the Antichrist, as depicted in Daniel 7 and Daniel 8. Then proceeding on to Daniel 8:10, we see the Antichrist's evil desire manifested through pride as he waxes great, even to the host of heaven. This correlates to Revelation 12:3–4 and 7–9, Isaiah 14:12–14, and Ezekiel 28:16–17, as these verses tell a similar story. In them all, a "war" occurs in heaven, caused by the devil's desire "to be like the most High." The Scriptures in the table below describe these events.

Daniel 7	Revelation 12	Isaiah 14
(8) I considered the horns, and, behold, *there came up among them another little horn,* before whom there were three of the first horns plucked up by the roots: and, behold, in this horn were eyes like the eyes of man, and a mouth speaking great things.	(3) And behold a great red dragon, having seven heads and ten horns, and seven crowns upon his heads. (4) And *his tail drew the third part of the stars of heaven, and did cast them to the earth:* (7) and *there was war in heaven:* Michael and his angels fought against the dragon; and the dragon fought and his angels, (8) and prevailed not; neither was their place found any more in heaven. (9) And *the great dragon was cast out, that old serpent, called the Devil, and Satan,* which deceiveth the whole world: he was cast out into the earth, and his angels were cast out with him.	(12) *How art thou fallen from heaven,* O Lucifer, son of the morning! *how art thou cut down to the ground,* which didst weaken the nations! (13) For thou hast said in thine heart, *I will ascend into heaven,* I will exalt my throne above the stars of God: I will sit also upon the mount of the congregation, in the sides of the north: (14) *I will ascend above the heights of the clouds; I will be like the most High.*

Daniel 8	Ezekiel 28:16	Ezekiel 28:17
(9) And out of one of them came forth *a little horn*, which waxed exceeding great, toward the south, and toward the east, and toward the pleasant land. (10) And it waxed great, *even to the host of heaven; and it cast down some of the host and of the stars to the ground*, and stamped upon them. (11) Yea, *he magnified himself even to the prince of the host.*	By the multitude of thy merchandise they have filled the midst of thee with violence, and thou hast sinned: therefore *I will cast thee as profane out of the mountain of God:* and I will destroy thee, O covering cherub, from the midst of the stones of fire.	Thine heart was lifted up because of thy beauty, thou hast corrupted thy wisdom by reason of thy brightness: *I will cast thee to the ground*, I will lay thee before kings, that they may behold thee.

Please note that the composite beast image of Daniel 7:4–7, with seven heads and ten horns, is the same beast depicted in Revelation 13 and 17 (more detail on this is in the chapter on Revelation). This very same description of seven heads and ten horns is also given to the great red dragon of Revelation 12, who is called the devil and Satan (Revelation 12:9). This is a clear indication that the beast, Antichrist, or little horn has a symbiotic relationship with Satan. In what form, fashion, or manner, I don't know. I only know that they are on the same team and are fighting for the same purposes.

I find it difficult to fathom that as a man, the Antichrist himself will have the ability to ascend into heaven and into the throne room of God. But with the full support and influence of Satan, many things beyond my comprehension may be possible! With ruling power and authority given to the Antichrist as the new leader of Satan's beast kingdom, could Antichrist's rise to power on earth stir up and embolden Satan to disrupt the heavenly realm in an attempt to usurp and overthrow God? Or could it be possible that this is some type of a spiritual ascent into heaven by Antichrist and not a physical ascent? Or could Antichrist's ability to rise into heaven be a result of a death (i.e. the deadly wound referenced in Revelation 13:3 and Revelation 13:12, with the deadly wound healed when Satan is cast out of heaven)?

I don't know the answer. The Scripture indicates that this ascent into heaven is because of self-magnification and pride. That doesn't seem to correlate with a temporary death experience on earth. Something similar to the Godhead Trinity may be happening here, only it is Satan's trinity, comprised of Satan, Antichrist, and the False Prophet. However it happens, the key to the current discussion is that a disruption will occur in heaven and will have dramatic ramifications.

Here's an overview of the events:

- The little horn, or Antichrist, will rise up to power as ruler of the beast kingdom.
- The little horn will wax great with personal pride, ruling territory, kingship authority, and great aspirations. His great aspirations of heart, according to Isaiah 14, include the following statements: "*I will* ascend into heaven," "*I will* exalt my throne above the stars of God," and "*I will* be like the most High."
- Satan will attempt to take the throne from God but he will experience defeat. The devil/Satan, the accuser of the brethren, and all of his angels are then cast out into the earth by Michael.

Part 2: Heavenly Alterations and the Courtroom Judgment

Daniel gives us more insight into the scene from Daniel 7 and 8:

- As a result of the battle in heaven between Satan and Michael, physical structures in the throne room of God are ransacked (Daniel 7:9 and Daniel 8:11–12).
- The daily (continual, perpetual) worship of God in heaven is altered by reason of Satan's pride and the ensuing altercation (Daniel 8:11, 13).
- The angel says it will be 2300 days (the Hebrew says 2300 "evenings and mornings") before the sanctuary will be "made right" again (Daniel 8:14).
- God Almighty sits, the judgment is set, and the books of evidence are opened (Daniel 7:9–10, 22, 26).
- The Son of Man, the Lord Jesus Himself, comes with the clouds of heaven (which most likely is a large number of angels) and is brought before God (Daniel 7:13). The verdict is read, and Jesus is given glory, a kingdom that will never be destroyed, and an everlasting dominion (Daniel 7:14, 27). In other words, 2300 evenings and mornings after the war in heaven, Satan and Antichrist are no longer going to have authority on the earth. Satan will experience his defeat! The court in heaven will rule, and judgment will be made!

Let's take a closer at Daniel 7:13–14, 27.

> I saw in the night visions, and, behold, one like the Son of man came with the clouds of heaven, and came to the Ancient of days, and they brought him near before him. And there was given him dominion, and glory, and a kingdom, that all people, nations, and languages, should serve him: his dominion is an everlasting dominion, which shall not pass away, and his kingdom that which shall not be destroyed. And the kingdom and dominion, and the greatness of the kingdom under the whole heaven, shall be given to the people of the saints of the most High, whose kingdom is an everlasting kingdom, and all dominions shall serve and obey him. (Daniel 7:13–14, 27)

It appears that Jesus, accompanied by the clouds of heaven, comes from a distance when He approaches the seat where the Ancient of Days sits. As such, it appears that during this time of 2300 evenings and mornings when normal sanctuary activities are discontinued in heaven, our Lord Jesus will not be on the "right hand of God." This could be due to the fact that Michael will have effectively cast Satan out of heaven and the "accuser of the brethren" will no longer have the ability to come before God. Jesus's intercessory position to counter the accusations of Satan will no longer be necessary! If true, this is an incredible consideration. But where could our Lord Jesus go during this time? His possible whereabouts are discussed in detail in the chapter on Revelation when we look at chapter 10.

To summarize

Would God give us this much insight? Could the Holy Scriptures actually reveal, not with conjecture or hypothesis but with the actual and specific time periods in the text itself, that the time clock of the end will kick off at some point in the future on Purim and that thirty days later, on Passover, the allotted 3.5-year time period of the Antichrist, the two witnesses, the Jewish exile, and Jerusalem's being trod under foot will begin?

I have confidence in the Word of God. Humanly, my understanding could be in error. But to me, all of the eschatological time periods given in Daniel and Revelation, when taken at face value, appropriately and reasonably fit within the Jewish holidays and the appointed times of Leviticus 23. And based on the historical fact that our Lord Jesus perfectly fulfilled the spring feasts with His first coming, should we easily dismiss the idea that such a correlation, fit, and alignment is revealed by the Scripture in regard to the second coming?

At a high level, this is what I believe has been revealed:

Day 1	Destruction in Jerusalem and the removal of the daily sacrifice/worship on Purim
Day 30	The beginning of tribulation and the 3.5-year eschatological period on Passover
Day 112/113	The casting out of Satan by Michael on Tisha B'Av
Day 1287	The beginning of the seventieth week
Day 1290.5	The resurrection of the two witnesses and the abomination of desolation
Day 1293	The last day of the seventieth week
Day 1294	The day of the Lord on the Day of Atonement
Day 1295	The beginning of the forty-day tabernacle period
Day 1335	The formal inauguration of the millennium

V: DID JESUS SAY THAT NO ONE WILL EVER KNOW THE DAY OF HIS RETURN?

All of the above should lead us to a fairly obvious conclusion: to some degree, once events have begun, the day of the Lord's return can be accurately calculated. But wait! Are you saying to yourself that the author has missed something major? Did he just state that an expected day could one day be calculated? Doesn't he understand that no one knows the day or hour of Jesus's return? Not even the Lord Jesus Himself! Only the Father knows!

We'll look in detail at Jesus's words on the subject in a moment, but first, let's review the biblical support for a calculable day.

If Jesus perfectly fulfilled the spring feast days with His death, burial, resurrection, and sending of the Holy Spirt, it seems appropriate that the fall feast days of repentance (Trumpets) and fasting and mourning (the Day of Atonement) contain a similar prophetic meaning. Then, based on the 1335 days of Daniel 12:12, Jesus may "tabernacle" with His people for forty days leading up to that wondrous thousand-year reign.

Calendar dates for upcoming Jewish holidays and feast days are available to anyone with Internet access. For study, I developed a spreadsheet of the Jewish holidays out to the year 2050. It is interesting to note that the scriptural alignment discussed in section 4 above doesn't occur every year. In other words, it isn't every year that you end up with 1260 days between Passover and the Day of Atonement, when taking into account the 3.5-day adjustment back to the abomination of desolation. For reference, there are eighteen times between the year 2020 and 2050 when the time between the Jewish feast days and the abomination of desolation calculates perfectly to the day.

We shouldn't miss how supernatural this is. The precise connection between the Jehovah-instituted holidays and feasts and the timing-related Scriptures in Daniel and Revelation is simply incredible. It magnifies the glory of God in my heart. My yearning grows stronger to be in the presence of the Omniscient one day. And not least of all, my smallness grows smaller as I consider these things. Isn't it true that the more we see God for who He is— how detailed, how all-knowing, how loving, how merciful, how powerful, and how perfect—the more insignificant we become? How did the apostle John respond when he beheld the perfect beauty and majesty of the glorified Lamb in heaven (Revelation 1:17)? How did the prophet Isaiah react when he saw the Lord upon the throne in heaven (Isaiah 6:5)? What was Daniel's response to his visions (Daniel 10:8)? What did Ezekiel do when he saw into the heavens and witnessed the glory of the Lord (Ezekiel 1:28)?

Today, I don't know when the Son of Man will come. However, I believe that wise and prepared servants of God will grow in understanding and expectancy as the time draws near. I strongly believe that as future events occur, He will enable us to have a maturing understanding of these things—along with a God-directed ability to align them with Scripture. It is much like childbirth. Today, a woman who is not pregnant has no clue when or if she may give birth to another baby. But once she is pregnant, an expected due date is established.

Just as with expectant mothers, the day could arrive sooner or come later. While I have confidence in the perfect alignment given in the testimony of Scripture, only God knows the very hour of the second coming. As time moves along and gets nearer to the due date, the anticipation grows, the signs increase, and the pangs strengthen until it is absolutely certain that childbirth may be days, or even hours away. This is much the way I handle the information above. If eschatological events occur as I believe they will in the "set time" that God has designated, on Purim and then again on Passover in some upcoming year, we will be able to wisely calculate an expected day of the Lord on Yom Kippur. Then, we will tune in to the developing signs and bear witness to their occurrences as we travel through the path of tribulation.

As we soberly keep our finger on the pulse of world events, may the

Spirit guide our lives so that Christ is magnified in those dark days. What an incredible opportunity awaits followers of the Word of God! More than ever, fulfillments of end-time prophecies will provide a remarkable source text for Bible followers to testify to unbelievers of the Word's veracity and pertinence and to proclaim to unbelievers the need to repent and believe in the One who is able to deliver us from sin and eternal condemnation!

Now, let us look at Jesus's words concerning the day and the hour. He did indeed speak of this time being unknown—but perhaps He did not quite say what many of us think He did.

Below are the Scriptures which speak to the day and hour of the Lord's return. Let's take a fresh look at the applicable texts with eyes fully open, and not skewed by our tradition.

All of the examples below are from Jesus Christ in what is termed the Olivet Discourse, which is recorded in Matthew 24, Luke 21, and Mark 13. In these passages, the Lord Jesus set forth a substantial list of details and events that would precede His second coming. Each of the verses below is in the latter portion of His discourse, after the events and signs (or "these things," Matthew 24:33, Mark 13:29, and Luke 21:31) have come to pass. Jesus says that at this time, "Know that it is near, even at the doors" (Matthew 24:33).

Let's closely review these Scriptures to see what restriction God has placed upon mankind's knowledge of this day. Additionally, let us ask: are the restrictions the same for both the servants of God and for those who aren't obedient followers of God?

The Parable of the Servants

> Who then is a faithful and wise servant, whom his lord hath made ruler over his household, to give them meat in due season? Blessed is that servant, whom his lord when he cometh shall find so doing. Verily I say unto you, That he shall make him ruler over all his goods. *But and if that evil servant* shall say in his heart, My lord delayeth his coming; and shall begin to smite his fellowservants, and to eat and drink with the drunken; *the lord of that servant shall come in a day when he looketh not for him, and in an hour that he is not aware of,* and shall cut him asunder, and appoint him his portion with the hypocrites: there shall be weeping and gnashing of teeth. (Matthew 24:45–51)

What does Jesus teach us from the parable of the faithful and wise servant and the evil servant? If we are walking faithfully to our Lord, with godly wisdom, we will be blessed at the return of the Son of Man. On the contrary, if we are not concerned with the Lord's coming, and if we are not obedient to the Scripture in our lifestyle, the coming of the Lord will catch us unawares, in a day and in an hour that we are not looking for and when we are unprepared. Simply stated, the wise and faithful servant will be ready and prepared; the evil servant will suffer for his lack of readiness and preparation.

The Parable of the Virgins

> Then shall the kingdom of heaven be likened unto ten virgins, which took their lamps, and went forth to meet the bridegroom. And five of them were wise, and five were foolish. They that were foolish took their lamps, and took no oil with them: but the wise took oil in their vessels with their lamps. While the bridegroom tarried, they all slumbered and slept. And at midnight there was a cry made, Behold, the bridegroom cometh; go ye out to meet him. Then all those virgins arose, and trimmed their lamps. And the foolish said unto the wise, Give us of your oil; for our lamps are gone out. But the wise answered, saying, Not so; lest there be not enough for us and you: but go ye rather to them that sell, and buy for yourselves. And while they went to buy, the bridegroom came; and *they that were ready went in with him to the marriage*: and the door was shut. *Afterward came also the other virgins*, saying, Lord, Lord, open to us. But he answered and said, *Verily I say unto you*, I know you not. Watch therefore, *for ye know neither the day nor the hour* wherein the Son of man cometh. (Matthew 25:1–13)

What does Jesus teach us from the parable of the ten virgins, of whom five were wise and five foolish?

First, the wise took oil in their vessels with their lamps. Some may say this was faith, or faithfulness, or that the oil was the Spirit of God, or that it is watchfulness or readiness. Whatever the oil represents, the wise virgins took possession and retained it. On the contrary, the foolish virgins were not compelled to harbor or retain the valuable commodity.

Second, this oil is so precious and personal that it cannot be borrowed from someone else. The example that I think of is this: we cannot borrow readiness and preparation for the Lord's return from someone else any more than we can sit down at a table and eat a meal for someone else. When we partake of a meal and become filled, it is our hunger that is satisfied. It is impossible for us to satisfy the hunger of another by eating on their behalf.

Third, Jesus is speaking to the unprepared, foolish virgins when He says "I know you not" and when He says "for ye know neither the day nor the hour wherein the Son of man cometh." From the Scriptures we understand that God provides a multitude of detail in regards to His second coming. As we grow closer to that great and notable day, the understanding of those who humbly persevere in faith will increase and not wane. Much like those labor pains of an expectant mother, the signs and symptoms will alert all who are sensitive and reliant upon the Spirit of God and who daily satiate their spiritual hunger with the Word of God. He calls all who don't currently have oil in their lamps to become wise and prepared for that day.

What if we neglect preparation and remain foolish? We won't have a clue. We will be ignorant of the signs and symptoms of the end times and the soon approaching day of the Lord. That day will come to us as a thief in the night! "But ye, brethren, are not in darkness, that that day should overtake you as a thief" (1 Thessalonians 5:4).

The Days of Noah

> But of that day and hour knoweth no man, no, not the angels of heaven, but my Father only. But as the days of Noe were, so shall also the coming of the Son of man be. For as in the days that were before the flood they were eating and drinking, marrying and giving in marriage, until the day that Noe entered into the ark, and knew not until the flood came, and took them all away; so shall also the coming of the Son of man be. (Matthew 24:36–39)

> But of that day and that hour knoweth no man, no, not the angels which are in heaven, neither the Son, but the Father. (Mark 13:32)

The coming of the Son of Man will be as in the days of Noah. What were the characteristics of those days? Evil continued in defiance of the righteous preaching of Noah. People will largely be deceived, like the evil servant in the first example, and comfort themselves that the Word of God is not relevant to them and that their earthly lives are more important than yielding to truth. This is a picture of blindness. The world was continually evil in Noah's days. This environment of deception, self-centeredness, and evil will be the backdrop for the time of the end.

Just prior to this example of Noah's day, the Lord Jesus stated that no man knows the day and hour, but my Father only. What are we to take from this?

First, it's evident that the evil and foolish will continue in their deception and self-centeredness until that day comes and it is too late. Second, we are told that only the Father knows the day *and* the hour. This is a precise, narrow window. Only the Father knows down to the very hour.

It is appropriate to note here that most Bible versions translate Matthew 24:36 and Mark 13:32 as "day *or* hour" instead of "day *and* hour." This is a dramatic difference, but which is correct? I am convinced that translating the Greek word *kai* (Strong's G2532) as "and" is correct. *Kai* is the most common conjunction used in the New Testament (used over nine thousand times). According to Thayer's Greek Lexicon it has "a copulative and sometimes also a cumulative force." It is always connective and never adversative (i.e. it joins, correlates, adds, or augments). It is extremely rare (only eleven instances) that *kai* is translated as "or." It always joins two things that can both be true, with one never nullifying the other.

Moreover, the Scripture routinely defines itself. The "day and hour" of Matthew 24:36 is consistent with and is further reiterated and defined by the "hour" restriction a few verses later in verse 42 and verse 44. And the "day and hour" restriction of Mark 13:32 is reiterated and supported by the "hour" restriction just three verses later in verse 35. The unknown *hour* of the Lord's return is a consistent message from the Scripture. Only God knows the "set time."

One Shall Be Taken, The Other Left

> Then shall two be in the field; the one shall be taken, and the other left. Two women shall be grinding at the mill; the one shall be taken, and the other left. Watch therefore: for ye know not what hour your Lord doth come. (Matthew 24:40–42)

The point of this example is that no one knows what hour the Lord will return. Consistent with the example above, we are told that the Father is the only one who knows the exact hour. (It is beyond the scope of this section, but more is written about the context of this verse in the chapter on the Olivet Discourse.)

The Thief in the Night

> But know this, that if the goodman of the house had known in what watch the thief would come, he would have watched, and would not have suffered his house to be broken up. Therefore be ye also ready: for in such an hour as ye think not the Son of man cometh. (Matthew 24:43–44)

If the head of the family knew what hour the thief would come, he would have been watching at that hour. Again, note the emphasis here on the *hour*. The Lord tells us to be watchful and ready; He will return in an hour that we think not.

Watch!

> Watch ye therefore: for ye know not when the master of the house cometh, at even, or at midnight, or at the cockcrowing, or in the morning: lest coming suddenly he find you sleeping. And what I say unto you I say unto all, Watch. (Mark 13:35–37)

These verses sum up the whole discussion. Because of the breadth of detail provided in the Scripture, we will have a keen understanding that the great day is drawing near, even at the door. We may even know the very day. However, the key lesson is to watch! It is reiterated again that we do not know the hour. We only know that it will be sudden. It may take place at even, or at midnight, or at the cockcrowing, or in the morning! Don't be caught off guard because of the cares of this life, or the second coming will be to you like a thief in the night. Walk in the light. Be children of the day. Watch and be prayerful always that you can be accounted worthy to escape the wrath of God and vengeance against evil!

Below is a category summary of the Scripture examples reviewed above. In my opinion, the Scripture does not restrict us from knowing the day of the Lord's return, only the specific hour of the day. Jesus didn't say "Watch because you don't know if it will be in April or May, or on a Tuesday or Wednesday." He referred specifically to times within a twenty-four hour period. The wise and faithful, watchful and prepared servants of God Almighty may very well know (almost unbelievably so) the expected day of the Lord well in advance. Especially after the following events occur during the first half of Daniel's seventieth week, we will know that the time is very near:

- the two witnesses die at the beginning of the week and lie in the street for 3.5 days
- the two witnesses are resurrected
- the abomination of desolation occurs
- a great earthquake in Jerusalem kills seven thousand people (Revelation 11:13)

To the evil, foolish, intoxicated, and burdened with the cares of this life:	To the wise and faithful servant and wise virgins:	To everyone:
1. The Lord will come in a day and in an hour that you are not aware of.	1. Blessed is that servant!	1. No one except the Father knows *the day* and *the hour* of the second coming.
2. You will know neither the day nor the hour.	2. We will find entrance with the bridegroom into the marriage supper of the Lamb.	2. *We know not what* hour the Lord comes.
3. That day will come upon you unawares.		3. Watch and be ready, for *in such an hour* we think not the Son of Man will come.
		4. Watch, for we know not if the Lord will suddenly come at evening, at midnight, at the cockcrowing, or in the morning.

Although it isn't what the Scripture explicitly states for the wise and faithful servants of God, I concur that as of 2016 we are restricted in our understanding, and we don't know the "day or hour." But one day we will know the expected day (not "the day *and* the hour," but the expected day). We need to trust the Scriptures with complete confidence and not add restrictions that are intended for foolish ones whose priorities are with the things of this life. We shouldn't dismiss the depths and details of what God can and will reveal from sola scriptura regarding the Lord's second coming and other eschatological matters. We will be able to see the signs unfolding and the end drawing near if we are children of light.

I will admit: even as write these words, to me they are almost unfathomable. It is deep within the fibers of my mind and soul that we really don't have a clue; that we simply need to be watching and ready *every day*. I still hold dearly to this end-times doctrine of preparedness. We need to be ever-ready. None of us knows when our last breath will be taken. Daily we need to keep close to the Lord and walk in grace and truth with the guidance of the Spirit. As stated, today I don't have a clue what day to expect the Lord to return. But one day this will change. As we see events in the Middle East align with Scripture, as they ultimately lead to profound, prophetic events that occur on Purim and then thirty days later on Passover, the time clock of the end will be running—and we will have the ability to understand as never before.

Even though it directly goes against my traditional view and understanding, I believe God is revealing a new framework of understanding from the Holy Scripture that will provide a clear understanding of these matters as the end approaches and as saints of God unite around a wholly Bible-based eschatological framework void of human assumption. Human assumptions do not lead to increased unity. Others can always find some valid fault and weakness in the foundation of an assumption. To be very specific, I cannot go forward on the foundational framework of a future seven-year tribulation, no matter how widespread and popular it may be. To me its foundation was built with pure intent, but it is faulty. The human assumptions implicit in the framework require a whole lot of faith in human assumptions! Personally, I would rather place my complete faith in an eschatological framework that requires faith to use the literal words of Daniel's seventy weeks, where those seventy weeks mean 490 days and where no mention of a gap means no gap is required. Once this hump is crossed, God reveals the time of the end with precision and clarity.

I understand that everyone who has set a date or claimed foreknowledge of when the Lord is going to return has only made a fool of themselves. So why am I willing to go out on that seemingly foolish and treacherous limb and state confidently that God will allow His wise servants to calculate the expected day once the expected trigger events occur at Purim and thirty days later on Passover?

For the following reasons:

- It is no personal, special "revelation" from God we are talking about, but a prediction based on faith in God's Word.
- Using literal hermeneutics and eliminating the need for human assumptions cause the eschatological truths of Scripture to come together like hands folded together in prayer, as it was meant to be.
- My confidence rests with the Holy Scripture, taking the words at their face value. At least this is my pure desire and intent, because I know that our weak, frail human interpretations and opinions can unknowingly add or take away what the text intends.
- A plain childlike reading (i.e., how long is seventy weeks?) opens up to us a sound end-times framework that meshes with all of Scripture and unclouds our understanding.
- God is not the author of confusion. He is authoritative and all-knowing.

- God tells us precisely how many months the Antichrist will have power (forty-two).
- God tells us precisely how many days the two witnesses will have power (1260).
- God teaches us to look for the removal of the daily sacrifice, and that if we count precisely 1290 days forward, the abomination of desolation will occur on that very day.
- God tells us precisely when the day of the Lord is going to occur (Daniel 9:24).
- God tells us precisely that the abomination of desolation will occur in the middle of the last week (Daniel 9:27). Thus we can expect the second coming at the end of that last week, just 3.5 days later.

The more hours and days I spend in quiet study, the more my confidence in the Word of God only builds. I can testify that the philosophy and practice of sola scriptura has been the most effective means of growing my understanding. It is through this quiet time that God has blessed my heart with inspiration and understanding, more than I could have imagined. He has allowed the nonchronological chapters of Revelation to become clear and sorted out in my mind. He has made me fully appreciate that comparing Scripture to Scripture is a field ripe with blessings. He has taught me that the day of the Lord is more complete, more complex, more rich, more sober, more alarming, and more glorious than I had ever envisioned. He has opened my eyes to the abundant overlay of prophetic truth that is in the Scripture and has shown me that we have the opportunity to uncover these layers of truth, which add detail upon detail to a common time period or event.

But I also must say this from the bottom of my heart: the more time that I spend in the Word, the more keenly aware I become of how little I know and how much there is to know. I have a deepened desire to continue growing, to increase in wisdom and understanding.

> O the depth of the riches both of the wisdom and knowledge of God! how unsearchable are his judgments, and his ways past finding out! For who hath known the mind of the Lord? or who hath been his counsellor? Or who hath first given to him, and it shall be recompensed unto him again? For of him, and through him, and to him, are all things: to whom be glory for ever. Amen. (Romans 11:33–36)

Chapter 3

THE REVELATION OF JESUS CHRIST

Before proceeding into a study of the book we know as the Revelation of Jesus Christ, let's now consider that a framework has been constructed for our prophetic understanding. A structure has been outlined according to the specific measurements provided by the "Master plan," and the dimensions of 1260, 1290, 1150, 1335, and 490 have been identified according to God's design.

The prophetic house is generally square, but it has some variety. The elaborate details of the most complex part of the framework have been left to the last week of the project, but it all beautifully and precisely comes together, almost supernaturally so. After the framework is completed, we will understand that it is diligent faithfulness to the original terms outlined on the plans that cause things to dovetail so perfectly in the end. It is now time to unveil some of the details that will make the prophetic house functional and usable and that will comprise its overall character.

In the pages of this book, a simple, solid, and precise framework for the end times has been built on the solid foundation of God's Word. It is now up to us as Bereans, with the help of God, to see if these things are so. The Lord has promised a blessing to those who read, hear, and keep the words of this prophecy (Revelation 1:3). The Scripture provides us with all we need. We must not add to it, nor can we take away or ignore certain passages (Revelation 22:18–19).

Consistent with what has been mentioned several times, in multiple passages throughout the book of Revelation we will be taken all the way to the magnificent day of the Lord through the visions of the apostle John. With all of that said, let's begin a study of this wonderful book. May it become alive in our hearts!

I. BRIEF HIGHLIGHTS OF REVELATION CHAPTERS 1–5

Revelation 1

The purpose of the book of Revelation is to reveal Jesus Christ, the Lamb of God, who will one day physically rule the world from Jerusalem as Lord of lords and King of kings. According to Revelation 1:8, Jesus is the Alpha and Omega, the beginning and the ending, who is, and who was, and who is to come, the Almighty! When John was in the isle of Patmos and in the Spirit on the Lord's day, it was for a special purpose, explained as "for the word of God, and for the testimony of Jesus Christ" (Revelation 1:2, 9).

Prophecy is truly synonymous with Jesus Christ. It purely reveals to us and testifies of who He is, what He has done, and what He will do. When the angel rebukes John in Revelation 19:10 for falling at his feet to worship him, he says "worship God: for the testimony of Jesus is the spirit of prophecy."

I want to ask an important question: can we relegate the majority of this book as not applicable to the church? This we must do if we cleave to a pretribulation rapture doctrine. But to whom was this testimony of Jesus Christ written, according to Revelation 1:1? The servants of the Lord Jesus. Are you a servant of Jesus Christ, like Paul, James, Peter, Jude, and John (Romans 1:1, James 1:1, 2 Peter 1:1, Jude 1:1, Revelation 1:1), or a fellowservant like Epaphras and Tychicus (Colossians 1:7, 4:7)? The church is often called the servants of God (Acts 4:29, 16:17; Ephesians 6:6; 2 Timothy 2:24; 1 Peter 2:16). Additionally, the term "saints" is repetitively used in the book of Revelation, even up to the end, just prior to the harvest of the earth we read about in Revelation 14:12: "Here is the patience of the saints: here are they that keep the commandments of God, and the faith of Jesus." Are you confident that these saints of God have been "left behind" by the church? Should we blatantly dismiss the fact that the church is referred to as "saints" on numerous occasions throughout the New Testament—there are too many references to cite! Or to flip this around, should we dismiss the applicability of some chapters in the New Testament that barely mention the word "church" or don't use the term at all? That would be absurd!

Regardless of the incredible patience and faith necessary to endure hardship and persecution, my desire to experience the harvest of Revelation 14:14–16 and the marriage to the Lamb of Revelation 19:5–9 is fervent! God is faithful! He has a proven, historical track record of pouring sufficient grace and peace into the hearts of persecuted believers. No, we cannot make the events of Revelation irrelevant to ourselves. We are the church, and we must enter the kingdom through much tribulation.

> Confirming the souls of the disciples, and exhorting them to continue in the faith, and that we must through much tribulation enter into the kingdom of God. (Acts 14:22)

Revelation 2 and 3

These chapters are solely the words of Jesus to seven churches located in Asia Minor. These were active churches at the time. Both positive and negative statements are made, to some churches more and to some less. The main exhortation by Christ is to repent, to overcome, and to hear what the Spirit says.

There is merit to equating these local churches to church "ages" throughout history. This leads to the common idea that our modern church age may be that of Laodicea, the lukewarm church. However, it appears most valid and applicable to consider Revelation 2 and Revelation 3 as a composite image of the church as she can be described when the end times are approaching. The body of Christ can generally be categorized into these seven types, each with varying degrees of positive and negative attributes. To say that the bride of Christ prior to His glorious return will be entirely Laodicean (lukewarm, rich and satisfied with life, but shamefully deficient and in need of faith and revival) isn't accurate. While this may seem an appropriate description of the general status of Christianity in America, aren't there churches in America that still demonstrate a true love, holiness, and faith? And what about the flourishing movements in places like China and Iran, where the governments do not offer religious freedom? Could we describe the present-day persecuted church as Laodicean in their faith? And then you have the fact that even within a Laodicean-like congregation, there may be individual congregants who exhibit primarily Philadelphia-like attributes or Ephesus-like attributes.

That being said, when the end times are upon the final generation and the heat of persecution is turned up, it is quite likely that the true, born-again, Holy Spirit–dependent, humble, loving, and obedient church will become more noticeable, and a true dichotomy between true and untrue, faithful and unfaithful, hot and cold will become clearly evident. The flames of persecution tend to produce these results. While persecution shouldn't be necessary to purify us, the end result of it may ultimately yield the glorious, pure, and faithful bride that Jesus Christ so richly deserves.

The last verse of Revelation 1 says this:

> The mystery of the seven stars which thou sawest in my right hand, and the seven golden candlesticks. The seven stars are the angels of the seven churches: and the seven candlesticks which thou sawest are the seven churches. (Revelation 1:20)

Jesus is seen by the apostle John in Revelation 1:13 as being "in the midst of the seven candlesticks" and in Revelation 1:16 holding "in his right hand seven stars." This to me is an image not of different church types at different historic church ages, but rather of all church types together at the end of the age. If Laodicea exclusively represents the church at the time of the end, we should eventually see Jesus in the presence of only one star and one candlestick. On top of that, the exhortations to the first several churches to repent, to hear, and to overcome would be irrelevant to end-times believers if that church age had long ago passed into the history books. Rather, each "church" has a need to hear what Jesus is speaking, each has a need to listen to the Spirit, each has a need to improve (whether in a minor or major fashion), and each has a calling to overcome self and the enemy that we might dwell with the LORD forever one day!

Another reason I believe these churches are a composite image of the whole church during the time of the end is the warning that Jesus gives to those at Sardis of His "thief-like" second coming. Why warn them to strengthen those things that are ready to die out and be watchful, if they will not exist at the time of the end? He exhorts them just as any of us need to be exhorted today: be watchful, be awake, and hold fast to the truths and promises of God. Why? Because if you aren't awake and don't watch, I will come as a thief. It is the same warning we find throughout Scripture, and it especially applies to the evil and disobedient, the unwatchful, the foolish, and those intoxicated and burdened with the cares of this life. As discussed earlier, to these unwatchful and unprepared, the Lord's return will be unexpected and like a thief in the night (Matthew 24:36–39, 24:43–44, 24:48–51, 25:11–13).

Jesus says to the rich and satisfied church of Laodicea that if they don't experience a true revival and develop a genuine trust in God, they will remain wretched, miserable, poor, blind, and naked. Many think that the church will have long been raptured prior to the judgments of Revelation 16. But what warning do the words of Scripture still cry out at the time between the sixth and seventh vial judgments of wrath in Revelation 16:15? The thief-like coming is "near," but it is still not "here" prior to Revelation 16:15!

If we are not watchful, and if in the end we are not wearing the garment of faith, we will be found wretched, miserable, poor, and blind when the Lord returns! This was the Lord's counsel to the church of Laodicea, and the warning is repeated in Revelation 16:15:

> Behold, I come as a thief. Blessed is he that watcheth, and keepeth his garments, lest he walk naked, and they see his shame. (Revelation 16:15)

The primary message of chapters 2 and 3 is this: "he that hath an ear, let him hear what the Spirit saith unto the churches." It is wise for all of us to hear and receive this message from the Spirit of the Lord. Whoever we are and wherever we are, the Lord has counsel ready to be delivered into our hearts.

Believers throughout all times could learn and benefit from these words of Jesus. The message for the child of God in these chapters is one of warning, soberness, and faithfulness, not splendor, tranquility, ease, comfort, and complacency.

Revelation 4

This chapter presents a special and majestic view into the throne room of God. The vision given to the Apostle John was simply incredible. If only our hearts would echo the words of the four beasts round about the throne, which rest not day and night, and which say, "Holy, holy, holy, Lord God Almighty, which was, and is, and is to come"!

> And the four beasts had each of them six wings about him; and they were full of eyes within: and they rest not day and night, saying, *Holy, holy, holy, Lord God Almighty, which was, and is, and is to come.* And when those beasts give glory and honour and thanks to him that sat on the throne, who liveth for ever and ever, the four and twenty elders fall down before him that sat on the throne, and worship him that liveth for ever and ever, and cast their crowns before the throne, saying, *Thou art worthy, O Lord, to receive glory and honour and power: for thou hast created all things, and for thy pleasure they are and were created.* (Revelation 4:8–11)

Think for a moment about the words of the twenty-four elders before the throne. They especially worship the Lord because of His worthiness to receive glory and honor and power. But why? Because of the Genesis account of creation! This is a powerful fact. All things were made by Him first and foremost *for His pleasure*. For one additional moment, I ask you to pause and consider the earth, the animal kingdom, the plant kingdom, humankind, and all that was "very good," all that God fashioned by His Word. It is *all* for the pleasure of God.

Will God comprehensively abandon the present earth? Will the new earth and the new heavens be totally unrelated to what we know today? Wouldn't that be a great victory for Satan? Or will God restore, renew, and regenerate His existing creation?

We have already reviewed the restoration principle in the Scripture. The "new" earth will be vibrant as before the fall. But we find two overarching truths in Scripture that we cannot dismiss—each offers persuasive evidence that God will not forsake his creation.

One, the climax of the end times is in and around the city of Jerusalem, and this is the physical location where the Lord Jesus Christ will reign and rule over all the earth. Physical people will live here on physical land.

> And *his feet shall stand in that day upon the mount of Olives, which is before Jerusalem on the east,* and the mount of Olives shall cleave in the midst thereof toward the east and toward the west, and there shall be a very great valley; and half of the mountain shall remove toward the north, and half of it toward the south. And it shall be in that day, that *living waters shall go out from Jerusalem*; half of them toward the former sea, and half of them toward the hinder sea: in summer and in winter shall it be. *And the* LORD *shall be king over all the earth: in that day shall there be one* LORD, *and his name one*. And men shall dwell in it, and there shall be no more utter destruction; but Jerusalem shall be safely inhabited. (Zechariah 14:4, 8, 9, 11)

> . . . for *the earth* shall be full of the knowledge of the LORD, as the waters cover the sea. (Isaiah 11:9)

> The sun shall be no more thy light by day; neither for brightness shall the moon give light unto thee: but the LORD shall be unto thee an everlasting light, and thy God thy glory. Thy sun shall no more go down; neither shall thy moon withdraw itself: for the LORD shall be thine everlasting light, and the days of thy mourning shall be ended. Thy people also shall

be all righteous: they shall inherit *the land* for ever, the branch of my planting, the work of my hands, that I may be glorified. (Isaiah 60:19–21)

For as the new heavens and the new earth, which I will make, shall remain before me, saith the LORD, so shall your seed and your name remain. And it shall come to pass, that from one new moon to another, and from one sabbath to another, shall *all flesh* come to worship before me, saith the LORD. (Isaiah 66:22–23)

One generation passeth away, and another generation cometh: but *the earth abideth for ever*. (Ecclesiastes 1:4)

Two, a new Jerusalem will come down from God out of heaven, and God will dwell with men forever.

And I John saw the holy city, new Jerusalem, *coming down from God out of heaven*, prepared as a bride adorned for her husband. And I heard a great voice out of heaven saying, Behold, the tabernacle of God is with men, and he will dwell with them, and they shall be his people, and God himself shall be with them, and be their God. And God shall wipe away all tears from their eyes; and there shall be no more death, neither sorrow, nor crying, neither shall there be any more pain: for the former things are passed away. And he that sat upon the throne said, Behold, I make all things new. And he said unto me, Write: for these words are true and faithful. (Revelation 21:2–5)

Ever since God provoked a deep passion and thirst within my heart to learn more about and study the end times, I have been transformed in my thinking. It seems innate for us to think of eternity as a spirit realm where we float and move about in some faraway, remote, and unearthly place where God dwells. Rather, in the Scriptures we see Jesus coming to earth to rule and reign. And ultimately, we see the God of the heavens coming down from heaven to dwell with us forever. According to Romans 8:19–23, do you think the whole creation is groaning and travailing for a future destruction or a future restoration?

Revelation 5

This chapter provides one of the most important visions given to John. It pertains to a special book in the right hand of God. According to Revelation 5:1, John saw in the right hand of God a book written within and on the back side, sealed with seven seals. John wept because no man was found worthy to open the book, neither to look on it. Ah, but there was one found worthy—the Lion of the tribe of Judah, the Root of David! He has prevailed to open the book and to loose the seven seals that keep it closed. As John heard these words, he saw a Lamb that had been slain, with seven horns and seven eyes, which are the seven Spirits of God sent forth into all the earth. He came and took the book out of God's right hand, and a new song was sung. The song reveals the Lamb's worthiness and also turns our view to that ultimate point in time when "we shall reign on the earth" with Him after His second coming. Though many difficult steps need to be taken to reach that time when Jesus is king on earth, it is the core of our yearning and hope.

> And they sung a new song, saying, Thou art worthy to take the book, and to open the seals thereof: for thou wast slain, and hast redeemed us to God by thy blood out of every kindred, and tongue, and people, and nation; and hast made us unto our God kings and priests: and we shall reign on the earth. (Revelation 5:9–10)

II. CHRONOLOGY OF THE BOOK OF REVELATION

At this point, the statement needs to be made that throughout the Revelation of Jesus Christ we are tossed to and fro on the chronological timeline. The book never claims to be chronological, and it clearly is not. A plain reading from chapter 1 to chapter 22 doesn't naturally flow, especially beginning at chapter 6. This is a point of confusion for many, and many have tried to fit it into a chronological flow. Much of the confusion is due to how these events were revealed to the apostle John.

- He experienced several visions throughout the book, witnessing one vision at a time. John would bear witness to a vision and then proceed to describe what he saw from beginning to end. In some cases the vision may cover only a snapshot in time, and in other cases the vision may cover multiple years of time from beginning to end. Then John would be chronologically pulled back in time to witness another vision that was then revealed to him from beginning to end.
- Because of the phenomenon described above, if we read Revelation from beginning to end, we need to hit a mental "reset" and reorient ourselves several times. We need to pull ourselves back

on the chronological timeline to where the next event begins that John is describing. This is not a simple task, but it is necessary in order for us to make sense of the things revealed to John.
- At all times it is required that we consider the context and pay close attention to the details given. Using Scripture comparison is a necessity if we are to understand the book of Revelation.

In my personal experience, certain insights in regards to the chronology and timing of John's visions began when I noticed a few key citations in the Scripture pertaining to the resurrection. I had been studying the Revelation and specifically spending time trying to understand what the trumpets and vials were, and then trying to decipher where they could fit in the overall time frame of the end (i.e. do they happen back-to-back-to-back in a chronological fashion, etc.). Then one evening, it stood out to me. I saw the preresurrection cosmic events in Revelation 6:12 at the sixth seal. The preresurrection thief-like coming mentioned in Revelation 16:15 just prior to the seventh vial. The "finished" language of Revelation 10:7 at the seventh thunder. And then the postresurrection time of judging the dead in Revelation 11:18 at the seventh trumpet. Like a puzzle, one connection led to another which led to another.

The seals, trumpets, and vials are not contained within one chapter or a sequence of chapters in a neat and tidy fashion. Again, John simply wrote them down as he saw the visions pertaining them. This can make it difficult to decipher correctly what we are reading. Below is a helpful reference to the specific texts for each of the seven seals, seven trumpets, and seven vials. As you look these over, note that the seventh seal includes verses 3–5 of Revelation 8. Many people may not realize this. This is additional evidence for the importance of comparing Scripture to Scripture. The language consistency between the seventh seal, seventh trumpet, and seventh vial is unmistakable when Revelation 8:3–5 is included as part of the seventh seal.

- Seals: One through six are found in Revelation 6:1–17. The seventh seal is described in Revelation 8:1, 3–5.
- Trumpets: One through four are found in Revelation 8:2, 6–13. Five through six are found in Revelation 9:1–21. The seventh trumpet is described in Revelation 11:15–19.
- Vials: One through seven are found in Revelation 15:1–8 and Revelation 16:1–21.

Before we proceed through a detailed review of the seals, trumpets, and vials, let us first walk through a big-picture overview of the tribulation and when it begins.

III. A BIG-PICTURE OVERVIEW OF THE TRIBULATION AND ITS TIMING

The rise of the Antichrist marks the beginning of the tribulation. However, before the tribulation, several events must occur to ripen the way for the rise of Antichrist. These events are primarily described in Daniel 7 and Daniel 8. (The events of Daniel 7 and Daniel 8 appear to be linked to the first four horsemen of Revelation 6. This is discussed in more detail in the chapter on Daniel.)

The Antichrist, or little horn as he is described in Daniel 7 and Daniel 8, will rise from a dreadful and terrible "beast kingdom" (the eighth kingdom, which is "of the seven," Revelation 17:11). This kingdom is the "feet and toes" kingdom referred to in Daniel 2, made of part iron and part clay. It is also the fourth beast described in Daniel 7 and the final kingdom referred to in Daniel 8. These Scriptures all refer to the same entity or end-times beast kingdom.

Once this beast kingdom comes to power, it will lend its power to the Antichrist, a "little horn" who rises from this kingdom.

Generally speaking, the tribulation is the period when the Antichrist and false prophet, along with the evil spirits of Satan, exhaust themselves in an attempt to defeat God's plan and purposes using all their might and power. Their goal is to steal away the glory due Him. The beast/Antichrist, the beast's kingdom, and Satan will not be defeated easily. The tribulation will consist of much persecution led by Antichrist against those who are unwilling to worship him and his image and to receive a "mark of the beast" in their right hand or in their foreheads. Life will become sober and difficult for the follower of God.

> And it was given unto him to make war with the saints, and to overcome them: and power was given him over all kindreds, and tongues, and nations. (Revelation 13:7)

> And he [the false prophet] exerciseth all the power of the first beast before him, and causeth the earth and them which dwell therein to worship the first beast, whose deadly wound was healed. (Revelation 13:12)

And he [the false prophet] causeth all, both small and great, rich and poor, free and bond, to receive a mark in their right hand, or in their foreheads: and that no man might buy or sell, save he that had the mark, or the name of the beast, or the number of his name. (Revelation 13:16–17)

Meanwhile, during the tribulation God will counter the persecution of Antichrist and his followers with several terrible plagues (called "the wrath of God"). The followers of God will be immune from these plagues much like in the days of Moses, when the children of Israel were delivered out of Egypt. The wrath of God's plagues will not go against His followers! However, if we are alive and following God during the tribulation, we are bound to be openly targeted by Satan and the Antichrist. This we can appropriately define as persecution, not the wrath of God. Persecution has always impacted the church, and this pattern will continue until the very end.

Toward the end of the 3.5 years of tribulation, this difficult period will climax to a point where Antichrist stands in the holy place and blasphemously claims to be God (2 Thessalonians 2:4; Daniel 9:27, 11:31, 11:36). While the death of the two witnesses of God will bring about a euphoric time for the Antichrist and his followers, their so-called victory and associated reprieve from the wrath of God will be short-lived. This evil and blasphemous act will lead to the Antichrist's sudden downfall. Paul says it this way in 2 Thessalonians 2:8–9: "And then shall that Wicked be revealed, whom the Lord shall consume with the spirit of his mouth, and shall destroy with the brightness of his coming: even him, whose coming is after the working of Satan with all power and signs and lying wonders."

I believe that many Jews will be dislodged from Jerusalem (Daniel 11:16) when the glorious land experiences a destructive event shortly prior to the time when Antichrist rises to power (Daniel 11:21). The great tribulation, which will occur nearly 3.5 years later, will result in another disbursement just prior to the second coming. It will be a swift set of gut-wrenching events for regathered Jews (Ezekiel 38:12) who falsely dwell in peace (Jeremiah 4:10, Ezekiel 38:8, 11, 14; I Thessalonians 5:3). The enemies of God will wreak destruction on Jews like never before in history. It will be the time of Jacob's trouble. Read Zechariah 14:1–2, Jeremiah 30:5–7, and Isaiah 13:7–8, 15–18 for an idea of the depth of misery to be inflicted against the people of God.

Then the day of the Lord will come: a tremendous transition event that changes everything. This is the time of the first resurrection. It will be the time of remnant Israel's salvation. It is also the time wherein the fury, wrath, and fierce anger of God are unleashed in a day of slaughter against the enemies of God in the battle of Armageddon. Believers will be delivered from this outpouring of wrath much as Noah's family was spared in the ark (Matthew 24:36–39). Essentially, those dead in Christ and the living followers of the Lord Jesus will be *lifted off the earth* and taken to heaven to stand before the throne of God. All living believers will be translated at this time and will not be subject to this unprecedented and ultimate *day* of wrath. This is what is commonly called the resurrection/rapture. It could also be pictured much like the time when Lot fled Sodom (Luke 17:28–30).

> But as the days of Noe were, so shall also the coming of the Son of man be. For as in the days that were before the flood they were eating and drinking, marrying and giving in marriage, until the day that Noe entered into the ark, and knew not until the flood came, and took them all away; so shall also the coming of the Son of man be. (Matthew 24:37–39)

> Likewise also as it was in the days of Lot; they did eat, they drank, they bought, they sold, they planted, they builded; but the same day that Lot went out of Sodom it rained fire and brimstone from heaven, and destroyed them all. Even thus shall it be in the day when the Son of man is revealed. (Luke 17:28–30)

This is the time that was in view when the new song was sung in Revelation 5:9–14, when the twenty-four elders praised the Lamb for what would occur once the seventh and final seal would be opened. The twenty-four elders will be made kings and priests, and they will reign on the earth. Worthy is the Lamb who was slain to receive power, and riches, and wisdom, and strength, and honor, and glory, and blessing! Satan will be bound and defeated!

What is the timing of the day of the Lord? It will occur when the seventh seal is opened, when the seventh thunder speaks, when the seventh trumpet sounds, and when the seventh vial is poured out. The seventh thunder, seventh trumpet, and seventh vial declare it with these wonderful words:

> **Seventh Thunder:** Revelation 10:7: "But in the days of the voice of the seventh angel, when he shall begin to sound, *the mystery of God should be finished,* as he hath declared to his servants the prophets."

> **Seventh Trumpet:** Revelation 11:15: "And the seventh angel sounded; and there were great voices in heaven, saying, *The kingdoms of this world*

are become the kingdoms of our Lord, and of his Christ; and he shall reign for ever and ever."

Seventh Vial: Revelation 16:17: "And the seventh angel poured out his vial into the air; and there came a great voice out of the temple of heaven, from the throne, saying, *It is done.*"

Below is a general, high-level sketch of end-times events as I see them occurring.

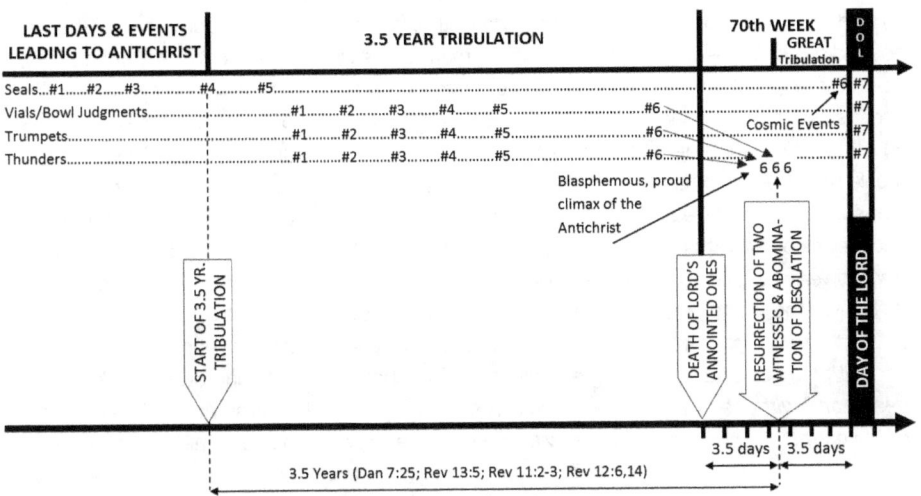

IV. SEALS, TRUMPETS, AND VIALS— A DETAILED COMPARISON AND STUDY

Revelation 6, 8, 9, 11, 15, and 16 introduce us to the seals, trumpets, and vials. As indicated by the high-level sketch, I believe the first three seals will occur in the last days leading up to the time of Antichrist's arrival, prior to the tribulation. Descriptions of the first three seals are recorded in Revelation 6:2–6 and depict the sights and sounds the apostle John saw and heard in the vision given him, as the seals were opened by the Lamb. The first three seals reveal a colored horse each with rider on steed. The first is white, the second is red, and the third is black. A detailed analysis of these horses and their riders is covered in the chapter on Daniel, where we can read of events that lead to the rise of Antichrist.

In this section, we'll focus on the time period beginning with the fourth seal and onward. I believe the fourth seal represents the time when Antichrist comes into view and the tribulation begins, as indicated by the vertical, dashed line at the fourth seal in the abbreviated chart above.

The Fourth Seal

The following Scriptures contain a comparison of the fourth rider (Death) in Revelation 6:7–8 with the little horn of Daniel 7:8, 21, 25 and Daniel 8:9, 23–25.

Revelation 6:7–8	Daniel 7:8, 21, 25	Daniel 8:9, 23–25
(7) And when he had opened the *fourth seal*, I heard the voice of the fourth beast say, Come and see. (8) And I looked, and behold a pale horse: and his name that sat on him was *Death*, and *Hell* followed with him. *And power was given unto them* over the fourth part of the earth, *to kill with sword, and with hunger, and with death, and with the beasts of the earth.*	(8) I considered the horns, and, behold, *there came up among them another little horn,* before whom there were three of the first horns plucked up by the roots [i.e. he subdued three of the ten kings, Revelation 17:12–13]: and, behold, in this horn were eyes like the eyes of man, and a mouth speaking great things. (21) I beheld, and *the same horn made war with the saints, and prevailed against them;* (25) and he shall speak great words against the most High, and shall wear out the saints of the most High, and think to change times and laws: and *they shall be given into his hand until a time and times and the dividing of time* [i.e. 3.5 years].	(9) And out of one of them *came forth a little horn,* which waxed exceeding great, toward the south, and toward the east, and toward the pleasant land. (23) And in the latter time of their kingdom, when the transgressors are come to the full, *a king of fierce countenance,* and understanding dark sentences, shall stand up. (24) And his power shall be mighty, *but not by his own power:* and *he shall destroy wonderfully,* and shall prosper, and practise, and *shall destroy the mighty and the holy people.* (25) And through his policy also he shall cause craft to prosper in his hand; and he shall magnify himself in his heart, and by peace shall destroy many: he shall also stand up against the Prince of princes; but he shall be broken without hand.

The fourth seal (or fourth horseman) of Revelation 6:7–8 indicates the time when the Antichrist comes into view. It describes two entities, Death and Hell. The horse rider's name is Death, and Hell is his counterpart who follows him. Death is given power over a fourth part of the earth to kill with the sword. This matches up very well with the little horn description in Daniel 7 and Daniel 8, which says that he makes war with the saints and prevails against them, that his power will be mighty, and that he shall destroy the mighty and the holy people.

It seems that these two evil entities are filled with the power and evil spirit of Satan. Note that Revelation 6:8 says "power was given unto them," and in Daniel 8:24 the little horn is described as having mighty power, "but not by his own power."

It appears reasonable to connect the proud, stout, deceptive, saint-destroying little horn with the fourth horsemen, whose name is Death and who is given power to kill and cause misery over a fourth part of the earth.

Isaiah 28:15 and 18 seem to fortify the interpretation that "death" and "hell" in the last days are legitimate parties with whom a covenant and agreement can be made. We know that Antichrist joins in a league with others at the beginning of his reign (Daniel 11:23) and that he "confirms a covenant" at the beginning of the seventieth week of Daniel (Daniel 9:27). Also, we know that he has "intelligence with them that forsake the holy covenant" (Daniel 11:30).

> Because ye have said, We have made a covenant with *death*, and with *hell* are we at agreement; when the overflowing scourge shall pass through, it shall not come unto us: for we have made lies our refuge, and under falsehood have we hid ourselves: therefore thus saith the Lord GOD, Behold, I lay in Zion for a foundation a stone, a tried stone, a precious corner stone, a sure foundation: he that believeth shall not make haste. Judgment also will I lay to the line, and righteousness to the plummet: and the hail shall sweep away the refuge of lies, and the waters shall overflow the hiding place. And your covenant with *death* shall be disannulled, and your agreement with *hell* shall not stand; when the overflowing scourge shall pass through, then ye shall be trodden down by it. (Isaiah 28:15–18)

> And *after the league made with him* he shall work deceitfully: for he shall come up, and shall become strong with a small people. (Daniel 11:23)

> *And he shall confirm the covenant with many for one week:* and in the midst of the week he shall cause the sacrifice and the oblation to cease, and for the overspreading of abominations he shall make it desolate, even until the consummation, and that determined shall be poured upon the desolate. (Daniel 9:27)

> For the ships of Chittim shall come against him: therefore he shall be grieved, and return, and have indignation against the holy covenant: so shall he do; *he shall* even return, and *have intelligence with them that forsake the holy covenant.* (Daniel 11:30)

According to Revelation 19:20 and 20:10, the beast and false prophet are cast into the lake of fire at the second coming of Jesus. Likewise, death and hell are connected with ungodliness and the lake of fire from the Scripture below. Also, the devil has the "power of death" (Hebrews 2:14). The connections between death and hell and the beast, false prophet and the devil are numerous.

> And the sea gave up the dead which were in it; and *death and hell* delivered up the dead which were in them: and they were judged every man according to their works. And *death and hell* were cast into the lake of fire. This is the second death. And whosoever was not found written in the book of life was cast into the lake of fire. (Revelation 20:13–15)

The Fifth Seal

The fifth seal of Revelation 6:9–11 clearly indicates that it is opened during the tribulation period due to the persecution of the saints by Antichrist and his followers "for the word of God, and for the testimony they held."

> And when he had opened the *fifth seal*, I saw under the altar the souls of *them that were slain for the word of God, and for the testimony which they held:* and they cried with a loud voice, saying, How long, O Lord, holy and true, dost thou not judge and avenge our blood on them that dwell on the earth? And white robes were given unto every one of them; and it was said unto them, *that they should rest yet for a little season, until their fellowservants also and their brethren, that should be killed as they were, should be fulfilled.* (Revelation 6:9–11)

The verses cited previously from Daniel 7 and Daniel 8 correlate with the evil actions of the Antichrist and his followers very well:

> I beheld, and the same horn *made war with the saints, and prevailed against them.* (Daniel 7:21)

> And his power shall be mighty, but not by his own power: and *he shall destroy wonderfully, and shall prosper, and practise, and shall destroy the mighty and the holy people.* (Daniel 8:24)

No more seals are opened until the very end of the tribulation period, just prior to the day of the Lord. So now our attention can be turned to the seven trumpets and the seven vial plagues.

Before diving right into a study of the trumpets and vial plagues, it is imperative to step back and lay some groundwork by reviewing the testimony of the two witnesses. It is my belief that the two witnesses will play a significant role with respect to the plagues of God's wrath that will target Antichrist and his followers. The following review will cover what some of their role and responsibilities may include, and who the two witnesses might be.

The Two Witnesses

The power of the two witnesses involve the a) heavens, b) seas, and c) earth. Note the language in Revelation 11:6: they are given "power . . . to smite the earth with *all* plagues." During this 3.5-year period, the two witnesses exhibit tremendous God-given powers. It appears that these two witnesses will have the capacity to carry out the plagues described in Revelation.

I liken this time period very closely to how God demonstrated His wrath against Pharaoh and Egypt through the willing hands of Moses and Aaron. The tribulation period, which will climax at the day of the Lord, has strong correlations to Israel's release and escape from Egypt.

Let's review the text. Revelation 11:3–6 describes some details and circumstances pertaining to the lives of the two witnesses during their 3.5-year testimony. Although extremely interesting, we'll skip a full review of Revelation 11:7–13 for now. Those verses, verses 7–13, contain details pertaining to the end of the two witnesses' lives (their deaths and subsequent resurrection 3.5 days later) that are critical to understanding the events that occur during the sixth seal, sixth trumpet, and sixth vial plague. But for now, we'll stick with a review of verses 3–6.

> And I will give power unto my two witnesses, and they shall prophesy a thousand two hundred and threescore days, clothed in sackcloth. These are the two olive trees, and the two candlesticks standing before the God of the earth. And if any man will hurt them, fire proceedeth out of their mouth, and devoureth their enemies: and if any man will hurt them, he must in this manner be killed. These have power to shut heaven, that it rain not in the days of their prophecy: and have power over waters to turn them to blood, and to smite the earth with all plagues, as often as they will. (Revelation 11:3–6)

Note several facts:

- The two witnesses will have power and will prophesy for 1260 days on the earth.
- They are described as two olive trees and two candlesticks.
- Enemies of the two witnesses, or those who hurt them, will be killed by the fire that the two witnesses will have the ability to bring forth. The fire will devour their adversaries.
- The two witnesses will have the power to prevent the heavens from providing rain during their 3.5 years.
- The two witnesses will have power to turn the waters (seas and rivers) into blood.
- The two witnesses will have the power to smite the earth with *all* plagues, as often as they will.

We will begin a review of the seven plagues in short order, but suffice it to say the above powers characterize many aspects of the plagues described by John in the vial and trumpet judgments. You can come to your own conclusions after our review, but for now I simply want you to see that to connect the involvement of the two witnesses with the trumpet blasts and vial plagues, to the extent that God desires their participation, seems reasonable and fitting.

Who might the two witnesses be? First, let's make the connection that the two witnesses of Revelation 11 are the same as the two anointed ones referred to in chapter 4 of Zechariah. The language is exactly the same as that used in Revelation 11:4.

| Revelation 11:4: These are the *two olive trees,* and the *two candlesticks standing before the God of the earth.* | Zechariah 4:11–14: Then answered I, and said unto him, *What are these two olive trees upon the right side of the candlestick and upon the left side thereof?* And I answered again, and said unto him, *What be these two olive branches* which through the two golden pipes empty the golden oil out of themselves? And he answered me and said, Knowest thou not what these be? And I said, No, my lord. Then said he, *These are the two anointed ones, that stand by the Lord of the whole earth.* |

It is my personal opinion that these two witnesses are none other than Elijah and Moses. After all, it was Elijah and Moses who appeared (and talked) with Jesus when He was transfigured before Peter, James, and John (Matthew 17:1–8). That event tells us that Moses and Elijah are living today. It appears that the two witnesses, though not on earth today, are alive today in the presence of God—Revelation 11:4 and Zechariah 4:14 both say that they are "standing," in present tense, by the Lord of the whole earth.

The miraculous powers these men display are reminiscent of Moses's day in Egypt and Elijah's time on earth when it didn't rain for 3.5 years (see Exodus 1–14, 1 Kings 17:1, James 5:17). Elijah also was a prophet very familiar with supernatural fire (see 1 Kings 18:38–39, 2 Kings 1:10, 2:11).

In an end-times context, Malachi 3:1 speaks of a messenger the Lord will send to prepare the way before Himself. Malachi 4:5–6 states it similarly and finishes, "Behold, I will send you Elijah the prophet before the coming of the great and dreadful day of the LORD."

> Behold, *I will send my messenger*, and he shall prepare the way before me: and the LORD, whom ye seek, shall suddenly come to his temple, even the messenger of the covenant, whom ye delight in: behold, he shall come, saith the LORD of hosts. But who may abide the day of his coming? and who shall stand when he appeareth? for he is like a refiner's fire, and like fullers' soap. (Malachi 3:1–2)

> Behold, *I will send you Elijah the prophet before the coming of the great and dreadful day of the* LORD: and he shall turn the heart of the fathers to the children, and the heart of the children to their fathers, lest I come and smite the earth with a curse. (Malachi 4:5–6)

Before too long, the weight of the text adds up, and it is hard to dismiss the evidence. As strange as it may seem, Moses and Elijah will most likely walk the earth again to stand against the Antichrist.

With that background in place, let's turn our attention to a review of each of the trumpet blasts and vial plagues.

The Trumpet Blasts and the Vial Plagues of God's Wrath Upon Evildoers

When we read about the trumpet blasts and vial plagues, one of the most natural questions regards their timing. Do they happen back-to-back in chronological fashion? Or is it possible that the trumpets and the vial plagues can be synchronized, one through seven, and occur at the same time? Could the thunders also be synchronized along with the trumpets and vials?

As I have already touched on, one evening it stood out to me as I was quietly studying. I noticed two peculiar verses that used resurrection language. First, there were the preresurrection cosmic events in Revelation 6:12, which happen at the sixth seal. Then there was the preresurrection thief-like coming mentioned in Revelation 16:15, just prior to the seventh vial in Revelation 16:17, where the statement is made that "It is done." Looking further, I realized this lined up with the "finished" language of Revelation 10:7 at the seventh thunder. And lastly, there was the postresurrection time of judging the dead in Revelation 11:18 at the seventh trumpet.

What did this mean?

Revelation 16:15: Between the sixth and seventh vials, this verse uses resurrection language, describing the thief-like coming and the day of God. This verse, Revelation 16:15, told me that the resurrection was *near*, but it still wasn't *here*.

Revelation 11:18: Language at the seventh trumpet referred to the time of judgment of the dead and rewards for saints. This verse, Revelation 11:18, told me that the resurrection had *just occurred*.

Revelation 6:12: Here we find the clear preresurrection language of the sixth seal and its reference to the cosmic events. These cosmic events correlate with numerous other day of the Lord and second coming passages, such as Isaiah 13:9–10, Acts 2:19–21, Joel 2:31, Joel 3:13–15, Matthew 24:29–31, Luke 21:25–28, and Isaiah 2:10–21. The cosmic events, I knew, would occur just prior to the day of the Lord.

It seemed that the Lord was impressing something to me that I had never before considered. I had always heard the vials, trumpets, and seals described as separate chronological events—but that could not be.

- Using the very basic chart outline I'd made at the time, I wrote out what was starting to become clear. I couldn't help but see how the sixth seal, the sixth trumpet, and the sixth vial all seemed to line up together and how they coincided with the peak event of the Antichrist's blasphemous exaltation of himself as God (i.e. the abomination of desolation). Not only that, but I couldn't help but see how perfect it was to have the resurrection and day of the Lord coincide with the seventh seal, the seventh thunder, the seventh trumpet, and the seventh vial.

The next day, I put the side-by-side comparison of the verses together (seven angels with trumpets and seven angels with vials), and it became obvious that the trumpets and vials referenced the same seven plague events. I saw that these were simultaneous events and descriptions, not separate. This was a wonderful experience that I will never forget! Because of the Scripture commonalities and the overall alignment and fit, I personally can only conclude that this is God's design for the end.

If you are skeptical about a synchronization between the trumpets and vials, I simply ask you to read through the following comparison of these Scriptures with an open heart and mind.

Keep in mind as you do that while the vials are clearly plagues according to Revelation 15:1, nowhere does the Scripture tell us that the trumpets are "plagues" in and of themselves. The apostle John is certainly describing a plague event after each of the trumpets sound forth. But we are not told specifically that the trumpets are somehow filled with plagues. Light may be shed on this if we ask what is the general purpose of a trumpet call in Scripture. Often the trumpet blast was a herald or an announcement. In Ezekiel 33, the watchman is to sound the trumpet to warn the people of a sword that is coming upon the land. It is a warning of impending judgment.

While it may appear that the trumpet blasts are in and of themselves a series of seven "trumpet plagues," this is a mere assumption and is not proven by the text itself. It is my opinion that the trumpets are *not* plagues, but rather are heralds that announce the pouring out of the vial plagues.

- I believe that after John hears the trumpet blast, he describes the plague that comes forth from the poured vial. The poured vial comes right on the heels of the trumpet blast. They are connected events! The apostle John simply wrote what he saw after the trumpet sounded. We naturally connected the "plague" impact with the warning blast of the trumpet, but they are not the same thing.
- John may have described the plague effects in a slightly different fashion when he wrote about the trumpets versus when he wrote about the vials. But events can be seen from different angles and vantage points. He could have had more of a worldwide, panoramic view in the case of the seven trumpets and a narrower focus or view in the case of the vial plagues, for example. He might also have caught different details of the plagues from the different viewing points. What was seen by John was slightly different in each vision, yet he was describing the same event. This is much like the testimony of witnesses to a theft or an accident. Each witness may see it

differently and pick up on unique details. Or it could be compared to someone witnessing a football play from an end-zone seat and another person witnessing the same play thirty rows up from the fifty-yard line. I believe we can add the two different descriptions together to gain a fuller understanding of each plague.

- As time has passed, I have become more convinced that the sixth thunder, sixth trumpet, and sixth vial plague line up identically and will occur toward the beginning of the final week, the seventieth week of Daniel. It seems reasonable to me for these events to initiate and begin on the Feast of Trumpets, a few days prior to the seventieth week. These three notorious 6s primarily connote the climatic events during the final week of this current world. The emphasis is on man's pride and power against the plans of God. The two witnesses of God will be murdered, the Antichrist will commit his blasphemous abomination, and the great gathering of evil enemies will surround Jerusalem, bringing a flood of destruction like at no other time in history. I see the sixth seal being opened at the very tail end of the seventieth week of Daniel, representing the cosmic events that occur prior to the day of the Lord at the seventh seal, seventh thunder, seventh trumpet, and seventh vial plague.

Let's go forward with an in-depth review of these Scriptures.

TRUMPET AND VIAL PLAGUE #1	
Revelation 8:6–7: And the seven angels which had the seven trumpets prepared themselves to sound. *The first angel sounded,* and there followed hail and fire *mingled with blood, and they were cast upon the earth:* and the third part of trees was burnt up, and all green grass was burnt up.	**Revelation 16:1–2:** And I heard a great voice out of the temple saying to the seven angels, Go your ways, and pour out the vials of the wrath of God upon the earth. *And the first went, and poured out his vial upon the earth; and there fell* a noisome and *grievous sore* upon the men which had the mark of the beast, and upon them which worshipped his image.
Similarities: Hail and fire were cast upon the earth Resulted in blood	"Upon the earth there fell" Resulted in a grievous sore

A summation of the first vial plague would be as follows:

Hail and fire were cast upon the earth, resulting in grievous, bloody sores upon the men who had the mark of the beast and upon them who worshipped his image. The hail and fire also caused a third part of the trees and all green grass to burn up. This plague of God was targeted at those who bore the mark of the beast and worshipped the image of the beast.

TRUMPET AND VIAL PLAGUE #2	
Revelation 8:8–9: And *the second angel sounded,* and as it were a great mountain burning with fire was cast into *the sea:* and the third part of *the sea became blood;* and the third part of *the creatures which were in the sea, and had life, died;* and the third part of the ships were destroyed.	**Revelation 16:3:** And *the second angel poured out his vial* upon *the sea; and it became as the blood of a dead man:* and *every living soul died in the sea.*
Similarities: A plague was upon the sea The seawaters became blood The creatures in the sea died	A plague was upon the sea The water became as the blood of a dead man Every living soul died in the sea

As stated previously, the viewing angle that John had while witnessing the angels blowing their trumpets could have been more of a panoramic view of the earth, and thus the destruction that he witnessed only encompassed roughly a third of all the seas that he could see. Then, his viewing angle when witnessing the angels pouring out the vials could have been a more narrow view, so that all of the seas that he could see were impacted by the pouring out of the vial.

A summation of the second vial plague would be as follows:

The seas were disturbed greatly by what looked like a mountain of fire that was cast into the sea. This caused the seawater to become like blood, which caused death to all creatures living in those seas and also destruction to the ships in them. (I picture red flowing lava in my mind, as this has a bloody look and would cause devastation not only to sea creatures but to ships also).

TRUMPET AND VIAL PLAGUE #3	
Revelation 8:10–11: And *the third angel sounded,* and there fell a great star from heaven, burning as it were a lamp, and it fell upon *the third part of the rivers, and upon the fountains of waters;* and the name of the star is called Wormwood: and the third part of the waters became wormwood; and *many men died of the waters, because they were made bitter.*	Revelation 16:4–7: And *the third angel poured out his vial* upon *the rivers and fountains of waters;* and they became blood. And I heard the angel of the waters say, Thou art righteous, O Lord, which art, and wast, and shalt be, because thou hast judged thus. For they have shed the blood of saints and prophets, and *thou hast given them blood to drink; for they are worthy.* And I heard another out of the altar say, Even so, Lord God Almighty, true and righteous are thy judgments.
Similarities:	
A plague upon the rivers and fountains of waters	A plague upon the rivers and fountains of waters
The waters caused men to die	The waters were a judgment against those who opposed God.

What is wormwood? Wormwood is referred to in seven places in Scripture besides Revelation 8:11. It is generally related to judgment (Jeremiah 9:15, Proverbs 5:1–8); to a poisonous curse (Deuteronomy 29:18); to trouble, affliction, and misery (Lamentations 3:15, 19); and to bringing judgment upon yourself by helping evil to prosper and good to diminish (Jeremiah 23:13–20, Amos 5:7–27). Two of the seven Scripture examples are shown below.

Proverbs 5:1–8 correlates the bitterness of wormwood to judgment upon a "strange woman" speaking words that do not reflect the wisdom of God and whose evil path of life leads to death and hell:

> My son, attend unto my wisdom, and bow thine ear to my understanding: that thou mayest regard discretion, and that thy lips may keep knowledge. For the lips of a strange woman drop as an honeycomb, and her mouth is smoother than oil: *but her end is bitter as wormwood, sharp as a twoedged sword. Her feet go down to death; her steps take hold on hell.* Lest thou shouldest ponder the path of life, her ways are moveable, that thou canst not know them. Hear me now therefore, O ye children, and depart not from the words of my mouth. *Remove thy way far from her, and come not nigh the door of her house.* (Proverbs 5:1–8)

Jeremiah 23:13–20 also correlates wormwood to judgment, this time against prophets who speak falsely, cause people to err, and grow in disobedience against God:

And I have seen *folly in the prophets* of Samaria; *they prophesied in Baal, and caused my people Israel to err.* I have seen also in the prophets of Jerusalem an horrible thing: they commit *adultery,* and *walk in lies:* they *strengthen also the hands of evildoers,* that none doth return from his wickedness: they are all of them unto me as Sodom, and the inhabitants thereof as Gomorrah. *Therefore thus saith the* LORD *of hosts concerning the prophets;* Behold, *I will feed them with wormwood, and make them drink the water of gall:* for from the prophets of Jerusalem is profaneness gone forth into all the land. Thus saith the LORD of hosts, Hearken not unto the words of the prophets that prophesy unto you: they make you vain: they speak a vision of their own heart, and not out of the mouth of the LORD. They say still unto them that despise me, The LORD hath said, Ye shall have peace; and they say unto every one that walketh after the imagination of his own heart, No evil shall come upon you. For who hath stood in the counsel of the LORD, and hath perceived and heard his word? who hath marked his word, and heard it? Behold, a whirlwind of the LORD is gone forth in fury, even a grievous whirlwind: it shall fall grievously upon the head of the wicked. The anger of the LORD shall not return, until he have executed, and till he have performed the thoughts of his heart: *in the latter days ye shall consider it perfectly.* (Jeremiah 23:13–20)

A summation of the third vial plague would be as follows:

A star, like a burning lamp, fell upon the rivers and fountains of waters, turning the water into blood, making it bitter to drink and having a poisonous impact. Those who were caused to drink the water were the enemies of God, and they were afflicted, suffered, and died from the tainted waters. This plague was a true and righteous judgment of God targeted at those who afflicted the people of God by shedding the blood of the saints and prophets.

TRUMPET AND VIAL PLAGUE #4	
Revelation 8:12: And *the fourth angel sounded,* and the third part of *the sun* was smitten, and the third part of the moon, and the third part of the stars; so as the third part of them was darkened, and the day shone not for a third part of it, and the night likewise.	Revelation 16:8: And *the fourth angel poured out his vial* upon *the sun;* and power was given unto him to scorch men with fire. And men were scorched with great heat, and blasphemed the name of God, which hath power over these plagues: and they repented not to give him glory.
Similarities: The plague affected the sun	The plague was upon the sun

A summation of the fourth vial plague would be as follows:

The vial substance was poured upon the sun, and it was smitten. This caused a third of the day not to receive normal sunlight and a third of the night not to receive normal moonlight and starlight. Also, the angel of the Lord with the fourth vial was given power to scorch men with fire and great heat. God targeted this plague of scorching heat and fire at those who blasphemed the name of God and did not repent of their evil ways.

Before the fifth plague starts, an angel announces "woe, woe, woe" because of the three angels that are yet to sound:

> And I beheld, and heard an angel flying through the midst of heaven, saying with a loud voice, Woe, woe, woe, to the inhabiters of the earth by reason of the other voices of the trumpet of the three angels, which are yet to sound! (Revelation 8:13)

Praise to God that at the same time the Antichrist and Satan and his evil spirits are fighting against the saints on earth, our Holy God is countering those who blaspheme the God of heaven, who worship the image of the beast, and who have the mark of the beast! Three woes are mentioned, and the first woe takes place as the fifth trumpet sounds.

TRUMPET AND VIAL PLAGUE #5

Revelation 9:1–12: And *the fifth angel sounded,* and I saw a star fall from heaven unto the earth: and to him was given the key of *the bottomless pit.* And he opened the bottomless pit; and there arose a smoke out of the pit, as the smoke of a great furnace; and *the sun and the air were darkened by reason of the smoke of the pit.* And there came out of the smoke locusts upon the earth: and *unto them was given power, as the scorpions of the earth have power.* And it was commanded them that they should not hurt the grass of the earth, neither any green thing, neither any tree; but only those men which have not the seal of God in their foreheads. And to them it was given that they should *not* kill them, *but that they should be tormented five months: and their torment was as the torment of a scorpion, when he striketh a man.* And in those days shall men seek death, and shall not find it; and shall desire to die, and death shall flee from them. And the shapes of the locusts were like unto horses prepared unto battle; and on their heads were as it were crowns like gold,	Revelation 16:10–11: And *the fifth angel poured out his vial* upon *the seat of the beast;* and *his kingdom was full of darkness;* and *they gnawed their tongues for pain,* and blasphemed the God of heaven *because of their pains and their sores,* and repented not of their deeds.

and their faces were as the faces of men. And they had hair as the hair of women, and their teeth were as the teeth of lions. And they had breastplates, as it were breastplates of iron; and the sound of their wings was as the sound of chariots of many horses running to battle. And they had tails like unto scorpions, and there were stings in their tails: and their power was to hurt men five months. And they had a king over them, which is the angel of the bottomless pit, whose name in the Hebrew tongue is Abaddon, but in the Greek tongue hath his name Apollyon. *One woe is past; and, behold, there come two woes more hereafter.*	
Similarities:	
The bottomless pit was opened The sun and the air were darkened by the smoke Locusts tormented men for five months so much that men sought to die, but they were unable to flee from the torment and die	The vial was poured upon the seat of the beast His kingdom was full of darkness Men gnawed their tongues in pain because of their pains and sores

A summation of *the first woe*, or the fifth vial plague, would be as follows:

A deep pit near the location of Antichrist's headquarters was opened up and spewed forth immense black smoke into the region of the end-times beast kingdom. Locusts came out of the smoke and for five months tormented the blasphemers of God, or those who did not have the seal of God in their foreheads, with horrible pains and sores.

TRUMPET AND VIAL PLAGUE #6—PART A	
Revelation 9:13–21: And *the sixth angel sounded,* and I heard a voice from the four horns of the golden altar which is before God, saying to the sixth angel which had the trumpet, Loose the four angels which are bound *in the great river Euphrates.* And the four angels were loosed, *which were prepared for an hour, and a day, and a month, and a year, for to slay the third part of men.* And the number of the army of the horsemen were two hundred thousand thousand: and I heard the number of them. And thus I saw the horses in the vision, and them that sat on them, having breastplates of fire, and of jacinth, and brimstone: and the heads of the horses were as the heads of lions; and out of their mouths issued fire and smoke	Revelation 16:12–16: And *the sixth angel poured out his vial* upon *the great river Euphrates;* and the water thereof was dried up, that the way of the kings of the east might be prepared. And I saw three unclean spirits like frogs come out of the mouth of the dragon, and out of the mouth of the beast, and out of the mouth of the false prophet. For they are the spirits of devils, working miracles, *which go forth unto the kings of the earth and of the whole world, to gather them to the battle of that great day of God Almighty.* Behold, I come as a thief. Blessed is he that watcheth, and keepeth his garments, lest he walk naked, and they see his shame. *And he gathered them together into a place called in the Hebrew tongue Armageddon.*

and brimstone. *By these three was the third part of men killed, by the fire, and by the smoke, and by the brimstone, which issued out of their mouths.* For their power is in their mouth, and in their tails: for their tails were like unto serpents, and had heads, and with them they do hurt. And the rest of the men which were not killed by these plagues yet repented not of the works of their hands, that they should not worship devils, and idols of gold, and silver, and brass, and stone, and of wood: which neither can see, nor hear, nor walk: neither repented they of their murders, nor of their sorceries, nor of their fornication, nor of their thefts.	
Similarities: The plague affected the great river Euphrates	The plague was upon the great river Euphrates

Revelation 9 describes an army of 200,000,000 horsemen. Is that possible? According to an October 2013 article at www.horsetalk.co.nz, the world's equine population was 60,001,310 in 2009; 59,585,428 in 2010; and 58,472,151 in 2011. It appears this plague of 200,000,000 horsemen will be created by the Lord for the specific purpose of killing a third of men who do not worship God but instead worship devils and idols of gold, silver, brass, stone, and wood; those who are murderers, fornicators, thieves, and users of sorcery. The description is unlike a natural horse, as these horses' mouths issue fire and smoke and brimstone, and they will have power to hurt men both with their mouths and their tails.

A summation of part A of *the second woe,* or the sixth vial plague, would be as follows:

The vial was poured upon the great river Euphrates. It dried up the water, allowing preparations of the gathering of the ungodly to Armageddon. At the same time, it caused the loosing of four angels who were prepared for this exact moment in time to bring forth a plague of death-causing horsemen, 200 million in number, which killed a third part of ungodly men.

TRUMPET AND VIAL PLAGUE #6—PART B	
Revelation 11:7–14: And when they shall have finished their testimony, the beast that ascendeth out of the bottomless pit shall make war against them, and shall overcome them, and kill them. And their dead bodies shall lie in the street of the great city, which spiritually is called Sodom and Egypt, where also our Lord was crucified. And they of the people and kindreds and tongues and nations shall see their dead bodies three days and an half, and shall not suffer their dead bodies to be put in graves. And they that dwell upon the earth shall rejoice over them, and make merry, and shall send gifts one to another; because these two prophets tormented them that dwelt on the earth. And after three days and an half the Spirit of life from God entered into them, and they stood upon their feet; and great fear fell upon them which saw them. And they heard a great voice from heaven saying unto them, Come up hither. And they ascended up to heaven in a cloud; and their enemies beheld them. And the same hour was there *a great earthquake,* and the tenth part of the city fell, and in the earthquake were slain of men seven thousand: and the remnant were affrighted, and gave glory to the God of heaven. *The second woe is past; and, behold, the third woe cometh quickly.*	Revelation 16:12–16: And the sixth angel poured out his vial upon the great river Euphrates; and the water thereof was dried up, that the way of the kings of the east might be prepared. And I saw three unclean spirits like frogs come out of the mouth of the dragon, and out of the mouth of the beast, and out of the mouth of the false prophet. For they are the spirits of devils, working miracles, which go forth unto the kings of the earth and of the whole world, to gather them to the battle of that great day of God Almighty. *Behold, I come as a thief. Blessed is he that watcheth, and keepeth his garments, lest he walk naked, and they see his shame.* And he gathered them together into a place called in the Hebrew tongue Armageddon.

It is important to review Revelation 11:7–14 to learn what happens with the two witnesses just prior to the conclusion of the second woe. Also, I have restated Revelation 16:12–16 in Part B above simply because these events will occur in the same time frame.

- The two witnesses will be overcome and killed by the Antichrist at the conclusion of their 3.5-year "ministry." According to my understanding of end times events, this will mark the beginning of the seventieth week of Daniel.

- The two witnesses will lie in the streets of Jerusalem for 3.5 days, and people of the earth will *rejoice* at their deaths and *send gifts* to one another because the causes of their many torments are now dead.
- After their bodies have lain in the street dead for 3.5 days, the Spirit of life from God will enter them, and they will be resurrected! This causes great fear in their enemies.
- A great voice from heaven will tell them to "Come up hither," and they will ascend up to heaven in a cloud.
- Their enemies will behold them ascending to heaven.
- Within one hour, there will be a great earthquake in the city, killing seven thousand people.

The murder of God's beloved two witnesses by Antichrist will lead to the dreadful abomination of desolation. Since the two witnesses die at the beginning of the seventieth week and lie dead in the street for 3.5 days, their resurrection will essentially occur "in the middle of the week." This will be *exactly* 1260 days after their ministry began at Passover 3.5 years earlier.

The Scripture says in Revelation 11:11 that their resurrection caused great fear, no doubt because the Antichrist's chief adversaries were alive again! However, there was probably joy on earth again when they ascended up to heaven in a cloud. The Scripture says in Revelation 11:12 that "their enemies beheld them" as they ascended to heaven.

It is most likely that *right after* God's voice calls the two witnesses into heaven, the Antichrist will enter the temple of God in Jerusalem, place his image inside as the object for humankind to worship, and desolate the temple. Why so soon after the resurrection and ascension of the two witnesses? Because the Scripture tells us in Daniel 9:27 that the abomination of desolation will occur in the middle of the week, the same time as the witnesses are resurrected. The Scripture says in Revelation 11:13 that *in the same hour* as their resurrection, there will be a great earthquake.

What does the Scripture tell people living in Jerusalem to do when they see Antichrist stand in the holy place? The message is to *flee into the mountains*. Why is there not time to linger? Because within that very hour, a great earthquake will occur, causing seven thousand people to die! And, the enemies are gathered! It will be a frantic and confusing time. Read Matthew 25:15–31 from the Olivet Discourse for more information.

In part A, looking at the sixth trumpet and vial, we saw the plague of 200 million death-causing horsemen and the gathering of the enemies of God to Armageddon due to the inducements of evil spirits.

In part B, we have encountered the events of the first 3.5 days of Daniel's seventieth week, which include:

- The death of the two witnesses at the beginning of Daniel's seventieth week
- The resurrection of the two witnesses in the middle of Daniel's seventieth week
- The abomination of desolation in the middle of Daniel's seventieth week
- The call to flee Jerusalem immediately when you see the abomination of desolation
- The great earthquake in the same hour that the two witnesses are resurrected

Let's go a bit deeper into the great end-time gathering that occurs during the sixth plague, as well as the call to flee Jerusalem in Luke 21:20–21. Most believe that this great gathering of armies and the call to flee Jerusalem pertain to the mid-point of a future seven-year tribulation. However, the seven-year tribulation is a shaky framework. I believe the end-time gathering of the sixth plague is inextricably connected to the call to flee Jerusalem in Luke's gospel. Please seriously consider that the context of these Scriptures is very near the second coming of Jesus and the cosmic events.

> And *when ye shall see Jerusalem compassed with armies*, then know that the desolation thereof is nigh. Then let them which are in Judaea *flee to the mountains*; and let them which are in the midst of it depart out; and let not them that are in the countries enter thereinto. For these be the *days of vengeance*, that all things which are written may be fulfilled. But woe unto them that are with child, and to them that give suck, in those days! for there shall be great distress in the land, and wrath upon this people. And they shall fall by the edge of the sword, and shall be led away captive into all nations: and Jerusalem shall be trodden down of the Gentiles, until the times of the Gentiles be fulfilled. And there shall be *signs in the sun, and in the moon, and in the stars*; and upon the earth distress of nations, with perplexity; the sea and the waves roaring; men's

hearts failing them for fear, and for looking after those things which are coming on the earth: for the powers of heaven shall be shaken. And *then shall they see the Son of man coming in a cloud with power and great glory.* (Luke 21:20–27)

I am fully aware that many Jews will be exiled to the wilderness and experience a miraculous provision of God for 1260 days (Revelation 12:6, 14). And while this destructive event in Jerusalem will occur approximately 3.5 years prior to the day of the Lord, that is not what is in view here. This is very important to sort out.

While Jerusalem and the surrounding area will experience desolation for a time, at some point the population of Jews in the land will revive once more (Ezekiel 38:12). This revival may occur for two primary reasons. One, the apparent willingness of some Jews to cooperate with the deceiver Antichrist (Daniel 11:23, 30, 32). Recall that Antichrist will come onto the scene peaceably, skillfully using flattery and deception (Daniel 11:21, 23–24). Two, seventy weeks prior to the day of the Lord, a commandment will go forth to restore and to build Jerusalem. In troublous times, great efforts will be made to rebuild a plaza area and wall. As such, a degree of prosperity will return to Jerusalem and its inhabitants. Unfortunately, it appears that such prosperity won't yield humble and fruitful hearts that honor God (Jeremiah 4:1–4).

In my opinion, the great end-time gathering will begin on the Feast of Trumpets ten days prior to the day of the Lord. The gathering has the purpose of robbing and spoiling, and due to the pride and arrogance of Antichrist and his followers, it ultimately has the evil intent of usurping Almighty God. But, this final gathering is in God's plan! We can read several Scriptures that depict this provocation and gathering in the last days prior to the return of Jesus (Luke 21:20, Revelation 16:12–14, Isaiah 10:5–6, 12; 42:24; Ezekiel 38:4, 9–12; Joel 3:2, 11–12; Zephaniah 3:8; Zechariah 12:2–3; 14:2).

Perhaps no Scripture summarizes it as well as Jeremiah 4. Let's review some key elements of this passage.

- The Jews have a hard heart and have not turned to the Lord (Jeremiah 4:1–4; 14, 17–18, 22). This parallels with the reason for the provocation given in Isaiah 10:6; 42:24.
- The inhabitants of Jerusalem have been deceived into a false peace (Jeremiah 4:10). This false peace is consistent with Ezekiel 38:8, 11, 14.

- The enemies will generally come from the north (Jeremiah 4:6). Likewise, this same fact is described in Ezekiel 38:15.
- The inhabitants of Jerusalem will become swiftly surrounded by their enemies. The gathering will happen as fast as storm clouds moving in, or a whirlwind, or a swift eagle (Jeremiah 4:13). This same swiftness is described in Ezekiel 38:9–10; 15–16.
- There will be a great gathering, a spoil, and travail (Jeremiah 4:6, 13, 17, 19–20, 30–31). These facts parallel with numerous Scriptures, including Ezekiel 38:12–13.
- Due to the impending tumult, the Jews will feel a need to leave their "unprotected" state (i.e. Ezekiel 38:11) and go find a fortified and protected place (Jeremiah 4:5).

Then, in context of this great gathering and the general chaos and fright of this time, we see the following notable fact.

- The whole city will flee because of the noise of the great gathering and the horsemen (Jeremiah 4:29–31). This is a climax point. The great tribulation that begins in the middle of the seventieth week will cause severe confusion, turmoil, and anguish.

We find further context for this fleeing (Jeremiah 4:29-31) to occur only *days* prior to the return of the Lord. What other characteristics can we identify from Jeremiah 4?

- We see evidence of cosmic events and a great shaking in the land (Jeremiah 4:23–24, 28). This same great shaking is evident in numerous Scriptures, including Ezekiel 38:19–20.
- There is the sound of the trumpet and the alarm of war (Jeremiah 4:21). I believe this gathering begins at the Feast of Trumpets, ten days prior to the Day of Atonement. The ten days leading up to Yom Kippur, or the Day of Atonement are called the ten days of repentance. Prophetically, the connection is obvious. This is a time of awakening and soul searching because the Lord is going to return soon and judgment day is coming!
- A striking reference is made regarding the physical presence of the Lord (Jeremiah 4:26). This is not a Scripture to avoid. The word for "presence" is *paniym* (Strong's H6440) and it means the actual face of a person in this context. This same physical presence of the Lord is depicted in Ezekiel 38:20.

In summary of our review of Jeremiah 4, we find solid scriptural support that the call to flee in Luke 21:20–21 is but a few *days* prior to the day of the Lord. It is when Jerusalem is compassed with armies (verse 20), during the great tribulation or days of vengeance (verse 22), when travail and great distress are in the land (verses 23–24), and when cosmic events occur and the Son of man comes with power and great glory (verses 25–27). This fleeing occurs at the end of this age just *days* prior to the day of the Lord, not 3.5 *years* prior!

Continuing on with our study of the sixth vial, we must note again the preresurrection/prerapture message in Revelation 16:15. This message refers to the thief-like coming of Jesus Christ: "Behold, I come as a thief." Not only will Jesus Christ return like a thief, but the day of the Lord will come like a thief (1 Thessalonians 5:2, 2 Peter 3:10). Both events are one and the same, much like how the resurrection and rapture will occur nearly simultaneously (1 Thessalonians 4:15–17). As stated before, the resurrection/rapture is *near but not here* at the time of the sixth vial plague.

This brings us to the sixth seal (Revelation 6:12–17). The sixth seal describes the cosmic events that precede the second coming of Jesus Christ. Consistent with the message and context of other Scriptures, my conclusion is that the second coming will occur just after great cosmic events in the heavens and earth. In other words, we should expect the second coming *right after* the sixth seal.

> And I beheld when he had opened the sixth seal, and, lo, there was a great earthquake; and the sun became black as sackcloth of hair, and the moon became as blood; And the stars of heaven fell unto the earth, even as a fig tree casteth her untimely figs, when she is shaken of a mighty wind. And the heaven departed as a scroll when it is rolled together; and every mountain and island were moved out of their places. And the kings of the earth, and the great men, and the rich men, and the chief captains, and the mighty men, and every bondman, and every free man, hid themselves in the dens and in the rocks of the mountains; And said to the mountains and rocks, Fall on us, and hide us from the face of him that sitteth on the throne, and from the wrath of the Lamb: For the great day of his wrath is come; and who shall be able to stand? (Revelation 6:12–17)

In addition to Matthew 24:29, Mark 13:24, and Luke 21:25, the following Scriptures agree that the cosmic events will occur just *before* the second coming of Jesus Christ:

And I will shew wonders in heaven above, and signs in the earth beneath; blood, and fire, and vapour of smoke: the sun shall be turned into darkness, and the moon into blood, before that great and notable day of the Lord come. (Acts 2:19–20)

The sun shall be turned into darkness, and the moon into blood, before the great and the terrible day of the Lord come. (Joel 2:31)

Behold, *the day of the Lord cometh*, cruel both with wrath and fierce anger, to lay the land desolate: and he shall destroy the sinners thereof out of it. *For the stars of heaven and the constellations thereof shall not give their light: the sun shall be darkened in his going forth, and the moon shall not cause her light to shine.* And I will punish the world for their evil, and the wicked for their iniquity; and I will cause the arrogancy of the proud to cease, and will lay low the haughtiness of the terrible. I will make a man more precious than fine gold; even a man than the golden wedge of Ophir. Therefore *I will shake the heavens*, and the earth shall remove out of her place, in the wrath of the Lord of hosts, and in the day of his fierce anger. (Isaiah 13:9–11)

When all of these Scriptures are taken together, it is very difficult to see anything other than the second coming of our Lord Jesus Christ and our gathering together unto Him at the conclusion of the sixth seal, even as the seventh seal, trumpet, and vial begin. We cannot ignore the preresurrection warning contained late in the book of Revelation in chapter 16. The weight of the scriptural evidence is substantial. In summary:

- **Sixth Vial:** The language in Revelation 16:15 refers to the famously recited verse of 1 Thessalonians 5:2: "The day of the Lord so cometh as a thief in the night." At the time of the sixth vial, the resurrection is *near but not here*.
- **Sixth Seal:** The language in Revelation 6:12–17 is almost identical to Matthew 24:29, Mark 13:24–25, Luke 21:25–26, Acts 2:19–20, Joel 2:31, Isaiah 13:9–11, and Isaiah 2:10–21. The cosmic events will occur *before* the resurrection.

This peak of evil at the dreadful and difficult time of the 6s leads us to the day of the Lord at the time of the 7s. The last trumpet will bring forth the long-awaited resurrection/rapture! So let's move to the last and final seal, trumpet, and vial plague. It is also the time of the seventh *thunder*, which we will look at in more detail below. Using Scripture to compare Scripture provides my heart with abundant assurance that these events will occur in the same time frame. The events line up and fit with an entirely biblically based eschatological framework, and the language is strikingly similar, as the text expresses a finality with the words "finished" and "it is done." And finally—it just makes plain sense to read them this way.

SEAL, TRUMPET, AND VIAL PLAGUE #7

The message of the sevens is conclusive, final, consistent, and complete. The parallels are distinct and obvious if we study the text closely. We will examine the seventh thunder here as well (Revelation 10:7).

Revelation 8:1, 3–5: And when he had opened *the seventh seal*, there was silence in heaven about the space of half an hour. And another angel came and stood at the altar, having a golden censer; and there was given unto him much incense, that he should offer it with the prayers of all saints upon the golden altar which was before the throne. And the smoke of the incense, which came with the prayers of the saints, ascended up before God out of the angel's hand. And the angel took the censer, and filled it with fire of the altar, and cast it into the earth: and there were *voices, and thunderings, and lightnings, and an earthquake.* Revelation 10:7: But in the days [Strong's G2250—"the time space between dawn and dark, or the whole twenty-four hours"] of *the voice of the seventh angel, when he shall begin to sound, the mystery of God should be finished, as he hath declared to his servants the prophets.*	Revelation 11:15–19: And *the seventh angel sounded;* and there were great voices in heaven, saying, *The kingdoms of this world are become the kingdoms of our Lord, and of his Christ; and he shall reign for ever and ever.* And the four and twenty elders, which sat before God on their seats, fell upon their faces, and worshipped God, saying, We give thee thanks, O Lord God Almighty, which art, and wast, and art to come; because thou hast taken to thee thy great power, and hast reigned. And the nations were angry, and thy wrath is come*, and the time of the dead, that they should be judged, and that thou shouldest give reward unto thy servants the prophets, and to the saints, and them that fear thy name, small and great*; and shouldest destroy them which destroy the earth. And the temple of God was opened in heaven, and there was seen in his temple the ark of his testament: and *there were lightnings, and voices, and thunderings, and an earthquake, and great hail.*	Revelation 16:17–21: And *the seventh angel poured out his vial into the air;* and there came a great voice out of the temple of heaven, from the throne, saying, *It is done.* And *there were voices, and thunders, and lightnings; and there was a great earthquake,* such as was not since men were upon the earth, so mighty an earthquake, and so great. And the great city was divided into three parts, and the cities of the nations fell: and great Babylon came in remembrance before God, to give unto her the cup of the wine of the fierceness of his wrath. And every island fled away, and the mountains were not found. And *there fell upon men a great hail out of heaven*, every stone about the weight of a talent: and men blasphemed God because of the plague of the hail; for the plague thereof was exceeding great.

Before moving on, let's highlight several of the details from the seventh seal, seventh thunder, seventh trumpet and seventh vial passages.

I believe that Jesus the Lamb will first open the seventh seal. Due to the far-reaching consequences of the seventh seal, there will be silence in heaven for thirty minutes. What a sober moment of time! The prophesies of the resurrection and rapture will soon occur. The prophesies of the salvation of corporate remnant Israel will soon occur. The prophesies of the fury, vengeance and the "fierceness of His wrath" will soon occur. And then it happens, the thunder voice begins to sound. When he begins to sound the mystery of God will come to an end and be accomplished! The seventh and final trumpet will sound to declare the transfer of all authority to Jesus Christ. The seventh vial will be poured out and a great voice *from the throne* in heaven will say "It is done." There will be great joy and worship in heaven resulting from the resurrection and rapture, and great anger and fear on earth because God's wrath "is come." When the temple of God is opened in heaven there will be voices, thunderings, lightnings and a mighty earthquake. The plague of hail that will fall out of heaven will be unbelievably massive.

While each of the seven vial plagues are called "the wrath of God," the final plague and the "cup of the wine of the fierceness of His wrath" (Revelation 16:19) will lead the ungodly on earth to understand that "Thy wrath is come" (Revelation 11:18). In other words, the day of the Lord will be the *ultimate wrath*, the fulfillment of the consistent message of the fury and wrath that God "declared to His servants the prophets" to occur on the great and notable *day* of the Lord. This ultimate wrath is what we studied in the chapter on the day of the Lord.

V. REVELATION 10— THE MYSTERY OF THE SEVEN THUNDERS

This passage is truly a mystery. When John was about to write down what the seven thunders uttered, a voice from heaven said, "seal up those things which the seven thunders uttered,and write them not." If not sealed, I believe that synchronization between the thunders, trumpets, and vials would be obvious. Though sealed, what we do know is that the seventh verse confirms to us the importance of the seventh angel. In essence, when the seventh angel begins to sound, the mystery of God (i.e. the present church age via the gospel) will be accomplished! This correlates with the great voice in Revelation 16:17

declaring "It is done" and the great voice in Revelation 11:15 declaring that Jesus Christ now has dominion, and He shall reign for ever and ever.

Let's now peer into a great mystery of Revelation 10.

> And I saw another mighty angel come down from heaven, clothed with a cloud: and a rainbow was upon his head, and his face was as it were the sun, and his feet as pillars of fire: And he had in his hand a little book open: and he set his right foot upon the sea, and his left foot on the earth, And cried with a loud voice, as when a lion roareth: and when he had cried, seven thunders uttered their voices. (Revelation 10:1–3)

Who might the mighty angel described in Revelation 10:1–3 be? Prior to evaluating the characteristics given in the first three verses, it is necessary to review a somewhat complicated episode found in Daniel 7 and Daniel 8. Once this is done, we can make some connections to at least bring forth a candidate for the mighty angel using biblical support.

The altercation in heaven between Satan and Michael is the event that we need to hone in on.

Daniel 8:9–14 relates a disruption in heaven, not on earth. I believe this event is connected to the "war in heaven" as described in Revelation 12 and also the accounts in Isaiah 14:12–14 and Ezekiel 28:16–17. Daniel 7:7–10, 13–14, 22, and 26–28 also shed additional light and detail about this event. What we see from these four Scriptures is summarized as follows:

- The little horn, or Antichrist, will rise up to power as ruler of the beast kingdom.
- The little horn will wax great with personal pride, ruling territory, kingship authority, and great aspirations. His great aspirations of heart, according to Isaiah 14, include the following statements: "*I will* ascend into heaven," "*I will* exalt my throne above the stars of God," and "*I will* be like the most High."
- Satan will attempt to take the throne from God but he will experience defeat. The devil/Satan, the accuser of the brethren, and all of his angels are then cast out into the earth by Michael.
- As a result of the battle in heaven between Satan and Michael, physical structures in the throne room of God are ransacked (Daniel 7:9 and Daniel 8:11–12).
- The daily (continual, perpetual) worship of God in heaven is altered by reason of Satan's pride and the ensuing altercation (Daniel 8:11, 13).

- The angel says it will be 2300 days (the Hebrew says 2300 "evenings and mornings") before the sanctuary will be "made right" again (Daniel 8:14).
- God Almighty sits, the judgment is set, and the books of evidence are opened (Daniel 7:9–10, 22, 26).
- The Son of Man, the Lord Jesus Himself, comes with the clouds of heaven (which most likely is a large number of angels) and is brought before God (Daniel 7:13). The verdict is read, and Jesus is given glory, a kingdom that will never be destroyed, and an everlasting dominion (Daniel 7:14, 27). In other words, 2300 evenings and mornings after the war in heaven, Satan and Antichrist are no longer going to have authority on the earth. Satan will experience his defeat! The court in heaven will rule, and judgment will be made!

If you recall from section IV of chapter 2, the time period of 2300 "evenings and mornings" of Daniel 8:14 is in a sanctuary context. This carries with it the likelihood that the 2300 evenings and mornings imply a number of sacrifices, a morning and an evening sacrifice. This would mean 1150 morning sacrifices and 1150 evening sacrifices, or 1150 days. I strongly believe we should interpret this as 1150 days instead of 2300 days due to the following hard facts:

- This episode occurs *after* the little horn comes to power, and his power lasts 1260 days.
- 1150 days from Tisha B'Av takes us to one to two days after the abomination of desolation, which is particularly interesting timing in light of the End-Times Chart and the events of the seventieth week of Daniel!

We previously noted that Jesus comes with the clouds of heaven and is brought before God to hear the verdict (Daniel 7:13). This seems to imply that the Son of Man is not at the Father's right hand during this time of 1150 days when normal sanctuary activities have been discontinued in heaven. If so, where is our Lord Jesus going to be during this time? This brings us back to the initial question of "who might the mighty angel be that is described in Revelation 10:1–3"?

First, let's review one more fact of Scripture before analyzing the characteristics of the mighty angel. According to Revelation 15:8, during the time when the seven vial plagues are poured out, *no man* is able to enter the temple. Does this include the Son of Man, Jesus Christ?

> And the temple was filled with smoke from the glory of God, and from his power; and no man was able to enter into the temple, till the seven plagues of the seven angels were fulfilled. (Revelation 15:8)

And if He is not at the right hand of God, where does our Lord Jesus go during this time of 2300 evenings and mornings? My suspicion is that Revelation 10 could be a picture of Jesus Christ surrounded by a cloud of angels. The text reads that the angel is "clothed with a cloud," and as was mentioned, this is the "clothing" that the Son of Man is wearing as He is brought near the Ancient of Days at the conclusion of the 1150 days, perhaps being led back from His position on earth enshrouded by an angelic host.

Let's review the details given in Revelation 10:1–3 and then review comparable passages to see if there are sufficient parallels to conclude that this is the image of the Lord Jesus.

> And I saw another mighty angel come down from heaven, clothed with a cloud: and a rainbow was upon his head, and his face was as it were the sun, and his feet as pillars of fire: and he had in his hand a little book open: and he set his right foot upon the sea, and his left foot on the earth, and cried with a loud voice, as when a lion roareth: and when he had cried, seven thunders uttered their voices. (Revelation 10:1–3)

Notice that there is a rainbow upon his head. The only places in Scripture that we find a rainbow in relation to a person are in John's description of the heavenly throne room in Revelation 4 and Ezekiel's description of the glory of the LORD.

> . . . and there was *a rainbow round about the throne,* in sight like unto an emerald. (Revelation 4:3)

> *As the appearance of the bow that is in the cloud in the day of rain,* so was the appearance of the brightness round about. *This was the appearance of the likeness of the glory of the* LORD. And when I saw it, I fell upon my face, and I heard a voice of one that spake. (Ezekiel 1:28)

The mighty angel's face was like the sun. Look at these descriptions of Jesus in other places in Scripture:

His head and his hairs were white like wool, as white as snow; and *his eyes were as a flame of fire*. (Revelation 1:14)

... and was transfigured before them: and *his face did shine as the sun*, and his raiment was white as the light. (Matthew 17:2)

And he had in his right hand seven stars: and out of his mouth went a sharp twoedged sword: and *his countenance was as the sun shineth in his strength*. (Revelation 1:16)

And I saw as the colour of amber, as *the appearance of fire* round about within it, from the appearance of his loins even upward. (Ezekiel 1:27)

And it came to pass in the sixth year, in the sixth month, in the fifth day of the month, as I sat in mine house, and the elders of Judah sat before me, that the hand of the Lord GOD fell there upon me. Then I beheld, and lo a likeness as the appearance of fire: from the appearance of his loins even downward, fire; and *from his loins even upward, as the appearance of brightness*, as the colour of amber. (Ezekiel 8:1–2)

His feet were as pillars of fire:

And *his feet* like unto fine brass, *as if they burned in a furnace*; and his voice as the sound of many waters. (Revelation 1:15)

... *and from the appearance of his loins even downward, I saw as it were the appearance of fire*, and it had *brightness* round about. (Ezekiel 1:27)

And it came to pass in the sixth year, in the sixth month, in the fifth day of the month, as I sat in mine house, and the elders of Judah sat before me, that the hand of the Lord GOD fell there upon me. Then I beheld, and lo a likeness *as the appearance of fire: from the appearance of his loins even downward, fire*; and from his loins even upward, as the appearance of brightness, as the colour of amber. (Ezekiel 8:1–2)

His voice was loud, as when a lion roars:

And one of the elders saith unto me, Weep not: behold, *the Lion of the tribe of Juda*, the Root of David, hath prevailed to open the book, and to loose the seven seals thereof. (Revelation 5:5)

In Ezekiel 1:28, we read that the prophet Ezekiel's reaction to seeing the appearance of the likeness of the glory of the LORD was equivalent to John's when he saw the Lord Jesus in Revelation 1. In addition, Ezekiel was caused to eat the roll of a book, just as John was made to eat the book in the hand of the mighty angel in Revelation 10, and the impact of sweetness in the mouth and bitterness afterward was identical! Lastly, the figure in Revelation 10 has an open book in his hand. According to Revelation 5:5–7, the one who is able to take the book from the Father's right hand is none other than the Lamb of God!

> As the appearance of the bow that is in the cloud in the day of rain, so was the appearance of the brightness round about. *This was the appearance of the likeness of the glory of the* LORD. And when I saw it, *I fell upon my face*, and I heard a voice of one that spake. (Ezekiel 1:28)

> And when I looked, behold, *an hand* was sent unto me; and, lo, *a roll of a book* was therein; and he spread it before me; and it was written within and without: and there was written therein lamentations, and mourning, and woe. Moreover he said unto me, Son of man, eat that thou findest; *eat this roll*, and go speak unto the house of Israel. So I opened my mouth, and he caused me to eat that roll. And he said unto me, Son of man, cause thy belly to eat, and fill thy bowels with this roll that I give thee. Then did I eat it; and *it was in my mouth as honey for sweetness*. So the spirit lifted me up, and took me away, and *I went in bitterness*, in the heat of my spirit; but the hand of the LORD was strong upon me. (Ezekiel 2:9–10; 3:1–3, 14)

> And one of the elders saith unto me, Weep not: behold, *the Lion of the tribe of Juda*, the Root of David, hath prevailed to open the book, and to loose the seven seals thereof. And I beheld, and, lo, in the midst of the throne and of the four beasts, and in the midst of the elders, stood a Lamb as it had been slain, having seven horns and seven eyes, which are the seven Spirits of God sent forth into all the earth. And *he came and took the book out of the right hand of him that sat upon the throne*. (Revelation 5:5–7)

> And the voice which I heard from heaven spake unto me again, and said, Go and take *the little book* which is open in the hand of the angel which standeth upon the sea and upon the earth. And I went unto the angel, and said unto him, Give me the little book. And he said unto me, *Take it, and eat it up*; and it shall make thy belly *bitter*, but it shall be in thy mouth *sweet as honey*. And I took the little book out of the angel's hand, and ate it up; and it was in my mouth sweet as honey: and as soon as I had eaten it, my belly was bitter. (Revelation 10:8–10)

If it is Jesus standing with His right foot upon the sea and His left foot on the earth, the seven thunders could potentially correlate with the timing of the trumpets and vials, since during this time we expect that the wrath of God is being dispensed upon earth in the form of the vial plagues. Revelation 15:8 notes that the temple is literally filled with smoke from the glory and power of God during the time when the plagues are released. This could be related to the description given by Daniel, which states that God's throne was like the fiery flame and His wheels as burning fire, and a fiery stream issued and came forth from before Him. Thousands upon thousands of angels bore witness to this sight, but no man was able to be in the presence of God at this time, as His mighty power was overwhelming.

> And *the temple was filled with smoke* from the glory of God, and from his power; and no man was able to enter into the temple, till the seven plagues of the seven angels were fulfilled. (Revelation 15:8)

> I beheld till the thrones were cast down, and the Ancient of days did sit, whose garment was white as snow, and the hair of his head like the pure wool: his throne was like the *fiery flame*, and his wheels as *burning fire*. A *fiery stream* issued and came forth from before him: thousand thousands ministered unto him, and ten thousand times ten thousand stood before him: the judgment was set, and the books were opened. (Daniel 7:9–10)

A separation between Jesus and God the Father at this time would not appear to violate Scripture. We are told in Matthew 5:35 that the earth is the footstool of the Lord. Also, several New Testament passages hearken back to David's Psalm 110:1, quoted below. If Jesus truly is the mighty angel standing upon earth, then all of the enemies of the Lord would *literally* be the footstool of the Lord Jesus.

> But I say unto you, Swear not at all; neither by heaven; for it is God's throne: nor by the earth; for it is his footstool: neither by Jerusalem; for it is the city of the great King. (Matthew 5:34–35)

> The Lord said unto my Lord, *Sit thou* at my right hand, *until* I make thine enemies thy footstool. (Psalm 110:1)

> This Jesus hath God raised up, whereof we all are witnesses. Therefore being by the right hand of God exalted, and having received of the Father the promise of the Holy Ghost, he hath shed forth this, which ye now see

and hear. For David is not ascended into the heavens: but he saith himself, The LORD said unto my Lord, *Sit thou* on my right hand, *until* I make thy foes thy footstool. (Act 2:32–35)

The timing of the war in heaven and the 1150 days fit marvelously with the End-Times Chart, as noted in the "Eschatological Framework" chapter. During the 1150 days there would be no seals to unloose, as the fifth seal essentially represents the bulk of the 3.5-year tribulation and in all likelihood would be opened prior to the trumpet blasts and vial plagues. And if the Son of Man is unable to be in the temple during this time, a likely destination is to fulfill the position of the mighty angel seen by John.

I noted previously that the beginning point of the 1150 days and the "war in heaven" correlates with the sober fast day Tisha B'Av. Tisha B'Av is an annual day of mourning on the ninth of Av. Numerous Jewish tragedies, such as the destruction of the first temple by the Babylonians in 586 BC and the destruction of the second temple by the Romans in 70 AD, occurred on this exact date. I think it is sobering and amazing that this also will correlate with the time Satan mounts up with pride and ransacks the heavenly temple.

This again is another example of the fit and alignment of the eschatological framework. Counting 1150 days from Tisha B'Av results in a date that is just after the abomination of desolation and just prior to the Day of Atonement, or what I believe to be the future day of the Lord.

Since the 1150-day time period extends just beyond the abomination of desolation, it would enable this "angel," perhaps the Lord Jesus Himself, to witness the despicable and blasphemous act of the Antichrist's abomination of desolation and then turn to Jehovah God and "lift up his hand to heaven, and sware by him that liveth for ever and ever, who created heaven, and the things that therein are, and the earth, and the things that therein are, and the sea, and the things which are therein, *that there should be time no longer*" (Revelation 10:6). He appears to be referencing the evil and blasphemous act of Antichrist and declaring that his time is *done* and *finished*. The evidence against Antichrist and Satan himself, topped off by the climatic and blasphemous abomination of desolation, is sufficient.

The Lord Jesus is depicted in Daniel 7:13 as coming with the clouds of heavens to the Ancient of days to receive the verdict. This fits with the description of the angel in Revelation 10:1. Not long after the verdict is given, we will have the sixth seal being opened by the Lamb (just prior to the seventh seal, seventh thunder, seventh trumpet and seventh vial), and the cosmic events will occur as the second woe is finished. Then, at some unknown hour after the great cosmic events, the Lord Jesus will come to gather His elect at the command of God, and the day of the Lord will commence.

VI. REVELATION 13— THE BEASTS AND THE MARK, NAME, AND NUMBER OF ANTICHRIST

Let's review Revelation 13 in three parts. Part 1 is an analysis of the end-times beast kingdom and the beast/Antichrist, part 2 is a review of another beast that arises called the false prophet, and part 3 is my attempt to understand the mark, the name, and number of Antichrist.

Part 1: The End-Times Beast Kingdom and the Beast/Antichrist

Let's begin at the beginning of Revelation 13, where the vision of the seven-headed, ten-horned beast is given. Both Daniel and the apostle John were given visions pertaining to the latter days. I believe that the beast witnessed by the apostle John is the same beast witnessed by Daniel in his second vision. The descriptions are identical. As summarized below, Revelation 13:1–2 is a composite image of the beasts described in Daniel 7:3–7. This same beast is also seen by John in Revelation 17:3.

> And I stood upon the sand of the sea, and saw a beast rise up out of the sea, having *seven heads and ten horns*, and upon his horns ten crowns, and upon his heads *the name of blasphemy*. And the beast which I saw was *like unto a leopard, and his feet were as the feet of a bear, and his mouth as the mouth of a lion*: and the dragon [i.e. Satan] gave him his power, and his seat, and great authority. (Revelation 13:1–2)

> So he carried me away in the spirit into the wilderness: and I saw a woman sit upon *a scarlet coloured beast, full of names of blasphemy, having seven heads and ten horns*. (Revelation 17:3)

Daniel 7:4–7	Revelation 13 & 17
v4. A lion .... with 1 Head and 0 Horns	The mouth of a lion (loud roar)
v5. A bear .... with 1 Head and 0 Horns	The feet of a bear (fast runner)
v6. A leopard .... with 4 Heads and 0 Horns	Like a leopard (leaps, strong, hides well)
v7. A 4th Beast .. with 1 Head and 10 Horns	A Beast having 7 Heads and 10 Horns
Composite beast with 7 Heads and 10 Horns =	7 Heads and 10 Horns

The beast described in Revelation incorporates all of the same animals mentioned in Daniel 7. In addition, the total number of heads and horns on the Revelation beast/beast kingdom equals the sum of the heads and horns on Daniel's beast/beast kingdom. In my opinion, both Scriptures are referring to the same end-times beast/beast kingdom since the composite image of Daniel's beast *is the same as* Revelation's beast.

Some key characteristics of the beast, the Antichrist or the beast kingdom are noted in Revelation 13:3–10 as follows:

> And I saw one of his heads as it were wounded to death; and his deadly wound was healed: and all the world wondered after the beast. And they worshipped the dragon which gave power unto the beast: and they worshipped the beast, saying, Who is like unto the beast? who is able to make war with him? And there was given unto him a mouth speaking great things and blasphemies; and power was given unto him to continue forty and two months. And he opened his mouth in blasphemy against God, to blaspheme his name, and his tabernacle, and them that dwell in heaven. And it was given unto him to make war with the saints, and to overcome them: and power was given him over all kindreds, and tongues, and nations. And all that dwell upon the earth shall worship him, whose names are not written in the book of life of the Lamb slain from the foundation of the world. If any man have an ear, let him hear. He that leadeth into captivity shall go into captivity: he that killeth with the sword must be killed with the sword. Here is the patience and the faith of the saints. (Revelation 13:3–10)

Notice:

- He experienced some type of cure or revival from a deadly wound
- All the world (either a specific region or the entire globe) wondered (marveled, admired) after him
- He is a great orator who can speak great things, including blasphemies against God and God's people
- He will have power for forty-two months
- He will make war with the saints and overcome them
- He will have influence and power over all kindreds, and tongues, and nations

This will be discussed in greater detail in the chapter on Daniel, but for our high-level review now, the "beast" appears to represent a kingdom (i.e. the beast kingdom) and a person (i.e. the beast/Antichrist). We should not expect

THE REVELATION OF JESUS CHRIST • 187

to see a person rise up from the sea with seven actual heads and ten actual horns. The great red dragon in Revelation 12 is also described as having seven heads and ten horns. This beast kingdom is a worldly, ungodly, Satan-influenced power. As the chapter on Daniel will indicate, the heads represent past kingdoms that have persecuted and afflicted God's people throughout history. A final leader, the Antichrist, will arise in the future to lead a final end-times beast kingdom during the 3.5-year tribulation.

Part 2: The False Prophet

Another beast, one with two horns, is seen in Revelation 13:11–18. Key characteristics and activities of the two-horned beast are as follows:

> And I beheld *another beast* coming up out of the earth; and he had two horns like a lamb, and he spake as a dragon. And he exerciseth all the power of the first beast before him, and causeth the earth and them which dwell therein to worship the first beast, whose deadly wound was healed. And *he doeth great wonders*, so that he maketh fire come down from heaven on the earth in the sight of men, and *deceiveth them that dwell on the earth* by the means of *those miracles which he had power to do* in the sight of the beast; saying to them that dwell on the earth, that they should make an image to the beast, which had the wound by a sword, and did live. And he had power to give life unto the image of the beast, that the image of the beast should both speak, and cause that as many as would not worship the image of the beast should be killed. And he causeth all, both small and great, rich and poor, free and bond, to receive a mark in their right hand, or in their foreheads: and that no man might buy or sell, save he that had the mark, or the name of the beast, or the number of his name. Here is wisdom. Let him that hath understanding count the number of the beast: for it is the number of a man; and his number is Six hundred threescore and six. (Revelation 13:11–18)

- He is the one Scripture defines in Revelation 19:20 as the "false prophet"
  - Revelation 19:20: "And the beast was taken, and with him *the false prophet* that wrought *miracles* before him, with which *he deceived* them that had received the mark of the beast, and them that worshipped his image. These both were cast alive into a lake of fire burning with brimstone."
- He has the same powers as the first beast, the Antichrist

- He causes earth dwellers to worship Antichrist
- He performs mighty miracles, such as calling fire to come down from heaven onto the earth in the sight of men
- He deceives earth dwellers because of the miracles that he has the power to perform alongside the Antichrist
- He causes earth dwellers to create an image to the Antichrist
- He has the miraculous power to give life to the image of the Antichrist so that the image can speak
- He causes those who do not worship the image of Antichrist to be killed
- He causes all (i.e. "all manner of person," whether small, great, rich, poor, etc.) to receive a mark of the beast in their right hand or in their forehead, which enables that person to buy and sell

The false prophet is one with enormous satanic influence and power, very much like the Antichrist (whom Revelation simply calls "the beast"). They work in tandem. Similar to the Godhead Trinity, this all may be a part of Satan's trinity, comprised of Satan, Antichrist, and the False Prophet. In fact, it wouldn't surprise me if this miracle-working figure, who speaks like a dragon, rises to power in connection with Michael's overthrow of Satan to the earth.

Part 3: The Mark, Name, and Number of Antichrist

What is the mark, the name, and the number of the beast? There are actually four forms that denote the beast, since there is also an image raised of him. The analogy I can think of is this. Pick the college you attended. In my case, that is Kansas State University. I would equate the image, the mark, the name, and the number of Kansas State University as follows:

- The name: Kansas State University
- The number: KSU
- The mark: Powercat logo
- The image: Willie the Wildcat mascot

Readers of the Scripture are told in Revelation 13:18 that the number of Antichrist is 666. However, why does it say "here is wisdom" and "let him that hath understanding count the number of the beast" when it tells us in plain sight that his number is 666? How much counting do we have to do, or how much wisdom do we need to have, in order to decipher six hundred threescore and six? Not much. But that is not the point.

I don't believe for a moment that Antichrist will go parading around with a 666 moniker on his shirt. He will not tout himself as "the Antichrist" but rather as someone to be lauded as a god himself. Likely, the Antichrist will be deceived into believing that he truly has an opportunity to seize power and authority from God and to thwart the plans of God if only he makes the right calculations and performs wisely and valiantly. Thanks be to God, we know how the story ends.

Let's review some clues to see what we may or may not be able to understand today about this mysterious mark, name, and number of Antichrist.

Clue 1: Deceitfulness of Antichrist

One of the main attributes of the Antichrist is deception. He is tightly knit with Satan, who is an angel of light and a deceiver at his core, able to make that which is false appear true (Revelation 20:3). I believe that followers of Antichrist will believe that they are on the right path, and doing the right thing. Let's review these deceitful attributes.

- Antichrist will obtain rule of the beast kingdom by "flatteries" (Daniel 11:21). From Strong's Concordance, this means he will use smooth, soft, and affectionate words, when in reality he is anything but smooth, soft, and affectionate!
- Antichrist will understand "dark sentences" (Daniel 8:23). From Strong's Concordance, this means he is an expert in puzzles, tricks, conundrums, proverbs, riddles, and hard questions.
- Antichrist will corrupt by flatteries (Daniel 11:32). From Strong's Concordance, this means that he will pollute and profane by smoothness.
- Antichrist will forecast his devices against established strongholds (Daniel 11:24). From Strong's Concordance, this means he will weave, fabricate, and plot his cunning plans and purposes to accomplish his desires.
- Antichrist will be able to give people false security when his real intent is to steal, kill, and destroy (Daniel 11:24, John 10:10).
- Antichrist will "have intelligence with them that forsake the holy covenant" (Daniel 11:30). From Strong's Concordance, this means that he will deal with these people in a cunning, eloquent, and skillful manner.

Clue 2: Deceitfulness of the False Prophet

> . . . and deceiveth them that dwell on the earth by the means of those miracles which he had power to do in the sight of the beast; saying to them that dwell on the earth, that they should make an image to the beast, which had the wound by a sword, and did live. (Revelation 13:14)

The false prophet will deceive by means of the miracles that he is able to perform. These miracles will cause people to make an image to the beast. The miracles will also cause people to receive the mark of the beast and worship the image of the beast (Revelation 19:20).

What we can we learn from these first two clues? Based on the deception inherent in Antichrist and the false prophet, and the evil they represent as allies of Satan, we shouldn't expect people who have the number 666 or a logo of a red dragon with a pitchfork emblazoned on their forehead or wrist. Remember, the beast's ways are deceptive, smooth, and subtle.

Those people who are:

a) unarmed with the Sword of the Lord (i.e. the Holy Scriptures)
b) not walking in a trusting, diligent, and faithful relationship with God and our Lord Jesus Christ
c) without faith, and
d) not under the influence and guidance of the Spirit of God

will risk falling prey to this evil influence and pledging their allegiance and alliance to Antichrist. To them it will seem right, proper, and maybe even moral to do so. The "great words" that Antichrist speaks will lead them to surrender to this "almighty," miracle-working figure, so much so that in their eyes he will be worthy of an image to be created and worshipped! We can call this spiritual darkness, or blindness. What a terrible fate to those who take the mark or bear the name or worship the image!

Based on these first two clues alone, if there is a physical mark, I don't have any idea what the "mark" will look like, nor do I know what Antichrist's "name" will be—or even if the "name" of Antichrist is the actual name of the person or possibly the religious/governmental entity that he represents. However, the Scripture doesn't teach us to decipher, in advance of its arrival, what the mark or name of the beast might be.

So what *are* we supposed to know? The Scripture says plainly these three things:

Here is wisdom.

1: Let him of understanding *count his number*.
2: His number is *the number of a man*.
3: His number is 666.

Let's move to the third clue of Antichrist and see if this clue will help us move closer to understanding his number of 666.

Clue 3: Antichrist Is an Arrogant Blasphemer Against God

According to Webster's Dictionary, to "blaspheme" means "to speak of the Supreme Being in terms of impious irreverence; to revile or speak reproachfully of God, or the Holy Spirit." We know that Jesus was accused of blasphemy against God by stating truthfully that He was the Son of God (Mark 14:62).

> But he held his peace, and answered nothing. Again the high priest asked him, and said unto him, Art thou the Christ, the Son of the Blessed? *And Jesus said, I am*: and ye shall see the Son of man sitting on the right hand of power, and coming in the clouds of heaven. Then the high priest rent his clothes, and saith, What need we any further witnesses? *Ye have heard the blasphemy*: what think ye? And they all condemned him to be guilty of death. (Mark 14:61–64)

Blasphemy is one of Antichrist's most prominent qualities. He is a blasphemer in his very nature.

> And I stood upon the sand of the sea, and saw a beast rise up out of the sea, having seven heads and ten horns, and upon his horns ten crowns, and *upon his heads the name of blasphemy*. (Revelation 13:1)

> And there was given unto him a mouth *speaking great things and blasphemies*; and power was given unto him to continue forty and two months. And *he opened his mouth in blasphemy against God*, to blaspheme his name, and his tabernacle, and them that dwell in heaven. (Revelation 13:5–6)

> So he carried me away in the spirit into the wilderness: and I saw a woman sit upon a scarlet coloured beast, *full of names of blasphemy*, having seven heads and ten horns. (Revelation 17:3)

In addition, Scripture tells us the Antichrist is filled with arrogance and pride.

> And *he shall speak great words against the most High*, and shall wear out the saints of the most High, and think to change times and laws: and they

shall be given into his hand until a time and times and the dividing of time. (Daniel 7:25)

And through his policy [intelligence/wisdom] also he shall cause craft [deceit/fraud] to prosper in his hand; and *he shall magnify himself* [pride] *in his heart*, and by peace [false security] shall destroy many: *he shall also stand up against the Prince of princes*; but he shall be broken without hand. (Daniel 8:25)

The ultimate blasphemy will be carried out when Antichrist in his great pride commits the abomination of desolation.

When ye therefore shall see the abomination of desolation, spoken of by Daniel the prophet, *stand in the holy place*, (whoso readeth, let him understand:) . . . (Matthew 24:15)

At the time appointed he shall return, and come toward the south; but it shall not be as the former, or as the latter. For the ships of Chittim shall come against him: therefore he shall be grieved, and return, and have indignation against the holy covenant: so shall he do; he shall even return, and have intelligence with them that forsake the holy covenant. And arms shall stand on his part, and *they shall pollute the sanctuary of strength, and shall take away the daily sacrifice, and they shall place the abomination that maketh desolate*. And such as do wickedly against the covenant shall he corrupt by flatteries: but the people that do know their God shall be strong, and do exploits. (Daniel 11:29–32)

It is likely that the Antichrist and the false prophet will enter the temple in Jerusalem and "place" the image of the beast there as a blasphemous object to be worshipped.

And the king shall do according to his will; and *he shall exalt himself, and magnify himself above every god*, and shall speak marvellous things against the God of gods, and shall prosper till the indignation be accomplished: for that that is determined shall be done. Neither shall he regard the God of his fathers, nor the desire of women, nor regard any god: for *he shall magnify himself above all*. (Daniel 11:36–37)

And he shall confirm the covenant with many for one week: and *in the midst of the week he shall cause the sacrifice and the oblation to cease, and for the overspreading of abominations he shall make it desolate*, even until the consummation, and that determined shall be poured upon the desolate. (Daniel 9:27)

Who opposeth and exalteth himself above all that is called God, or that is worshipped; *so that he as God sitteth in the temple of God, shewing himself that he is God.* (2 Thessalonians 2:4)

We know without any doubt that Antichrist will be a proud blasphemer. And one day he will commit the ultimate, horrible, and abominable sin of desolating the temple of God with his person and his image as THE ONE and THE OBJECT to be worshipped above all that is in the world, even the God of heaven Himself. Let's couple this understanding with my proposed eschatological framework.

A Look at the Numbers

I personally cannot see the benefit in using a code methodology to decipher the identity of Antichrist. Is it the Lord's preference for us to read and comprehend the book of Revelation or to go around using various formulas to see if we can find a match between this person or that organization with the dreaded number of 666? Many organizations and men have fit the bill of such calculations—but to what benefit? Is this the way of God? Rather, Scripture provides sufficient detail that will aid sincere believers in identifying the Antichrist when he rises to power.

So here is my take on the purpose and benefit—indeed the wisdom—of this number. The number has given me a measure of peace and assurance, sort of a stamp of approval, that its real value is not in identifying a particular person but in understanding how this number is scripturally tied to the peak of a man's pride and blasphemy. While the eschatological framework I have put together may be a unique perspective compared to traditional interpretations, I believe it is as biblically sound and literal as one can be with these end-times Scriptures. That being said, the right framework also allows for a fascinating alignment of the sixth and seventh seals, thunders, trumpets, and vials to become clear and plain. And here we find another fascinating alignment, because when we consider that the blasphemous abomination of desolation occurs just prior to the day of the Lord in the middle of the seventieth week of Daniel—a time when *man* exalts himself literally and physically as God in the temple of God—we can also count the number of this time and see that it is 666. We can see that the sixth thunder, sixth trumpet, and sixth vial also occur (likely on the Feast of Trumpets) near the start of the seventieth week of Daniel, which leads directly to the day of the Lord. By counting from one to six three separate times, we can make the connection between these collective events and conclude that the ultimate blasphemy—*man* declaring himself as God in the temple—is directly connected to the number 666. As I look back on my personal experience, I really believe the number is for the purpose of scriptural understanding as opposed to deciphering a connection with a specific man using codes or formulas.

To Recap and Conclude

Will we know who the Antichrist is before he rises to power? Not necessarily. But once he does, the key is not to join rank in any way with the Antichrist, because he will be a deceitful, blasphemous, proud *man* who will think that he is as good or better than Almighty God. Despite the cost, we must remain loyal to God. Any obedience to the Antichrist will come at a great eternal cost, even though it might provide an appearance of temporary fulfillment through an abatement of persecution or the ability to gain financially. We should avoid anything (his name, his initials, his logo, or his image) that could link or affiliate us with his "team."

The crescendo of Antichrist's performance will climax at the time of the dreaded sixes, but we must persevere, steadfast in our faith, all the way until the second coming of Jesus Christ at the time of the sevens. A wise practice is to look at the lives of the early church leaders. They realized that their "light affliction" was for a season, and it wasn't to be compared to the eternal weight of glory that stood before them (2 Corinthians 4:17). In the early church, being a "witness" for Christ was the same as being a "martyr."

For the glory of God, we should always live with an eternal mindset. May He provide sufficient grace to help in our times of need.

VII. REVELATION 7 AND 14— THE 144000 AND THE HARVEST OF THE EARTH

As you are aware by now, the book of Revelation jumps around chronologically. Studying the book by topic or by vision is the most effective way to comprehend it. This section includes two main topics, the 144000 servants of God and the harvest of the earth. Regarding the 144000, it is important to consider: who are they, when will they be sealed for service, and what will happen when their service is done? Regarding the resurrection/rapture, it is important from a timing standpoint to look at the great multitude in Revelation 7 through the lens of the harvest-of-the-earth events in Revelation 14.

Let's begin with the topic of the 144000.

The Sealing of the 144000

In Revelation 7:1–8 we read that 144000 of Israel are given the seal of God. The 144000 servants of God seen in this passage will be from all the tribes of the children of Israel (Revelation 7:4), twelve thousand from each tribe.

When will the 144000 become active in their service to God? A clue is given that tells us that this sealing of the 144000 occurs *prior to* the seven trumpets and seven vials. The important phrase is "hurt not . . . till we have sealed" the 144000.

> And after these things I saw four angels standing on the four corners of the earth, holding the four winds of the earth, that the wind should not blow on the earth, nor on the sea, nor on any tree. And I saw another angel ascending from the east, having the seal of the living God: and he cried with a loud voice to the four angels, to whom it was given to hurt the earth and the sea, Saying, *Hurt not the earth,* neither the *sea,* nor the *trees, till we have sealed* the servants of our God in their foreheads. (Revelation 7:1–3)

The four angels standing on the four corners of the earth will play an integral role with the plagues of God according to Revelation 7:1–2. The two witnesses, like Moses and Aaron in Egypt, will also work in conjunction with God as the plagues are dispensed toward the Antichrist and his followers. The Scripture says the two witnesses will have power over "waters" and "the earth":

> These have power to shut heaven, that it rain not in the days of their prophecy: and have power over waters to turn them to blood, and to smite the earth with all plagues, as often as they will. (Revelation 11:6)

Because of the powers of the two witnesses, the sealing of the 144000 will likely occur prior to the arrival of the two witnesses at the beginning of the 3.5-year tribulation.

The 144000: Their Purpose

What does Revelation tell us about the work and labor of the 144000? Nothing! However, a curious verse in Matthew 10:23 says, "Ye shall not have gone over the cities of Israel, till the Son of man be come."

When comparing the Olivet Discourse with Matthew 10:17–39, numerous parallels can be seen. I believe we can learn something from this. Matthew 10 was Jesus's message to the twelve disciples. The disciples were sent out to proclaim the truth and heal the sick. While this passage was for them, it is also alive and active in our day and time, and I believe Matthew 10 will be significantly relevant for both Christians and the 144000 sealed servants of God during the tribulation period!

Therefore, these passages quite possibly reveal the purpose of the 144000: to pass through many cities proclaiming the truth of Jesus Christ, all the while enduring persecution as part of the "least of these my brethren."

Matthew 10 and the Olivet Discourse share the following commonalities:

> But beware of men: for they will deliver you up to the councils, and they will scourge you in their synagogues. (Matthew 10:17)

> And ye shall be brought before governors and kings for my sake, for a testimony against them and the Gentiles. (Matthew 10:18)

> But when they deliver you up, take no thought how or what ye shall speak: for it shall be given you in that same hour what ye shall speak. For it is not ye that speak, but the Spirit of your Father which speaketh in you. (Matthew 10:19–20)

> And the brother shall deliver up the brother to death, and the father the child: and the children shall rise up against their parents, and cause them to be put to death. For I am come to set a man at variance against his father, and the daughter against her mother, and the daughter in law against her mother in law. And a man's foes shall be they of his own household. He that loveth father or mother more than me is not worthy of me: and he that loveth son or daughter more than me is not worthy of me. And he that taketh not his cross, and followeth after me, is not worthy of me. He that findeth his life shall lose it: and he that loseth his life for my sake shall find it. (Matthew 10:21, 35–39)

> And ye shall be hated of all men for my name's sake: but he that endureth to the end shall be saved. (Matthew 10:22)

> But the very hairs of your head are all numbered. (Matthew 10:30)

The Redemption of the 144000 as the Firstfruits of God

Aside from Revelation 7, the only Scripture that specifically mentions the 144000 is Revelation 14:1–5. In this passage, we read of three noteworthy facts. First, at this point the 144000 have been redeemed from the earth. Second, they have been redeemed from among men, being the firstfruits unto God and to the Lamb. Third, the scene appears to move from earth in verse 1 to heaven in verses 3 and 5, where the 144000 are singing a new song before the throne of God.

> And I looked, and, lo, a Lamb stood on the mount Sion, and with him an hundred forty and four thousand, having his Father's name written in their foreheads. And I heard a voice from heaven, as the voice of many waters, and as the voice of a great thunder: and I heard the voice of harpers harping with their harps: and they sung as it were a new song before the throne, and before the four beasts, and the elders: and no man could learn that song but the hundred and forty and four thousand, which were redeemed from the earth. These are they which were not defiled with women; for they are virgins. These are they which follow the Lamb whithersoever he goeth. These were redeemed from among men, being the firstfruits unto God and to the Lamb. And in their mouth was found no guile: for they are without fault before the throne of God. (Revelation 14:1–5)

Is the mighty angel in view in Revelation 14:1? I don't understand this verse except to say that in some visionary way, the apostle John saw the Lamb of God on earth with the 144000 and he witnessed their actual ascension from earth to heaven. Their ascension would be similar to the rapture of the two witnesses to heaven when a great voice from heaven called, "Come up hither." In this particular account, John hears a "voice from heaven, as the voice of many waters, and as the voice of a great thunder," and then he immediately hears music around the throne of God.

The mission of the 144000 now accomplished, they stand without fault before the throne of God! A special group indeed, they will be "redeemed from among men as the firstfruits to God and the Lamb," the main harvest yet upcoming.

Having now seen the firstfruits of God that will be redeemed from among men, let's now proceed to that topic of the main harvest of the earth. We'll continue on in Revelation 14 and then move back to Revelation 7.

The Angelic Warning

Prior to the harvest of the earth we read of three angels, each of whom proclaims a specific message. These three warnings appear to come near the end of the Antichrist's reign, not long before the second coming of the Lord Jesus. The Almighty is trying to stir up the hearts of humankind to repent and turn to the everlasting God in faith. Torment and wrath and fire and brimstone await those who worship the beast or his image, or who receive the mark of his name. The warnings are given in Revelation 14:6–11 and are summarized below:

- Angel 1: Preaches the everlasting gospel to them that dwell on the earth, to every nation, and kindred, and tongue, and people. Says with a loud voice, "Fear God, and give glory to him; *for the hour of his judgment is come:* and worship him that made heaven, and earth, and the sea, and the fountains of waters."
- Angel 2: Says "Babylon is fallen, is fallen, that great city, because she made all nations to drink of the wine of the wrath of her fornication."
- Angel 3: Proclaims a final warning to the inhabitants of earth. If you worship the beast and his image or receive the mark of his name, you will drink of the wine of the wrath of God, which is poured out into the cup of his indignation!

Through angelic means we see that the Lord will mercifully cry out to unbelievers even to the last hours. His desire is to gather as much wheat into the barn as possible. This is a marvelous teaching moment for us. Do we share God's heart in this? In context of the soon thief-like return, we read how the Lord remains "longsuffering to us, not willing that any should perish, but that all should come to repentance" (2 Peter 3:9).

Encouragement to the Followers of God

The message from Revelation 14:12–13, which now is very near the return of Jesus Christ, is to patiently continue to worship God, keep his commandments, and remain unrelenting in your faith in Jesus. The voice from heaven told John to write, "Blessed are the dead which die in the Lord from henceforth: Yea, saith the Spirit, that they may rest from their labours; and their works do follow them." Don't lose faith now! Even if it means your death at the hands of the enemies of God!

The First Sickle: The Harvest of Believers

In these key verses of Revelation 14:14–16, the *Son of Man* has a sharp sickle in His hand, not a sword in His mouth like in Revelation 19:15. An angel cries out that the time is come, for the harvest of the earth is ripe. "Then *he that sat on the cloud* thrust his sickle on the earth; and the earth was reaped!" This is the great harvest of the righteous, the resurrection and rapture!

The Second Sickle: The Harvest of the Wicked

A far different picture is portrayed in Revelation 14:17–20. An angel cries with a loud cry saying, "Thrust in thy sharp sickle, and gather the clusters of the vine of the earth; for her grapes are fully ripe." Then the vine of the earth is cast into the great winepress of the wrath of God, and blood comes out of the winepress up to the bridles of the horses. This portion of Scripture, with its terrible picture of the harvest of the wicked (see Jesus's parable of the tares in Matthew 13) is very similar to Revelation 19:15, Isaiah 34:1–9, Isaiah 63:1–6, and Joel 3:13.

Resurrection and Rapture: The Wheat Gathered into the Barn

Revelation 7:9–17 pertains to a scene in heaven. As we read this passage, it is important to recall what was mentioned previously: that when reading the book of Revelation the reader is often tossed to and fro on the chronological time frame. This is why we have now moved from Revelation 14 back to Revelation 7. The apostle John views the following scene. I might add that this scene is one of the most beautiful pictures I can envision in my heart.

> After this I beheld, and, lo, a great multitude, which no man could number, of all nations, and kindreds, and people, and tongues, stood before the throne, and before the Lamb, clothed with white robes, and palms in their hands; and cried with a loud voice, saying, Salvation to our God which sitteth upon the throne, and unto the Lamb. And all the angels stood round about the throne, and about the elders and the four beasts, and fell before the throne on their faces, and worshipped God, saying, Amen: Blessing, and glory, and wisdom, and thanksgiving, and honour, and power, and might, be unto our God for ever and ever. Amen. And one of the elders answered, saying unto me, What are these which are arrayed in white robes? and whence came they? And I said unto him, Sir, thou knowest. And he said to me, These are they *which came out of great*

tribulation, and have washed their robes, and made them white in the blood of the Lamb. (Revelation 7:9–14)

The Great Multitude
- So great a number that no man could number it
- People from all nations (Strong's G1484—*ethnos*: from all ethnicities)
- People from all kindreds (Strong's G5443—*phule*: from all offshoots of races)
- People from all people (Strong's G2992—*laos*: from all people in general)
- People from all tongues (Strong's G1100—*glossa*: from all languages)

The Location and Characteristics of the Great Multitude
- Standing before the throne of God and the Lord Jesus Christ
- Clothed with white robes
- Palms in their hands
- They cried with a loud voice to God, sitting upon the throne, and to the Lamb

The Great Multitude is the Harvest of Believers on the Day of the Lord

In verse 14, the context of the resurrection of the great multitude to heaven is "out of great tribulation." The Lord Jesus describes this period of "great tribulation" taking place after the abomination of desolation (Matthew 24:21). The great tribulation then leads directly to His second coming in the clouds with the great sound of a trumpet (Matthew 24:30–31). Some believe that this great multitude represents only the saints who are killed during the tribulation period. But the scene depicts people with physical bodies (they have feet, hands, and mouths, and are wearing clothes) standing before God's throne with palm branches in their hands. This is not a picture of anything other than physical, resurrected bodies that possess the ability to do all that Jesus Christ did after He was resurrected from the dead. He was able to stand and walk, He was able to speak, He was able to wear clothes, and He was able to hold objects in His hands.

When are followers of God given new bodies and changed from mortality to immortality? Is it at the time of our death, or at the resurrection of the dead? Since new bodies are given at the resurrection, it is difficult to conclude that this countless multitude represents tribulation saints alone and not the entire body of Christ.

I believe this vast throng is a picture of the resurrected/raptured in heaven, moments after having been gathered in the clouds when the Lord returns after a short period of great tribulation. This is a massive group of all peoples. The following Scriptures describe this great harvest of souls from earth: Matthew 24:31, Mark 13:27, 1 Corinthians 15:50–54, 1 Thessalonians 4:15–17, Revelation 14:14–16, Isaiah 26:19, and Job 14:12.

Where do we go when we die? What happens to our fleshly bodies? What about our souls? I won't go deep into this subject except to make a few points to help us understand the context of the picture given to us in Revelation 7:9.

Does Job Confirm the Timing of the Harvest of Believers on the Day of the Lord?

Everyone I know of who dies on this earth experiences a destruction of the flesh. As Job says in Job 19:26, worms destroy this body. The mortal frame is corrupted, it decays, and it vanishes away. In Job's discourse on death in Job 14, he writes "man dieth, and wasteth away" . . . and then he marvelously confirms a posttribulation resurrection at a "set time"! He states the following:

> So man lieth down, and riseth not: *till the heavens be no more*, they shall not awake, nor be raised out of their sleep. O that thou wouldest hide me in the grave, that thou wouldest keep me secret, *until thy wrath be past*, that thou wouldest appoint me *a set time*, and remember me! If a man die, shall he live again? All the days of my appointed time will *I wait, till my change come*. (Job 14:12–14)

Did you catch the details? Job mentions three items that I want to address:

- Man will "rise not, until the heavens are no more"
- Man will "hide in the grave . . . until God's wrath is past"
- Man will wait until "a set time . . . when his change comes"

Man will "rise not, until the heavens are no more." With this statement, Job definitively equates the timing of the resurrection of the dead to the passing away of the heavens. This exactly aligns with 2 Peter 3:7, 10–12:

> But the heavens and the earth, which are now, by the same word are kept in store, reserved unto fire against the day of judgment and perdition of

ungodly men. But the day of the Lord will come as a thief in the night; in the which *the heavens shall pass away with a great noise*, and the elements shall melt with fervent heat, the earth also and the works that are therein shall be burned up. Seeing then that all these things shall be dissolved, what manner of persons ought ye to be in all holy conversation and godliness, looking for and hasting unto the coming of the day of God, wherein *the heavens being on fire shall be dissolved*, and the elements shall melt with fervent heat? (2 Peter 3:7, 10–12)

According to Job and Peter, the resurrection and rapture will occur on the day of the Lord when the heavens will pass away. Additionally, through the Holy Spirit's inspiration, Peter fully acknowledges that the church will still be on earth until the great and notable day of the Lord when he exhorts us, "Knowing these facts, how should we behave? You should maintain a godly, holy lifestyle while looking for and eagerly awaiting the coming of the day of the Lord!" (my paraphrase). Still today, we are "looking for that blessed hope, and the glorious appearing of the great God and our Saviour Jesus Christ" (Titus 2:13).

Man will "hide in the grave . . . until God's wrath is past." This statement corroborates the eschatological timing I have discussed several times. The resurrection will occur just as the seventh and final vial of wrath is poured out. Then, as the great multitude is resurrected and raptured from earth, the ultimate wrath, or the "day of judgment," will commence on the day of the Lord. Just as it was with Noah and Lot, be assured that the Lord knows how to deliver the godly (2 Peter 2:5–9)! As taught by Jesus, the resurrection will occur "at the last day" (John 6:40, 44, 54).

Note that the children of God are frequently taught to endure trouble and tribulation. Numerous Scriptures depict a close association in timing between the resurrection/rapture and the "day of judgment," perhaps none so well as 2 Thessalonians 1:4–12. The backdrop is persecution, tribulation, and trouble experienced by believers. In one breath the apostle Paul writes of the coming of the Lord Jesus "to be glorified in his saints" and "to be admired" in those who believe "in that day." And in the next breath he speaks of the Lord Jesus coming from heaven "with his mighty angels, in flaming fire" to take vengeance on those who do not know God and do not obey the gospel of Jesus Christ.

Man will wait until a "set time . . . when his change comes." We read in 1 Corinthians 15:52–55 that the point of change, when immortal, incorruptible bodies are given, is at the time of the resurrection. We have reviewed the *moedim*, or appointed times, in detail. At the "set time" on the Day of Atonement, the LORD will appear in His glory at the second coming! And then "in a moment, in the twinkling of an eye, at the last trump: for the trumpet shall sound, and the dead shall be raised incorruptible, and we shall be changed."

Oh, what a day that will be! My prayer and my desire echoes that of the apostle Paul when he prayed that the "eyes of our understanding" would be enlightened to understand "the hope" and "the power" of the resurrection and rapture:

> That the God of our Lord Jesus Christ, the Father of glory, may give unto you the spirit of wisdom and revelation in the knowledge of him: the eyes of your understanding being enlightened; that ye may know what is the hope of his calling, and what the riches of the glory of his inheritance in the saints, and what is the exceeding greatness of his power to us-ward who believe, according to the working of his mighty power, which he wrought in Christ, when he raised him from the dead, and set him at his own right hand in the heavenly places. (Ephesians 1:17–20)

The Blessings and Promises for Those Resurrected and Raptured on the Day of the Lord

> Therefore are they before the throne of God, and serve him day and night in his temple: and he that sitteth on the throne shall dwell among them. They shall hunger no more, neither thirst any more; neither shall the sun light on them, nor any heat. For the Lamb which is in the midst of the throne shall feed them, and shall lead them unto living fountains of waters: and God shall wipe away all tears from their eyes. (Revelation 7:15–17)

In verse 15 we see a clear picture of the immortal state of the resurrected:

- Standing before the presence of Almighty God and the Lamb is clearly a picture of having been changed into an immortal state.
- The elder tells John that the great multitude will always and forever render worship to God (who sits on the throne in his temple).

Verse 16 tells us they shall no more hunger or thirst, neither will the sun or heat ever be too severe upon them. And verse 17 depicts the Lamb of God feeding the saints and leading them to living fountains of waters, with God wiping away all tears. This depicts a true, lasting, and satisfied state, where there are no more toils, burdens, or want of material provisions such as food. Let's ponder the riches of the glory of this inheritance!

Of course, this Scripture is not the only witness to these future realities. Luke 6:21 says, "Blessed are ye that hunger now: *for ye shall be filled.*" In Matthew 5:6 we likewise read, "Blessed are they which do hunger and thirst after righteousness: *for they shall be filled.*" The warning today is Luke 6:25: "Woe unto you that are full! For ye shall hunger."

Isaiah 49:10 describes the future of the redeemed: "They shall not hunger nor thirst; neither shall the heat nor sun smite them: for he that hath mercy on them shall lead them, even by the springs of water shall he guide them." Living fountains of waters flowing from the temple, the house of the Lord, in Jerusalem are depicted in Joel 3:18, Zechariah 14:8, and Ezekiel 47. God wiping away all tears is referenced by Isaiah as well, in conjunction with the resurrection of the dead (Isaiah 25:8). And finally, Revelation 21:4 connects this with the eternal state in the holy city, the new Jerusalem.

To summarize, the great harvest of the earth will occur at the set time on the day of the Lord. The primary blessings and promises for the great harvest of believers will be to enjoy the millennium, where we will live and reign with Jesus Christ in the kingdom of God. After the one thousand years are accomplished, we look forward to the ultimate defeat of Satan when, soon after he is "loosed out of his prison," he will be cast into the lake of fire and brimstone and tormented day and night for ever and ever. We then look forward to the eternal state, when God Himself will descend from heaven with the new Jerusalem, the City of God, and proceed to dwell with the redeemed on earth for ever and ever (Revelation 21:2–3, 10).

In contrast, the harvest of the wicked is a plight altogether different. The emotions of its recipients are anger, fear, and distress. On this day of judgment, the indignation and fury of the LORD will be upon the ungodly, and the sword of the LORD will be filled with blood (Isaiah 34:2, 6; 63:2–3, 6). The host of heaven will be dissolved and the heavens rolled together as a scroll (Isaiah 34:4). Not only will the ungodly experience death, but the "host of heaven" (i.e. the evil powers of the air) will be annihilated! In other words, the day of the Lord will bring victory to Jesus Christ and His redeemed and defeat to Satan and his followers.

VIII. REVELATION 19—A GLARING DICHOTOMY

This chapter represents some of the Bible's most stirring images, and it pertains entirely to the great and notable day of the Lord. A stark dichotomy is evident between events on earth and in heaven.

Some of the earthly events will be:

- A raining down of great hail (Revelation 16:17–21, Isaiah 30:30, Ezekiel 38:22)
- Darkness and gloom during the daytime (Zechariah 14:6–7; Zephaniah 1:15; Amos 5:18, 20; Joel 2:2)
- The Lord will cause men to kill each other as in the day of Midian (Isaiah 10:26, Zechariah 14:13, Ezekiel 38:21–22)
- A flesh-consuming plague will smite all people who have fought against Jerusalem (Zechariah 14:12)
- Distress, fear, pestilence, confusion, and blindness among sinners (Zephaniah 1:15–17, Isaiah 24:17–18, Habakkuk 3:5)
- A fiery judgment on the earth (2 Peter 3:7; Isaiah 9:19, 24:6, 34:4, 9; Ezekiel 39:6; Zephaniah 1:15–18; Malachi 4:1)

Meanwhile, in heaven we see a scene of rejoicing:

And after these things I heard a great voice of much people in heaven, saying, Alleluia; Salvation, and glory, and honour, and power, unto the Lord our God: for true and righteous are his judgments: for he hath judged the great whore, which did corrupt the earth with her fornication, and hath avenged the blood of his servants at her hand. And again they said, Alleluia. And her smoke rose up for ever and ever. And the four and twenty elders and the four beasts fell down and worshipped God that sat on the throne, saying, Amen; Alleluia. And a voice came out of the throne, saying, praise our God, all ye his servants, and ye that fear him, both small and great. (Revelation 19:1–5)

Pay special attention to whom the message is given in verse 5: "all ye his servants, and ye that fear him, both small and great." This is the great multitude of the resurrected/raptured! The language is exactly how the seventh trumpet in Revelation 11:18 describes the resurrected/raptured:

And the nations were angry, and thy wrath is come, and the time of the dead, that they should be judged, and that thou shouldest give reward unto *thy servants the prophets, and to the saints, and them that fear thy name, small and great*; and shouldest destroy them which destroy the earth. (Revelation 11:18)

With the voice of a great multitude, the resurrected and raptured appropriately respond to the voice from the throne by praising God and saying, "Alleluia: for the Lord God omnipotent reigneth. Let us be glad and rejoice, and give honour to him: for the marriage of the Lamb is come, and his wife hath made herself ready" (Revelation 19:6–7). Notice how the above seventh-trumpet passage further confirms the great contrast on the day of the Lord: either vengeance and wrath on earth or rewards from God in heaven!

Now, for a moment, I want to bring us back full circle to principle 1 from the introduction where I stated, "The ultimate trajectory of the Bible's prophetic accounts takes us all the way to the day of the Lord." Truly, the heart of the message of prophecy is Jesus Christ. It is here in Revelation 19 where we find the relevant passage:

And I fell at his feet to worship him. And he said unto me, See thou do it not: I am thy fellowservant, and of thy brethren that have the testimony of Jesus: worship God: for the testimony of Jesus is the spirit of prophecy. (Revelation 19:10)

The placement of this verse in the Holy Bible is telling. The seventh angel has just declared that "the mystery of God should be finished, as he hath declared to his servants the prophets" and the great voice from the throne has stated "It is done" (Revelation 10:7, 16:17). We have come to "that day" as declared by the prophets. Jesus Christ is the heart of Scripture, and He is the heart of this great and notable day. The harvest of believers has occurred, the marriage of the Lamb is taking place in heaven, the ungodly on earth are being punished, and soon the Lord Jesus will personally descend with His wife for the battle of Armageddon. Besides the Almighty, who is in focus at this time? Jesus Christ. It is the day of the *Lord!*

The Marriage Supper of the Lamb

For the marriage, the saints are arrayed in fine linen, clean and white. No longer the "bride" of Christ, verse 7 uses the term wife as she has "made herself ready."

And to her was granted that she should be arrayed in fine linen, clean and white: for the fine linen is the righteousness of saints. And he saith unto me, write, blessed are they which are called unto the marriage supper of the Lamb. And he saith unto me, these are the true sayings of God. And I fell at his feet to worship him. And he said unto me, see thou do it not: I am thy fellowservant, and of thy brethren that have the testimony of Jesus: worship God: for the testimony of Jesus is the spirit of prophecy. (Revelation 19:8–10)

After the marriage, the saints are called to the marriage supper of the Lamb. From a timing perspective, I expect the wedding feast to occur toward the tail end of the day of the Lord. It seems most appropriate for the feast to occur after the resurrection, after the bride of Christ is fitted with fine, white linen garments and united with their Lord in marriage, after Israel's salvation, and after the destruction of the wicked.

I believe that Isaiah 25:6–9 sheds light on the marriage supper of the Lamb. Isaiah 25:6 indicates that the LORD of hosts will make for all people "a great feast in this mountain." Based on Isaiah 24:23, it seems reasonable to conclude that the feast will occur on Mount Zion, in Jerusalem, since the context of Isaiah 24 and Isaiah 25 is the day of the Lord:

And in this mountain shall the LORD *of hosts make unto all people a feast of fat things, a feast of wines on the lees, of fat things full of marrow, of wines on the lees well refined.* And he will destroy in this mountain the face of the covering cast over all people, and the vail that is spread over all nations. He will swallow up death in victory; and the Lord GOD will wipe away tears from off all faces; and the rebuke of his people shall he take away from off all the earth: for the LORD hath spoken it. *And it shall be said in that day,* Lo, this is our God; we have waited for him, and he will save us: this is the LORD; we have waited for him, we will be glad and rejoice in his salvation. (Isaiah 25:6–9)

Then the moon shall be confounded, and the sun ashamed, when the LORD of hosts shall reign *in mount Zion,* and in Jerusalem, and before his ancients gloriously. (Isaiah 24:23)

The flow of events from Revelation 19 doesn't indicate space and time for a marriage feast until after Armageddon. Rather, Jesus and the saints descend on their horses to earth, the enemies of God are destroyed by the sword of the LORD coming out of the mouth of Jesus, and then there is celebration. Feasting and joy is appropriate after evil is defeated! This is a celebration of Christ's victory and the great transfer of dominion and power over earth from Satan to the Lord Jesus! Isaiah 25:9 says, "And it shall be said *in that day*, Lo, this is our God; we have waited for him, and he will save us: *this is the* LORD; *we have waited for him, we will be glad and rejoice in his salvation.*"

The Harvest of the Wicked

The main events of Revelation 19:11–21 are:
- Jesus is seen upon a white horse with a sharp sword coming out of His mouth, ready to tread the winepress of the fierceness and wrath of Almighty God.
- Jesus is clothed with a vesture dipped in blood, His name is called the The Word of God, and on His vesture is the name, KING OF KINGS AND LORD OF LORDS.
- No longer the bride, but the *wife* of Christ is now seen following Jesus upon white horses.
- An angel shouts to the fowls of the air to gather themselves for a supper of the great God, where they may eat the flesh of men and horses.
- The beast, the kings of the earth, and their armies are depicted as gathered together to make war against Jesus and His army of followers on white horses.
- The beast and false prophet are cast alive into a lake of fire burning with brimstone. The rest are slain with the sword of Jesus, and the fowls are filled with their flesh.

In this powerful imagery, we have Jesus clothed with a vesture dipped in blood and His wife arrayed in fine linen, white and clean. They descend from heaven to earth on white horses, and subsequently the battle of Armageddon takes place. It is pictured as a slaughter. Revelation 14:18–20 describes the event as follows:

> And another angel came out from the altar, which had power over fire; and cried with a loud cry to him that had the sharp sickle, saying, Thrust in thy sharp sickle, and gather the clusters of the vine of the earth; for *her grapes are fully ripe. And the angel thrust in his sickle into the earth, and gathered the vine of the earth, and cast it into the great winepress of the wrath of God. And the winepress was trodden without the city, and blood came out of the winepress, even unto the horse bridles, by the space of a thousand and six hundred furlongs.* (Revelation 14:18–20)

This personal encounter of Jesus Christ with the enemies of God on earth is depicted in many Scriptures. I'll highlight a few.

> . . . and to you who are troubled rest with us, when the Lord Jesus shall be revealed from heaven with his mighty angels, in flaming fire taking vengeance on them that know not God, and that obey not the gospel of our Lord Jesus Christ: who shall be punished with everlasting destruction *from the presence of the Lord, and from the glory of his power;* when he shall come to be glorified in his saints, and to be admired in all them that believe (because our testimony among you was believed) in that day. (2 Thessalonians 1:7–10)

> And it shall come to pass at the same time when Gog shall come against the land of Israel, saith the Lord God, that my fury shall come up in my face. For in my jealousy and in the fire of my wrath have I spoken, Surely in that day there shall be a great shaking in the land of Israel; so that the fishes of the sea, and the fowls of the heaven, and the beasts of the field, and all creeping things that creep upon the earth, and *all the men that are upon the face of the earth, shall shake at my presence,* and the mountains shall be thrown down, and the steep places shall fall, and every wall shall fall to the ground. And I will call for a sword against him throughout all my mountains, saith the Lord God: every man's sword shall be against his brother. And I will plead against him with pestilence and with blood; and I will rain upon him, and upon his bands, and upon the many people that are with him, an overflowing rain, and great hailstones, fire, and brimstone. (Ezekiel 38:18–22)

> Behold, the day of the Lord cometh, cruel both with wrath and fierce anger, to lay the land desolate: and he shall destroy the sinners thereof out of it. For the stars of heaven and the constellations thereof shall not give their light: the sun shall be darkened in his going forth, and the moon shall not cause her light to shine. And *I will punish the world for their evil, and the wicked for their iniquity; and I will cause the arrogancy of the proud to cease, and will lay low the haughtiness of the terrible.* I will make a man more precious than fine gold; even a man than the golden wedge of Ophir. Therefore I will shake the heavens, and the earth shall remove out of her place, in the wrath of the Lord of hosts, and in the day of his fierce anger. (Isaiah 13:9–13)

I beheld the earth, and, lo, it was without form, and void; and the heavens, and they had no light. I beheld the mountains, and, lo, they trembled, and all the hills moved lightly. I beheld, and, lo, there was no man, and all the birds of the heavens were fled. *I beheld, and, lo, the fruitful place was a wilderness, and all the cities thereof were broken down at the presence of the LORD, and by his fierce anger.* For thus hath the LORD said, The whole land shall be desolate; yet will I not make a full end. For this shall the earth mourn, and the heavens above be black: because I have spoken it, I have purposed it, and will not repent, neither will I turn back from it. (Jeremiah 4:23–28)

This wraps up our review of the book of Revelation. We could proceed on with a deeper look into Revelation 21 and 22, but those are well-known passages, and I don't feel they need to be treated here. I'll likewise pass at making predictions about Babylon the Great in Revelation 18—she is still a mystery to me.

In summary, the message of this wonderful book of Holy Scripture is about the day of the Lord. The day of the Lord is the endpoint of the seals, the thunders, the trumpets, and the vials. It all ends with a great harvest. May we all consider deeply this great day of reaping!

Chapter 4

THE BOOK OF DANIEL

Due to its numerous links with other prophetic texts, several Scriptures from the book of Daniel have already been reviewed in this book. Much remains, however. Five dynamic and powerful visions were given to Daniel, inspired by the God he served faithfully. Each of Daniel's visions share the common trajectory that we have discovered many times. They take us to the finality of prophecy when Jesus is given everlasting dominion on earth. In Daniel 2:44–45 we see Jesus and the kingdom of God consuming and destroying earthly kingdoms and powers. In Daniel 7:13–14 and 27, we see the same picture of Jesus and the kingdom of God with an everlasting dominion and kingdom. Daniel 8:25 takes us all the way to the end of tribulation, when the Antichrist is broken and defeated. Of course, as we have already reviewed extensively, the seventy weeks of Daniel 9 end at the day of the Lord and the victory of Jesus. And finally, Daniel's last vision takes us all the way to day 1335 and the millennial kingdom! Such hope is contained in these passages, even if the subject matter leading up to the beautiful victory of Christ is difficult and hard to understand in its fullness.

Before we begin our study of Daniel's visions, let me be up front. History isn't my strong suit, and I haven't read the works of Flavius Josephus. I do appreciate and understand the many historical fulfillments of Daniel—yet I maintain that there is good reason to see them as partial and as types, rather than as full fulfillments. My reasoning will be contained below.

That said, let's begin by diving right into the topic of historical versus future applicability.

I. THE FUTURITY OF DANIEL'S VISIONS

Daniel 7

Is the vision given to Daniel in chapter 7 historical (already fulfilled) or future (yet to be fulfilled)? My Bible has the year 555 BC written next to Daniel 7:1. Daniel 7:1 tells us that Daniel was given this vision in the first year of Belshazzar king of Babylon. Belshazzar was a successor to Nebuchadnezzar, who reigned from approximately 605–562 BC. Let's look at two Scriptures in particular:

> These great beasts, which are four, are four kings, which *shall arise* out of the earth. (Daniel 7:17)

> This is the dream; and we will tell the interpretation thereof before the king. Thou, O king, art a king of kings: for the God of heaven hath given thee a kingdom, power, and strength, and glory. And wheresoever the children of men dwell, the beasts of the field and the fowls of the heaven hath he given into thine hand, and hath made thee ruler over them all. *Thou art this head of gold.* (Daniel 2:36–38)

Many name the Babylonian empire as the first of four beasts in Daniel's vision in chapter 7. But what does the Scripture say? Daniel 2:38 clearly interprets the Babylonian empire ruled by King Nebuchadnezzar as an *existing, powerful kingdom*. Many years later, Daniel 7:17 gives us an interpretation of the four great beasts as four kingdoms which *shall arise* out of the earth. If this is true, it is not possible for Babylon to arise out of the earth either during or after the time of Belshazzar's reign, because the kingdom had already been thriving and in existence for decades!

Although the four beasts of Daniel 7 appear to match up with Daniel 2, the first beast of Daniel 7 is most likely not referring to the Babylonian empire. As with much of prophecy, history may have provided us with a type of fulfillment, but the ultimate fulfillment could be targeted for the end times.

Daniel 8

Is the vision given to Daniel in chapter 8 historical or future? This passage, which contains the third vision given to Daniel, has also been viewed in a historical context by many over the years, linked to the Greek empire and particularly to the terrible rule of Antiochus Epiphanes. But is this valid? The text provides two distinct clues as to whether we should allow the vision to be tied to historical events or if we should reserve application for the end times.

> And I heard a man's voice between the banks of Ulai, which called, and said, Gabriel, make this man to understand the vision. So he came near where I stood: and when he came, I was afraid, and fell upon my face: but he said unto me, Understand, O son of man: *for at the time of the end shall be the vision.* Now as he was speaking with me, I was in a deep sleep on my face toward the ground: but he touched me, and set me upright. And he said, Behold, I will make thee know what *shall be* in the last end of the indignation: *for at the time appointed the end shall be.* (Daniel 8:16–19)

The above phrases are clear enough! The vision is for the end times. Further, it also makes sense to expect a continuity from the beginning of Daniel's vision in chapter 8 to the end of that same vision, which reveals the doom of Antichrist. Unless otherwise specified by Scripture (as in Daniel 2), it is unnatural to truncate a singular vision of Daniel's and apply the beginning stages of the vision to historical figures and events, then insert a gap of hundreds or thousands of years and await a future fulfillment of the latter portion of the vision. What purpose does that serve?

While we can be understanding and sympathetic toward many Bible readers and commentators who have found historical alignment with various aspects of the vision, our expectation should rest in a latter-days future fulfillment because of Gabriel's words. We simply need to have faith and trust in the words of Gabriel, the same messenger who revealed truth regarding the first coming of Jesus Christ in Luke 1.

Are there in fact ties between Daniel 8 and the reign of Antiochus Epiphanes? Yes. They are types, partial fulfillments that point ahead to the final fulfillment. Historical ties are wonderful, and they have inspired many over the course of history to have a deeper faith in the Word of God, but rest assured that the last generation will yet encounter a greater, richer, and more complete fulfillment in the end times as we near the second coming of Jesus Christ. Even if there are types and figures of prior fulfillment, our Lord Jesus is the spirit of prophecy! Christ is the focal point!

Based on Daniel 8:17 and 8:19, we need to interpret this prophecy as predicting events which are near to the time of the end and the second coming of Jesus.

Daniel 9

This fourth vision given to Daniel, the prophecy of seventy weeks, has been discussed at length in the "Eschatological Framework" chapter. Based on the evidences cited, it is my understanding and conclusion that we should view this vision of the seventy weeks as future.

Daniel 10–12

The last three chapters of Daniel comprise one entire message. They contain the fifth and final vision given to Daniel. Daniel 10 provides a marvelous and touching account. The vision was revealed to Daniel in verse 1. It caused Daniel to mourn for three full weeks, during which time he ate no pleasant bread, neither flesh, nor wine, nor did he bathe himself for those twenty-one days. It appears that the Lord Jesus Himself was the one who gave the vision to Daniel. It caused great human weakness and sorrow in Daniel, but in time he was strengthened by the words spoken from one who was sent to answer his prayer and give him understanding. Consistent with Luke 1:19 and Daniel 8:16–19 and 9:21–23, most likely it was Gabriel the messenger angel who came and touched Daniel and gave him understanding (Daniel 10:10–14).

Regarding Daniel 11, many Bible scholars would contend that Daniel 11 has been *perfectly and historically fulfilled up to Daniel 11:35*. At that point, they claim, the prophecy takes a turn and the Antichrist comes into view at verse 36. Others believe the Antichrist comes into view at verse 21 but provide for historical fulfillment of the first twenty verses only.

I concur that historical events do align with amazing precision to Daniel 11:1–20. And I concur that a great deal of historical alignment exists with Daniel 11:21–35. But for the reasons below, I question whether these historical fulfillments are more than an antetype, a near-term fulfillment for what will one day be a chain of continuous events that lead to the time of the second coming and the establishment of the kingdom of God.

I can't declare without a doubt, nor with full confidence, that the entirety of Daniel's final vision should be understood as 100 percent focused on the latter days. But the question persists in my mind. Why truncate the vision and apply half of the verses to historical fulfillment, insert a long, unexplained gap, and then suddenly pick the vision back up when the Antichrist appears in the latter days? Is this the way of God? How does complete historical fulfillment of the first twenty verses provide clarity, focus, and vision in leading humankind to the time of the end and the second coming of Jesus?

Based on the eschatological focus of Daniel 7, Daniel 8, and Daniel 9, therefore, my preference and leaning is to consider the entirety of Daniel 10–12 as relating to the time of the end. However, we cannot rely on inklings and personal preferences. Does the text allow for this possibility?

> In the third year of Cyrus king of Persia a thing was revealed unto Daniel, whose name was called Belteshazzar; and the thing was true, *but the time appointed was long:* and he understood the thing, and had understanding of the vision. (Daniel 10:1)

> Now I am come to make thee understand *what shall befall thy people in the latter days:* for yet the vision is for many days. (Daniel 10:14)

> But thou, O Daniel, shut up the words, and seal the book, *even to the time of the end:* many shall run to and fro, and knowledge shall be increased. (Daniel 12:4)

> And he said, Go thy way, Daniel: *for the words are closed up and sealed till the time of the end.* (Daniel 12:9)

This final prophecy of Daniel is bookended by four verses that provide clues to the time of its application. Daniel 10:1 states that the time appointed is long, meaning that the vision is applicable to a time that was a long way off from Daniel's day. Daniel 10:14 makes a summary statement that the vision is in regard to what shall befall the Israelites in the latter days. Daniel 12:4 says the words of the book are related to the time of the end. And Daniel 12:9 restates that the words of prophecy pertain to the time of the end.

These clues give me pause to consider the historical alternative. They don't allow me to comfortably rest in a conclusion that Daniel 11:1–20 wholly pertains to history, despite how perfectly the details align with past events. Historical fulfillment of Daniel 11:1–20 (or even worse, Daniel 11:1–34) runs counter to a basic principle of prophecy. That basic principle is that generally speaking, the spirit of prophecy pertains to the Lord Jesus Christ. Why in Daniel 11:1–20 would God reveal to us an ultimate fulfillment in someone or something other than what Daniel 7 and Daniel 8 show us? Daniel 7 and 8 reveal to us a continuous road map that will ultimately lead to Antichrist and then the second coming of Jesus. An ultimate fulfillment of Daniel 11:1–20 in something disconnected from the events starting in verse 21 that pertain to Antichrist is an unexpected and unanticipated change of plot and circumstance for the common Bible reader.

You may counter my analysis above and say that the Scriptures provide numerous examples of prophecies that have a near or contemporary fulfilment close to the time of the prophet but then suddenly turn to events that lead to the return of Jesus Christ at the day of the Lord. This is quite true. However, unlike this fifth vision of Daniel, these prophecies do not have timing parameters placed upon them by the Scripture itself (Daniel 10:1, 14; Daniel 12:4, 9)!

II. THE KINGDOMS OF DANIEL 2 AND REVELATION 17

Daniel's First Vision

Daniel 2:19, 31–45 describes King Nebuchadnezzar's dream of a statue, which represented five Middle Eastern empires generally situated around Babylon. Though greatly disturbed by it, the king had forgotten what the dream was about, so Daniel sought God in prayer, desiring the mercies of the God of heaven concerning this secret (Daniel 2:18). God heard the prayers of Daniel and his three companions and revealed to Daniel the dream itself and the interpretation of the dream ("But there is a God in heaven that revealeth secrets, and maketh known to the king Nebuchadnezzar what shall be in the latter days." Daniel 2:28). Based on Daniel's interpretation in Daniel 2:37–38, we know that this vision stretches from the time of the Babylonian kingdom to the latter days and ultimately to the time when the final kingdom, God's everlasting kingdom, is established with the second coming of Jesus Christ. The substances of the statue (gold, silver, etc.) and their durable qualities make sense when considering this span of time, which so far has exceeded 2600 years.

> Thou, O king, sawest, and behold a great image. This great image, whose brightness was excellent, stood before thee; and the form thereof was terrible. This image's *head was of fine gold, his breast and his arms of silver, his belly and his thighs of brass, his legs of iron, his feet part of iron and part of clay.* Thou sawest till that *a stone* was cut out without hands, which smote the image upon his feet that were of iron and clay, and brake them to pieces. Then was the iron, the clay, the brass, the silver, and the gold, broken to pieces *together,* and became like the chaff of the summer threshingfloors; and the wind carried them away, that no place was found for them: and *the stone that smote the image became a great mountain, and filled the whole earth.*

This is the dream; and we will tell the interpretation thereof before the king. Thou, O king, art a king of kings: for the God of heaven hath given thee a kingdom, power, and strength, and glory. And wheresoever the children of men dwell, the beasts of the field and the fowls of the heaven hath he given into thine hand, and hath made thee ruler over them all. Thou art this head of gold. And after thee shall arise another kingdom inferior to thee, and another third kingdom of brass, which shall bear rule over all the earth. And the fourth kingdom shall be strong as iron: forasmuch as iron breaketh in pieces and subdueth all things: and as iron that breaketh all these, shall it break in pieces and bruise. And whereas thou sawest the feet and toes, part of potters' clay, and part of iron, the kingdom shall be divided; but there shall be in it of the strength of the iron, forasmuch as thou sawest the iron mixed with miry clay. And as the toes of the feet were part of iron, and part of clay, so the kingdom shall be partly strong, and partly broken. And whereas thou sawest iron mixed with miry clay, they shall mingle themselves with the seed of men: but they shall not cleave one to another, even as iron is not mixed with clay.

And in the days of these kings shall the God of heaven set up a kingdom, which shall never be destroyed: and the kingdom shall not be left to other people, but it shall break in pieces and consume all these kingdoms, and it shall stand for ever. Forasmuch as thou sawest that the stone was cut out of the mountain without hands, and that it brake in pieces the iron, the brass, the clay, the silver, and the gold; the great God hath made known to the king what shall come to pass hereafter: and the dream is certain, and the interpretation thereof sure. (Daniel 2:31–45)

Let's break this vision down.

- First Kingdom: Head of fine gold—This represents King Nebuchadnezzar's existing Babylonian empire (Daniel 2:37–38).
- Second Kingdom: Breast and arms of silver—This is the kingdom that shall arise after the Babylonian empire, which we know to be the Medo-Persian empire.
- Third Kingdom: Belly and thighs of brass—This is the kingdom that arises after the Medo-Persian empire, which we know to be the Greek empire.
- Fourth Kingdom: Legs of iron—This is the kingdom that shall arise after the Greek empire. Most would say this is the Roman

empire; however the text (and history) indicates a better fit with the Islamic empire, as we will discuss shortly.
- Fifth Kingdom: Feet and toes of part iron and part clay—This is the final Middle Eastern kingdom, the beast kingdom that will exist at the end of the age and which will be smitten and broken by the stone cut out without hands, which is a representation of the millennial kingdom of Jesus Christ.

To connect this further to our prior studies, let's go to Revelation 17, specifically verses 9–10. Revelation 17 presents an overview of the primary kingdoms and geography from which blasphemous religions and religious practices spawned that were directly harmful to God's people in Bible times. It also represents the kingdoms that have persecuted and afflicted the children of Israel. Persecution and ill treatment of God's people were an attribute of these ancient kingdoms, and they will continue to be a key identifying characteristic of the modern Middle Eastern kingdom era, especially the time when the final beast kingdom finds its place in history.

The final beast kingdom will be drunk with the blood of the saints and the blood of the martyrs of Jesus:

> And I saw the woman drunken with the blood of the saints, and with the blood of the martyrs of Jesus: and when I saw her, I wondered with great admiration. And the angel said unto me, Wherefore didst thou marvel? I will tell thee the mystery of the woman, and of the beast that carrieth her, which hath the *seven heads and ten horns*. The beast that thou sawest was, and is not; and shall ascend out of the bottomless pit, and go into perdition: and they that dwell on the earth shall wonder, whose names were not written in the book of life from the foundation of the world, when they behold the beast that was, and is not, and yet is. And here is the mind which hath wisdom. *The seven heads are seven mountains*, on which the woman sitteth. And *there are seven kings: five are fallen, and one is, and the other is not yet come; and when he cometh, he must continue a short space. And the beast that was, and is not, even he is the eighth, and is of the seven, and goeth into perdition.* (Revelation 17:6–11)

Revelation 17:9 describes the seven heads as seven mountains. As Scripture often does, it then helps to define itself by saying that these represent seven kings (Strong's G935—the image of mountains implies a foundation of power). Kings rule kingdoms, and it is not uncommon for a mountain to represent a kingdom in Scripture. We see this very usage in Daniel 2:35:

> Then was the iron, the clay, the brass, the silver, and the gold, broken to pieces together, and became like the chaff of the summer threshingfloors; and the wind carried them away, that no place was found for them: and *the stone* that smote the image *became a great mountain, and filled the whole earth*. (Daniel 2:35)

So what are the primary Middle Eastern kingdoms of secular history that have significantly and negatively impacted God's people throughout history? The Spirit revealed to John that up to this point, five had already come and gone, and one was currently in power. Which kingdoms were these?

A good starting point is the *Egyptian empire* (#1) and their enslavement of the people of God. Next in line is most likely the *Assyrian empire* (#2), who fought against and eventually conquered the ten northern tribes of Israel. After this, the *Babylonian empire* (#3) conquered Judea and took the people captive to Babylon. Following Babylon, the *Medo-Persian empire* (#4) ruled Judea. Then the *Greek empire* (#5), led initially by Alexander the Great, ruled Judea. After the Greek empire the *Roman empire* (#6) controlled Judea.

Who came after the Roman empire? Revelation 17:9–10 references seven kingdoms and then states that the beast empire is the eighth. The text says "the beast that was, and is not, even he is the eighth, and is of the seven." The "beast" in this context is referring to the beast kingdom, since the text is relating the beast with the previous mountains or kingdoms. In other words, the beast kingdom will be *related to* or in some way *revived from* the prior kingdoms. However, the Scripture is also personalizing the beast and beast kingdom to some extent by using the personal pronoun "he" in the text. This helps to explain what Revelation 17:10 means when it says "and when *he* cometh, *he* must continue a short space." And the text further uses the personal pronoun by saying in Revelation 17:11 that "*he* is the eighth, and is of the seven, and goeth into perdition." The "*he*" of Revelation 17:10 refers to Antichrist himself and personifies his kingdom, and it refers to the short duration and rule of the beast kingdom and the beast. Both are committed to the persecution and ill treatment of God's people. It won't take long, only 3.5 years, and he will go into perdition (ruin, waste, damnation, death, loss).

To help understand the seventh and eighth kingdoms, we can compare Revelation 17 with Daniel 2. We know from Revelation that the eighth kingdom is related to one of the former kingdoms, because the eighth is "of the seven." In Daniel, we can see a similarity between the legs of iron and the feet/toes of iron and clay.

The description of *iron* legs and feet/toes of *part iron* necessitate that we put these two related empires as the final two empires in human history. Why? Because the Scripture tells us that God's kingdom, the everlasting kingdom, will directly smite the image upon his feet of iron and clay (Daniel 2:34). The stone, Christ's kingdom, will crush the entire kingdom footprint—it consumes all these previous kingdoms together so there is no residue left, becomes a great mountain, and fills the whole earth. This is comparable with the eighth kingdom in Revelation 17:11. Revelation tells us that the Antichrist and the final beast kingdom, the eighth kingdom, will go into perdition due to the mighty power of God at the day of the Lord. The ninth kingdom shall never be destroyed and shall stand for ever. This is the *kingdom set up by the God of heaven with the Lord Jesus, the Lamb, as King of kings* (Revelation 17:14). These similarities cannot be dismissed. Therefore, it is reasonable to connect the seventh and eighth kingdoms in Revelation 17:11 with the legs of iron and the feet/toes of iron and clay.

The language of Revelation 17:10–11 tells us that the sixth empire was in power at the time John wrote Revelation circa AD 95. That empire was Rome. Then, two empires, the seventh and eighth, were to come after AD 95. If Rome was in view as the legs of iron in King Nebuchadnezzar's dream, the Roman empire would not only be the sixth empire of Revelation 17:10 but also the seventh and a "relative" of the eighth. How is this possible? It appears that a kingdom other than Rome needs to represent the legs of iron and the revived feet/toes kingdom made of part iron and part clay. Carefully analyzing the word sequence of "five are fallen, and one is, and the other is not yet come" in Revelation 17:10 forms a strong case for the absence of Rome in Daniel 2.

The first three kingdoms in Daniel 2 also share geographic similarities, each had a Middle East and Babylon-centered land "footprint." Therefore, we should expect the legs of iron and the feet/toes of iron and clay to share a similar ruling territory. When comparing a map of the Roman empire to the Islamic empire, a stark contrast is easily identified. The Roman empire was primarily concentrated around the perimeter of the Mediterranean Sea, while the Islamic empire's geographic area of control was Middle East and Babylon-centered.

Most importantly, insight can be gained by studying the kingdom characteristics used by Daniel. Daniel 2:40 states, "And the fourth kingdom shall be strong as iron: forasmuch as iron breaketh in pieces and subdueth all things: and as iron that breaketh all these, shall it break in pieces and bruise."

- Strong as iron
- Breaketh in pieces (i.e. crumbles)
- Subdueth all things

History proves that while the Roman empire was stout and dominant, it didn't "break in pieces" or "crumble" the prior three kingdoms. In fact, the Romans built and constructed more than they destroyed. They allowed existing customs and cultures to generally continue on as they had been. Early Christians were persecuted and suppressed, but not en masse.

In contrast, the Islamic empire which sprung into power in the seventh century dealt a severe blow to early Christianity and trampled underfoot and destroyed with convincing "iron leg" force much of the Middle East. It brought not only a new religion, but a new language and culture. Their conquests were marked by pillaging raids. However, lives and property of those who wouldn't convert to Islam were spared when they submitted and paid the jizya tax. The effect of this "iron leg" trampling is evident still today. I recommend two authors who have written extensively on this subject: Joel Richardson in his book *Mideast Beast* and Mark Davidson in his book *Daniel Revisited*.

Let's summarize by comparing Daniel's vision with the eight kingdoms of Revelation 17 in chart format:

	Daniel's Description:	Revelation 17:10–11, the eight empires	Revelation 17:10–11, a chronology as of 95 AD:
#1	N/A—not in dream	Egyptian empire	Is pre-95 AD because "five are fallen"
#2	N/A—not in dream	Assyrian empire	Is pre-95 AD because "five are fallen"
#3	Head of fine gold	Babylonian empire	Is pre-95 AD because "five are fallen"
#4	Breast/Arms of silver	Medo-Persian empire	Is pre-95 AD because "five are fallen"
#5	Belly/Thighs of brass	Greek empire	Is pre-95 AD because "five are fallen"
#6	N/A—not in dream	Roman empire	Is current because "one is"
#7	Legs of iron	Islamic empire	Is post-95 AD because "not yet come"
#8	Feet/Toes of iron and clay	Revived Islamic/Beast empire	"he is the eighth, and is of the seven"

III. LINKING THE DANIEL AND REVELATION BEAST KINGDOMS

Daniel's Second Vision

> And *four great beasts came up from the sea*, diverse one from another. The first was like *a lion*, and had eagle's wings: I beheld till the wings thereof were plucked, and it was lifted up from the earth, and made stand upon the feet as a man, and a man's heart was given to it. And behold another beast, a second, like to *a bear*, and it raised up itself on one side, and it had three ribs in the mouth of it between the teeth of it: and they said thus unto it, Arise, devour much flesh. After this I beheld, and lo another, like *a leopard*, which had upon the back of it four wings of a fowl; *the beast had also four heads*; and dominion was given to it. After this I saw in the night visions, and behold *a fourth beast*, dreadful and terrible, and strong exceedingly; and it had great iron teeth: it devoured and brake in pieces, and stamped the residue with the feet of it: and it was diverse from all the beasts that were before it; *and it had ten horns*. I considered the horns, and, behold, there came up among them another *little horn*, before whom there were three of the first horns plucked up by the roots: and, behold, *in this horn were eyes like the eyes of man, and a mouth speaking great things.* (Daniel 7:3–7)

The "little horn" or "Antichrist" or "beast" or "vile person" will be the ruler of this final beast kingdom.

> And I stood upon the sand of the sea, and saw *a beast rise up out of the sea*, having *seven heads* and *ten horns*, and upon his horns ten crowns, and upon his heads the name of blasphemy. And *the beast* which I saw *was like unto a leopard*, and his feet were as the feet of *a bear*, and his mouth as the mouth of *a lion*: and the dragon [i.e. Satan] gave him his power, and his seat, and great authority. (Revelation 13:1–2)

> So he carried me away in the spirit into the wilderness: and I saw a woman sit upon *a scarlet coloured beast, full of names of blasphemy, having seven heads and ten horns.* (Revelation 17:3)

For reference, these passages were compared in chart format in our review of Revelation 13, where we concluded that both Daniel and Revelation depict the same end-times beast kingdom.

The end-times beast kingdom will arise from within and rule the same land mass as the kingdoms depicted in King Nebuchadnezzar's statue dream, all of them centered on Babylon and the Middle East. We conclude this from Daniel 2:34–35: when God's everlasting kingdom, led by the Lamb, comes to destroy the "feet/toes" kingdom, all of the current substances (iron and clay) and prior substances (brass, silver, and gold) are consumed together and at the same time. The land area of these prior kingdoms is taken over completely by God's kingdom, and ultimately to the ends of the earth. From this, we can understand the location from which the four beasts of Daniel 7 will arise. The lion, bear, and leopard kingdoms will arise from within the Middle East.

The contrast of the beast vision in Daniel 7 to the statue vision in Daniel 2 is notable in this regard. The statue image was comprised of substances characterized by durable, long-lasting qualities—substances that can be passed down from generation to generation. However, the beast images of Daniel 7 and 8 imply brevity. Beasts can live many years, even decades, and at other times only a few short months. And in regards to the final beast kingdom comprised of seven heads and ten horns, the personal pronoun used in Revelation 17:10–11 says that "he" must continue a short space. This short space is further defined in Daniel 7:25 and Revelation 13:5 as 3.5 years.

As described previously, the seven heads of the beast kingdom depict seven kingdoms. The consolidated kingdom territory depicted by the seven heads is the Middle Eastern land mass that empires ruled in ancient times. In the future, this rule will be revived again with formal kingdom status. Said another way, we can reasonably conclude that this seven-headed beast kingdom will be fully related to and integrated with the seven major kingdoms or empires that went before it: Egypt, Assyria, Babylon, Medo-Persia, Greece, Rome, and the Islamic empire. This eighth kingdom will be "of the seven" and therefore will most likely be a revived Islamic empire as discussed above.

This is not to say that the beast kingdom will be completely restricted to the Middle East. Perhaps the land area under governmental dominance will be primarily Middle Eastern, but the outstretching of religious and/or economic power and influence could and very likely will extend well beyond the Middle East, and potentially to the four corners of the earth.

The ten horns are leaders or kings who will with "one mind" give their power and strength to the beast (Revelation 17:13). This has been ordained by the heavenly Father. Revelation 17:17 states, "For God hath put in their hearts to fulfil his will, and to agree, and give their kingdom unto the beast, until the words of God shall be fulfilled." Yet, despite the eighth kingdom's mighty strength, there will be severe infighting and acrimony within it. After all, this revived kingdom is a disunified mixture of iron and clay, typified by the historic acrimony between religious factions in the Middle East that we can read about frequently in the news today.

IV. STUDY AND COMPARISON OF DANIEL 7–8

At this point we have reviewed:

a) The futurity of Daniel's visions given in Daniel 7, 8, 9 and 10–12.
b) The kingdoms pertaining to King Nebuchadnezzar's dream as well as the eight kingdoms noted in Revelation 17:10–11.
c) The beast descriptions of Daniel 7 and how they link to Revelation 13 and 17.

It is noteworthy that all of the visions given to Daniel (five in total) have this commonality: they take us to the time when Antichrist is defeated and God establishes His everlasting kingdom upon earth. This kingdom will be ruled by the Lamb, who is Lord of lords and King of kings. This is consistent with the general purpose of prophecy in the Scriptures, as prophecy is geared ultimately to reveal to us more about Jesus Christ and specifically His first and second comings.

We should note also that prophecy is often given in segments and pieces, each one a layer that can be put upon the others according to subject and context. Practically, this means we are unable to go to a single Scripture to read and understand the fullness of Christ's first coming or His second coming. Multiple Scriptures provide hints and details of these occurrences. When we consolidate and overlay these accounts, we are able to gain a full comprehension of all that God has revealed through the prophets. This is especially true with respect to the second coming of our Lord Jesus. The Scriptures contain copious information regarding the end times. It is a seemingly overwhelming task to grasp even a portion of it, let alone achieve a full understanding. However, we do well to bear in mind the concept that God regularly provides us multiple layers of information regarding the same prophetic events. When this is understood, the overwhelm abates and a clearer picture begins to come to view.

We will continue to keep in mind the above two important principles in our study of Daniel 7 and 8.

Besides linking the beast of Revelation to the beast of Daniel 7, what else could we possibly glean from Daniel 7 and 8? We know from reading Daniel 7 and 8 that each describes the emergence of the little horn, the Antichrist. What then do these Scriptures reveal to us about the events leading up to the time when the little horn rises and the tribulation commences? That is, how will God orchestrate events on earth that ripen the way for an end-times ruler to rise to prominence? Are there certain signs to look for? Could these chapters help us to correlate events with the four horsemen of Revelation 6, which likewise appear to bring us to the rise of Antichrist and the 3.5-year tribulation period? What needs to occur in our world for us to reach this point in our history?

Let's begin with the rise of the Antichrist, or little horn.

In Daniel 7, the little horn arises from what is described by Daniel 7:23 as the "fourth kingdom upon earth." In our review of the kingdoms of Daniel 2, the fourth kingdom, comprised of legs of iron, was identified as the Islamic empire. And from the connections made with the eight kingdoms referred to in Revelation 17, we understood that the seventh kingdom of Revelation 17:10 was the Islamic empire as well, and the eighth kingdom—the beast kingdom ruled by Antichrist—will be the revived Islamic empire. Revelation 17:11 says the eighth is a distinct kingdom, but it is "of the seven." This is the same relationship defined by Daniel 2 between the legs of iron and the feet/toes made of part iron and part clay. There is consistency between not only Daniel 2 and Revelation 17, but also within Daniel 7. Plus, we know that the beast kingdom of Daniel 7 is equivalent to the beast/beast kingdom of Revelation 13 and 17 based on the earlier analysis. In many ways, the book of Revelation provides meaningful insight to the book of Daniel, and vice versa.

What we know:

- The final, eighth kingdom of Revelation 17:11 is the last kingdom before Jesus Christ's kingdom.
- The final feet/toes kingdom of Daniel 2 is the last kingdom before Jesus Christ's kingdom.
- The Daniel 7 beast is the same as the seven-headed, ten-horned beast of Revelation 13 and 17.
- The fourth beast kingdom of Daniel 7:23, from which the little horn or Antichrist rises, will be the final kingdom of man. Its end will be met directly by the dominion of Jesus Christ. Jesus and the saints will receive authority and dominion from the Ancient of Days (Daniel 7:22, 25–27) after the little horn rules for a period of 3.5 years.

Due to the tight-knit association between the seventh and eighth kingdoms of Revelation 17, it is completely reasonable that Daniel 7:23 states the beast kingdom will be the "fourth" kingdom upon earth, with no reference to it being in a revived form. The revived final kingdom will be different, yet one and the same as the former. I believe we can become comfortable assuming that the fourth kingdom of Daniel 7:23 is equivalent to the eighth kingdom of Revelation 17 and the feet/toes kingdom of Daniel 2 for the following reasons:

- Daniel 7:25 refers to a rule of 3.5 years for the little horn that rises from this fourth kingdom. This correlates with the short-term nature of the eighth kingdom in Revelation 17:10, which says "when he cometh, he must continue a short space." This also correlates with the strong yet crumbly mixture of iron and clay from the feet/toes kingdom of Daniel 2, which does not suggest a long-lasting mixture.
- The attributes of the fourth beast kingdom of Daniel 7 are very similar to the description of the fourth kingdom of Daniel 2:40 with its legs of iron, and the feet/toes kingdom is also made partly of iron. The beast kingdom of Daniel 7, from which the Antichrist rises, is described as dreadful, terrible, and "strong exceedingly"; it had great iron teeth, it devoured, it broke in pieces, and it stamped the residue with its feet. Again, the relationship between the original and the revived is very close. They are essentially one and the same.
- Daniel 7 says the little horn will come up from within a power structure of ten kings. Likewise, Revelation 17:12 says that ten kings (i.e. "horns") will receive power as kings one hour with the beast. Likely, we should expect an Islamic coalition of ten kings or leaders to be in power for a very brief period of time before the Antichrist rises out of this power structure.

It isn't necessary to make a concrete conclusion that the final and dreadful beast kingdom of Daniel 7:23 will devour the "whole earth," even though that is the exact language contained in verse 23. There is biblical precedent that the "whole earth" can be regional in context. All we need to do is look at the similar language used in Daniel 2:35 and Daniel 2:39. Even though "filled the whole earth" and "shall bear rule over all the earth" are used in those two verses, we know that the Babylonian empire and the Greek empire, respectively, did not cover the entire earth. Please note that I am not saying the Antichrist's kingdom will *not* "devour the whole earth"; I am simply stating that it is not a requirement of the Scriptures. From a governmental ruling perspective, it appears to me unlikely.

In Daniel 8 the little horn rises from a nation that has been divided into four kingdoms or territories. Because this sounds different than a power structure of ten kings, should we dismiss this and the other correlations with Revelation and conclude that Daniel must be speaking about a different little horn or Antichrist? Or should we implement the "layering" method of interpretation and take from these verses an additional layer of detail that will help boost our understanding of the entire dynamic from which the little horn or Antichrist will be officially birthed?

If we review and compare the attributes and characteristics of the little horn from Daniel 8 with the attributes and characteristics of Daniel 7 (and Daniel 11 also), we find great commonality and consistency. Therefore, I believe it is prudent to make an effort to embed the additional information from Daniel 8 into our overall picture of understanding.

Daniel 7	Daniel 8
The kingdom from which the Antichrist rises . . .	
From Daniel 7:7–8, 20, 24: Out of a dreadful, terrible, strong, and devouring beast kingdom led by a ten-king leadership structure, a little horn (i.e. Antichrist) will rise. The Antichrist will immediately subdue three of the ten kings, plucking them up by the roots.	From Daniel 8:8–9, 22–23: Four kingdoms/territories will stand up out of a nation. In the latter time of their kingdom, when the transgressors are come to the full, a little horn, a king of fierce countenance and understanding dark sentences, shall stand up.

In summary, the Antichrist appears to rise from a four kingdom/nation/territory that is led by ten kings/leaders. The kingdom overall is depicted as strong, diverse, and damaging. Immediately after coming onto the scene, the Antichrist will subdue and remove three of the ten kings.

The little horn or Antichrist . . .	
From Daniel 7:8, 20–21, 25: Eyes like the eyes of a man and a mouth speaking great things. A look more stout than his fellows. He made war with the saints, and prevailed against them. He shall speak great words against the most High, wear out the saints of the most High, think to change times and laws, and power shall be given into his hand for 3.5 years.	Daniel 8:23–25: A king of fierce countenance and understanding dark sentences. His power shall be mighty (but not by his own power), he shall destroy wonderfully, shall prosper, practice and destroy the mighty and the holy people. He shall cause deception to prosper, he will be proud, he will destroy many by means of peace and security.

What an alarming and dreadful list of characteristics describe the Antichrist, or little horn! The little horn of Daniel 7 is clearly the same as the little horn of Daniel 8. I also believe a connection can be made with the fourth horseman of Revelation 6:

> And when he had opened the fourth seal, I heard the voice of the fourth beast say, Come and see. And I looked, and behold a pale horse: and his name that sat on him was Death, and Hell followed with him. And power was given unto them over the fourth part of the earth, to kill with sword, and with hunger, and with death, and with the beasts of the earth. (Revelation 6:7–8)

Revelation 6:8 says "power was given unto them," and in Daniel 8:24 the little horn is described as having mighty power, "but not by his own power." It appears reasonable to connect the proud, stout, deceptive, saint-destroying little horn with the fourth horseman, whose name is Death and who is given power over a quarter of the earth. In fact, Isaiah 28:15, 18 seems to confirm that "death" and "hell" are parties with which a covenant and agreement can be made, and we know that Antichrist will do these very things (Daniel 9:27, 11:23).

Because I have such a strong belief that the Scripture itself contains most, if not all, of the answers necessary to understand the end times, I have come to the conclusion that the events and descriptions *leading up to* the little horn/Antichrist in Daniel 7 and Daniel 8 are linked. In addition, I believe that the first three horsemen in Revelation 6 are connected to those events, just as I believe the fourth horseman is a picture of the little horn/Antichrist.

We have already compared the little horn beast kingdom of Daniel 7 and Daniel 8 with the fourth seal of Revelation 6, the pale horse and his rider, whose name is Death, and his counterpart, Hell, who follows him. Before comparing the Scriptures and going through the events that lead to the rise of the Antichrist, I want to note that I recently read a book that helped me significantly. The book, *Daniel Revisited*, by author Mark Davidson, gave me a supreme boost of confidence about correlating Daniel 7 and 8 with the four horsemen (i.e. seals 1–4) of Revelation 6—all applied to a Middle East context. While I was trying to connect dots and put pieces together, my confidence level was not high.

Daniel Revisited goes into intricate historic detail and specificity that far exceeds my ability. I don't possess a deep understanding of world history, and I would never be considered a librarian's best friend! But reading *Daniel Revisited* buoyed my belief that making connections between Daniel 7, Daniel 8 and Revelation 6 is reasonable.

The following is a high-level overview of the main events of Daniel 7–8 and Revelation 6:

Daniel 7	Daniel 8	Revelation 6
Beast #1 – Like a lion	N/A	A white horse
Beast #2 – Like a bear	Ram (Media/Persia)	A red horse
Beast #3 – Like a leopard	Male goat (Greece)	A black horse
Beast #4 – Little horn beast kingdom	Little horn beast kingdom	A pale horse

What can we learn from the above connections? Derived largely from *Daniel Revisited*, but in my own words, the following appear to be events to watch for on the march toward the rise of the Antichrist. However, let me say this: I am far from dogmatic about the specifics surrounding the events that lead up to the Antichrist. This is an example of where we as Bereans need to search the Scriptures and seek wisdom from God. Then, as future events unfold, time and events will bring consensus and confirmation regarding the actual fulfillment of prophetic events that are yet future.

Like a Lion	N/A	A White Horse
Daniel 7:4: The first was *like a lion,* and had eagle's wings: I beheld till the wings thereof were plucked, and it was lifted up from the earth, and made to stand upon the feet as a man, and a man's heart was given to it.		Revelation 6:2: And I saw, and behold a white horse: and he that sat on him had a bow; and a crown was given unto him: and he went forth conquering, and to conquer.

First event: The first horseman and lion event. It is difficult for me to find a striking correlation between these two. Perhaps these passages depict an event that is necessary to create the proper environment for the second beast to do his work but on its own doesn't stand out as significant. If the author of *Daniel Revisited* is correct and this event was the Iraq War, this may have already occurred. It is speculation, but it is not wild speculation. Based on the scriptural descriptions of this event, something unnatural had to occur (signified by the plucked lion that was made to stand on its feet as a man). In

Iraq, there was indeed an unnatural change when the United States assisted Iraq's transition to a democratic government. This was the lasting result of the United States' invasion in 2003 over what they thought was a fierce lion with weapons of mass destruction. Instead, those WMDs were found to be nonexistent—much like a bow without any arrows, or the roar of a lion without the bite. One more tidbit is that President George W. Bush is quoted as saying that God spoke to him and said, "'George, go and end the tyranny in Iraq,' and I did." I personally wouldn't discount this possibility.

All credit for this possible identification goes to Mark Davidson in his book *Daniel Revisited*. *Daniel Revisited* also notes additional historical connections with Saddam's "crown" and some of Iraq's prior quests in battle. Time and events will bear out whether this deduction is correct or not. This will be the test: if the next main event in the Middle East is Iran (i.e. the kings of Media and Persia) storming out to the north, west, and south, we can have great confidence that indeed the Iraq War was the first horseman and lion event. Let's read about this next event.

Like a Bear	Ram (Media/Persia)	A Red Horse
Daniel 7:5: And behold another beast, a second, *like to a bear*, and it *raised up itself on one side*, and it had three ribs in the mouth of it between the teeth of it: and they said thus unto it, *Arise, devour much flesh.*	Daniel 8:3: Then I lifted up mine eyes, and saw, and, behold, there stood before the river a ram which had two horns: and the two horns were high; but *one was higher than the other,* and the higher came up last. Daniel 8:4: I saw the ram pushing westward, and northward, and southward; so that no beasts might stand before him, *neither was there any that could deliver out of his hand; but he did according to his will, and became great.* Daniel 8:20: The ram which thou sawest having two horns are the kings of Media and Persia.	Revelation 6:3: And when he had opened the second seal, I heard the second beast say, Come and see. Revelation 6:4: And there went out another horse that was red: and power was given to him that sat thereon to *take peace from the earth,* and that they should kill one another: and there was given unto him *a great sword.*

Second event: The red horse, ram, and bear event. Note that the bear was raised up on one side as compared to the ram that had two horns, one higher than the other. Also, three ribs were pointing out of the bear's mouth, as compared to the ram, which pushed out in three directions. Lastly, the bear seemed swift and invincible in its devouring of much flesh, as compared to the ram's actions, where he charged so fast that no one could stand in his way. There also seems to be a possible connection between the red horse rider and the bear/ram because of the great sword, which has power to create fear and cause death. Both the bear and ram depict a swift, destructive, and deadly force that could not be stopped.

The Scriptures provide a clear identification for the two horns of the ram. From Daniel 8, we are told that the two horns of the ram represent Media and Persia.

Kings of Media and Persia: If we take the scripture literally, we should also try to keep the interpretation as simple as possible. This means when the scripture says "kings of Media and Persia," we simply conclude that the modern-day equivalent nation is Iran. The Medes were an ancient Iranian people who lived in the northwestern portion of present-day Iran. And Persia is modern-day Iran.

Thus, modern-day Iran, led by two powerful leaders, will one day launch out to the north, west, and south, and no one will dare stand in their path. This seems to fit with the trajectory of current events. Iran has an open disdain for many of their neighbors. They are making massive military purchases, and billions of frozen dollars are being released into their coffers due to the nuclear deal made possible by President Obama and Secretary of State John Kerry. This is a possibility. Time will tell. Now, let's read the Scriptures pertaining to the "third event."

Like a Leopard	Male Goat (Greece)	A Black Horse
Daniel 7:6: After this I beheld, and lo another, *like a leopard,* which had upon the back of it *four wings of a fowl;* the beast had also four heads; and dominion was given to it.	Daniel 8:5: And as I was considering, behold, an he goat came from the west on the face of the whole earth, and *touched not the ground:* and the goat had a notable horn between his eyes. Daniel 8:6: And he came to the ram that had two horns, which I had seen standing before the river, and ran unto him in the fury of his power.	Revelation 6:5: And when he had opened the third seal, I heard the third beast say, Come and see. And I beheld, and lo a black horse; and he that sat on him had a pair of balances in his hand.

Daniel 8:7: And I saw him come close unto the ram, and he was moved with choler against him, and smote the ram, and brake his two horns: and there was no power in the ram to stand before him, but he cast him down to the ground, and stamped upon him: and there was none that could deliver the ram out of his hand. Daniel 8:8: Therefore the he goat waxed very great: and when he was strong, the great horn was broken; and for it came up four notable ones toward the four winds of heaven. Daniel 8:21: And the rough goat is the king of Grecia: and the great horn that is between his eyes is the first king.	Revelation 6:6: And I heard a voice in the midst of the four beasts say, A measure of wheat for a penny, and three measures of barley for a penny; and see thou hurt not the oil and the wine.

Third event: The black horse, male goat, and leopard event. Some similarities appear between the leopard with four wings (denoting flight) and the male goat that comes from the west without his feet touching the ground. The leopard is given dominion, and the he-goat waxes great and strong. But how could the black horse rider connect with the leopard and male goat? With the leopard, the Scripture doesn't specify the animal characteristic we should use for comparison purposes as it does with the lion (mouth) and bear (feet). But one trait of a leopard is to kill its prey and then climb a tree, sometimes with a very large and heavy kill in its mouth, to eat his food in hidden seclusion. Perhaps there are more connections, but this one stands out as something self-serving humans would do in time of severe famine, if they were fortunate enough to procure a good supply of food.

The Scriptures also provide a known identification for the male goat. From Daniel 8, we are told that the male goat is from "Grecia."

King of Grecia: Grecia (Strong's H3120—"Javan, the name of a son of Joktan, and of the race (Ionians, that is, Greeks) descended from him, with their territory"). In a simple way, we could conclude that the king of Grecia will come from somewhere in the ancient Greek empire. However, Strong's Concordance gives us more detail by noting the Hebrew word Javan is the territory of Ionia within the ancient Greek kingdom. Ionia was located in southwest Asia Minor, in what is present-day Turkey. Most likely the nation led by the king of Grecia will be a Turkish-led force led by a very strong leader.

This male goat will retaliate against Iran and create another major power shift in the Middle East. After the counterattack and ultimate destruction of Iran (the two horns of Media/Persia are broken) and the victor waxes great and strong, there will eventually be a division of the single great horn of dominance as it breaks and turns into four horns of power.

This event leads to the rise of the little horn/Antichrist as we discussed previously. But when does the rise of the little horn/Antichrist occur within the overall eschatological framework of the end times? For that, let's move to section V.

V. THE RISE OF THE LITTLE HORN/ANTICHRIST

We have already seen quite a bit of detail about this as we looked at the eschatological framework, so this section will serve as a brief review.

Daniel 7 and 8 both refer to someone they call the "little horn." Daniel 11 refers to this same person as a "vile person." Revelation 13 calls him a "beast." These are all alternate names for the Antichrist. From Revelation 13:1–9 we read the following: Satan, or the dragon, will give the beast/Antichrist his power, and his seat, and great authority. He will be a great blasphemer, as upon his seven heads is the name of blasphemy. He will be the king of the end-times beast kingdom. He will have power for forty-two months, or 3.5 years. He will persecute the saints of God. Great deception will be upon the earth in his days.

This time of the Antichrist or little horn rising out of the end-times revived beast kingdom is indicated at seal #4 by the vertical, dashed black line in this mini, condensed version of the End-Times Chart:

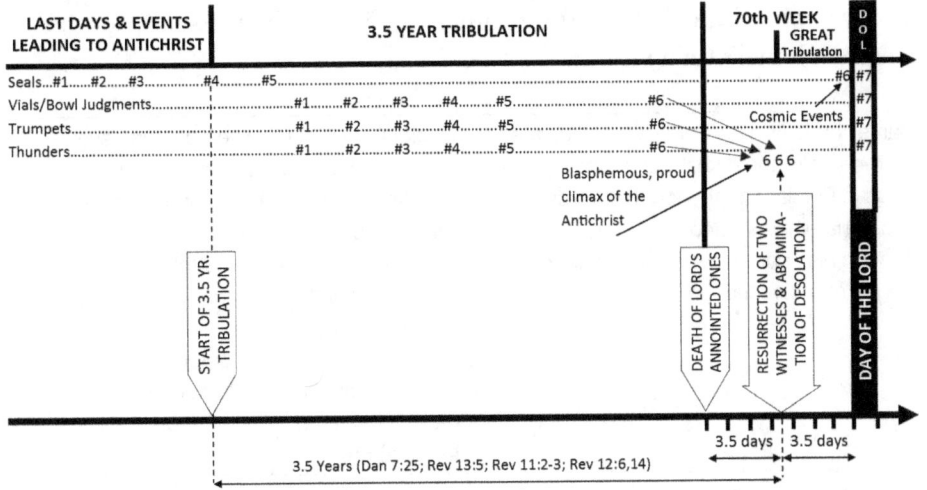

The calling for the believer at the time when the Antichrist comes to power—as it is in all times—is to love *not* our lives but pour out our affections toward God and our Lord Jesus, praying and desiring that His will alone be done. The reign of Antichrist will indeed be a time of purification and refining for the followers of Jesus Christ.

> And they overcame him by the blood of the Lamb, and by the word of their testimony; and they loved not their lives unto the death. (Revelation 12:11)

VI. DANIEL 10–12, THE FIFTH VISION

As noted previously, the last three chapters of Daniel comprise one entire message. It contains the fifth and final vision given to Daniel. In the section on the futurity of Daniel's visions, I contended that to see a purely or even primarily historical fulfillment of these chapters runs counter to a basic principle of prophecy: that generally speaking, prophecy pertains to the Lord Jesus Christ, either His first coming or His second coming. And not to belabor the point, but we cannot dismiss what the text explicitly tells us about the timing of the vision. Daniel 10:1 states that the time appointed was long, meaning that the vision was applicable to a time that was a long way off from Daniel's day. Daniel 10:14 makes a summary statement that the vision is in regard to what shall befall the Israelites in the latter days. Daniel 12:4 says the words of the book are related to the time of the end, as Daniel 12:9 restates. Even if we don't understand how the events of Daniel 10–12 will specifically play out in the future, this is one more set of Scriptures to be vividly tuned in to as we see the day approaching. Let's start at Daniel 11:2 where the messenger begins to interpret Daniel's final vision.

Daniel 11:2: And now will I shew thee the truth. Behold, there shall stand up yet three kings in Persia; and the fourth shall be far richer than they all: and by his strength through his riches he shall stir up all against the realm of Grecia.	**Daniel 8:3–4:** Then I lifted up mine eyes, and saw, and, behold, there stood before the river a ram which had two horns: and the two horns were high; but one was higher than the other, and the higher came up last. I saw the ram pushing westward, and northward, and southward; so that no beasts might stand before him, neither was there any that could deliver out of his hand; but he did according to his will, and became great.

Daniel 11:2 may hint at the bear, ram, and red horse event referred to earlier. We know that Iran has had two supreme leaders since the 1979 revolution in their country. Their sitting supreme leader has cancer and could be near the end of his reign. A possibility exists that the next supreme leader could be the third king in Persia mentioned here, to be followed or accompanied by a fourth, unknown leader with abundant financial resources and military strength, who could come up later and rise up as the larger horn per Daniel 8:3.

Daniel 11:3: And a mighty king shall stand up, that shall rule with great dominion, and do according to his will.	Daniel 8:5–7: And as I was considering, behold, an he goat came from the west on the face of the whole earth, and touched not the ground: and the goat had a notable horn between his eyes. And he came to the ram that had two horns, which I had seen standing before the river, and ran unto him in the fury of his power. And I saw him come close unto the ram, and he was moved with choler against him, and smote the ram, and brake his two horns: and there was no power in the ram to stand before him, but he cast him down to the ground, and stamped upon him: and there was none that could deliver the ram out of his hand.

Daniel 11:3 may indicate the leopard, male goat, and black horse event referred to earlier. If so, a mighty king (the single notable horn) will be able to retaliate with anger against Iran's military attack and smite the ram, break his two horns, cast him to the ground, and stamp upon him.

Daniel 11:4: And when he shall stand up, his kingdom shall be broken, and shall be divided toward the four winds of heaven; and not to his posterity, nor according to his dominion which he ruled: for his kingdom shall be plucked up, even for others beside those.	Daniel 8:8: Therefore the he goat waxed very great: and when he was strong, the great horn was broken; and for it came up four notable ones toward the four winds of heaven.

Daniel 11:4 could align with Daniel 8:8 and the eventual breaking apart of the single notable horn into four notable horns that spread out toward the four winds of heaven. The language is very similar between the two Scriptures.

The Kings of North and South

In Daniel 11, our attention quickly turns to two rulers called the "king of the north" and the "king of the south." Daniel 11:5–12 seems to indicate a dominant king of the south and various dealings back and forth with the king of the north. Then, Daniel 11:13–16 says that the king of the north will return after certain years with a great army and riches to come against the king of the south, and no one, not even the chosen people, will be able to withstand his power.

> For the king of the north shall return, and shall set forth a multitude greater than the former, and shall certainly come after certain years with a great army and with much riches. And in those times there shall many stand up against the king of the south: also the robbers of thy people shall exalt themselves to establish the vision; but they shall fall. So the king of the north shall come, and cast up a mount, and take the most fenced cities: and the arms of the south shall not withstand, neither his chosen people, neither shall there be any strength to withstand. But he that cometh against him shall do according to his own will, and none shall stand before him: and he shall stand in the glorious land, which by his hand shall be consumed. (Daniel 11:13–16)

Who are these kings, and what do these events signify?

The storyline through a large portion of Daniel 11 is acrimony between the north and the south. Most would say that the bulk of Daniel 11 represents battles and events that occurred between Antiochus Epiphanes (ruler of the Seleucid Kingdom in the north) and the Ptolemaic Kingdom in the south during the Greek empire. I could be off-base, but I prefer to see these events as the byproduct of a crumbly composition of iron mixed with clay in the latter days. Most assuredly, a great deal of in-fighting will occur as the eighth kingdom works into a "revived" status, and then while it dominates for a "short space" of 3.5 years. Until the coming kingdom led by Jesus Christ, we should expect ongoing turmoil and upheaval in the Middle East.

Daniel 11:16–17 says that the king of the north will stand in the glorious land, which by his hand will be consumed. He will enter with power and domination. This appears to be a devastating blow against Jerusalem in some future day. The glorious land most likely is Jerusalem and Judea. Glorious is that land because it is God's promised land, and it is the place from which the glorious reign of Christ will flow one day. If my guess is true that the Western Wall is the place of "daily sacrifice" that will be removed, this could be the time when the treasured and holy site of the Western Wall will be destroyed, not leaving one stone upon another, thus starting the time clock of the end with the 1290 days of Daniel 12:11 and the 1335 days of Daniel 12:12. (Consult the "Eschatological Framework" chapter for detailed discussion of this topic.)

Daniel 11:18–20 could very well be a swift set of events when the king of the north turns his face back toward his own land. But he stumbles and falls and is not to be found. In his place stands up another, a raiser of taxes, but within a few days that person is destroyed, neither in anger nor in battle:

> After this shall he turn his face unto the isles, and shall take many: but a prince for his own behalf shall cause the reproach offered by him to cease; without his own reproach he shall cause it to turn upon him. Then he shall turn his face toward the fort of his own land: but he shall stumble and fall, and not be found. Then shall stand up in his estate a raiser of taxes in the glory of the kingdom: but within few days he shall be destroyed, neither in anger, nor in battle. (Daniel 11:18–20)

This brings us to verse 21. In my opinion, Daniel 11:21 marks the arrival of the Antichrist. We can perform a simple exercise starting at verse 21 with the phrase "he shall." By tracing this phrase from verse to verse, we find an unbroken chain of the pronoun "he" (i.e. Antichrist) from verse 21 all the way to verse 45.

When Antichrist rises to power, his initial target is not Jerusalem. Rather, he will first target leaders and land within the beast kingdom itself. We read that he will come in peaceably, and obtain the kingdom by flatteries (Daniel 11:21). Ten kings will pledge their loyalty to him and the beast kingdom, but he will subdue three of them (Revelation 17:13, Daniel 7:8). The initial target of Antichrist's great army appears to be the king of the south (Daniel 11:25). Many will be slain (Daniel 11:26). When Antichrist returns to his land, he does so with great riches, which he distributes among his people (Daniel 11:24, 28). Joel Richardson writes in *Mideast Beast*, pages 122–123: "The Ancient Christians believed that the three nations of Egypt, Libya, and Sudan correspond to the three horns that would first be uprooted by the Antichrist according to Daniel 7:8." I think this makes a great deal of sense and is a simple way to summarize Daniel 11:24–28 as well as Daniel 11:43.

In the latter days, Egypt and some surrounding nations will experience a great fall (Ezekiel 30:3–5). Daniel 11:24–28 may be depicted in the following Scriptures where we see Egypt given into the hand of a cruel king from the north:

- Isaiah 19:4: "And the Egyptians will I give over into the hand of a cruel lord; and a fierce king shall rule over them, saith the Lord, the LORD of hosts."
- Ezekiel 30:10–11: "Thus saith the Lord GOD; I will also make the multitude of Egypt to cease by the hand of Nebuchadrezzar king of Babylon. He and his people with him, the terrible of the nations, shall be brought to destroy the land: and they shall draw their swords against Egypt, and fill the land with the slain."

It will be a time of drought in Egypt where the rivers become dried up.

- Isaiah 19:5: "And the waters shall fail from the sea, and the river shall be wasted and dried up."
- Ezekiel 30:12: "And I will make the rivers dry, and sell the land into the hand of the wicked: and I will make the land waste, and all that is therein, by the hand of strangers: I the LORD have spoken it."

And it will be a time of civil war.

- Isaiah 19:2: "And I will set the Egyptians against the Egyptians: and they shall fight every one against his brother, and every one against his neighbour; city against city, and kingdom against kingdom."

Thankfully, the Scripture portrays hope beyond the desperate situation that we have just reviewed. It appears from Isaiah 19:21–22 and Ezekiel 30:26 that many Egyptians will eventually come to a full understanding of the Lord!

We'll conclude this chapter with a high-level summary of Antichrist's actions and attributes as recorded in Daniel 11. Please note that a chronological sketch of events in the life of Antichrist is included in chapter 5 on the Olivet Discourse.

The Characteristics of Antichrist

He will have a "great army" that has power to overthrow many. However, it appears to me that he will have a "soft" edge. The description that frequently comes to my mind is that he will be a "wolf in sheep's clothing."

As you know, I favor an interpretation that depicts Jerusalem falling at the hands of an earlier leader (Daniel 11:16) just thirty days prior to the rise of the Antichrist. I believe this sets the table for a "soft" entrance, in regards to Antichrist's relationship with the Jews, and will enhance his ability to work deceitfully.

He will flatter and corrupt by flatteries; he will destroy many by peace (a false security); he will make fine promises and speak great things. He will work deceitfully and will enter peaceably even into rich, secure places. He will fabricate plans and divide the land for gain. His heart will be against the holy covenant, and he will have intelligence with those that forsake the holy covenant. He will do exploits, speak lies, and do mischief.

He will be proud and will plant his dwelling place in the glorious holy mountain, where he will exalt himself and magnify himself above all, speaking marvelous things against God. Despite his pride and blasphemies, he will prosper in his actions for a time. He will honor a god of forces, a foreign god, and will experience resistance from the king of the south and other nations.

Then, after forty-two months of deceitful wickedness, Antichrist's time will be over. His time of rule will have been marked by his cunningness and his evil ability to trick and corrupt people by deception and flattery. As if the people of God will not have enough to deal with from his hand of physical persecution, they will also have to deal with someone who is a master deceiver and who has the backing of Satan's evil devices, the false prophet, and evil signs and wonders. This is a phenomena that is difficult to fully grasp. Evil will be completely unleashed. Oh, how needful in those days to cry out to the Almighty at every moment for wisdom, for patience, for faith, and for grace to endure to the end!

Thanks be to God, the powerful might of God will also counter the enemy during this time, sending difficult plagues throughout the tenure of the Antichrist's 3.5-year rule that are specifically targeted at Antichrist and his followers. Even in these darkest days of human history, God's faithfulness and power will be evident to those who look.

Chapter 5

THE OLIVET ROAD MAP OF THE END TIMES: WHAT DID JESUS SAY?

I n this chapter we will take a remarkable journey through the words of Jesus Christ. From the Mount of Olives, He privately told His disciples of the "sign of His coming" and "of the end of the world." This discourse of our Lord Jesus is truly a road map of the end times. And where does it lead? You guessed it—to the day of the Lord, when He returns in power and great glory!

> Immediately after the tribulation of those days shall the sun be darkened, and the moon shall not give her light, and the stars shall fall from heaven, and the powers of the heavens shall be shaken: and then shall appear *the sign* of the Son of man in heaven: and then shall all the tribes of the earth mourn, and they shall see *the Son of man coming* in the clouds of heaven with power and great glory. And he shall send his angels with a great sound of a trumpet, and they shall gather together his elect from the four winds, from one end of heaven to the other. (Matthew 24:29–31)

Without further delay, let's begin the journey. But first, I implore you. Unless you want to bypass a rich blessing, do not gloss over the comparative Scriptures from Jesus's sermon that are laid out in the charts!

COMPARISON AND REVIEW OF MATTHEW 24, MARK 13, AND LUKE 21

NOT ONE STONE UPON ANOTHER		
Matthew 24:1: And Jesus went out, and departed from the temple: and his disciples came to him for to shew him the buildings of the temple.	Mark 13:1: And as he went out of the temple, one of his disciples saith unto him, Master, see what manner of stones and what buildings are here!	Luke 21:5: And as some spake of the temple, how it was adorned with goodly stones and gifts, he said,
Matthew 24:2: And Jesus said unto them, See ye not all these things? verily I say unto you, There shall not be left here one stone upon another, that shall not be thrown down.	Mark 13:2: And Jesus answering said unto him, Seest thou these great buildings? there shall not be left one stone upon another, that shall not be thrown down.	Luke 21:6: As for these things which ye behold, the days will come, in the which there shall not be left one stone upon another, that shall not be thrown down.
Matthew 24:3: And as he sat upon the mount of Olives, the disciples came unto him privately, saying, Tell us, when shall these things be? and what shall be the sign of thy coming, and of the end of the world?	Mark 13:3–4: And as he sat upon the mount of Olives over against the temple, Peter and James and John and Andrew asked him privately, Tell us, when shall these things be? and what shall be the sign when all these things shall be fulfilled?	Luke 21:7: And they asked him, saying, Master, but when shall these things be? and what sign will there be when these things shall come to pass?

The disciples, with wonder and awe, looked at the stones and the buildings in the temple complex. Then Jesus declared, "there shall not be left *one stone upon another, that shall not be thrown down.*"

The prophecy of "there shall not be left one stone upon another" was fulfilled in 70 AD, correct? Maybe, maybe not. I don't want to be too nitpicky, but what did the disciples say to Jesus. In awe, they said to Jesus, "Master, see what manner of stones and what buildings are here!" It is possible that they were only focused on one section of the temple complex and the present-day Western Wall was not in view. But are we fully confident that this prophecy has been 100 percent fulfilled?

All of us have viewed pictures of the Western Wall and its beautiful stone wall, each one upon the other. The Western Wall was not a part of the temple itself, but an outer wall surrounding the Temple Mount. This remnant of what was the most sacred building in the Jewish world is possibly the holiest place for Jews today. Other parts of the Temple Mount retaining wall also remain standing, but the Western Wall is especially dear, as it is the spot closest to the Holy of Holies—the central focus of the temple that was destroyed in 70 AD.

The Western Wall is the site of ongoing daily prayers and worship in Jerusalem today. While we can be satisfied that Jesus's prophecy of the stones and the buildings being thrown down was generally fulfilled in 70 AD, it seems to me a likely possibility that the destruction of this holy site could very well be day 1 of the 1290 days in Daniel 12:11. Thus, a greater and ultimate fulfillment of this prophecy may lie ahead! According to the eschatological framework of the Scriptures, this would occur on Purim on some appointed year in the future. The daily activities of prayer at this holy site meet the requirement of Daniel 12:11. All it would take is a destructive event, such as that intimated in Daniel 11:16, to occur on Purim, thirty days prior to the rise of the 3.5-year term of Antichrist.

THE BEGINNING OF BIRTH PANGS

Matthew 24:4: And Jesus answered and said unto them, Take heed that no man deceive you.	Mark 13:5: And Jesus answering them began to say, Take heed lest any man deceive you:	Luke 21:8: And he said, Take heed that ye be not deceived:
Matthew 24:5: For many shall come in my name, saying, I am Christ; and shall deceive many.	Mark 13:6: For many shall come in my name, saying, I am Christ; and shall deceive many.	for many shall come in my name, saying, I am Christ; and the time draweth near: go ye not therefore after them.
Matthew 24:6: And ye shall hear of wars and rumours of wars: see that ye be not troubled: for all these things must come to pass, but the end is not yet.	Mark 13:7: And when ye shall hear of wars and rumours of wars, be ye not troubled: for such things must needs be; but the end shall not be yet.	Luke 21:9: But when ye shall hear of wars and commotions, be not terrified: for these things must first come to pass; but the end is not by and by.
Matthew 24:7: For nation shall rise against nation, and kingdom against kingdom: and there shall be famines, and pestilences, and earthquakes, in divers places.	Mark 13:8: For nation shall rise against nation, and kingdom against kingdom: and there shall be earthquakes in divers places, and there shall be famines and troubles:	Luke 21:10–11: Then said he unto them, Nation shall rise against nation, and kingdom against kingdom: And great earthquakes shall be in divers places, and famines, and pestilences; and fearful sights and great signs shall there be from heaven.
Matthew 24:8: All these are the beginning of sorrows.	these are the beginnings of sorrows.	

The signs leading to the second coming of Jesus Christ include deception, wars and commotions, famines, earthquakes, and troubles. These signs are the beginning of labor or birth pangs. The word used for "sorrows" in Matthew 24:8 is a pang or throe (Strong's G5604—"a pang or throe, especially of childbirth:—pain, sorrow, travail"). The equating of the days near the day of the Lord to "birth pangs" is common throughout the Scripture. Since the Olivet Discourse is a story line that takes the reader to the second coming of Jesus and the resurrection of the dead, it is not unexpected, or out of line, for Jesus to bring the thought of childbirth pain into His teaching at this point. Rather, it is the very description of the prophets Isaiah and Jeremiah being carried forward.

Isaiah 26:17–18 refers to "birth pangs" in context with the resurrection. The following verse in Isaiah 26:19 reads: "Thy dead men shall live, together with my [Isaiah's] dead body shall they arise. Awake and sing, ye that dwell in dust: for thy dew is as the dew of herbs, and the earth shall cast out the dead."

The apostle Paul also refers to birth pains in 1 Thessalonians 5:3 in context of the day of the Lord: "For when they shall say, Peace and safety; then sudden destruction cometh upon them, as travail upon a woman with child; and they shall not escape."

Jeremiah 30:6–7 also refers to birth pains (travail). Jeremiah 30:6–7: "Ask ye now, and see whether a man doth travail with child? wherefore do I see every man with his hands on his loins, as a woman in travail, and all faces are turned into paleness? Alas! for that day is great, so that none is like it: it is even the time of Jacob's trouble; but he shall be saved out of it."

Isaiah 13:8–9 echoes this image once more: "And they shall be afraid: pangs and sorrows shall take hold of them; they shall be in pain as a woman that travaileth: they shall be amazed one at another; their faces shall be as flames. Behold, the day of the LORD cometh, cruel both with wrath and fierce anger, to lay the land desolate: and he shall destroy the sinners thereof out of it."

These passages in Isaiah 13 and Jeremiah 30 are in context of the time of Jacob's trouble and the subsequent destruction of the wicked that will occur at the day of the Lord. Isaiah 26:17 and 1 Thessalonians 5:3 depict a time when the labor pains are great and the time for delivery of the child is near. In contrast to the time noted by Christ in the Olivet Discourse, which He calls the "beginning" of labor pains, the pangs and sorrows in Isaiah and Jeremiah are strong and severe due to the nearness and proximity of the second coming—it is the difference between the early contractions of labor and the tremendous transition at the end.

THE OLIVET ROAD MAP OF THE END TIMES: WHAT DID JESUS SAY?

ENDURING PERSECUTION FOR THE GOSPEL

Matthew 24:9: Then shall they deliver you up to be afflicted, and shall kill you: and ye shall be hated of all nations for my name's sake.	Mark 13:9: But take heed to yourselves: for they shall deliver you up to councils; and in the synagogues ye shall be beaten: and ye shall be brought before rulers and kings for my sake, for a testimony against them.	Luke 21:12–13: But before all these, they shall lay their hands on you, and persecute you, delivering you up to the synagogues, and into prisons, being brought before kings and rulers for my name's sake. And it shall turn to you for a testimony.
	Mark 13:11: But when they shall lead you, and deliver you up, take no thought beforehand what ye shall speak, neither do ye premeditate: but whatsoever shall be given you in that hour, that speak ye: for it is not ye that speak, but the Holy Ghost.	Luke 21:14: Settle it therefore in your hearts, not to meditate before what ye shall answer: Luke 21:15: For I will give you a mouth and wisdom, which all your adversaries shall not be able to gainsay nor resist.
Matthew 24:10: And then shall many be offended, and shall betray one another, and shall hate one another. Matthew 24:11: And many false prophets shall rise, and shall deceive many.	Mark 13:12: Now the brother shall betray the brother to death, and the father the son; and children shall rise up against their parents, and shall cause them to be put to death.	Luke 21:16: And ye shall be betrayed both by parents, and brethren, and kinsfolks, and friends; and some of you shall they cause to be put to death.
Matthew 24:12–13: And because iniquity shall abound, the love of many shall wax cold. But he that shall endure unto the end, the same shall be saved.	Mark 13:13: And ye shall be hated of all men for my name's sake: but he that shall endure unto the end, the same shall be saved.	Luke 21:17: And ye shall be hated of all men for my name's sake.
		Luke 21:18–19: But there shall not an hair of your head perish. In your patience possess ye your souls.
Matthew 24:14: And this gospel of the kingdom shall be preached in all the world for a witness unto all nations; and then shall the end come.	Mark 13:10: And the gospel must first be published among all nations.	

As indicated above, persecution, family betrayal, and diminished love one for another will prevail. The Lord foretells of much division in the end times, but that fact isn't to dissuade the people of God from proclaiming and representing truth! The truth can bring a blessed unity with God, but it can also divide (Luke 12:49–53). Jesus says these difficulties and persecution will occur for "my name's sake." But Jesus also encourages us to fully trust in Him for wisdom, promising that in tough environments He will provide words to speak that no one can oppose. I am reminded of the sobering passage in Daniel 11:32–33, which is in context of this tribulation time period, which states, "but the people that do know their God shall be strong, and do exploits. And they that understand among the people shall instruct many: yet they shall fall by the sword, and by flame, by captivity, and by spoil, many days." This theme of persecution also lines up with Revelation 12:17, which tells us that one of the primary targets of Satan are those who keep the commandments of God and have the testimony of Jesus Christ.

So what are the people of God to do? The answer is provided in Revelation 12:11, which says "And they overcame him by the blood of the Lamb, and by the word of their testimony; and they loved not their lives unto the death." This is a sober reminder. But God is fully capable of providing sufficient grace and strength for any circumstance that may arise. And in the end, through patience and endurance of faith, ultimate salvation (Luke 21:28) will come when Jesus returns in the clouds.

As we studied in the chapter on Revelation regarding the 144000, many similarities were noted between the Olivet Discourse and Matthew 10:17–37. Matthew 10:23 says "Ye shall not have gone over the cities of Israel, till the Son of man be come." I believe that Jesus's exhortation here, and in Matthew 10, is not only a prophetic example of the ongoing work and labor of the church, but also of the 144000 "servants of God" during the tribulation.

All of this then ties in with the sheep and goat judgment from Matthew 25, which appears to be a separate event from the judgment seat of Christ in heaven. The audience is "all nations," and it seems to be a judgment predicated on how the nations of the earth treat the brethren of Christ—not only the church, but also the 144000 servants of God. The location of this judgment appears to be on earth after Jesus is sitting on the throne of glory (Matthew 19:28, Matthew 25:31). How will the nations treat the 144000 in the last days, and what will the response be to their message of truth? Jesus says that "inasmuch as ye have done it unto one of the least of these my brethren, ye have done it unto me"—that is, the giving of food, drink, shelter, and clothing, and the visiting in prison of the brethren of Jesus has also been done to Jesus Himself.

In my estimation, the timing of the end times is such that the work and labor of the 144000 will occur largely throughout the entire tribulation period. While little information is given, it appears that the 144000 are sent on a mission similar to that of the twelve disciples. As "servants of God," they are a direct extension of Christ, much like the church is today, and are called to spread the message of truth, and to convey the urgency of the hour. I believe these 144000 are sealed by God and sent out onto the mission field (as in Matthew 10:23) because of the mercy of God. The Lord will go to great lengths to ensure that His truth is made available to the hearts of men—not only through the efforts of the church and the 144000 servants of God, but also by means of an angel flying in the midst of heaven (Revelation 14:6), and preaching the everlasting gospel message to souls far and wide!

> And I saw another angel fly in the midst of heaven, having the everlasting gospel to preach unto them that dwell on the earth, and to every nation, and kindred, and tongue, and people, saying with a loud voice, Fear God, and give glory to him; for the hour of his judgment is come: and worship him that made heaven, and earth, and the sea, and the fountains of waters. (Revelation 14:6–7)

I am awed at how the Scripture is so alive! Not only does the missional message of Matthew 10 apply to the time of the disciples, but it is relevant to us today, and it will be supremely relevant during the time of the end. It is for "their time," it is for "our time," and it is for the "end time."

THE GREAT END-TIME GATHERING AND CLIMAX OF EVIL

Matthew 24:15: When ye therefore shall see *the abomination of desolation*, spoken of by Daniel the prophet, stand in the holy place, (whoso readeth, let him understand:)	Mark 13:14: But when ye shall see *the abomination of desolation*, spoken of by Daniel the prophet, standing where it ought not, (let him that readeth understand,)	Luke 21:20: And when ye shall see Jerusalem compassed with armies, then know that *the desolation* thereof is nigh.

The sixth plague (the second woe) will cause the drying up of the river Euphrates. It is one last plague that will cause an enormous death toll, killing a third of men who worship devils and repent not of their evil deeds, and gathering the evil ones together to a place called Armageddon (see Revelation

16:12–16 and Revelation 9:13–21). This gathering is what we see in Luke 21:20 just prior to the abomination of desolation. I believe it is the same gathering we read about in Zechariah 14:1–2, Zechariah 12:2, Jeremiah 4:6 and 17, and Ezekiel 38:9 and 16. It is recorded in 1 Thessalonians 5:3 that the Jews remaining in the land will feel safe and at peace when sudden destruction comes upon them. This is exactly the condition—dwelling safely in a false peace from the deceptive flatterer Antichrist—that we find at the time when the armies start to gather toward Jerusalem, per Ezekiel 38:11 and 14.

At a high level, I see the following rough sketch of events that bring us to this point in time in the life of Antichrist:

- Destruction caused by the king of the north occurs in the glorious land, which sends many Jews into captivity (Daniel 11:16).
- The arrival of Antichrist (a vile person, the little horn) occurs soon after. Antichrist comes in peaceably and by flatteries (he makes great promises and is very articulate) to begin his rule of 3.5 years (Daniel 11:21, Daniel 7:8, Revelation 13:5). As a "little horn," it appears that Antichrist begins his rule without a great deal of strength or political capital, but he quickly becomes strong (Daniel 11:23).
- Antichrist immediately subdues three of the ten leaders and spoils and plucks up the treasures from their lands (Daniel 7:8, Daniel 11:24–25). The target of Antichrist's great army appears to be the king of the south (Daniel 11:25). When Antichrist returns back to his land, he does so with great riches, which he distributes among his people (Daniel 11:24, 28).
- A tribulation period (deception, killing, famines, earthquakes, and troubles) will ensue. True followers are called to patiently endure for Jesus's sake. Meanwhile, God will dispense difficult plagues against the followers of Antichrist.
- Through deceit and craftiness, it appears that Antichrist fashions some sort of a league or peace agreement with the Jews remaining in Jerusalem and the surrounding region (Daniel 11:23). I believe this is possible because the glorious land so recently suffered devastation. The current Jewish residents will be looking for relief from the constant oppression they have experienced throughout history, and perhaps the dialogue with this new leader seems

acceptable. However, Antichrist enters the scene as a wolf in sheep's clothing.
- This agreement may involve a division of the land for gain (Daniel 11:39). To me, this makes sense, since Scripture implies that a third temple structure will exist at some point (2 Thessalonians 2:4, Revelation 11:2) and that this area might be under Jewish control, whereas the outer court will be given to the Gentiles.
- Toward the end of the tribulation, Antichrist is provoked to go toward the south. This is all a part of God's plan. Isaiah 10:5 implies that the provoking comes from the Lord as a harsh chastisement against a hypocritical Jerusalem. Isaiah 42:24 says that Jacob and Israel are given up for a spoil by the Lord. Why? Because they would not walk in His ways and were disobedient. Ezekiel 38:4 says the Lord will put hooks into Antichrist's jaws to perform what He deems necessary. Being spurred to go to the land of Israel where the people are at rest and dwelling safely (see pages 172–173) will be very acceptable to the Antichrist and will align with his evil mind (Ezekiel 38:10). In other words, Antichrist will be a willing participant. He will pleasure in gaining riches and taking a great spoil (Jeremiah 4:13, Ezekiel 38:13).
- He also will be angry against God and His holy covenant (Daniel 11:30), in addition to a desire to take a spoil.
- It appears that Antichrist will confirm an existing peace covenant at the beginning of the seventieth week (Daniel 9:27) while at the same time killing or cutting off the ruler/anointed one and his companion (Revelation 11:4, Zechariah 4:14, Daniel 9:26). In my opinion the two witnesses will have played an earthly role in helping to administer the God-powered plague assaults against Antichrist and his followers (Revelation 11:6).
- Antichrist will also "have intelligence" with them that forsake the holy covenant (Daniel 11:30) and corrupt many to act wickedly against the holy covenant based on his powers of flattery and deception (Daniel 11:32).
- When the two witnesses lie in the street for 3.5 days (i.e. the first half of the seventieth week; Revelation 11:9), it will be a joyous time for Antichrist and his followers as Antichrist does according to his will (Revelation 11:10, Daniel 11:36).

- God will then resurrect the lifeless bodies of the two witnesses (Revelation 11:11). A great voice from heaven will say "Come up hither," and they will ascend up to heaven in a cloud (Revelation 11:12). Within the hour, a great earthquake will bring fright and devastation to Jerusalem (Revelation 11:13).
- Either just prior to, at the same time as, or right after the two witnesses are resurrected by God at the middle of the seventieth week, Antichrist will commit the blasphemous abomination of desolation (Daniel 11:31, 36–37). It is my conjecture that the abomination of desolation will occur just prior to the great earthquake, which will frighten the Jewish remnant and gives opportunity for God to be glorified (Revelation 11:13).

Many Scriptures depict this horrible, proud, blasphemous act of the Antichrist. Jesus specifically refers to it, calling it "the act spoken of by the prophet Daniel."

> . . . who opposeth and exalteth himself above all that is called God, or that is worshipped; so that he as God sitteth in the temple of God, shewing himself that he is God. (2 Thessalonians 2:4)

And he shall confirm the covenant with many for one week: and in the midst of the week he shall cause the sacrifice [denotes animal sacrifice specifically] and the oblation to cease, and for the overspreading of abominations he shall make it desolate, even until the consummation, and that determined shall be poured upon the desolate. (Daniel 9:27)

And arms shall stand on his part, and they shall pollute the sanctuary of strength, and shall take away the daily sacrifice and they shall place the abomination that maketh desolate. (Daniel 11:31)

And the king shall do according to his will; and he shall exalt himself, and magnify himself above every god, and shall speak marvellous things against the God of gods, and shall prosper till the indignation be accomplished: for that that is determined shall be done. (Daniel 11:36)

As can be seen below when we continue reading further in Jesus's Olivet Discourse, the days after the abomination of desolation are utter distress and chaos. The warning is very sharp and urgent to immediately flee!

THE OLIVET ROAD MAP OF THE END TIMES: WHAT DID JESUS SAY?

QUICKLY FLEE—A GREAT TRAVAIL AND TRIBULATION

Matthew 24:16: Then let them which be in Judaea *flee* into the mountains: Matthew 24:17: Let him which is on the housetop not come down to take any thing out of his house: Matthew 24:18: Neither let him which is in the field return back to take his clothes.	Mark 13:14: then let them that be in Judaea *flee* to the mountains: Mark 13:15: And let him that is on the housetop not go down into the house, neither enter therein, to take any thing out of his house: Mark 13:16: And let him that is in the field not turn back again for to take up his garment.	Luke 21:21: Then let them which are in Judaea *flee* to the mountains; and let them which are in the midst of it depart out; and let not them that are in the countries enter thereinto. Luke 21:22: For these be *the days of vengeance*, that all things which are written may be fulfilled.
Matthew 24:19: And woe unto them that are with child, and to them that give suck in those days!	Mark 13:17: But woe to them that are with child, and to them that give suck in those days!	Luke 21:23: But woe unto them that are with child, and to them that give suck, in those days!
Matthew 24:20: But pray ye that your flight be not in the winter, neither on the sabbath day:	Mark 13:18: And pray ye that your flight be not in the winter.	
Matthew 24:21: For then shall be *great tribulation*, such as was not since the beginning of the world to this time, no, nor ever shall be.	Mark 13:19: For in those days shall be *affliction, such as was not from the beginning of the creation* which God created unto this time, neither shall be.	for there shall be *great distress in the land*, and wrath upon this people.
Matthew 24:22: And except *those days* should be shortened, there should no flesh be saved: but for the elect's sake those days shall be shortened.	Mark 13:20: And except that the Lord had shortened *those days*, no flesh should be saved: but for the elect's sake, whom he hath chosen, he hath shortened the days.	Luke 21:24: And they shall fall by the edge of the sword, and shall be led away captive into all nations: and Jerusalem shall be trodden down of the Gentiles, until the times of the Gentiles be fulfilled.

Immediately following the abomination of desolation, the indignation of Antichrist and his followers will be at peak level, and a flood of destruction will occur during the great tribulation, a time of intense travail (Isaiah 59:19; Daniel 9:26; Matthew 24:21; Zechariah 14:2; Jeremiah 30:5–7; Isaiah 13:7–8, 15–18).

Antichrist knows that his time is short, and the Scriptures indicate an unleashing of severe indignation and savagery. This is why such an urgent warning to flee is proclaimed to the residents of Jerusalem and Judea when they see the abomination of desolation. Not only will there immediately be a great earthquake near the time of the abomination, but the greatest tribulation and travail ever known to man is coming!

Antichrist will prosper until the indignation is accomplished (Daniel 11:36). Fortunately, the great tribulation of those days will soon end (approximately 3.5 days after the abomination of desolation) but not until after great affliction, distress, and wrath has been poured out by Antichrist and his armies.

The call to flee (Matthew 24:16, Mark 13:14, Luke 21:21) is in context of the great end-time gathering around Jerusalem (Luke 21:20) and the *days of vengeance* (Luke 21:22) that lead to the second coming. We reviewed this event in detail in chapter 3, section IV when studying the sixth trumpet and sixth vial plague. I believe this urgent call to flee in the Olivet Discourse is the same as described in Jeremiah 4:29–31. The day of the Lord is very near!

To summarize, once the abomination of desolation occurs, the message is urgent, and it calls for immediate action. If you happen to be in Jerusalem or Judea at this time, flee. Quickly depart, as in, fly away without getting an extra change of clothes, don't retrieve your iPad, don't even go into your house to retrieve anything! There will be severe affliction such as never before. There will be great confusion and deception. This is Satan's final assault and attempt to usurp the plan of God.

Fortunately, for the elect's sake, *those days* will be shortened. Based on my understanding, the great tribulation of those days will last for approximately 3.5 days.

It is given to us in Luke 17 that as it was in the days of Lot, even so shall it be in the day when the Son of Man is revealed in the clouds. How did the events at Sodom and Gomorrah occur? Over a period of 3.5 years, or over a short time period? The destruction of these cities occurred immediately after Lot and his family fled and ran away from the city! The devastation quickly followed.

> Likewise also as it was in the days of Lot; they did eat, they drank, they bought, they sold, they planted, they builded; but *the same day* that Lot went out of Sodom it rained fire and brimstone from heaven, and destroyed them all. Even thus shall it be in the day when the Son of man

THE OLIVET ROAD MAP OF THE END TIMES: WHAT DID JESUS SAY?

is revealed. In that day, he which shall be upon the housetop, and his stuff in the house, let him not come down to take it away: and he that is in the field, let him likewise not return back. Remember Lot's wife. Whosoever shall seek to save his life shall lose it; and whosoever shall lose his life shall preserve it. (Luke 17:28–33)

The great tribulation of those days is a time of soberness, distress, and heartache. How does the apostle Paul say it? "For when they shall say Peace and safety; then sudden destruction cometh upon them, as travail upon a woman with child; and they shall not escape" (1 Thessalonians 5:3). The following Scriptures portray a horrible travail. It is an event often spoken of by the prophets of old (Ezekiel 38:17).

Behold, the day of the LORD cometh, and thy spoil shall be divided in the midst of thee. For I will gather all nations against Jerusalem to battle; and the city shall be taken, and the houses rifled, and the women ravished; and half of the city shall go forth into captivity, and the residue of the people shall not be cut off from the city. (Zechariah 14:1–2; see also Luke 21:20, Zechariah 12:2, Ezekiel 38:9 and 16.)

For thus saith the LORD; We have heard a voice of trembling, of fear, and not of peace. Ask ye now, and see whether a man doth travail with child? wherefore do I see every man with his hands on his loins, as a woman in travail, and all faces are turned into paleness? Alas! for that day is great, so that none is like it: it is even the time of Jacob's trouble; but he shall be saved out of it. (Jeremiah 30:5–7)

Therefore shall all hands be faint, and every man's heart shall melt: and they shall be afraid: pangs and sorrows shall take hold of them; they shall be in pain as a woman that travaileth: they shall be amazed one at another; their faces shall be as flames. Every one that is found shall be thrust through; and every one that is joined unto them shall fall by the sword. Their children also shall be dashed to pieces before their eyes; their houses shall be spoiled, and their wives ravished. Behold, I will stir up the Medes against them, which shall not regard silver; and as for gold, they shall not delight in it. Their bows also shall dash the young men to pieces; and they shall have no pity on the fruit of the womb; their eye shall not spare children. (Isaiah 13:7–8, 15–18)

Thanks to Almighty God, soon after Antichrist goes forth with great fury to destroy, slay, and mutilate many (Daniel 11:44), the day of the Lord will come with overwhelming power and bring an abrupt halt to the travail. Until those days are shortened, chaos, confusion, and great tribulation will continue.

DON'T BE DECEIVED: JESUS WILL COME IN POWER AND GLORY

Matthew 24:23: Then if any man shall say unto you, Lo, here is Christ, or there; believe it not.	Mark 13:21: And then if any man shall say to you, Lo, here is Christ; or, lo, he is there; believe him not:	Luke 17:23: And they shall say to you, See here; or, see there: go not after them, nor follow them.
Matthew 24:24: For there shall arise false Christs, and false prophets, and shall shew great signs and wonders; insomuch that, if it were possible, they shall deceive the very elect.	Mark 13:22: For false Christs and false prophets shall rise, and shall shew signs and wonders, to seduce, if it were possible, even the elect.	
Matthew 24:25: Behold, I have told you before. Matthew 24:26: Wherefore if they shall say unto you, Behold, he is in the desert; go not forth: behold, he is in the secret chambers; believe it not.	Mark 13:23: But take ye heed: behold, I have foretold you all things.	
Matthew 24:27: For as the lightning cometh out of the east, and shineth even unto the west; so shall also the coming of the Son of man be.		Luke 17:24: For as the lightning, that lighteneth out of the one part under heaven, shineth unto the other part under heaven; so shall also the Son of man be in his day.
Matthew 24:28: For wheresoever the carcase is, there will the eagles be gathered together.	Note: *Verses from Luke 17 are included in this section instead of Luke 21.*	Luke 17:37: And they answered and said unto him, Where, Lord? And he said unto them, Wheresoever the body is, thither will the eagles be gathered together.

The chaos of those days will continue but a short while, and then as the lightning flashes from the eastern sky to the western sky, so shall also the coming of the Son of Man be in His day! Until you witness His return yourself, if you hear someone say, "look, there is Christ," don't believe it. Antichrist and evilness will be raging, and deception will continue in full force in a final attempt to cause people to be wooed away from the true God by marvelous signs and wonders. But Jesus warns simply, if someone tells you that Christ is hiding out over in this secret place, or was seen walking in a desert place over there, don't believe it for a second! Why such a simple warning? Because the second coming of Jesus will be loud, visible, apparent without question, and it will come suddenly at any moment immediately after the tribulation of those days. Everyone will know without a doubt, just as surely as we can see lightning flash across the sky during a night storm. Lift up your heads. Don't be sleeping. Be watchful.

One final point that Jesus notes here is the physical realities of death. It is my understanding that the seventieth week largely represents the second woe, or the sixth trumpet and vial plague. I believe the second woe could begin on the Feast of Trumpets, ten days prior to the day of the Lord. This plague involves the drying up of the Euphrates, a great death toll of one-third of people who worship devils and don't repent of their evil deeds, and the gathering of evil ones toward Jerusalem for the battle of Armageddon. Carcasses of dead men will prevail over the landscape as a result of the sixth plague. By the time Jesus returns at the day of the Lord, which is the final day of the seventieth week, those carcasses will have been exposed to the open air for enough time that multitudes of eagles or vultures flying through the air will also provide a vivid signal for the soon approaching second coming.

COSMIC EVENTS AND THE DAY OF THE LORD

Matthew 24:29: Immediately after the tribulation of those days shall the sun be darkened, and the moon shall not give her light, and the stars shall fall from heaven, and the powers of the heavens shall be shaken:	Mark 13:24: But in those days, after that tribulation, the sun shall be darkened, and the moon shall not give her light, Mark 13:25: And the stars of heaven shall fall, and the powers that are in heaven shall be shaken.	Luke 21:25–26: And there shall be signs in the sun, and in the moon, and in the stars; and upon the earth distress of nations, with perplexity; the sea and the waves roaring; Men's hearts failing them for fear, and for looking after those things which are coming on the earth: for the powers of heaven shall be shaken.

Matthew 24:30: And then shall appear the sign of the Son of man in heaven: and then shall all the tribes of the earth mourn, and they shall see the Son of man coming in the clouds of heaven with power and great glory.	Mark 13:26: And then shall they see the Son of man coming in the clouds with great power and glory.	Luke 21:27: And then shall they see the Son of man coming in a cloud with power and great glory.
Matthew 24:31: And he shall send his angels with a great sound of a trumpet, and they shall gather together his elect from the four winds, from one end of heaven to the other.	Mark 13:27: And then shall he send his angels, and shall gather together his elect from the four winds, from the uttermost part of the earth to the uttermost part of heaven.	Luke 21:28: And when these things begin to come to pass, then look up, and lift up your heads; for your redemption draweth nigh.

The second coming of Jesus and the resurrection and rapture will occur very soon after the abomination of desolation, after the tribulation of those days, and after great cosmic events in the sky. Jesus will then come in the clouds, His second coming accompanied by the sound of a trumpet. Then the angels will gather together the resurrected dead and raptured living in the sky and proceed to the throne in heaven. This is the day of the Lord and the time for the harvest of the earth!

According to 2 Thessalonians 2:1–4, the resurrection and rapture will occur after the man of sin (i.e. the Antichrist) is revealed and after he exalts himself as God in the temple of God, showing himself that he is God (i.e. the abomination of desolation). This agrees with the Olivet Discourse, where the abomination of desolation precedes the second coming of Jesus.

> Now we beseech you, brethren, by the coming of our Lord Jesus Christ, and by *our gathering together unto him*, that ye be not soon shaken in mind, or be troubled, neither by spirit, nor by word, nor by letter as from us, as that the day of Christ is at hand. Let no man deceive you by any means: for *that day shall not come, except* there come a falling away first, and that man of sin be revealed, the son of perdition; who opposeth and exalteth himself above all that is called God, or that is worshipped; so that he as God sitteth in the temple of God, shewing himself that he is God. (2 Thessalonians 2:1–4)

In addition to Matthew 24:21, Mark 13:19, and Luke 21:23, the Scripture of Daniel 12:1–2 agrees that the great tribulation will occur prior to the resurrection.

And at that time shall Michael stand up, the great prince which standeth for the children of thy people: and there shall be a time of trouble, such as never was since there was a nation even to that same time: and at that time thy people shall be delivered, every one that shall be found written in the book. And many of them that sleep in the dust of the earth shall awake, some to everlasting life, and some to shame and everlasting contempt. (Daniel 12:1–2)

In addition to Matthew 24:29, Mark 13:24, and Luke 21:25, other Scriptures agree that the cosmic events will occur just *before* the second coming of Jesus Christ.

And I will shew wonders in heaven above, and signs in the earth beneath; blood, and fire, and vapour of smoke: the sun shall be turned into darkness, and the moon into blood, *before* that great and notable day of the Lord come. (Act 2:19–20)

The sun shall be turned into darkness, and the moon into blood, *before* the great and the terrible day of the LORD come. (Joel 2:31)

And I beheld when he had opened the sixth seal, and, lo, there was a great earthquake; and the sun became black as sackcloth of hair, and the moon became as blood; and the stars of heaven fell unto the earth, even as a fig tree casteth her untimely figs, when she is shaken of a mighty wind [i.e. the cosmic events]. And the heaven departed as a scroll when it is rolled together [i.e. the powers of the heavens shall be shaken]; and every mountain and island were moved out of their places. (Revelation 6:12–14)

Behold, the day of the LORD cometh, cruel both with wrath and fierce anger, to lay the land desolate: and he shall destroy the sinners thereof out of it. For the stars of heaven and the constellations thereof shall not give their light: the sun shall be darkened in his going forth, and the moon shall not cause her light to shine. And I will punish the world for their evil, and the wicked for their iniquity; and I will cause the arrogancy of the proud to cease, and will lay low the haughtiness of the terrible. I will make a man more precious than fine gold; even a man than the golden wedge of Ophir. Therefore I will shake the heavens, and the earth shall remove out of her place, in the wrath of the LORD of hosts, and in the day of his fierce anger. (Isaiah 13:9–11)

In addition to Matthew 24:31, other Scriptures agree that the second coming will be accompanied with a great sound of a trumpet.

> For the Lord himself shall descend from heaven with a shout, with the voice of the archangel, and *with the trump of God*: and the dead in Christ shall rise first: then we which are alive and remain shall be caught up together with them in the clouds, to meet the Lord in the air: and so shall we ever be with the Lord. (1 Thessalonians 4:16–17)

> In a moment, in the twinkling of an eye, *at the last trump: for the trumpet shall sound*, and the dead shall be raised incorruptible, and we shall be changed. For this corruptible must put on incorruption, and this mortal must put on immortality. So when this corruptible shall have put on incorruption, and this mortal shall have put on immortality, then shall be brought to pass the saying that is written, Death is swallowed up in victory. (1 Corinthians 15:52–54)

The apostle Paul in 1 Corinthians 15:54 references the same resurrection that the prophet Isaiah references:

> He will swallow up death in victory; and the Lord GOD will wipe away tears from off all faces; and the rebuke of his people shall he take away from off all the earth: for the LORD hath spoken it. And it shall be said in that day, Lo, this is our God; we have waited for him, and he will save us: this is the LORD; we have waited for him, we will be glad and rejoice in his salvation. (Isaiah 25:8–9)

According to 1 Thessalonians 4:16–17, the resurrection and the rapture occur at the same time (or consecutively, one right after the other). The apostle John writes in Revelation 20 of the "first resurrection," and from a timing perspective, it is in context of the day of the Lord, prior to the start of the thousand-year reign of Christ.

> And I saw thrones, and they sat upon them, and judgment was given unto them: and I saw the souls of them that were beheaded for the witness of Jesus, and for the word of God, and which had not worshipped the beast, neither his image, neither had received his mark upon their foreheads, or in their hands; and they lived and reigned with Christ a thousand years. But the rest of the dead lived not again until the thousand years were finished. This is the first resurrection. *Blessed and holy is he that hath part in the first resurrection: on such the second death hath no power, but they shall*

be priests of God and of Christ, and shall reign with him a thousand years. (Revelation 20:4–6)

On the day of the Lord at the second coming, the powers of heaven will be shaken. This parallels with the message from 2 Peter 3:10–12 when the heavens shall "pass away" with a great noise. And according to Isaiah 34, the host of heaven will dissolve and fall to earth like a leaf! The "host of heaven" (i.e. evil powers of the air) will be annihilated!

> And all the host of heaven shall be dissolved, and the heavens shall be rolled together as a scroll: and all *their host shall fall down*, as the leaf falleth off from the vine, and as a falling fig from the fig tree. (Isaiah 34:4)

Job spoke of his personal resurrection (Job 19:25–27) in the context of Job 14 which states: "So man lieth down, and riseth not: till the heavens be no more, they shall not awake, nor be raised out of their sleep." Job marvelously confirms a post-tribulation resurrection at the second coming on the day of the Lord!

As I have stated before, I believe the Scriptures depict a post-tribulation resurrection and rapture: A resurrection and rapture that occurs on the day of the Lord, or the last day of Daniel's seventieth week, which I believe is the very day of the second coming of Jesus Christ. A resurrection and rapture that occurs after the sixth plague inspires the ungodly to gather for the battle of Armageddon (Revelation 16:14, 16), at a time when the Lord Jesus still warns of His thief-like coming (Revelation 16:15). A resurrection and rapture that occurs right after the cosmic events of the sixth seal (Revelation 6:12–14, and parallels). A resurrection and rapture that occurs at the time of the seventh seal when there is silence in heaven for half an hour, of the seventh trumpet when it is time for the dead to be judged, (Revelation 11:18), of the seventh vial when "it is done," and of the seventh thunder when the mystery of God is "finished" (Revelation 8:1, 11:18, 16:7, 10:7).

A resurrection on the "last day" is also consistent with the New Testament teachings of Jesus in places other than the Olivet Discourse. The following passages testify of the resurrection's occurrence on the last day:

> And this is the will of him that sent me, that every one which seeth the Son, and believeth on him, may have everlasting life: and I will raise him up at the last day. (John 6:40)

No man can come to me, except the Father which hath sent me draw him: and I will raise him up at the last day. (John 6:44)

Whoso eateth my flesh, and drinketh my blood, hath eternal life; and I will raise him up at the last day. (John 6:54)

Jesus saith unto her, Thy brother shall rise again. Martha saith unto him, I know that he shall rise again in the resurrection at the last day. (John 11:23–24)

Since Scripture shows the resurrection and rapture to be inseparably intertwined (1 Thessalonians 4:16–17, plus numerous other interconnected Scriptures that have already been mentioned), I believe we do a great injustice to the Holy Scripture if we attempt to come up with an alternate interpretation. To bifurcate the resurrection and rapture and create a rapture event for the church at some point prior to the tribulation is inconsistent with the teaching and themes of Scripture from the Old Testament prophets all the way to the book of Revelation. Another option, that of creating two separate resurrection/rapture events (one for "the church" and one for "the tribulation saints" at the last day), is an uncomfortable position for me also, as it adds tremendous complexity and confusion to an otherwise simple and consistent story line. This option clearly goes against the scriptural teaching of two resurrections, one prior to the millennium and one after (Revelation 20:5–6).

THE KINGDOM OF GOD IS NIGH AT HAND

Matthew 24:32: Now learn a parable of the fig tree; When his branch is yet tender, and putteth forth leaves, ye know that summer is nigh:	Mark 13:28: Now learn a parable of the fig tree; When her branch is yet tender, and putteth forth leaves, ye know that summer is near:	Luke 21:29–30: And he spake to them a parable; Behold the fig tree, and all the trees; When they now shoot forth, ye see and know of your own selves that summer is now nigh at hand.
Matthew 24:33: So likewise ye, when ye shall see all these things, know that it is near, even at the doors.	Mark 13:29: So ye in like manner, when ye shall see these things come to pass, know that it is nigh, even at the doors.	Luke 21:31: So likewise ye, when ye see these things come to pass, know ye that the kingdom of God is nigh at hand.
Matthew 24:34: Verily I say unto you, This generation shall not pass, till all these things be fulfilled.	Mark 13:30: Verily I say unto you, that this generation shall not pass, till all these things be done.	Luke 21:32: Verily I say unto you, This generation shall not pass away, till all be fulfilled.

THE OLIVET ROAD MAP OF THE END TIMES: WHAT DID JESUS SAY? • 261

Matthew 24:35: Heaven and earth shall pass away, but my words shall not pass away.	Mark 13:31: Heaven and earth shall pass away: but my words shall not pass away.	Luke 21:33: Heaven and earth shall pass away: but my words shall not pass away.
Matthew 24:36: But of that day and hour knoweth no man, no, not the angels of heaven, but my Father only.	Mark 13:32: But of that day and that hour knoweth no man, no, not the angels which are in heaven, neither the Son, but the Father.	
Matthew 24:37–41: But as the days of Noe were, so shall also the coming of the Son of man be. For as in the days that were before the flood they were eating and drinking, marrying and giving in marriage, until the day that Noe entered into the ark, and knew not until the flood came, and took them all away; so shall also the coming of the Son of man be. Then shall two be in the field; the one shall be taken, and the other left. Two women shall be grinding at the mill; the one shall be taken, and the other left.	Mark 13:33: Take ye heed, watch and pray: for ye know not when the time is. Mark 13:34: For the Son of man is as a man taking a far journey, who left his house, and gave authority to his servants, and to every man his work, and commanded the porter to watch	Luke 21:34: And take heed to yourselves, lest at any time your hearts be overcharged with surfeiting, and drunkenness, and cares of this life, and so that day come upon you unawares. Luke 21:35: For as a snare shall it come on all them that dwell on the face of the whole earth.

The mention of "these things" by Jesus in Matthew 24:33, Mark 13:29, and Luke 21:31 hearkens all the way back to Matthew 24:3, Mark 13:3, and Luke 21:7. Jesus is speaking of a trail of events that lead to His second coming. All of the signs and events will occur within one generation. The very words of Jesus will be fulfilled and come to fruition. His words of prophecy will never be replaced or changed, and they will live on forever as truth. This is in contrast to the enormous change and transition that will occur in the heavens and earth when they are made new by fire on the day of the Lord (2 Peter 3:7–13).

Jesus also tells us that the second coming will be like the time of Noah and the flood. For virtually all of humankind at the time of Noah, the flood overtook them as a "thief in the night." They were unaware and unsuspecting of what was going to come upon them. This was despite the fact that numerous warnings had been given to them by righteous Noah. The people simply failed to take heed and submit to the warnings. This same principle will be true with the coming of the Son of Man. Mankind has the choice to live and dwell in darkness and be overtaken as a thief or to walk in the light and be prepared (1 Thessalonians 5:4–6) for *that day!* Only God knows the very day and hour of the second coming, thus we need to be awake as children of light.

The lesson taught by Christ at this time is notably to watch and pray. Be ready. Unless we are in tune and heeding the Spirit of God, we could be caught unaware of the seriousness of the times and not be prepared for the second coming of Jesus.

I have heard many use the following Scripture to help justify an "any moment" rapture theory prior to the end-time Tribulation:

> Then shall two be in the field; the one shall be taken, and the other left. Two women shall be grinding at the mill; the one shall be taken, and the other left. Watch therefore: for ye know not what hour your Lord doth come. (Matthew 24:40–42)

But what is the context of these verses? It is the concluding portion of the Lord's Olivet Discourse, where numerous examples and parables are given to exhort the servants of God to be watchful, especially when we see "all these things be fulfilled" (Matthew 24:34). The context is the day of the Lord, which will come to pass when "all these things be fulfilled." "These things" are the signs of the times that we are to be watchful of. The most critical and intense sign, in my opinion, is the climax event of the abomination of desolation, an urgent time for all concerned.

Some may ask, if Christians are still going to be on earth during these troubled times, how could people be undergoing normal daily activities like farming or grinding flour? Won't the entire world be in chaos and confusion? To answer this question, we need to again consider the primary focal point of the end times. The evil armies are not going to gather around Dallas, Texas, in North America or Rome, Italy, in Europe. The focal point is the Middle East, and specifically Jerusalem, from which Jesus Christ will one day rule and reign.

We also need to consider that many pagans (Zechariah 14:18) will likely enter the millennium in mortal forms after the day of the Lord. In historical context, a "pagan" is a person who is not a Christian, a Jew, or a Muslim—in other words, someone not belonging to an Abrahamic religion. I would guess that many of these heathen peoples will surrender to the influence of the Antichrist during the latter days and ultimately suffer judgment on that great day, but it is apparent that some (or perhaps many) will be undergoing normal daily activities when they find themselves suddenly witness to the rapture from the earth of a believing neighbor or friend or spouse at the day of the Lord.

The timing of this sequence is consistent with all examples given in Scripture. First the righteous are "harvested," and then destruction comes to the ungodly. Consider the following:

- Noahic example (Matthew 24:37–39 and Luke 17:26–27)
  - First Noah enters the ark
  - Then the flood "took them all away" (i.e. the ungodly were destroyed)
    - "Took" is *airo* in Greek (Strong's G142; it means to take up or away; away with, put away, remove)
- Farming example (Matthew 24:40–41)
  - First one is taken
    - "Taken" is *paralambano* in Greek (Strong's G3880; it means to take with, to receive near; it implies intimacy).
  - Then one is left
    - Left is *aphiemi* in Greek (Strong's G863; it means to send, put away, lay aside, yield up)
- The evil and faithful servants (Matthew 24:45–51)
  - One is ready, watchful, looking for His coming = rewarded
  - One is not ready, unprepared for His coming = destroyed
- Ten virgins (Matthew 25:1–13)
  - Five are ready and prepared = go with the bridegroom to the marriage
  - Five are unprepared = the door is shut, and they are left out
- Lot and his family (Luke 17:28–29)
  - First Lot and his family leave Sodom
  - Then fire and brimstone from heaven destroy the city
- Harvest of Revelation 14:14–20
  - First reaping is of the ripe harvest (i.e. gathering the wheat into the barn). In verses 14–16 the context is Jesus on the clouds.
  - Second reaping is of the ungodly (i.e. tares thrust into the fire). In verses 17–20 the context is the winepress of the wrath of God.
- Harvest of Matthew 13:30, 37–43

- First, the Antichrist and his followers gather around Jerusalem (i.e. the tares are bundled together).
- Second, Jesus comes with the angels, and the faithful dead are resurrected and the faithful living raptured (i.e. the wheat is gathered into the barn).
- Third, God dispenses His wrath against the ungodly (i.e. the tares are thrust into the fire).
- Fourth, the righteous shine forth like the sun in the kingdom of their Father.

The physical and long-awaited kingdom of God will not begin until after Armageddon on the great day of God. Once Jesus is king of the earth, righteousness will prevail and eventually cover the whole earth like the waters cover the sea. This is depicted in my favorite "Christmas" song, *Joy to the World*.

WATCH AND PRAY		
Matthew 24:42–44: *Watch therefore*: for ye know not what hour your Lord doth come. But know this, that if the goodman of the house had known in what watch the thief would come, he would have watched, and would not have suffered his house to be broken up. *Therefore be ye also ready*: for in such an hour as ye think not the Son of man cometh.	Mark 13:34–36: For the Son of man is as a man taking a far journey, who left his house, and gave authority to his servants, and to every man his work, and commanded the porter to *watch*. *Watch ye therefore*: for ye know not when the master of the house cometh, at even, or at midnight, or at the cockcrowing, or in the morning: Lest coming suddenly he find you sleeping.	Luke 21:36: *Watch ye therefore, and pray always*, that ye may be accounted worthy to escape all these things that shall come to pass, and to stand before the Son of man.

The message could not be stronger: BE AWAKE! BE WATCHFUL! BE PRAYERFUL! BE READY! For what? The coming of the Son of Man on the day of the Lord!

It is time for us to be faithful and wise servants. Jesus says when you see "these things," know that it is near, even at the doors. In that day, our directive is not to be found sleeping, but to watch, pray, and be sober (1 Thessalonians 5:4–9). We won't know the hour of the day when he comes—whether at evening, or at midnight, or at the cockcrowing, or in the morning.

Chapter 6

THE EGYPTIAN COROLLARY OF THE END TIMES

We can sometimes read "Bible stories" and then keep them in that category—as just stories. Stories and miracles which are past our time. It can challenge us to think of them happening in our modern-day context. However, I believe that the time of the end, specifically the tribulation period, will in many ways present the final generation with experiences similar to those of the Egyptians and the children of Israel in the 1400s BC. Just as the plagues in that day hurt the adversaries of God's people, helped prepare the way for the exodus of the people of God, and declared the mighty name of God, so will the plagues from heaven in the end times. These are of course not exact parallels, but the Scriptures present a vivid correlation, summarized as follows:

- The rise of a new king over Egypt correlates to the rise of the Antichrist.
- The tribulation and affliction of God's people in Egypt correlates to the tribulation of God's people in the last days.
- The plagues of God against the Egyptians correlate to the plagues of God against the Antichrist and his followers. The Israelites received general immunity from the Egyptian plagues, and so will God's people receive immunity from the plagues of God in the last days. The plagues were administered by Moses in Egypt just as I believe the plagues will be administered by the two witnesses in the last days.

- The plagues exalt the might and power and name of God. The Egypt plagues led to the Israelites' escape and release from bondage. On that day, they saw the salvation (*yeshuah*—Strong's H3444) of the Lord (Exodus 14:13)! In correlation, the plagues of the last days will culminate in the escape of God's people from the gathering forces of evil and the salvation of remnant Israel as they look upon the One whom they pierced and mourn for their Savior.
- Pharaoh and his servants were inspired to pursue after the Israelites as they fled Egypt. Likewise, so will the evil ones be inspired to gather toward Jerusalem in the last days. And just as Pharaoh and his servants went into the midst of the sea and were then pressed by the waters as the sea returned to its strength so that none remained alive, so will the evil followers of Antichrist be found in the winepress of God in the last days.
- Moses and the children of Israel sang a song to the Lord that in many ways foreshadows Israel's deliverance at the great day of the Lord.

Let's look at these correlations in greater detail.

First, just as a new king arose in Egypt and made the lives of the Israelites burdensome and bitter with hard bondage, even charging that every son born to the Israelites should be cast into the river, the little horn, or Antichrist, will rise to rule the final, revived beast kingdom of the last days, and one of his chief missions will be to destroy the holy people and make war against the saints of God.

The Rise of a New King over Egypt	The End-Time Rise of the Antichrist
Exodus 1:8, 11–14, 22: (8) Now *there arose up a new king over Egypt, which knew not Joseph.* (11) Therefore they did set over them taskmasters to *afflict them with their burdens.* And they built for Pharaoh treasure cities, Pithom and Raamses. (13) And the Egyptians made the children of Israel to serve with rigour: (14) and *they made their lives bitter with hard bondage,* in morter, and in brick, and in all manner of service in the field: all their service, wherein they made them serve, was with rigour. (22) And Pharaoh charged all his people, saying, *every son that is born ye shall cast into the river,* and every daughter ye shall save alive.	Dan 8:23–25: (23) . . . *a king of fierce countenance,* and understanding dark sentences, *shall stand up.* (24) And his power shall be mighty, but not by his own power: and he shall destroy wonderfully, and shall prosper, and practise, and *shall destroy the mighty and the holy people.* (25) And through his policy also he shall cause craft to prosper in his hand; and he shall magnify himself in his heart, and by peace shall destroy many: he shall also stand up against the Prince of princes; but he shall be broken without hand. Daniel 7:21: I beheld, and *the same horn made war with the saints, and prevailed against them.*

Second, just as God told Moses that He had seen the affliction and oppression of His people in Egypt, that He had heard their cry, and that He desired to come down to deliver them out of the hand of the Egyptians and would do so through the hand of Moses, I believe the two witnesses will serve a similar role in dealing with the enemies of God by administering plagues directed at the Antichrist and his followers. I believe the plagues will help counter the fierce attack of Satan and the Antichrist against the Jews and Christians in the last days.

The Tribulation in Egypt	The Tribulation of the End Times
Exo 3:7–9, 15, 20: (7) And the Lord said, *I have surely seen the affliction of my people which are in Egypt, and have heard their cry by reason of their taskmasters; for I know their sorrows;* (8) and I am come down to deliver them out of the hand of the Egyptians, and to bring them up out of that land unto a good land and a large, unto a land flowing with milk and honey; unto the place of the Canaanites, and the Hittites, and the Amorites, and the Perizzites, and the Hivites, and the Jebusites. (9) Now therefore, behold, *the cry of the children of Israel is come unto me*: and I have also seen the oppression wherewith the Egyptians oppress them. (15) And God said moreover unto Moses, Thus shalt thou say unto the children of Israel, The Lord God of your fathers, the God of Abraham, the God of Isaac, and the God of Jacob, hath sent me unto you: this is my name for ever, and this is my memorial unto all generations. (20) And *I will stretch out my hand, and smite Egypt with all my wonders* which I will do in the midst thereof: and after that he will let you go.	Revelation 6:10: And *they cried with a loud voice, saying, How long, O Lord, holy and true, dost thou not judge and avenge our blood on them that dwell on the earth?* Revelation 11:3, 5–6: (3) And I will give power unto my two witnesses, and they shall prophesy a thousand two hundred and threescore days, clothed in sackcloth. (5) And if any man will hurt them, fire proceedeth out of their mouth, and devoureth their enemies: and if any man will hurt them, he must in this manner be killed. (6) *These have power to shut heaven, that it rain not in the days of their prophecy: and have power over waters to turn them to blood, and to smite the earth with all plagues, as often as they will.* Revelation 16:1–2: (1) And I heard a great voice out of the temple saying to the seven angels, Go your ways, and pour out the vials of *the wrath of God* upon the earth. (2) And the first went, and poured out his vial upon the earth; and there fell a noisome and grievous sore *upon the men which had the mark of the beast, and upon them which worshipped his image.*

Third, just as the Israelites received immunity from the plagues in Egypt, I believe the followers of God (and also those who don't bear the name, the mark, or the number of Antichrist) will experience immunity from the plagues of the last days. Based on the scriptural evidence, the plagues will constitute the wrath of God *expressly* targeted against the followers of Antichrist.

Ten Plagues of Egypt	The Vial Plagues of the Wrath of God
The children of Israel were immune to the repercussions of the ten plagues in Egypt.	The followers of God will be immune to the repercussions of the plagues from God.
1. *River water turned into blood.* Exodus 7:21: And the fish that was in the river died; and the river stank, and *the Egyptians could not drink of the water of the river; and there was blood* throughout all the land of Egypt.	*First trumpet/vial.* Revelation 8:7 and Revelation 16:2. *Bloody sores will come upon the followers of Antichrist* (those who have the mark of the beast, and upon them which worship his image), and the trees and grass will be burnt.
2. *Frogs.* Exodus 8:9–10: (9) And Moses said unto Pharaoh, Glory over me: when shall I intreat for thee, and for thy servants, and for thy people, to destroy the frogs *from thee and thy houses,* that they may remain in the river only? (10) And he said, To morrow. And he said, *Be it according to thy word: that thou mayest know that there is none like unto the Lord our God.*	*Second trumpet/vial.* Revelation 8:8–9 and Revelation 16:3. A great mountain burning with fire will be cast into the sea and *turn the seawater to blood,* causing death to fish and the destruction of ships. (With this plague there is no reference inferring this is targeted specifically against Antichrist and his followers)
3. *Lice.* There is no reference specifically inferring immunity from lice.	*Third trumpet/vial.* Revelation 8:10–11 and Revelation 16:4–7. A great burning star will fall from heaven, *causing the river waters to become blood,* and men will die because of the bitter water. Based on the angel's proclamation, *this is a judgment against those who shed the blood of God's people.*
4. *Flies.* Exodus 8:22: And I will sever in that day the land of Goshen, in which my people dwell, that *no swarms of flies shall be there; to the end thou mayest know that I am the Lord in the midst of the earth.*	*Fourth trumpet/vial.* Revelation 8:12–13 and Revelation 16:8–9. The plague of the sun. Also, the two witnesses will issue fire against their enemies. Men will be scorched by reason of a great heat. *This will be against the followers of Antichrist since the men injured will blaspheme the name of God and refuse to give Him glory.*
5. *Cattle.* Exodus 9:4: And the Lord shall sever between the cattle of Israel and the cattle of Egypt: and *there shall nothing die of all that is the children's of Israel.*	
6. *Boils.* Exodus 9:11: And the magicians could not stand before Moses because of the boils; for *the boil was upon the magicians, and upon all the Egyptians.*	*First woe—fifth trumpet/vial.* Revelation 9:1–12 and Revelation 16:10–11. *Darkness will come over the land* when the seat of the beast is opened. Also, *torment, pains, and sores from locusts* will be on those who do not follow God. *The recipients blaspheme the God of heaven because of their pains and sores and repent not of their deeds.*
7. *Hail.* Exodus 9:26: Only in the land of Goshen, *where the children of Israel were, was there no hail.*	

Ten Plagues of Egypt	The Vial Plagues of the Wrath of God
8. *Locusts.* Exodus 10:6: And they shall fill thy houses, and the houses of all thy servants, and *the houses of all the Egyptians; which neither thy fathers, nor thy fathers' fathers have seen, since the day that they were upon the earth unto this day.* And he turned himself, and went out from Pharaoh.	*Second woe—sixth trumpet/vial.* Revelation 9:13–21, 11:7–14 and Revelation 16:12–16. The great river Euphrates will dry up to prepare the way of the kings of the east. A plague of armies of 200,000,000 horsemen will kill one-third of men with fire, smoke, and brimstone. *The horsemen will target those who worship devils and idols and who are sinfully involved with murder, sorceries, fornication and theft.* At this time, evil spirits from the devil, Antichrist, and the false prophet will induce all those who oppose God to gather for the battle of Armageddon. As the horsemen are killing unbelievers and the evil spirits are gathering the troops to fight against God, the Antichrist will kill his two chief antagonists, the wonder-working witnesses of God, in the streets of Jerusalem.
9. *Darkness.* Exodus 10:23: They saw not one another, neither rose any from his place for three days: *but all the children of Israel had light in their dwellings.*	
10. *Death of firstborn.* Exodus 11:6–7: (6) And there shall be a great cry throughout all the land of Egypt, such as there was none like it, nor shall be like it any more. (7) But against any of the children of Israel shall not a dog move his tongue, against man or beast: *that ye may know how that the Lord doth put a difference between the Egyptians and Israel.*	
Exodus 12:12–13: (12) For I will pass through the land of Egypt this night, and will smite all the firstborn in the land of Egypt, both man and beast; and *against all the gods of Egypt I will execute judgment:* I am the Lord. (13) And the blood shall be to you for a token upon the houses where ye are: and when I see the blood, *I will pass over you, and the plague shall not be upon you to destroy you,* when I smite the land of Egypt.	*Third woe—seventh trumpet/vial.* Revelation 11:15–19 and Revelation 16:17–21. Armageddon and the great day of the wrath of the Lord. There will be voices, and thunders, and lightnings, and a great and mighty earthquake such as was not since men were upon the earth. There will be a great shaking of the earth and great hail will fall from heaven, every stone about the weight of a talent: and *men will blaspheme God because of the plague of the hail.*

Fourth, the plagues will exalt the mighty name of God. The plagues in Egypt culminated in the release of the Israelites through a dramatic and miraculous exit from the land so they could fulfill God's desire to bring them to the promised land. In this process, they "saw" the salvation of the LORD (Exodus 14:13). I believe the plagues of the last days will culminate with remnant Israel experiencing salvation on the day of the Lord and then experiencing their permanent restoration in the land promised to them. Remnant Israel will look to the Lord Jesus and "see" the One whom they pierced, repent of their sins, and experience salvation on that great day. They will go on to dwell in the promised land safely and forever with Jesus (Yeshua) as their king.

The plagues led to Israel's salvation out of the hand of the Egyptians, and the people feared the Lord and believed the Lord.	The plagues will lead to remnant Israel's salvation, and they will dwell safely in the promised land forever with King Jesus.
Exodus 9:13–16: And the Lord said unto Moses, Rise up early in the morning, and stand before Pharaoh, and say unto him, Thus saith the Lord God of the Hebrews, Let my people go, that they may serve me. *For I will at this time send all my plagues upon thine heart, and upon thy servants, and upon thy people; that thou mayest know that there is none like me in all the earth.* For now I will stretch out my hand, that I may smite thee and thy people with pestilence; and thou shalt be cut off from the earth. And in very deed for this cause have *I raised thee up, for to shew in thee my power; and that my name may be declared throughout all the earth.*	**Ezekiel 39:7:** *So will I make my holy name known in the midst of my people Israel;* and I will not let them pollute my holy name any more: and the heathen shall know that I am the Lord, the Holy One in Israel.
Exodus 10:1–2: And the Lord said unto Moses, Go in unto Pharaoh: for *I have hardened his heart,* and the heart of his servants, that I might shew these my signs before him: and *that thou mayest tell in the ears of thy son, and of thy son's son, what things I have wrought in Egypt, and my signs which I have done among them; that ye may know how that I am the Lord.*	**Ezekiel 39:26–29:** After that they have borne their shame, and all their trespasses whereby they have trespassed against me, when they dwelt safely in their land, and none made them afraid. *When I have brought them again from the people, and gathered them out of their enemies' lands,* and am sanctified in them in the sight of many nations; *then shall they know that I am the Lord their God,* which caused them to be led into captivity among the heathen: but I have gathered them unto their own land, and have left none of them any more there. *Neither will I hide my face any more from them: for I have poured out my spirit upon the house of Israel,* saith the Lord God.

Exodus 14:12–14: Is not this the word that we did tell thee in Egypt, saying, Let us alone, that we may serve the Egyptians? For it had been better for us to serve the Egyptians, than that we should die in the wilderness. And Moses said unto the people, Fear ye not, stand still, and *see the salvation* of the Lord, which he will shew to you to day: for the Egyptians whom ye have seen to day, ye shall see them again no more for ever.* The Lord shall fight for you, and ye shall hold your peace.	Zechariah 12:9–10: And it shall come to pass *in that day,* that *I will* seek to destroy all the nations that come against Jerusalem. And *I will* pour upon the house of David, and upon the inhabitants of Jerusalem, the spirit of grace and of supplications: and *they shall look upon me whom they have pierced,* and they shall mourn for him, as one mourneth for his only son,* and shall be in bitterness for him, as one that is in bitterness for his firstborn.
*Salvation, Strong's H3444—yeshua. The Hebrew word for Jesus Christ!	*They will look upon Jesus Christ, the one whom they pierced!
Exodus 14:29–31: But the children of Israel walked upon dry land in the midst of the sea; and the waters were a wall unto them on their right hand, and on their left. *Thus the Lord saved Israel that day out of the hand of the Egyptians;* and Israel saw the Egyptians dead upon the sea shore. *And Israel saw that great work which the Lord did upon the Egyptians: and the people feared the Lord, and believed the Lord, and his servant Moses.*	Isaiah 59:18–21: According to their deeds, accordingly he will repay, fury to his adversaries, recompence to his enemies; to the islands he will repay recompence. *So shall they fear the name of the Lord from the west, and his glory from the rising of the sun. When the enemy shall come in like a flood, the Spirit of the Lord shall lift up a standard against him.* And the Redeemer shall come to Zion, and unto them that turn from transgression in Jacob, saith the Lord. As for me, *this is my covenant with them, saith the Lord; My spirit that is upon thee,* and my words which I have put in thy mouth, shall not depart out of thy mouth, nor out of the mouth of thy seed, nor out of the mouth of thy seed's seed, saith the Lord, *from henceforth and for ever.*

Fifth, the Egyptians witnessed the mighty hand of God through devastating and horrific plagues, but they still pursued after the Israelites to the Red Sea. Then, all night long the LORD stood between the camp of the Egyptians and the Israelites' camp in a "pillar of fire and of a cloud" that was a "cloud and darkness" to the Egyptians and a "light by night" to the Israelites. After being kept at bay by this unusual presence, you would think that common sense would have told the Egyptians to back away because of this divine protection from God! However, this was not the case. They apparently were plagued one last time by some type of evil inspiration that enabled them to ignore any sense of reason—because after seeing the waters mount up like a wall on either side and the Israelites pass over the Red Sea on dry land, they went in after them to the midst of the sea, with all of their horses, horsemen, and chariots! The Egyptians were radically confused because the Lord "troubled" them. Likely this troubling came from thunder, lightning, rain, and a great earthquake (Psalm 77:17–20)! When they finally said "let us flee," it was far too late. Moses then stretched out his hand over the sea, and the waters came up over the Egyptians like a press, covering them and overthrowing them so that there remained not one living soul. We shouldn't be surprised. The power and ability of God is immeasurable. It is God who can effectively win our battles. When we trust in human strength we are easily defeated (Psalm 20:7).

In a striking correlation, during the last days an enormous gathering of evil will occur at a place called Armageddon. The gathering will result from inducements from the spirit world. They will pursue toward the holy city, Jerusalem, to make war against God's people. The evil adversaries of God will then witness enormous miracles when cosmic disturbances to the sun, moon, and stars occur, along with a great shaking of the earth.

Also, a final plague of great hail will torment men who blaspheme God. According to the seventh seal, seventh trumpet, and seventh vial, there will be "voices, thunderings, and lightnings." Then sudden destruction from the sword of the Lord (the fury, wrath, and vengeance of Almighty God) will come: the armies of those who oppose God will be thrust into the winepress, the blood will come out of the winepress even up to the horses' bridles, and the fouls of the air will be filled with much flesh.

Pursuit of the Egyptians to the Red Sea	Pursuit of the Ungodly toward Jerusalem
Exodus 14:8–10: And the Lord hardened the heart of Pharaoh king of Egypt, and he pursued after the children of Israel: and the children of Israel went out with an high hand. *But the Egyptians pursued after them, all the horses and chariots of Pharaoh, and his horsemen, and his army, and overtook them encamping by the sea,* beside Pihahiroth, before Baal-zephon. And when Pharaoh drew nigh, the children of Israel lifted up their eyes, and, behold, the Egyptians marched after them; and they were sore afraid: and the children of Israel cried out unto the Lord.	Revelation 16:12–14: And the sixth angel poured out his vial upon the great river Euphrates; and the water thereof was dried up, that the way of the kings of the east might be prepared. And I saw three unclean spirits like frogs come out of the mouth of the dragon, and out of the mouth of the beast, and out of the mouth of the false prophet. For they are the spirits of devils, working miracles, which go forth unto the kings of the earth and of the whole world, to gather them to the battle of that great day of God Almighty.

THE EGYPTIAN COROLLARY OF THE END TIMES • 273

Exodus 14:21–31: And Moses stretched out his hand over the sea; and the Lord caused the sea to go back by a strong east wind all that night, and made the sea dry land, and the waters were divided. And the children of Israel went into the midst of the sea upon the dry ground: and the waters were a wall unto them on their right hand, and on their left. *And the Egyptians pursued, and went in after them to the midst of the sea, even all Pharaoh's horses, his chariots, and his horsemen.* And it came to pass, that in the morning watch the Lord looked unto the host of the Egyptians through the pillar of fire and of the cloud, and troubled the host of the Egyptians, and took off their chariot wheels, that they drave them heavily: so that the Egyptians said, *Let us flee from the face of Israel; for the Lord fighteth for them against the Egyptians.* And the Lord said unto Moses, Stretch out thine hand over the sea, that the waters may come again upon the Egyptians, upon their chariots, and upon their horsemen. And Moses stretched forth his hand over the sea, and the sea returned to his strength when the morning appeared; *and the Egyptians fled against it; and the Lord overthrew the Egyptians in the midst of the sea. And the waters returned, and covered the chariots, and the horsemen, and all the host of Pharaoh that came into the sea after them; there remained not so much as one of them.* But the children of Israel walked upon dry land in the midst of the sea; and the waters were a wall unto them on their right hand, and on their left. *Thus the Lord saved Israel that day out of the hand of the Egyptians;* and Israel saw the Egyptians dead upon the sea shore. *And Israel saw that great work which the Lord did upon the Egyptians: and the people feared the Lord, and believed the Lord,* and his servant Moses.

Revelation 14:18–20: . . . and cried with a loud cry to him that had the sharp sickle, saying, Thrust in thy sharp sickle, and gather the clusters of the vine of the earth; for her grapes are fully ripe. And the angel thrust in his sickle into the earth, and gathered the vine of the earth, and cast it into the great winepress of the wrath of God. And the winepress was trodden without the city, and blood came out of the winepress, even unto the horse bridles, by the space of a thousand and six hundred furlongs.

Revelation 19:11, 15–21: And I saw heaven opened, and behold a white horse; and he that sat upon him was called Faithful and True, and in righteousness he doth judge and make war. And out of his mouth goeth a sharp sword, that with it he should smite the nations: and he shall rule them with a rod of iron: *and he treadeth the winepress of the fierceness and wrath of Almighty God.* And he hath on his vesture and on his thigh a name written, King Of Kings, And Lord Of Lords. And I saw an angel standing in the sun; and he cried with a loud voice, saying to all the fowls that fly in the midst of heaven, Come and gather yourselves together unto the supper of the great God; that ye may eat the flesh of kings, and the flesh of captains, and the flesh of mighty men, and the flesh of horses, and of them that sit on them, and the flesh of all men, both free and bond, both small and great. *And I saw the beast, and the kings of the earth, and their armies, gathered together to make war against him that sat on the horse, and against his army. And the beast was taken,* and with him the false prophet that wrought miracles before him, with which he deceived them that had received the mark of the beast, and them that worshipped his image. These both were cast alive into a lake of fire burning with brimstone. And the remnant were slain with the sword of him that sat upon the horse, which sword proceeded out of his mouth: and all the fowls were filled with their flesh.

The sixth correlation involves the song of the Lord. After witnessing their deliverance solely due to the mighty hand of God, Exodus 15 records a song that Moses and the children of Israel sang to the Lord. It is a song of deliverance and victory! The song and its celebration foreshadows the day of the Lord in many ways, including the mention of several Middle Eastern Nations who today harbor much resentment toward the Israelites and who will be destroyed at the battle of that great day of God. The song mentions the promised land, where Israel will truly and forever dwell safely after their final and complete deliverance at the day of the Lord. And the precious words "The LORD shall reign for ever and ever" are sung, depicting the defeat of Antichrist and Satan, and the ultimate and final handing over of earthly dominion and rule to Jesus Christ, the Lamb, who will reign as King of kings and Lord of lords forever!

> Then sang Moses and the children of Israel this song unto the LORD, and spake, saying, I will sing unto the LORD, for he hath triumphed gloriously: the horse and his rider hath he thrown into the sea. The LORD is my strength and song, and he is become my salvation: he is my God, and I will prepare him an habitation; my father's God, and I will exalt him. The LORD is a man of war: the LORD is his name. Pharaoh's chariots and his host hath he cast into the sea: his chosen captains also are drowned in the Red sea. The depths have covered them: they sank into the bottom as a stone. *Thy right hand, O LORD, is become glorious in power: thy right hand, O LORD, hath dashed in pieces the enemy. And in the greatness of thine excellency thou hast overthrown them that rose up against thee: thou sentest forth thy wrath, which consumed them as stubble.* And with the blast of thy nostrils the waters were gathered together, the floods stood upright as an heap, and the depths were congealed in the heart of the sea. The enemy said, I will pursue, I will overtake, I will divide the spoil; my lust shall be satisfied upon them; I will draw my sword, my hand shall destroy them. Thou didst blow with thy wind, the sea covered them: they sank as lead in the mighty waters. *Who is like unto thee, O LORD, among the gods? who is like thee, glorious in holiness, fearful in praises, doing wonders?* Thou stretchedst out thy right hand, the earth swallowed them. Thou in thy mercy hast led forth the people which thou hast redeemed: thou hast guided them in thy strength unto thy holy habitation. *The people shall hear, and be afraid:* sorrow shall take hold on the *inhabitants of Palestina.* Then the dukes of *Edom* shall be amazed; *the mighty men of Moab,* trembling shall take hold upon them; all *the inhabitants of Canaan shall melt away.* Fear and dread

shall fall upon them; by the greatness of thine arm they shall be as still as a stone; till thy people pass over, O Lord, till the people pass over, which thou hast purchased. *Thou shalt bring them in, and plant them in the mountain of thine inheritance, in the place, O* Lord, *which thou hast made for thee to dwell in, in the Sanctuary, O Lord, which thy hands have established. The* Lord *shall reign for ever and ever.* For the horse of Pharaoh went in with his chariots and with his horsemen into the sea, and the Lord brought again the waters of the sea upon them; but the children of Israel went on dry land in the midst of the sea. (Exodus 15:1–19)

From the depths of my heart, I believe that the Scriptures will "come alive" more than ever during the end times. Let's not relegate the miraculous works of God to Bible stories. Rather, let's look forward with hope! His right hand, glorious in power, will perform mighty wonders that lead to the future defeat of the ungodly and the arrival of the kingdom of God.

But the day of the Lord will come as a thief in the night;
in the which the heavens shall pass away with a great noise,
and the elements shall melt with fervent heat,
the earth also and the works that are therein shall be burned up.
Seeing then that all these things shall be dissolved,
what manner of persons ought ye to be
in all holy conversation and godliness,
looking for and hasting unto
the coming of the day of God,
wherein the heavens being on fire shall be dissolved,
and the elements shall melt with fervent heat?
Nevertheless we, according to his promise,
look for new heavens and a new earth,
wherein dwelleth righteousness.
Wherefore, beloved,
seeing that ye look for such things,
be diligent that ye may be found of him
in peace, without spot, and blameless.
(2 Peter 3:10–14)

❦

I thank my God always on your behalf,
for the grace of God which is given you by Jesus Christ;
that in everything ye are enriched by him,
in all utterance, and in all knowledge;
even as the testimony of Christ was confirmed in you:
so that ye come behind in no gift;
waiting for the coming of our Lord Jesus Christ:
who shall also confirm you unto the end,
that ye may be blameless
in the day of our Lord Jesus Christ.
(1 Corinthians 1:4–8)

CONCLUDING REMARKS

In Jesus's parable of the ten virgins, they *all* slumbered and slept while the bridegroom tarried.

Are we sleeping?

Is our life on autopilot?

I believe more than ever that now is a time of warning and a call to soberness. In some places around the world it is different, but we in America are especially caught up in a time and season that is hyperfocused on serving self and enjoying pleasures and luxuries in an instant-gratification society that is generally free of severe hardship. Our cars start up right away, and there is plenty of gas for the next trip. We casually gather to worship God in public assemblies without fear or threat of persecution. We are daily bombarded with innumerable opportunities for self-indulgence, and many of us pay an enormous sum of money to use phones that are rarely fatigued from actual phone calls. The list goes on and on.

Is a time of splendor and tranquility for the child of God what Jesus told us to strive toward? As stated earlier in this book, I believe the church descriptions in Revelation 2 and 3 present a composite overview of church conditions that will be present during the last days. Otherwise, why would Jesus warn those at Sardis of his "thief-like" second coming? Why would He warn them to strengthen those things that are ready to die out and to be watchful? He exhorts them just as any of us need to be exhorted today: be watchful, be awake, and hold fast to the truths and promises of God. Why? If you aren't awake and don't watch, I will come as a thief.

It is the same warning we find throughout Scripture, and it especially applies to the evil and disobedient, the unwatchful, the foolish, and those intoxicated and burdened with the cares of this life. To these unwatchful and unprepared, the day of the Lord's return will be unexpected and come as a thief in the night.

To the rich and satisfied church of Laodicea, Jesus says that if they don't experience a true revival and develop a genuine trust in God, they will remain wretched, miserable, poor, blind, and naked. Many think that the church will have long been raptured prior to the judgments of Revelation 16. But what warning do the words of Scripture still cry out at the time between the sixth and seventh vial judgments of wrath in Revelation 16:15? The thief-like coming is "near," but it is still not "here" prior to Revelation 16:15. If we are not watchful, and if we are shamefully lacking the garment of faith, we will be found wretched, miserable, poor, and blind when the Lord returns! This was the Lord's warning to the church of Laodicea in Revelation 3:18.

> Behold, I come as a thief. Blessed is he that watcheth, and keepeth his garments, lest he walk naked, and they see his shame. (Revelation 16:15)

Do you have a desire to hear counsel from the Holy Spirit today? The message to each church concludes with the following exhortation: "he that hath an ear, let him hear what the Spirit saith unto the churches."

It is wise for us to consider the message from the Spirit of the Lord in Revelation 2 and 3. Positive attributes are named, areas of deficiency are noted, warnings are given, repentance is emphasized, and in all cases a call to overcome and experience the forever promises of God sounds forth. Whoever we are and wherever we are, the Lord has counsel ready to be delivered into our hearts. The message for the child of God today is one of warning and soberness, not splendor and tranquility. One day the tables will be turned. Evil, pride, self-sufficiency, sinful pleasures, false peace, lukewarmness, and so on will bring a sober reality of judgment. On the other hand, the faithful overcomer who trusts in the Lord, listens to the Spirit, and walks by faith is called to endure, to labor with patience, face tribulation, love his enemy, live and proclaim the gospel, serve others, and remain obedient and devoted unto the end. Then, our blessed hope will become reality on the day of the Lord, when the dead in Christ are resurrected and living believers are translated into glorious, immortal bodies. Forever to be with the Lord!

The burden that presses on my heart today is real. But where did it come from? Is it prudent for me to desire that more and more fellow citizens of the household of God develop a thirst and longing to appreciate and grasp what the Lord has recorded in the Holy Scriptures pertaining to the time of the end?

To come off of autopilot and consider that the seventh trumpet may sound forth in our lifetime? To loosen our grip on the uncertain things of this world?

My personal burden in this area could be self-induced, but my intuition says that its flame was lit by God. Admittedly, for a long time I was content in my understanding of prophecy (or my lack thereof) because of the value and wisdom that I placed on the simple end-times doctrine of "be prepared." I was at peace with God and by His grace walking against sin, self, and Satan, and I knew this was sufficient. Yet, it became clear that God desired to move me away from my comfort zone and into a vast portion of the Scriptures that I respected and loved but in all honesty had neglected to study.

Please don't get me wrong. I am not saying that a simple "be prepared" philosophy for the end times is wrong or even insufficient. But let's not be slumbering! We must be awake and watchful. The prophecies in Scripture abound with instruction and detail and hope that can build our faith in the Word of God.

The second coming will not be obscure or happen by accident. Acts 15:18 says, "Known unto God are all his works from the beginning of the world." And from Isaiah we read that God has declared the end from the beginning. His counsel shall stand. He has purposed it, and He will do it. If there is one thing that we can wholeheartedly trust in and depend on in this day and time, it is the Word of God. It will stand until its complete fulfillment, and it will not pass away.

> Remember the former things of old: for I am God, and there is none else; I am God, and there is none like me, declaring the end from the beginning, and from ancient times the things that are not yet done, saying, My counsel shall stand, and I will do all my pleasure: calling a ravenous bird from the east, the man that executeth my counsel from a far country: yea, I have spoken it, I will also bring it to pass; I have purposed it, I will also do it. Hearken unto me, ye stouthearted, that are far from righteousness: I bring near my righteousness; it shall not be far off, and my salvation shall not tarry: and I will place salvation in Zion for Israel my glory. (Isaiah 46:9–13)

Believers in every generation since the first coming of the Lord Jesus have looked for His return. While future time and events will corroborate whether the hour truly is urgent, we very well could be the generation. Often, the teachings from Ezekiel 3 and 33 come to my mind. While today may not be the time for the trumpet to blow and for a warning to go out to the people, we know for sure that the time is ripe for the faithful, humble, and wise to fortify themselves with the Holy Scriptures and to ready themselves as watchmen.

We won't know the day until the time draws nearer. However, we are presented with two big-picture time periods of Scripture that are relevant to our day. The apostle Peter wrote in 2 Peter 3:8 that one day is with the Lord as a thousand years, and a thousand years as one day. If the world is about six thousand years old or six "days" old, could a day of millennial rest be coming soon?

The second time period comes from Hosea the prophet, who speaks of Israel seeking the face of the LORD in their affliction, a revival after two days, and being raised up to live in the sight of the LORD on the third day. All of this is in context with the mention of the coming as the latter and former rain, which is similarly mentioned in James 5:7:

> I will go and return to my place, till they acknowledge their offence, and seek my face: in their affliction they will seek me early. Come, and let us return unto the LORD: for he hath torn, and he will heal us; he hath smitten, and he will bind us up. After two days will he revive us: in the third day he will raise us up, and we shall live in his sight. Then shall we know, if we follow on to know the LORD: his going forth is prepared as the morning; and he shall come unto us as the rain, as the latter and former rain unto the earth. (Hosea 5:15–6:3)

> Be patient therefore, brethren, unto the coming of the Lord. Behold, the husbandman waiteth for the precious fruit of the earth, and hath long patience for it, until he receive the early and latter rain. Be ye also patient; stablish your hearts: for the coming of the Lord draweth nigh. (James 5:7–8)

It will soon be two thousand years, or two "days," since Christ died on the cross. The "third day" could be near. Not only is the Lord patient, but He charges us also to be patient and steadfast until the coming of the Lord. And that we must do.

Soon it may be time for the tribulation and Satan's final attempt to fulfill his prideful ambitions. His primary aim is to thwart the Word of God. This is the only way that he can win. The Word of God says that Jesus will rule and reign from Jerusalem upon His return. So where is Satan's ultimate focus? Jerusalem. And not only Jerusalem, but more particularly, Satan's focus will one day zero in on some type of rebuilt temple structure. The temple of God was always known as the dwelling place of God, and it is within this place that the Scripture says the Antichrist will exalt himself *above* God, so that he *as* God will sit in the temple of God declaring that he *is* God (2 Thessalonians 2:4). With all his might and power, we understand that until the very end Satan will work to usurp the position of God. It wouldn't be so bad if Antichrist operated as a lone wolf in sheep's clothing. But the sad reality is the Evil One has always had multitudes of willing followers who fall for his lies, deceit, and fateful promises. This will continue, and likely to a greater degree, as the rise of the Antichrist will be a final, fatal attempt on Satan's part. Through cunning and crafty ways and supernatural powers, he will effectively entice and amass a large contingent of followers as the battle between good and evil strides toward its climax.

As the end draws nearer, we need the truth of God's Word, the Spirit of God, and the grace of God (His divine influence) more than ever. Every tactic and weapon in the arsenal of Satan will be used as the end draws nigh. Much will be outright evil and obvious to our senses. But the Scripture strongly warns of deception, of the ability of Satan to transform into an angel of light (2 Corinthians 11:14), and of power, signs, great wonders, and miracles (2 Thessalonians 2:9–10 and Revelation 13:12–14).

The most effective means of detecting something counterfeit is to have a keen understanding of the authentic and original version. In this case, the key is our familiarity and understanding of the prophecies related to the time of the end. The greater our understanding of God's plan and the more serious our focus and desire to understand the events and circumstances pertaining to the second coming of Jesus Christ, the greater our ability to be effective ambassadors for Him, to shine truth and light in the midst of a dark world, and to impact the world for good, even as we are able to give appropriate and timely warning.

Praise God that we have the rich opportunity to experience the very indwelling of God in our hearts and lives in the present day! Praise God that the Scripture records how this blasphemous pursuit of the Evil One's will bring forth the judgment of God and Satan's ultimate defeat!

I believe that more than ever, the time referred to in Hebrews 10:25 is upon us: "and so much the more, as ye see the day approaching." What are we to do "so much the more"? Let us draw near with a true heart, let us hold fast the profession of our faith without wavering, let us provoke one another to love and to good works, and let us not go alone, but let us assemble together and exhort one another as the day approaches. It is time to set our eyes and hearts upon God and away from the nagging, temporal, and fleeting things of this world that often distract us from godly affection.

A charge goes out today for all of us to be as the Bereans. Should the time of the end come and prophetic events begin to unfold in our day, we need to be prepared.

There is always a need for the seed of truth to be sown into the hearts of unbelievers. Today is always the appropriate day to turn to the LORD in repentance and faith. However, the time of the end could provide a mighty tool for the followers of the Lord Jesus. Using the Holy Scripture as a checklist of sorts, as end-times prophetic events begin to unfold, we will find ourselves equipped with powerful evidence of the veracity of God's Word, the soon judgment of the LORD, and the need to repent and trust God. All this we may plant in the hearts of unbelievers.

Let's do our part to awaken as many as we can from stupor and sleepiness.

> I charge thee therefore before God, and the Lord Jesus Christ,
> who shall judge the quick and the dead at his appearing
> and his kingdom;
> preach the word; be instant in season, out of season; reprove, rebuke,
> exhort with all longsuffering and doctrine.
> For the time will come when they will not endure sound doctrine;
> but after their own lusts shall they heap to themselves teachers,
> having itching ears;
> and they shall turn away their ears from the truth,
> and shall be turned unto fables.
> But watch thou in all things, endure afflictions,
> do the work of an evangelist, make full proof of thy ministry.
> For I am now ready to be offered, and the time of my departure is at hand.
> I have fought a good fight,
> I have finished my course,
> I have kept the faith:
> henceforth there is laid up for me a crown of righteousness,
> which the Lord, the righteous judge, shall give me at that day:
> and not to me only, but unto all them also that love his appearing.
> (2 Timothy 4:1–8)

Appendix 1

THE KINGDOM OF GOD AT JESUS'S SECOND COMING

Today, we experience "competing kingdoms" on earth. Praise God, believers can spiritually be delivered from Satan's power into the power of Christ's existing kingdom (Colossians 1:13). However, we can look forward to a future defeat of the kingdoms of this world at the day of the Lord. This will lead to the absolute and forever dominion of the kingdom of God. Jesus will be King of the world! Let's explore some Scriptures that depict this future aspect of the kingdom, the "not yet" phase of the kingdom of God.

Matthew 4:8–10: *The kingdoms of this world are presently under the domain of the devil.*

Again, the devil taketh him up into an exceeding high mountain, and sheweth him all the kingdoms of the world, and the glory of them; and saith unto him, All these things will I give thee, if thou wilt fall down and worship me. Then saith Jesus unto him, Get thee hence, Satan: for it is written, Thou shalt worship the Lord thy God, and him only shalt thou serve.

Matthew 7:21: *Eligibility for kingdom entrance is following the Lord.*

Not every one that saith unto me, Lord, Lord, shall enter into the kingdom of heaven; but he that doeth the will of my Father which is in heaven.

Matthew 8:11: *This is an activity that we can look forward to.*

And I say unto you, That many shall come from the east and west, and shall sit down with Abraham, and Isaac, and Jacob, in the kingdom of heaven.

Matthew 25:34: *The "inheritance" comes after the second coming of Jesus.*

Then shall the King say unto them on his right hand, Come, ye blessed of my Father, inherit the kingdom prepared for you from the foundation of the world:

Mark 14:25: *Jesus will again partake of earthly drink when He rules from Jerusalem.*

Verily I say unto you, I will drink no more of the fruit of the vine, until that day that I drink it new in the kingdom of God.

Luke 9:62: *This infers that kingdom entrance is future, after we have sojourned by faith.*

And Jesus said unto him, No man, having put his hand to the plough, and looking back, is fit for the kingdom of God.

Luke 13:28: *What a regret to not be able to partake of the inheritance!*

There shall be weeping and gnashing of teeth, when ye shall see Abraham, and Isaac, and Jacob, and all the prophets, in the kingdom of God, and you yourselves thrust out.

Luke 19:11–27: *There will be roles and responsibilities for believers in the kingdom.*

And as they heard these things, he added and spake a parable, because he was nigh to Jerusalem, and because they thought that the kingdom of God should immediately appear. He said therefore, A certain nobleman went into a far country to receive for himself a kingdom, and to return.

And he called his ten servants, and delivered them ten pounds, and said unto them, Occupy till I come.

But his citizens hated him, and sent a message after him, saying, We will not have this man to reign over us. And it came to pass, that when he was returned, having received the kingdom, then he commanded these servants to be called unto him, to whom he had given the money, that he might know how much every man had gained by trading.

Then came the first, saying, Lord, thy pound hath gained ten pounds. And he said unto him, Well, thou good servant: because thou hast been faithful in a very little, have thou authority over ten cities. And the second came, saying,

Lord, thy pound hath gained five pounds. And he said likewise to him, Be thou also over five cities.

And another came, saying, Lord, behold, here is thy pound, which I have kept laid up in a napkin: for I feared thee, because thou art an austere man: thou takest up that thou layedst not down, and reapest that thou didst not sow.

And he saith unto him, Out of thine own mouth will I judge thee, thou wicked servant. Thou knewest that I was an austere man, taking up that I laid not down, and reaping that I did not sow: wherefore then gavest not thou my money into the bank, that at my coming I might have required mine own with usury? And he said unto them that stood by, Take from him the pound, and give it to him that hath ten pounds. (And they said unto him, Lord, he hath ten pounds.) For I say unto you, That unto every one which hath shall be given; and from him that hath not, even that he hath shall be taken away from him. But those mine enemies, which would not that I should reign over them, bring hither, and slay them before me.

Luke 21:27–31: *The kingdom, verse 31, is in context of the second coming.*

And then shall they see the Son of man coming in a cloud with power and great glory. And when these things begin to come to pass, then look up, and lift up your heads; for your redemption draweth nigh. And he spake to them a parable; Behold the fig tree, and all the trees; when they now shoot forth, ye see and know of your own selves that summer is now nigh at hand. So likewise ye, when ye see these things come to pass, know ye that the kingdom of God is nigh at hand.

Luke 22:16, 18, 29–30: *The disciples will have a large role/responsibility in the kingdom.*

For I say unto you, I will not any more eat thereof, until it be fulfilled in the kingdom of God. For I say unto you, I will not drink of the fruit of the vine, until the kingdom of God shall come. And I appoint unto you a kingdom, as my Father hath appointed unto me; that ye may eat and drink at my table in my kingdom, and sit on thrones judging the twelve tribes of Israel.

Act 14:22: *Kingdom entrance is after our life of faith is finished.*

Confirming the souls of the disciples, and exhorting them to continue in the faith, and that we must through much tribulation enter into the kingdom of God.

1 Corinthians 15:50: *Believers and saints of God will enter the millennium with new, immortal, resurrected or translated bodies.*

Now this I say, brethren, that flesh and blood cannot inherit the kingdom of God; neither doth corruption inherit incorruption.

2 Thessalonians 1:4–8: *Kingdom entrance, verse 5, is after a time of tribulation and in the context of the second coming of Jesus.*

So that we ourselves glory in you in the churches of God for your patience and faith in all your persecutions and tribulations that ye endure: which is a manifest token of the righteous judgment of God, that ye may be counted worthy of the kingdom of God, for which ye also suffer: seeing it is a righteous thing with God to recompense tribulation to them that trouble you; and to you who are troubled rest with us, when the Lord Jesus shall be revealed from heaven with his mighty angels, in flaming fire taking vengeance on them that know not God, and that obey not the gospel of our Lord Jesus Christ:

2 Timothy 4:1: *The kingdom is connected to the return of Jesus.*

I charge thee therefore before God, and the Lord Jesus Christ, who shall judge the quick and the dead at his appearing and his kingdom . . .

2 Timothy 4:18: *The Lord shall "keep" and "preserve" us unto the kingdom.*

And the Lord shall deliver me from every evil work, and will preserve me unto his heavenly kingdom: to whom be glory for ever and ever. Amen.

James 2:5: *Inheritance of the future kingdom is a promise of God.*

Hearken, my beloved brethren, Hath not God chosen the poor of this world rich in faith, and heirs of the kingdom which he hath promised to them that love him?

2 Peter 1:11: *We will enter the kingdom after our pilgrim journey of faith is finished.*

For so an entrance shall be ministered unto you abundantly into the everlasting kingdom of our Lord and Saviour Jesus Christ.

Revelation 11:15: *The seventh thunder, seventh trumpet, seventh vial, and seventh seal mark the day of the Lord, i.e. the second coming. This is the time of transition from evil dominion to Christ's dominion.*

And the seventh angel sounded; and there were great voices in heaven, saying, The kingdoms of this world are become the kingdoms of our Lord, and of his Christ; and he shall reign for ever and ever.

Daniel 2:44–45: *The "stone"—i.e. Jesus—will crush all existing powers of Satan and God will establish His kingdom forever.*

And in the days of these kings shall the God of heaven set up a kingdom, which shall never be destroyed: and the kingdom shall not be left to other people, but it shall break in pieces and consume all these kingdoms, and it shall stand for ever. Forasmuch as thou sawest that the stone was cut out of the mountain without hands, and that it brake in pieces the iron, the brass, the clay, the silver, and the gold; the great God hath made known to the king what shall come to pass hereafter: and the dream is certain, and the interpretation thereof sure.

Daniel 7:13–14, 27: *This chapter isn't easy to parse, but the final kingdom comes after the Antichrist/beast kingdom is destroyed—i.e. in an end-times context.*

I saw in the night visions, and, behold, one like the Son of man came with the clouds of heaven, and came to the Ancient of days, and they brought him near before him. And there was given him dominion, and glory, and a kingdom, that all people, nations, and languages, should serve him: his dominion is an everlasting dominion, which shall not pass away, and his kingdom that which shall not be destroyed. And the kingdom and dominion, and the greatness of the kingdom under the whole heaven, shall be given to the people of the saints of the most High, whose kingdom is an everlasting kingdom, and all dominions shall serve and obey him.

Parallel Accounts: *The Second Coming and the Kingdom*

Regarding the kingdom of God, I would like to cite one more passage to demonstrate its nature as a future kingdom. But first, let's back up to the Scripture previously noted in Luke's gospel, where the subject is summarized well. The context is the second coming of Jesus Christ, which is equated with power and great glory. Verse 31 says that when you see these things come to pass, know ye that the kingdom of God *is nigh* at hand.

And then shall they see the Son of man coming in a cloud with power and great glory. And when these things begin to come to pass, then look up, and lift up your heads; for your redemption draweth nigh. And he spake to them a parable; Behold the fig tree, and all the trees; when they now shoot forth, ye see and know of your own selves that summer is now nigh at hand. So likewise ye, when ye see these things come to pass, know ye that the kingdom of God is nigh at hand. (Luke 21:27–31)

From Luke 21, we can equate the second coming with "power and great glory" and with the day of the Lord. What next? In Matthew 25:31 we read, "When the Son of man shall come in his glory, and all the holy angels with him, then shall he sit upon the throne of his glory." This depicts the inauguration of the millennial kingdom, with Jesus as king! It is closely connected with the second coming. We can link the following events as follows:

The Day of the Lord → The Second Coming → Power and Great Glory → The Kingdom of God

The parallel Scriptures below emphatically demonstrate that the kingdom of God is associated with the return of Jesus. The message is virtually identical in the gospels of Matthew, Mark, and Luke. The context of the teaching in all three is the same, and therefore we can compare and layer all three of these Scriptures together to develop a more full and robust understanding of the teaching. Please especially review the italicized Scripture within the last two verses of the following accounts. The second coming is clearly connected to, and will usher in the kingdom of God. Can we honestly conclude otherwise?

Matthew 16:24: Then said Jesus unto his disciples, If any man will come after me, let him deny himself, and take up his cross, and follow me.	Mark 8:34: And when he had called the people unto him with his disciples also, he said unto them, Whosoever will come after me, let him deny himself, and take up his cross, and follow me.	Luke 9:23: And he said to them all, If any man will come after me, let him deny himself, and take up his cross daily, and follow me.
Matthew 16:25: For whosoever will save his life shall lose it: and whosoever will lose his life for my sake shall find it.	Mark 8:35: For whosoever will save his life shall lose it; but whosoever shall lose his life for my sake and the gospel's, the same shall save it.	Luke 9:24: For whosoever will save his life shall lose it: but whosoever will lose his life for my sake, the same shall save it.

Matthew 16:26: For what is a man profited, if he shall gain the whole world, and lose his own soul? or what shall a man give in exchange for his soul?	Mark 8:36: For what shall it profit a man, if he shall gain the whole world, and lose his own soul?	Luke 9:25: For what is a man advantaged, if he gain the whole world, and lose himself, or be cast away?
Matthew 16:27: For *the Son of man shall come in the glory of his Father with his angels;* and then he shall reward every man according to his works.	Mark 8:38: Whosoever therefore shall be ashamed of me and of my words in this adulterous and sinful generation; of him also shall the Son of man be ashamed, when *he cometh in the glory of his Father with the holy angels.*	Luke 9:26: For whosoever shall be ashamed of me and of my words, of him shall the Son of man be ashamed, when *he shall come in his own glory, and in his Father's, and of the holy angels.*
Matthew 16:28: Verily I say unto you, There be some standing here, which shall not taste of death, *till they see the Son of man coming in his kingdom.*	Mark 9:1: And he said unto them, Verily I say unto you, That there be some of them that stand here, which shall not taste of death, *till they have seen the kingdom of God come with power.*	Luke 9:27: But I tell you of a truth, there be some standing here, which shall not taste of death, *till they see the kingdom of God.*

All of the above Scriptures give us a firm footing to stand upon. The second coming of Jesus Christ will bring forth the "kingdom of God."

"Some Standing Here"

If you want to go further into these parallel accounts, I'll offer my guess as to what Christ meant when He said there were "some standing here," some who heard the words from His own mouth, who would "not taste of death" until the second coming. We know that all of them standing before Jesus that day, listening to the sound of His voice, experienced a physical death. So what does this mean? Two scriptures help point us to the answer. One is Hebrews 2:9, 14–15, and the other is John 8:52.

> Then said the Jews unto him, Now we know that thou hast a devil. Abraham is dead, and the prophets; and thou sayest, *If a man keep my saying, he shall never taste of death.* (John 8:52)

> *But we see Jesus,* who was made a little lower than the angels for the suffering of death, crowned with glory and honour; *that he by the grace of God*

should taste death for every man. Forasmuch then as the children are partakers of flesh and blood, he also himself likewise took part of the same; *that through death he might destroy him that had the power of death, that is, the devil;* and deliver them who through fear of death were all their lifetime subject to bondage. (Hebrews 2:9, 14–15)

What can be done in order for us to "never taste of death"? We must believe with all that is within us if we are to "never die" (John 11:25–26). If we lean wholly upon Jesus in faith, repent of our sins, and become converted, we can avoid the penalty and damnation of our sin because of the suffering and wrath that Jesus endured on our behalf, which culminated in the offering of His life and the shedding of His blood as a perfect sacrifice (Matthew 18:3, Mark 1:15, Luke 13:3, John 5:24, Acts 3:19, Romans 5:18, Romans 8:1).

But what if we don't repent of our sins and become converted? Then awaits judgment and the "taste of death."

So how did Jesus "taste death" for every man? I think we can put it this way. He drank every last drop of the cup (Matthew 26:39) so that mankind, whosoever would, could be passed from death to life and not have to endure, suffer, and experience the holy wrath of God against sin. This cup that he was drinking was the cup of God's wrath against sin (Psalm 75:8; Jeremiah 25:15, 49:12; Revelation 14:10, 16:19). Isaiah 53 speaks to why Jesus suffered on our behalf . . . because of *our* sins.

Some were "standing there" nearly two thousand years ago and at some point placed their faith in the Lord Jesus and repented of their sins. Thus, Jesus "tasted death" on their behalf. However, some who stood there would never trust in His precious atonement, and it is to those whom He said, "Verily I say unto you, There be some standing here, which shall not taste of death, till they see the Son of man coming in his kingdom." Likewise, if anyone today is not found abiding "in Him" at death or when Jesus returns, there will be a "tasting" of judgment on the day of the Lord. Unbelievers will suffer the wrath and judgment from God and bear the consequences of their sin on that great and notable day. Thanks be to God—He has provided a way of escape! He suffered the penalty of our sins and died in our place. It is for all who would believe that he endured the cross!

> And being found in fashion as a man, he humbled himself, and became obedient unto death, even the death of the cross. (Philippians 2:8)

Looking unto Jesus the author and finisher of our faith; who for the joy that was set before him endured the cross, despising the shame, and is set down at the right hand of the throne of God. (Hebrews 12:2)

My interpretation of Matthew 16:28 contends that the unrighteous dead will "taste of death" (i.e. indignation and wrath) and suffer in judgment at the second coming of Jesus and His kingdom. Other Scriptures, such as Matthew 12:36, Romans 2:5–9, and 2 Peter 2:9, support my contention that the unrighteous dead are indeed relevant on the "day of judgment."

How then will dead unbelievers "taste of death" when Jesus returns on the day of the Lord?

Logically, one needs to be alive to suffer. But, Revelation 20 seems to indicate that believers will be resurrected in the first resurrection (Revelation 20:6), while the unjust are reserved for the second resurrection after the millennial reign (Revelation 20:5, 12–13). This second resurrection is the time of the great white throne judgment, where judgment is made by the "books" (probably the books of the Bible), and those whose names are not found in the book of life will be cast into the lake of fire and tormented forever.

This presents difficulty if the unjust are not resurrected on the day of the Lord. How could the unrighteous dead "taste of death" (i.e. indignation and wrath) and suffer in judgment at the second coming of Jesus if they are not resurrected on the day of the Lord prior to the millennium?

- Could the unjust taste of death without being resurrected on the day of judgment when Christ returns?
    o We know that the bottomless pit can be opened (i.e. Revelation 9:1). Also, at the beginning of the millennium, an angel from heaven reopens the bottomless pit and throws Satan in. With an opening up of the bottomless pit, could the unrighteous dead have their consciences exposed to the judgment of God, where they experience the wrath and fury of God even without being resurrected?
- How can the unjust "give an account of every idle word" (Matthew 12:36) in the day of judgment if they aren't resurrected?

There are many questions here, but I'll offer my guess. The bottomless pit will be opened, and though not in bodily form, the souls of the unrighteous dead residing in Hades will have full cognition of their plight on the day of the Lord, thus exposing them to the wrath of the Almighty. They will have full awareness that God's hand of judgment has been placed upon them. It will be their "tasting" of death. Also, 2 Peter 3:10 says the elements will melt with a fervent heat, and the works that are therein shall be burned up. This could easily encompass the location of the unrighteous dead and potentially could be another mechanism for them to suffer wrath and figuratively gnash their teeth. In addition, another important consideration is that the devil has the "power of death" (Hebrews 2:14), and when the devil is thrust into the bottomless pit at the beginning of the millennium, the unrighteous dead will literally taste the presence of death and their eternal doom. Lastly, in their unresurrected state, the unrighteous dead will not have the ability to "give an account" on the day of the Lord. However, the Scripture does not contradict itself. The great white throne judgment will afford that opportunity. Though a thousand years later at the end of the millennium, the unrighteous dead will technically "give an account" in the "day of judgment," because with the Lord one thousand years is as one day, a statement Peter specifically makes in the context of the day of judgment (2 Peter 3:7–8).

The day of the Lord is both a single day and a thousand-year day! The focus of the single day (as we explored in detail throughout this book) is Jesus Christ. And, the focus of the millennial period, when the earth will be full of the knowledge of the LORD (Isaiah 11:9), is Jesus Christ!

So in conclusion of this sober topic of "tasting death", what is your choice? Will you regretfully partake of the bitter cup of wrath as judgment for your own sin on the day of judgment? Or will you take advantage of the wondrous gift from the One who willingly, out of great love, tasted death for us?

We have a high calling. Let's consider the words of Jesus at the beginning of these parallel passages. Are we willing to sacrifice, to deny ourselves, and to take up our cross daily? Are we willing to lose our life for His sake and the gospel's? In the words of Revelation 22:21, may the grace of our Lord Jesus Christ be with you all. Amen.

Appendix 2

ARE THERE MANSIONS IN HEAVEN?

Many interpret the words of Jesus in John 14:1–3 to mean that Jesus is going to heaven to build mansions in the sky that we will live in one day. However, this huge and far-reaching doctrine seems out of proportion and context with what Jesus is teaching in John 13 to 17.

> Let not your heart be troubled: ye believe in God, believe also in me. In my Father's house are many mansions: if it were not so, I would have told you. I go to prepare a place for you. And if I go and prepare a place for you, I will come again, and receive you unto myself; that where I am, there ye may be also. (John 14:1–3)

The context of these chapters is the time leading up to the departure of Jesus from the earth when He would be physically taken away from the presence of the disciples. His hour of departure was near (John 13:1; John 14:19; John 16:16, 28; John 17:11). Jesus wanted to prepare His disciples for the great transition that would occur: a transition from the moment when His physical presence would "go away" to the moment when His spiritual presence would "come again" in the Holy Spirit as the Comforter (John 13:19–20; John 14:20, 29; John 15:26–27; John 16:4; 22–23).

The themes of John 13 to 17 can generally be summed up in the following three categories:

1. An exhortation to love and serve one another.
2. A teaching about the great transition when Jesus would ascend

physically and then come again to earth via the Holy Ghost. He says, "Let not your heart be troubled, neither let it be afraid" and reiterates all throughout these Scriptures that in essence, "*I am going* to the Father that *I might come again* in Spirit and abide and dwell in your hearts."

3. The doctrine of the unification and oneness of the Father, the Son, and the Spirit.

What Jesus was teaching the disciples in John 14:1–3 was not a new doctrine outside of this context.. Staying within the context, we can properly interpret this teaching either literally or as an analogy. Let's start with the analogy.

Understanding Analogically

In my opinion, Jesus intended to further drive home the point He reiterated time and time again throughout these chapters. In this analogy, God would exit His former dwelling place (the temple) and enter into a new abode (the hearts of men).

"My Father's house" was a reference to the existing temple (John 2:16 and Matthew 12:4). His disciples would have understood Jesus's reference as being to the temple, not heaven. The temple had long been considered the house of God, or the dwelling place of God. Plus, there were many chambers or rooms surrounding the north, west, and south walls in this "house of the Lord" (1 Kings 6:5; Ezra 8:29; Jeremiah 35:2, 4; Jeremiah 36:10). The disciples would have understood this part of the analogy as well. In fact, the same Greek word (*mone'*—Strong's G3438) translated "mansions" in John 14:2 was used by Jesus later on in John 14:23 in the context of the Holy Spirit dwelling in our hearts. It was translated as "abode" in verse 23 compared to "mansions" in verse 2. The disciples would not so easily have gotten hung up on the word *mansion* like we can today. It simply meant "room"—one of "many rooms."

> Jesus answered and said unto him, If a man love me, he will keep my words: and my Father will love him, and we will come unto him, and make our abode with him. (John 14:23)

So what did the analogy mean? Basically, Jesus wanted to shift the disciples in their thinking—to turn them from thinking about the existing temple to the new dwelling place of God and the many abodes of the Spirit in the hearts and bodies of believers.

Today, there are many mansions (i.e. dwelling places, rooms, or abodes) where the Holy Spirit resides within the temples (i.e. our bodies) of born-again believers in Jesus Christ. Jesus was teaching that the physical temple structure where God dwelt with man in the Holy of Holies was going to become obsolete and irrelevant to the believer. Why? Because the Lord Jesus was soon going to die, but then He would come back again in Spirit to dwell in the hearts of His followers. This was the great transition! Christ's followers who love and serve God and one another and who keep the Lord's commandments provide a fit habitation for the indwelling of the Spirit in the temple of their hearts and bodies. This is the primary theme of these chapters!

This is very much what happened: Jesus ascended to the Father in heaven and made ready and prepared a specific place and time that He might come again in Spirit to attain a close union with His followers once again, only this is a spiritual union and not physical. (The place He prepared was the house where the disciples had gathered and the time was Pentecost—see Acts 2:1–2). These were truly comforting words to His disciples. He says "I will come to you" and "I will dwell with you and be in you"!

I love to think about and study the Scriptures pertaining to the day of the Lord and the second coming. However, the "I will come again" promise of John 14:2 is the same "come again" promise referred to in John 14:18 and John 14:28. In my opinion, Jesus is referring to His soon return on Pentecost as the Holy Spirit, who in essence is one and the same as the Father and the Son:

> And I will pray the Father, and he shall give you another Comforter, that *he may abide* [stay, dwell] *with you for ever; even the Spirit of truth; whom the world cannot receive, because it seeth him not, neither knoweth him: but ye know him; for he dwelleth with you, and shall be in you.* I will not leave you comfortless: *I will come to you.* Yet a little while, and the world seeth me no more; but ye see me: because I live, ye shall live also. *At that day ye shall know that I am in my Father, and ye in me, and I in you.* (John 14:16–20)

Jesus restates the same theme just a few verses later. He also states again the reassuring phrase, "Let not your heart be troubled." I believe He also refers back to John 14:1–3 when He says, "ye have heard how I said unto you." And he again declares the purpose of this teaching: "I'm telling you this now so that when it comes to pass and the Spirit descends on you, you might believe."

> But *the Comforter, which is the Holy Ghost,* whom the Father *will send in my name,* he shall teach you all things, and bring all things to your

remembrance, whatsoever I have said unto you. *Peace I leave with you, my peace I give unto you: not as the world giveth, give I unto you. Let not your heart be troubled, neither let it be afraid.* Ye have heard how I said unto you, *I go away, and come again unto you. If ye loved me, ye would rejoice, because I said, I go unto the Father: for my Father is greater than I. And now I have told you before it come to pass, that, when it is come to pass, ye might believe.* (John 14:26–29)

The terminology used to describe the actual "coming again" in these chapters is consistent with descriptions of God in the Old Testament. The rushing mighty wind (Acts 2:2) associated with the arrival of the Holy Spirit is consistent with how the presence of God was described in Job 38:1, 40:6; 2 Kings 2:1, 11; and Ezekiel 1:4. The description of cloven tongues like fire is likewise consistent with several Old Testament passages that describe God's presence, including Exodus 3:2, 19:18; Isaiah 6:4–6; Ezekiel 1:4; and Daniel 7:9.

I don't mean to be too lighthearted here. I realize that the Lord Jesus was the son of a carpenter while growing up with His earthly family. However, I don't believe it is His duty to erect mansions for us in heaven. I believe that His primary place and role is to intercede for us at the Father's right hand, because we have an evil adversary who is an "accuser of the brethren." This is a sober reality. But it is not only a sober reality: for the child of God, it is a precious truth and one of the most wonderful assets and privileges we could ever imagine to have such an advocate skillfully and lovingly countering an evil foe on our behalf.

Understanding Literally

We can also interpret the teaching literally while remaining within the context of John 13 to 17. How is this possible? First, let's consider the ten-day span of time between the ascension of Christ to the day of Pentecost (Shavu'ot). After the ascension, the disciples returned to Jerusalem and went into an upper room among a gathering of about 120 people (Acts 1:12–15). After prayer and discussion, they cast lots for an apostle to replace Judas and to regain the number of apostles to twelve. Now, were the apostles still in the upper room on the day of Pentecost or had they moved locations? It appears reasonable to me that Jesus had a special place prepared at the temple (i.e. the house of God) in one of the surrounding chambers or rooms. After all, where would the apostles naturally go to worship on a Jewish holiday? The place to be at Pentecost would have been the temple. Also, have you considered that when Peter stood up to preach after the Holy Ghost had come, a great multitude of over 3000 heard his sermon? Could this have been possible in the upper room?

So plainly, Jesus telegraphed His plans to the disciples in John 14:1–3. Jesus would divinely prepare a place for the disciples in one of the rooms of the temple. Jesus would arrange the specific time for their reunion (at Pentecost). And when Jesus came (as the Holy Ghost), He would meet the disciples in that exact spot. The Spirit of God would then be intimately joined with the disciples in unity.

Literally, for the sake of the great commission, it was expedient and necessary for Jesus to "go" to the Father that He could "come again" in Spirit. This great transition nearly 2000 years ago is still effective—enabling the Spirit of God to transform lives. This literal interpretation fits precisely with the way events truly panned out. Also, it is consistent with the overall context of these chapters. The Holy Spirit, even Jesus Himself, literally came (John 14:17–18) and His transforming power enables us to obey the Scripture, and to love God and each other (John 14:23)!

Final Thoughts

To extract the first three verses of John 14 and construct a doctrine of eternal life for the redeemed dwelling in mansions *in heaven* goes contrary not only to the context of John 14 and the surrounding chapters, but also to the following realities:

First: Jesus will be given an earthly dominion. Once the final judgment is made by the Ancient of Days in heaven, the Lord Jesus will be given dominion on earth (Daniel 7:13–14, 26–27; Revelation 11:15). The Lord Jesus will reign on earth during the millennial kingdom (Zechariah 14:9, Isaiah 11:9, Isaiah 60:19–21, Isaiah 66:22–23). The Scripture teaches us that after the resurrection we shall "ever" be with the Lord (1 Thessalonians 4:17). And during the millennium, we are to be priests of God and of Christ and reign with Him a thousand years (Revelation 20:6). It doesn't make sense that we would live in mansions in heaven while Jesus is reigning on earth. Wouldn't that require a separation, and wouldn't it inhibit our ability to live and reign with Him?

Most of our presuppositions lead us to view heaven and eternity as an ethereal, unfamiliar, and nonearthly place. Most do not recognize that this popular view was shaped by the Greek philosopher Plato. Should we have a view of heaven that originates from the Scriptures, or one that is heavily influenced by Greek philosophy?

One of the greatest rewards that I have received in studying eschatology is coming to a more biblically rooted understanding of eternity, including a restored earth, a physical resurrection, and a physical kingdom reign of Jesus Christ on earth. At the conclusion of the millennial reign of Jesus on earth, the time will come when every ounce of evil has been subdued and put under His feet and when death, the last enemy, is destroyed. At this time, Jesus will hand the keys over to God, so to speak, and God will be "all in all." This transition will occur after the new city of Jerusalem descends from heaven to earth and Almighty God Himself in His wondrous glory dwells on earth forever (Revelation 21:11). Recently, this passage in 1 Corinthians 15 struck me. It spoke to me as depicting this very transition of events at the end of the millennium and proceeding into eternity:

> Then cometh the end, when he shall have delivered up the kingdom to God, even the Father; when he shall have put down all rule and all authority and power. For he must reign, till he hath put all enemies under his feet. The last enemy that shall be destroyed is death. For he hath put all things under his feet. But when he saith all things are put under him, it is manifest that he is excepted, which did put all things under him. And when all things shall be subdued unto him, then shall the Son also himself be subject unto him that put all things under him, that God may be all in all. (1 Corinthians 15:24–28)

Second: New Jerusalem will come down from heaven. At the conclusion of the millennium, the tabernacle of God and a new Jerusalem will descend from heaven to the earth (Revelation 21:2–3). Again, the focus of eternity is *on the earth*. I think some interpret from Revelation 21:1–2 that a "new earth" will descend from heaven. But this is not what the text states. A new city of Jerusalem is the only thing that John describes as coming down from God out of heaven. This same trajectory is noted again by John in Revelation 21:10. This truth is also stated by our Lord in Revelation 3:12. It is the same message. The new city of God, new Jerusalem, will come down out of heaven. Do we definitively know the trajectory implied by this phrase "come down from God out of heaven"? Read Revelation 20:9, which uses the same expression. What was the direction of the fire? Clearly the fire came out of heaven and descended to the earth. The text is explicit. The men had surrounded the beloved city, but then were devoured by fire.

Third: The Scripture makes no mention of any ascension of King Jesus and the saints heading up toward heaven after the millennium. Rather, the tabernacle of God will be with men, and God Himself will dwell with man. We shall be His people, and God Himself shall be with us and be our God. This seems restorative, reminiscent of how things "used to be" in the garden, where it all began with humankind on earth.

> And I John saw the holy city, new Jerusalem, coming down from God out of heaven, prepared as a bride adorned for her husband. And I heard a great voice out of heaven saying, Behold, the tabernacle of God is with men, and he will dwell with them, and they shall be his people, and God himself shall be with them, and be their God. (Revelation 21:2–3)

What would be the purpose of eternal mansions in heaven if eternity is heaven on a new earth? I believe we can set our eternal sights on a reconstituted earth that will be restored and reformed to a paradise-like state after the fire of judgment occurs on the great day of God (2 Peter 3:10–12). Hebrews 1:11 says that the earth will perish. Does that mean the earth will be totally consumed and scrapped? In context, Hebrews 1:11 refers to Psalm 102:26 and Isaiah 51:6, which in both cases describe the earth in terms of clothing, as if the earth wears an outer garment. This fiery cleansing will result in the earth receiving a new outer garment where the old set of clothes is taken off, folded up, and changed into newness (Hebrews 1:11–12). The earth will be pure and refreshed into the fullness of radiant beauty and splendor, and the wolf and the lamb will lie down together. It is almost like the conversion of a soul who experiences salvation through repentance and faith. Second Corinthians 5:17 calls born-again believers a "new creation," where old things are passed away and all things become new. Yet we are not given a brand-new body. Rather, we are reborn and made new while keeping the same body.

Like Jesus after He was resurrected, we will undoubtedly have bodies that, while immortal, are capable of walking, talking, eating, drinking, and performing tasks similar to our abilities today. This will enable us to enjoy the goodness and perfectness of God's creation, along with new Jerusalem, without any of the burdens and toils and heartaches that are common in our day. How incredibly satisfying! We can also make a simple consideration of Adam and Eve in the garden. Isn't it true that while their bodies were natural, the Lord via the tree of life could have enabled their lives to go on forever? This is the future Scripture envisions for us.

Appendix 3

END-TIMES CHART

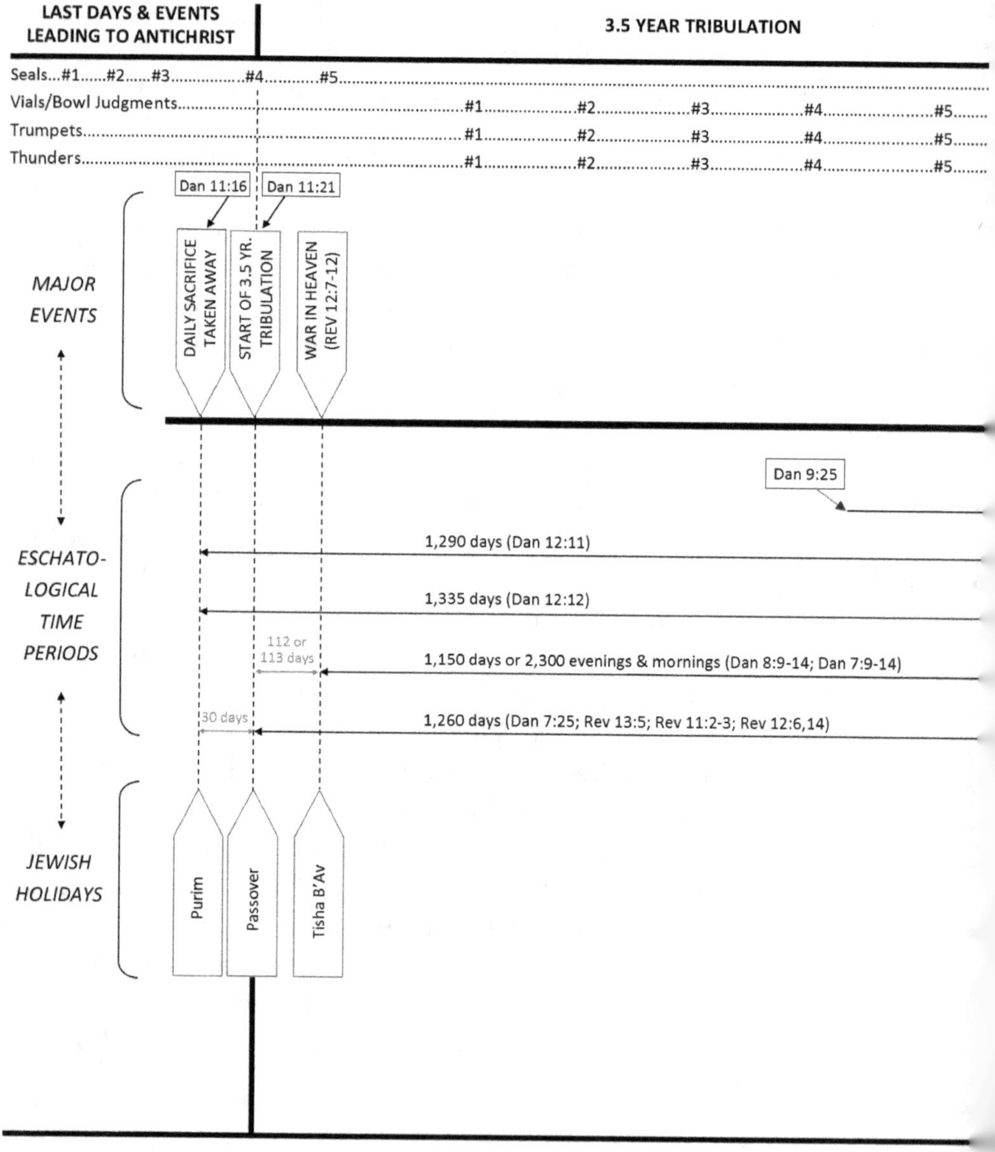

| LAST DAYS & EVENTS LEADING TO ANTICHRIST | 3.5 YEAR TRIBULATION |

Seals...#1......#2......#3.............#4........#5..
Vials/Bowl Judgments...#1............#2............#3............#4............#5
Trumpets...#1............#2............#3............#4............#5
Thunders...#1............#2............#3............#4............#5

MAJOR EVENTS
- Dan 11:16 → DAILY SACRIFICE TAKEN AWAY
- Dan 11:21 → START OF 3.5 YR. TRIBULATION
- WAR IN HEAVEN (REV 12:7-12)

ESCHATO-LOGICAL TIME PERIODS
- Dan 9:25
- 1,290 days (Dan 12:11)
- 1,335 days (Dan 12:12)
- 112 or 113 days
- 1,150 days or 2,300 evenings & mornings (Dan 8:9-14; Dan 7:9-14)
- 30 days
- 1,260 days (Dan 7:25; Rev 13:5; Rev 11:2-3; Rev 12:6,14)

JEWISH HOLIDAYS
- Purim
- Passover
- Tisha B'Av

END-TIMES CHART • 301

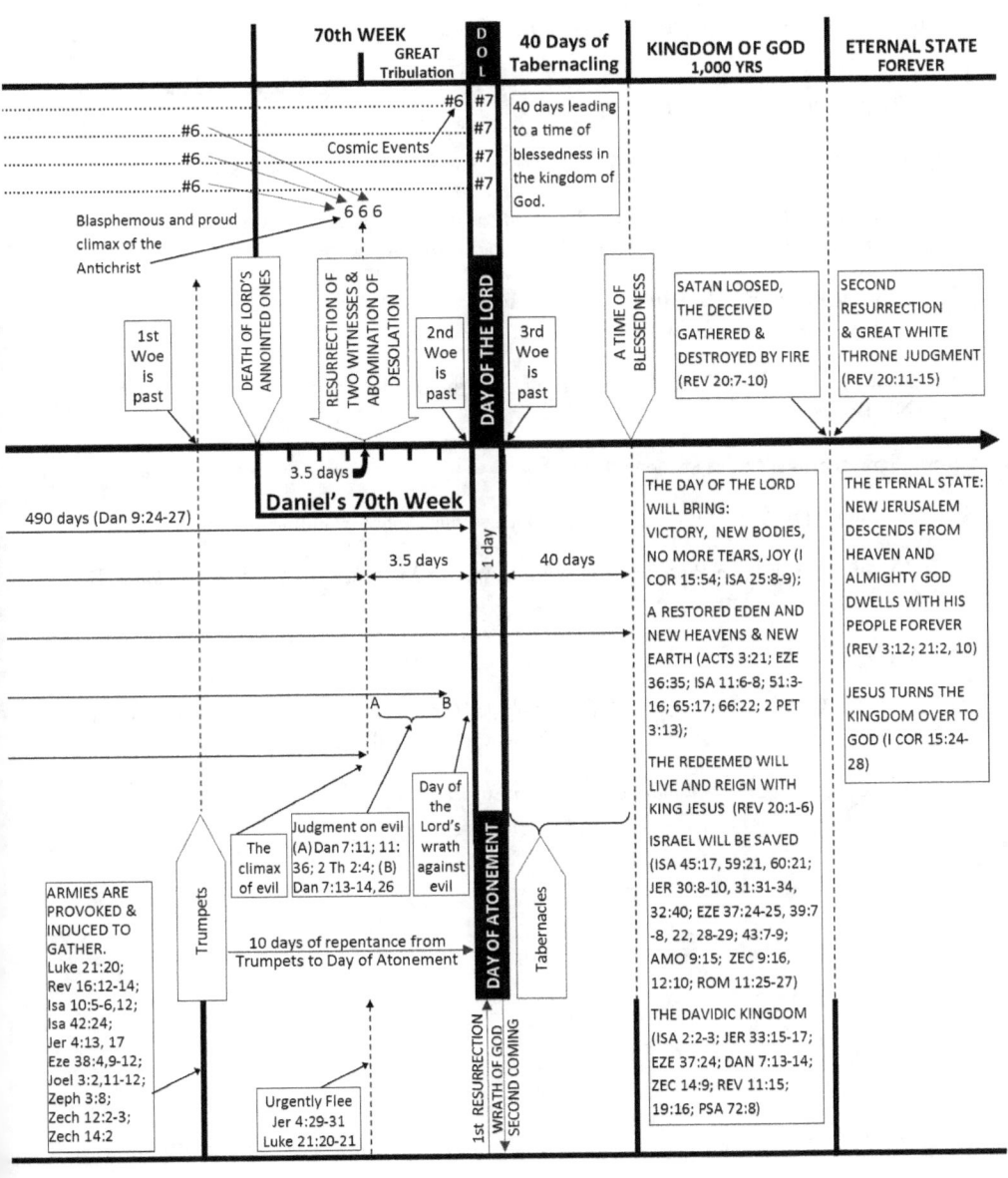

BIBLIOGRAPHY

Chisholm, Robert B. Jr., *Handbook on the Prophets*. Grand Rapids, MI: Baker Academic, 2002

Davidson, Mark, *Daniel Revisited: Discovering the Four Mideast Signs Leading to the Antichrist*. Nashville, TN: WestBow Press, 2015

Jacks, Dr. Noreen, *Feasts of the Lord*. http://www.trumpetcall2nations.com/feasts-lord

Parsons, John J., *The Jewish Holidays – A Simplified Overview of the Feasts of the LORD*. http://www.hebrew4christians.com/Holidays/Introduction/HolidaysIntro.pdf

Richardson, Joel, *When A Jew Rules the World: What the Bible Really Says about Israel in the Plan of God*. Washington, DC: WND Books, 2015

Richardson, Joel, *Mideast Beast: The Scriptural Case for an Islamic Antichrist*. Washington, DC: WND Books, 2012

Strong, James, *Strong's Bible Dictionary*. 1890

Struse, William, *Daniel's 70 Weeks: The Keystone of Bible Prophecy*. PalmoniQuest LLC, 2015

Swift, Kevin R., *Insights in Prophecy: Unlock the Ancient Mysteries of Daniel & Revelation Bible Discovery Series*. CreateSpace, 2012

Thayer, Joseph, *Thayer's Greek Definitions*. 1886

Van der Pool, Charles, *The Apostolic Bible Polyglot Greek-English Interlinear*, second edition. Newport, OR: The Apostolic Press, 2013 www.apostolicbible.com

Webster, Noah, *Webster's Dictionary of American English*. 1828

SCRIPTURE INDEX

GENESIS
1:14	31
3:15	5, 14-15, 25
6:5-7	13
15:4	10
15:5-21	17, 44

EXODUS
1:8, 11-14, 22	266
3:2	296
7:21	268
8:9-10	268
8:22	268
9:4	268
9:11	268
9:13-16	270
9:26	268
10:1-2	270
10:6	269
10:23	269
11:6-7	269
12:12-13	269
14:8-10	272
14:12-14	271
14:13	266, 270
14:21-31	273
14:29-31	271
15:1-19	274-275
19:18	296
20:1-18	46

LEVITICUS
Ch 23	8, 22, 124, 130
23:4	107
23:5-44	107
25:9	112
26:40-45	48

DEUTERONOMY
4:29-31	11, 44, 49
4:30-31	48

Ch 5	45
5:29	47
7:6-12	45
7:9, 12	44
Ch 28	46
29:4	47
29:18	164
30:1-6	50
30:4-6	11

JUDGES
19:26	126

2 SAMUEL
7:10-16	17, 47
7:12-13	5
13:4	126

1 KINGS
6:5	294
17:1	159
18:38-39	159

2 KINGS
1:10, 2:11	159
2:1, 11	296

1 CHRONICLES
17:11-14	5
17:11-15	17, 47

2 CHRONICLES
8:13	90

EZRA
1:1-4, 6:1-12	98
7:11-26	98
8:29	294

NEHEMIAH
2:1-9	98

ESTHER
9:26-27	124

JOB
14:12	36, 201, 259
14:12-14	201
19:23-27	41
19:25-27	35, 259
19:26	201
38:1, 40:6	296

PSALMS
2:6	79
20:7	272
24:7-10	79
47:5-7	79
48:1-2	18
51:7	112
68:1-4	79
72:8	16
72:9	19
75:8	290
77:17-20	272
102:13	7, 106, 123
102:26	299
110:1	183

PROVERBS
5:1-8	164

ECCLESIASTES
1:4	13, 147

ISAIAH
2:2-3	16
2:10-21	160, 175
2:10-22	33
6:4-6	296
6:5	132
7:14	5
9:4-5, 14-19	67

9:6-7	5	29:18-24	53	4:14, 17-18, 22	172
9:7	79	30:27-28, 31	68	4:17	248
9:19	30, 67, 205	30:27-33	71	4:19, 27-28, 31	56
10:5	73, 249	30:30	30, 205	4:19-31	57
10:5-6	68, 95, 172	31:4-9	71	4:21	173
10:12-21	68	34:1-9	199	4:23-28	74, 173, 210
10:20-21	18	34:1-17	72	4:26	173
10:20-23	52	34:2, 6	204	4:29-31	173, 252
10:22	83	34:4	78, 204, 259	4:30-31	173
10:26	30, 205	34:4, 9	30, 205	9:15	164
11:1-5	18	34:8	28	10:10	67
11:4	68	34:8-9	103	23:3-6	11, 57
11:4-5	15, 69, 83	35:10	18, 79	23:6	83
11:6, 8	18, 32	42:13-25	74	23:13-20	164-165
11:9	16, 18, 146, 292, 297	42:24	73, 95, 172, 249	25:15	290
11:9-12	53	45:17-25	54	25:29-38	40
11:11-12	18	46:9-13	279	30:1-10	49
13:7-8, 15-18	151, 251, 254	49:10	204	30:4-9	92, 94
13:8	93	51:3-16	15	30:5-7	151, 251, 253
13:8-9	244	51:6	299	30:6	93
13:8-18	92, 95	Ch 53	290	30:6-7	244
13:9-10	160	54:7, 13-17	54	30:7-11	18
13:9-11	175, 257	59:18-21	11, 54	30:8-22	58
13:9, 13	28	59:19	251	30:9	46, 48, 79
13:9-13	34, 67, 209	59:19-20	105, 115	30:17-22	18
13:9-19	7	59:20-21	18	31:10-11	18
13:9-22	70	Ch 60	79	31:12	18
14:3-7	70	60:18-22	55	31:31-33	18
14:12-14	127, 178	60:19-21	16, 147, 297	31:31-34	11, 17, 50
19:2	238	60:21	18	31:33	30
19:4	238	62:1-2	83	32:37-38	18
19:5	238	62:1-12	55	32:37-42	17, 51
19:21-22	238	62:7, 11-12	18	32:38-40	18
24:3-6, 17-21	70	63:1-6	199, 204	32:39	30
24:6	30, 205	65:17	15	33:14-17	46, 48
24:17-18	30, 205	65:20	19	33:15-16	5, 18
24:21	28	66:8	28	33:24-26	47
24:23	207	66:18-19	15	35:2, 4	294
25:6-9	38, 207	66:18-20	5, 16	36:10	294
25:7-9	53	66:18-24	56	49:12	290
25:8	35, 204	66:19-23	11		
25:8-9	258	66:22-23	16, 147, 297	**LAMENTATIONS**	
25:9	208	66:23	5, 15	3:15, 19	164
26:17	244				
26:17-18	244	**JEREMIAH**		**EZEKIEL**	
26:17-21	39	3:17	18	1:4	296
26:19	35, 201, 244	4:1-4	172	1:27	181
27:12	30	4:5	173	1:28	132, 180, 182
27:12-13	39, 53, 111	4:6	173, 248	2:9-10; 3:1-3, 14	182
27:13	35	4:10	151, 172	7:19	67
28:15-18	155, 228	4:13	173, 249	8:1-2	181
29:10-11	84-85	4:13, 17, 19-20	173	20:33-44	59

SCRIPTURE INDEX • 305

22:31	67	2:35	219, 223, 226	8:24	155, 156, 228
28:16-17	127-128, 178	2:36-38	212	8:25	192, 211
30:3-5	238	2:37-38	216, 217	9:21-23	214
30:10-11	238	2:39	226	9:24	83, 91, 101-102, 140
30:12	238	2:40	221, 225	9:24-27	82, 100, 102-105, 120
30:26	238	2:44	3, 14	9:25	83, 84, 98, 100-101
Ch 33	28, 161, 279	2:44-45	16, 211, 287	9:26	83, 84, 249, 251
36:22-38	17, 52	7:1	212	9:27	117, 118, 140, 151, 155, 170, 193, 228, 249, 250
36:24-29	11	7:3-7	222		
36:25-28	18	7:4	229	10:1	215, 234
36:26-27	30	7:4-7	128, 185	10:2-3	89
36:35	15	7:5	230	10:8	132
37:21-28	60	7:6	231	10:10-14	214
37:24	79	7:7	227	10:14	215, 234
37:25-28	18	7:8	127, 154, 227, 237, 248	11:1-20	214, 215
38:4	73, 172, 249	7:9	129, 296	11:2	234-235
38:8	151, 172	7:9-10	183	11:3	235
38:9-10	73, 95, 173	7:9-10,22,26	129 178, 179	11:4	235
38:9, 16	248, 253	7:13	184	11:5-12	236
38:10	249	7:13-14	3, 14, 16, 122, 129, 130, 178, 179, 211, 287, 297	11:13-16	236
38:11	173			11:16	115, 116, 118, 151, 236, 239, 243, 248
38:11, 14	151, 172, 248	7:17	212		
38:12	151, 172-173	7:20	227	11:17	236
38:13	173, 249	7:21	154, 156, 227	11:18-20	237
38:15-16	173	7:22	225	11:21	116, 151, 172, 189, 237, 248
38:17	253	7:23	225, 226		
38:18-22	209	7:24	227	11:21-35	214
38:18-23	75	7:25	92, 154, 192, 223, 225, 227	11:21-45	11
38:19	28, 173			11:23	91, 155, 172, 228, 248
38:20	74, 173	7:25-26	114, 121, 124	11:24	172, 189
38:21-22	30, 205	7:25-27	225	11:24-25	248
38:22	30, 205	7:26	115, 129	11:24-28	237–238, 249
39:1-8	75	7:26-27	16, 297	11:27	8, 107
39:6	30, 205	7:27	122, 129, 130, 179, 211	11:29-32	192
39:7	270	8:3	230, 234, 235	11:30	12, 155-156, 172, 189, 249
39:7, 22-29	60	8:4	230, 234		
39:8	28	8:5-8	231-232, 235	11:31	117, 151, 250
39:17-20	30	8:8	227	11:32	172, 189, 246, 249
39:22, 25-29	28	8:9	154, 227	11:33	246
39:26-29	270	8:9-11	128	11:35	8, 107
39:27-28	18	8:9-14	126, 178	11:36	151, 249, 252
Ch 43	19	8:10	127	11:36-37	192, 250
43:2-5, 13-17	19	8:11-12	129, 178	11:39	248
Ch 47	20, 204	8:13	129, 178	11:40-44	12
Ch 48	20	8:14	125, 126, 129, 179	11:43	237
48:35	18	8:16-19	213, 214	11:44	254
		8:19	8, 106, 123	12:1-2	256-257
DANIEL		8:20	230	12:1-3	40
2:18	216	8:21	232	12:4	83, 84, 215, 234
2:19	216	8:22	227	12:9	2, 84, 215, 234
2:28	216	8:23	189	12:11	114, 118, 119, 122, 124, 243
2:31-45	216-217	8:23-25	154, 227		
2:34	220, 223				

12:11-12	117, 237	3:8	172	5:34-35	183
12:12	119, 124, 131	3:11-20	63	6:1	13
		3:13-15	102	6:10	17

HOSEA

		3:14,17	79	7:13-14	13
2:14-23	61	3:15-16	28	7:21	283
2:19	83			8:11	17, 283
3:1-5	61	## ZECHARIAH		10:17-37	246
3:5	18, 46	4:11-14	104, 158	10:17-39	196
5:15-6:3	61, 280	4:14	87, 159, 249	10:23	195, 247
13:14	35	8:3	79	12:4	294
		9:14	112	12:36	291

JOEL

		9:14-16	40	13:23	6
2:2	30, 205	9:16	11, 28, 63	13:30	263
2:23-29	110	12:2	248, 253	13:37-43	263
2:31	160, 175, 257	12:2-3	95, 172	16:24-28	288-289
2:31-32	33	12:8-10	112-113	16:27	13
3:2, 11-12	172	12:8-11	17, 52	16:28	291
3:13	199	12:9-11	18, 28	17:1-8	159
3:13-15	160	12:10	11	17:2	181
3:13-16	33	12:10-11	30	18:3	290
3:15-21	62	13:8-9	11, 48-49	19:27-28	15, 32
3:16-20	11	14:1-2	151, 248, 253	19:28	246
3:18	204	14:1-4	92, 96	22:31-32	11
3:20-21	79	14:2	172, 251	23:37-39	63
		14:3-15	77	23:39	28, 50

AMOS

		14:4	146	24:1-3	242
5:7-27	164	14:6-7	30, 205	24:3	261
5:14	2	14:7	30	24:4-8	243
5:18,20	30, 205	14:8	146, 204	24:8	244
9:8-9	11	14:8-9	16, 30	24:9-14	245
9:11	79	14:9	16, 103, 146, 297	24:15	192, 247
9:11-15	18, 48	14:11	146	24:15-31	170
9:14-15	62	14:12	30, 205	24:16	252
		14:13	30, 205	24:16-22	251

MICAH

		14:16-19	19	24:19-22	92, 97
4:7	62	14:18	262	24:21	200, 251, 256
5:2	5, 90			24:21-22	94
5:9-15	76	## MALACHI		24:23-28	254
5:10	28	3:1-2	159	24:28	30
5:10-15	7	3:2-5	78	24:29	174, 175, 255, 257
		4:1	28, 30, 205	24:29-31	32, 36, 92, 97, 160, 241
## HABAKKUK		4:1-6	78	24:30-31	200, 256
3:3-19	76	4:2	83	24:31	34, 111, 201, 258
3:5	30, 205	4:5-6	159	24:32-34	260
3:12-13	30			24:33	133, 261
		## MATTHEW		24:34	262, 285
## ZEPHANIAH		1:20-23	5	24:35-41	262
1:1-18	7, 67	2:2	5, 17, 31, 46	24:36	136
1:14-18	76	2:5-6	5	24:36-39	135, 144, 152
1:15	28, 30, 205	4:8-10	283	24:37-39	263
1:15-17	30, 205	5:6	204	24:40-41	263
1:15-18	30, 40, 205	5:12	13		

SCRIPTURE INDEX • 307

24:40-42	136, 262	12:49-53	246	11:23-24	34, 260
24:42-44	264	13:3	290	11:24	10
24:43-44	136, 144	13:28	284	11:25-26	290
24:45-51	133, 263	13:34-35	63	13:1	293
24:48-51	144	14:14	41	13:19-20	293
25:1-13	134, 263	17:20-21	16	14:1-3	293, 294, 295, 297
25:11-13	144	17:23	254	14:2	295
25:14-30	42	17:24,37	254	14:16-20	295
25:31	246, 288	17:26-27	263	14:17-18	297
25:31-32	19	17:28-29	263	14:18	295
25:34	15, 284	17:28-30	152	14:19	293
26:29	16	17:28-33	253	14:20,29	293
26:39	290	19:11-27	42, 284	14:23	294, 297
27:45,54	31	19:15-19	16	14:26-29	296
28:2	31	20:35-36	16	14:28	295
		21:5-7	242	15:26-27	293
MARK		21:7	261	16:4,22-23	293
1:15	290	21:8-11	243	16:16,28	293
4:20	6	21:12-19	245	17:11	293
8:34-38	288-289	21:20	11, 105, 248, 253	19:14	109
9:1	291	21:20-21	171, 174		
13:1-4	242	21:20-22	95, 252	**ACTS**	
13:3	261	21:20-27	172, 174	1:3	110
13:5-8	243	21:21-24	251	1:6	32
13:9-13	245	21:22-27	92, 96	1:6-8	15
13:14	247, 252	21:23	256	1:12-15	296
13:14-20	251	21:25	257	2:1-2	295
13:19	256	21:25-26	175, 255	2:1-4	110
13:21-23	254	21:25-28	32, 36, 160	2:2	296
13:24	174, 257	21:27-28	256	2:19-20	175
13:24-25	175, 255	21:27-31	285, 288	2:19-21	160
13:24-27	32, 36	21:28	246	2:36-39	63
13:26-27	256	21:29-32	260	3:19	290
13:27	201	21:31	133, 261	3:21	15, 32
13:28-30	260	21:33-35	261	4:29	142
13:29	133, 261	21:36	64, 264	14:22	143, 285
13:31-34	261	22:16,18,29-30	285	15:18	8, 279
13:32	135, 136			16:17	142
13:34-36	264	**JOHN**		17:2-3	6
13:35-37	137	2:16	294	17:31	8, 107
14:25	284	2:24-25	42		
14:61-64	191	5:24	290	**ROMANS**	
		5:27-30	43	1:1	142
LUKE		6:32-33	109	2:5-9	291
1:19	214	6:39-40	10, 28	4:16	10
1:31-33	79	6:40	34, 202, 259	5:18	290
1:32-33	5, 17, 46	6:44, 54	10, 28, 34, 202, 260	6:4-5	109-110
6:21,25	204	6:48-51	109-110	8:1	290
8:15	6	8:52	289	8:19,21-22	18
9:23-27	288-289	8:58	11	8:19-23	147
9:62	284	10:9	109	9:1-5	63
12:33	14	10:10	189	9:27-28	63

10:17	31	
11:1-5	113	
11:11	18	
11:17,24	10	
11:21-22	18	
11:25-26	11	
11:25-27	17, 50	
11:25-29	113	
11:25-36	64	
11:26	28	
11:33-36	140	
14:7-12	43	
14:10	42	
16:20	25	
16:25	6	

1 CORINTHIANS

1:4-8	276
2:7	5
2:8	5
5:5	10
5:7	109
9:24	13
10:4	11
13:12	29
14:3	2
15:20	110
15:24-28	20, 298
15:42	42
15:50	286
15:50-54	201
15:51-55	37
15:52	26, 28, 34, 110, 111
15:52-54	258
15:52-55	202
15:54	35, 38
15:55	35

2 CORINTHIANS

1:14	10
4:4	5, 14
4:17	194
5:9-10	29, 43
5:10	13, 42
5:17	299
11:14	281

GALATIANS

1:4	5, 12
3:16,26,29	11
4:29	11
6:16	10

EPHESIANS

1:3	3
1:14	3
1:17-20	3, 203
2:2	5, 14, 78
2:12-14	5
2:12-22	11, 35
2:19-20	5
3:2-11	10
3:3-4,9	5
3:6	11, 35
4:4-6	11, 35
5:32	5
6:6	142
6:19	5

PHILIPPIANS

1:6,9-11	311
2:8	290
3:3	10
3:9-11	41
3:14	13

COLOSSIANS

1:5	13
1:7	142
1:13	16, 283
1:26-27	5
4:7	142

1 THESSALONIANS

4:13-18	111
4:15-17	174, 201
4:15-18	37
4:16	34
4:16-17	258, 260
4:17	16, 297
5:1-11	65
5:2	174, 175
5:2-3	92, 97
5:3	93, 151, 244, 248, 253
5:4	135
5:4-6	36, 262
5:4-9	264
5:9	29

2 THESSALONIANS

1:4-8	286
1:4-12	202
1:7-10	38, 209
2:1	34
2:1-4	256

2:2	35
2:3	35
2:3-4	34
2:4	151, 193, 248, 250, 281
2:8	15, 68, 115
2:8-9	151
2:9-10	281

1 TIMOTHY

6:14	3

2 TIMOTHY

2:24	142
4:1	286
4:1-8	282
4:8	3, 42
4:18	286

TITUS

2:12-13	42
2:13	3, 202

HEBREWS

1:11-12	299
2:9	289-290
2:14	20, 156, 292
2:14-15	290
7:16-17	19
10:25	2
12:2	291
13:12	112

JAMES

1:1	142
1:12	42
2:5	286
5:7-8	280
5:17	159

1 PETER

1:7	3
1:11	11
1:20	10
2:16	142
5:4	42

2 PETER

1:1	142
1:11	17, 286
2:5-9	202
2:9	291
3:6	12, 13

3:7	12, 30, 201, 205	6:12-14	257, 259	12:14	114
3:7-8	292	6:12-17	34, 174, 175	12:17	246
3:7,12	28	7:1-8	195	13:1	191
3:7-13	65, 261	7:9	201	13:1-2	185, 222
3:8	280	7:9-12	41	13:1-9	233
3:9	13, 198	7:9-17	199	13:3,12	128
3:10	14, 36, 174, 292	7:15-17	203	13:3-10	186
3:10-12	202, 259, 299	8:1	29, 259	13:5	91-92, 114, 121, 124, 223, 248
3:10-13	12, 78	8:1,5	26		
3:10-14	3, 276	8:1,3-5	149, 176	13:5-6	191
3:13	14, 83	8:2,6-13	149	13:7	12, 150
		8:6-7	162	13:8	5
1 JOHN		8:7-13	268	13:11-18	187
2:15-17	14	8:8-9	163	13:12	150
2:28	41-42	8:10-11	164	13:12-14	281
		8:12	165	13:14	190
JUDE		8:13	166	13:16-17	151
1:1	142	9:1	291	13:18	188
		9:1-12	166, 268	14:1-5	197
REVELATION		9:1-21	149	14:6	110
1:1	25, 142	9:13-21	167, 247-248, 269	14:6-7	247
1:2,8-9	142	10:1	184	14:6-11	198
1:3	141	10:1-3	178, 179, 180	14:10	290
1:7	11, 112	10:6	184	14:12	142
1:13,16	144	10:7	26, 37, 83, 104, 111, 149, 152, 160, 176, 206, 259	14:12-13	198
1:14	181			14:14-16	37-38, 66, 143, 199, 201, 259, 263
1:15	181	10:8-10	182		
1:16	181	11:2	116, 248	14:17-20	37, 66, 199, 263
1:17	132	11:2-3	121, 124	14:18-20	208, 273
1:20	144	11:3	267	14:19	12
2:20	42	11:3-6	115, 157	15:1	161
2:26-29	19	11:4	86-87, 104, 158, 159, 249	15:1-8	149
3:12	17, 298	11:5-6	267	15:8	179-180, 183
3:18	278	11:6	157, 195, 249	16:1-2	162, 267
3:21	16	11:7-13	157	16:1-21	149
4:3	180	11:7-14	104, 169, 269	16:2-11	268
4:8-11	145	11:9-10	249	16:3	163
5:1	147	11:11	120	16:4-7	164
5:5	181	11:11-13	86, 170, 250	16:7	206, 259
5:5-7	182	11:13	137	16:8	165
5:9-10	147	11:15	3, 5, 14, 16, 37, 103, 104, 111, 152, 178, 286, 297	16:10-11	166
5:9-14	152			16:12-14	172, 272
6:1-17	149	11:15-19	27, 43, 149, 176, 269	16:12-16	105, 167, 169, 247-248, 269
6:2	229	11:18	13, 14, 29, 37, 42, 149, 160, 177, 205-206, 259		
6:2-6	153			16:14	11, 28
6:3-4	230	12:3-4	127	16:14-16	65, 73, 95
6:5-6	231-232	12:6,14	116, 121, 124, 172	16:15	145, 149, 160, 174, 175, 259, 278
6:7-8	154, 228	12:6-7	115		
6:8	12, 155	12:7-9	127	16:17	83, 103, 153, 160, 177
6:9-11	156	12:9	128	16:17-21	27, 30, 65, 176, 205, 269
6:10	267	12:11	28, 234, 246		
6:12	149, 160	12:12,14	115	16:19	177, 290

17:3	185, 191, 222	19:10	3, 67, 142, 206	20:7-15	19
17:6-11	218	19:11	273	20:9	298
17:9-10	219	19:11-21	66-67, 208	20:10	156
17:10	226	19:15	12, 30, 69, 199	20:12-13	291
17:10-11	220, 221, 223, 224, 225	19:15-16	15	20:13-15	156
		19:15-21	273	21:1-3	298-299
17:11	150, 219	19:16	3, 16	21:2-3	20, 204
17:12	226	19:17	30	21:2-5	147
17:12-13	154	19:20	156, 187, 190	21:2,10	17
17:13	223, 237	19:21	30	21:4	204
17:14	220	20:1-6	44	21:9	17
17:17	223	20:3	189	21:10	20, 21, 204, 298
19:1-5	205	20:4	16	21:11	298
19:5-9	143	20:4-6	258-259	22:12	42
19:6-7	206	20:4,6	16	22:18	21
19:7-8	29	20:5-6	260, 291	22:18-19	141
19:7,14	17	20:6	17, 35, 41, 297	22:21	292
19:8-10	207	20:7-10	20		

ABOUT THE AUTHOR

Brandon Emch lives with his wife and seven children in Bucyrus, Kansas. After college, he assisted clients with financial and accounting matters as a CPA. Currently, he owns and operates a small business and is blessed to work at home alongside his family. Brandon is a member of the Apostolic Christian Church of Kansas City (apostolicchristian.org) where he has served as a lay minister for over seventeen years.

His greatest joys are faith and family. With this book, he reveals some of his heart while sharing and promoting the vibrant and inspiring picture of God's future plans.

You may email the author at **greatnotableday@gmail.com** or visit his website at **www.endtimessimplified.com**.

❋

Being confident of this very thing,
that he which hath begun a good work in you
will perform it until the day of Jesus Christ . . .
And this I pray,
that your love may abound yet more and more
in knowledge and in all judgment;
that ye may approve things that are excellent;
that ye may be sincere and without offence
till the day of Christ;
being filled with the fruits of righteousness,
which are by Jesus Christ,
unto the glory and praise of God.

(Philippians 1:6, 9–11)

www.ingramcontent.com/pod-product-compliance
Lightning Source LLC
Chambersburg PA
CBHW052133010526
44113CB00035B/2000